Publication Number 17

Duke University Commonwealth-Studies Center

The Nigerian Political Scene

Duke University Commonwealth-Studies Center Publications

The Nigerian Political Scene

Archibald Callaway, Taylor Cole, L. Gray Cowan, W. B. Hamilton, Frederick Harbison, Pendleton Herring, George P. Murdock, James O'Connell, Joseph J. Spengler, Francis X. Sutton

Edited by
Robert O. Tilman *and* Taylor Cole

Published for the
Duke University Commonwealth-Studies Center
Duke University Press, Durham, N.C.
Cambridge University Press, London
1962

Printed in the United States of America
by Vail-Ballou Press, Inc., Binghamton, N.Y.

Preface

In the decade 1951–60 twenty-three states on the African Continent gained political independence, and during the same period four new states joined the rapidly expanding Commonwealth. At one time these simple facts of independence and Commonwealth membership might immediately have suggested much about the economic system, the political structure, and the social order in each of these new states. Today, however, political independence and Commonwealth membership are much less suggestive than they were prior to World War II. Previous volumes in the *Commonwealth-Studies Series* have dealt in general with problems occasioned by the expansion of this now "multi-racial" Commonwealth,[1] and the collection of essays in the present volume will deal specifically with one of these new states, the twelfth member of the Commonwealth [2] and the twenty-sixth independent African state—the Federation of Nigeria.

As the title of this volume indicates, its focus is primarily political; but in the new areas of Asia and Africa disciplinary lines are difficult to draw, and the march lands between them are usually well traveled. Thus, contributions are drawn from the disciplines of anthropology, history, and economics, as well as from political science. The editors have attempted to arrange the essays in a logi-

---

[1] See Frank H. Underhill, *The British Commonwealth* (Durham, N.C., 1956) [publication no. 1]; Sir Ivor Jennings, *Problems of the New Commonwealth* (Durham, N.C., 1958) [publication no. 7]; Nicholas Mansergh, *et al.*, *Commonwealth Perspectives* (Durham, N.C., 1958) [publication no. 8]; T. H. Silcock, *The Commonwealth Economy in Southeast Asia* (Durham, N.C., 1959) [publication no. 10]; and Ralph Braibanti and J. J. Spengler, eds., *Traditions, Values, and Socio-Economic Development* (Durham, N.C., 1961) [publication no. 13].

[2] Nigeria and Sierra Leone were both the twelfth member of the Commonwealth, since between the times they entered South Africa withdrew, thus briefly reducing the number to eleven.

cal sequence, which, like Aristotles's description of a fable, has a beginning, a middle, and an end.

The beginning is supplied by the essay of George P. Murdock,[3] who surveys the traditional socio-political systems of Nigeria and classifies these, first, according to cultural and geographic area, and, second, according to the degree of political integration of these traditional systems. Although Mr. Murdock intends that his contribution should be primarily descriptive, he raises certain questions that will command the attention of social scientists in the years to come. Bridging the gap between the traditional and contemporary periods, W. B. Hamilton [4] seeks to analyze the historical evolution of British influence in Nigeria. Beginning his study in the early nineteenth century, almost a century before the name Nigeria was even coined, Mr. Hamilton provides an analysis of the historical forces and the men that contributed to the conversion of the diverse tribal societies into the modern state of Nigeria. At this point, we can therefore make the transition from the old to the new.

Viable government demands a degree of national integration, while political necessity often dictates the maximum decentralization of governmental functions. A compromise to these conflicting demands is often found in the establishment of a federal system of government, for it is the essence of the federal principle that the imperative of national cohesion should be balanced against the forces of disintegration. Taylor Cole,[5] in the first two essays of Part Two of this volume examines federalism in Nigeria. Beginning with an analysis of the centrifugal and centripetal forces affecting Nigerian federalism, Mr. Cole next proceeds to an examination of the present Constitution of the Federation of Nigeria. Though the emphasis is placed upon the legal questions that have arisen under the federal system, these problems can and must be placed in the setting of the unwritten constitution. During the colonial period, government was conducted primarily by the ad-

[3] Mr. Murdock is Mellon Professor of Anthropology at the University of Pittsburgh.
[4] Mr. Hamilton is Professor of History at Duke University.
[5] Mr. Cole is James B. Duke Professor of Political Science and Provost of Duke University.

ministrative services. When independence came to the new states of Africa and Asia, the bureaucracy, well established and with longer traditions of service than the other organs of government, quite naturally assumed great importance in the governance of the states, an importance perhaps out of proportion to that of the older bureaucracies of the West. In this light, the development, structure, and problems of the bureaucracy in Nigeria receive attention in Mr. Cole's third essay. An important part of the bureaucracy, and the element that is largely responsible for the portrayal of the national image abroad, is the external affairs service. L. Gray Cowan,[6] in the final essay dealing with the politics and government of modern Nigeria, explores problems related to the formulation and execution of foreign policy in the light of the colonial experience and the conflicting pressures of present-day international politics.

While politics constitutes the prime concern of the present volume, this subject cannot be considered in an academic vacuum, particularly in the new Afro-Asian states. These states approached independence with rising expectations as to their economic future, and their political stability depends in no small degree upon the extent to which these expectations can be fulfilled. Moreover, as the first essay of Part Three by Joseph J. Spengler[7] well demonstrates, the demographer who concerns himself with Africa must be prepared to evaluate phenomena that might not be classified in the strictest sense as purely economic in nature. As we can see in Mr. Spengler's contribution, the role of traditional forces must be carefully weighed along with the strictly economic factors in any evaluation of Nigerian development. Focusing upon the problem of manpower, the essays by Frederick Harbison[8] and Archibald C. Callaway[9] approach the question of the development of the Nigerian economy from two slightly different but complementary perspectives. For Mr. Harbison, the problem is how to

[6] Mr. Cowan is Associate Professor of Political Science and Director of the Program of Studies on Africa at Columbia University.
[7] Mr. Spengler is James B. Duke Professor of Economics at Duke University.
[8] Mr. Harbison is Professor of Economics and Director of the Industrial Relations Section of Princeton University.
[9] Mr. Callaway is a Research Associate in Economics at the Center for International Studies, Massachusetts Institute of Technology.

secure the human resources necessary for economic development. Mr. Callaway, on the other hand, is most concerned with what will happen to the school leavers, who have tasted enough Western education to become dissatisfied with the traditional way of life but who are not adequately trained to enter the category described by Mr. Harbison as "high-level manpower." Thus, the Nigerian political scene of the future will be affected in some way by the seeming contradiction of simultaneous labor shortages and unemployment, or underemployment.

In the final section of the present volume two authors seek to assess the political future of Nigeria in particular and of Africa in general. Pendleton Herring [10] addresses himself specifically to the future of democracy in Nigeria, while Francis X. Sutton [11] endeavors to analyze the historical roots of authority and authoritarianism in sub-Saharan Africa, and from this analysis offers several broad suggestions for the formulation of future western policies toward Africa. In a final essay James O'Connell,[12] provides a bibliographical study of materials related to Nigeria to guide the serious student in further research.

With the exception of two contributions,[13] the essays contained in this volume were presented before the annual Joint Seminar sponsored by the Duke University Commonwealth-Studies Center during the spring semester of 1961. In the light of the discussions at seminar meetings most of the contributors undertook substantial revisions of the original papers. Since most of these revisions were completed by the early summer of 1961, the studies presented here do not take into account any events occurring in Africa after this date. In the ever-changing African political scene this is a fact worth noting.

The Commonwealth-Studies Center was established at Duke University by a grant from the Carnegie Corporation in 1955,

[10] Mr. Herring is President of the Social Science Research Council.
[11] Mr. Sutton is Program Associate, Overseas Development Program, Near East and Africa, of the Ford Foundation.
[12] Father O'Connell is Lecturer in Government on the Faculty of Economics and Social Studies, University College, Ibadan, Nigeria.
[13] The essay by Mr. Callaway was previously published in *West Africa* and is reprinted here in revised form by permission of the publishers. The bibliographical study by Father O'Connell was prepared originally for inclusion in this volume.

which was renewed for a second five-year period in 1959. While it is the support of the Carnegie Corporation that has made possible the preparation and the publication of the *Commonwealth-Studies Series*, neither the Carnegie Corporation nor the Commonwealth-Studies Center is responsible for the views expressed by individual contributors to the volumes. Moreover, the individual authors occasionally may disagree among themselves. Since this is the privilege of academics, the editors have not felt it their duty to obscure these differences of opinion.

Several of the essays appearing in this volume have previously appeared in print in whole or in part in other publications. The Commonwealth-Studies Center and the Duke University Press are particularly indebted to the publishers of *West Africa, Public Administration* (London), the *South Atlantic Quarterly*, and the *Journal of International Affairs* for permission to use certain copyrighted material, and to the editors of *Constitutional Problems of Federalism in Nigeria* for permitting the publication in revised form of an essay that appeared in this volume. The full citation and an appropriate acknowledgement are given in each case where such material has been used.

Robert O. Tilman [14]

Taylor Cole

Duke University, January 18, 1962

[14] Mr. Tilman, Assistant Professor of Political Science, Tulane University, served as Executive Secretary to the Committee on Commonwealth Studies of the Duke University Commonwealth-Studies Center during 1960–62.

Contents

Contents

Appendix

Part One

The Background and Setting

The Traditional Socio-political Systems of Nigeria: An Introductory Survey

George P. Murdock

Nigeria offers the social scientist an excellent laboratory for research, since nowhere else in Negro Africa do the indigenous peoples reveal so much variation in their history and traditional organizations. Nigerian societies range from those that lack any political integration transcending the level of the local village of a few hundred inhabitants to organized aggregations of millions of people. Some of these great states are of a complexity unparalleled elsewhere south of the Sahara and have existed for centuries. Between these two extremes lies a spectrum consisting of every conceivable gradation.[1]

The important work of Coleman and others has demonstrated well the significant role of the modern Nigerian elite.[2] As these writers have recognized, behavior of the modern leaders of Nigeria has been governed in part by their past experiences in the traditional political systems in which they have been reared. It thus seems appropriate to preface the examination of the contemporary Nigerian political scene presented in later sections by this summary account of the traditional political and social orders.

[1] Material contained in this essay is not based on field investigations; it is drawn exclusively from published ethnographic literature, which is probably richer and fuller for Nigeria than for any other newly emerging Negro state. For specific bibliographical references, see George P. Murdock, *Africa: Its Peoples and Their Culture History* (New York, Toronto, and London, 1959), pp. 147–48, 242, and 250–51.

[2] See, for example, James S. Coleman, *Nigeria: Background to Nationalism* (Berkeley, 1958); and H. H. and M. M. Smythe, *The New Nigerian Elite* (Stanford, 1960).

Primarily descriptive in nature, this essay will serve to catalogue the tribal composition of present-day Nigeria, at the same time delineating the broad socio-political groupings with which these tribes were traditionally associated. Lastly, I shall attempt to point out several of the important characteristics of the traditional political systems that may influence the attitudes and outlook of some present-day Nigerians.

I

The traditional political systems of Nigeria will be regarded as those that were flourishing at the beginning of the nineteenth century, even though many of them, especially in Southern Nigeria, survived relatively intact for many decades thereafter. The time of the traditional systems is separated from the present by three major historical developments.

The first of these was the Fulani conquest of much of Northern Nigeria. Inspired by the religious fervor of Osman dan Fodio, the Fulani, a racially mixed people who originally came from Senegal, embarked on a series of holy wars of conquest in the early nineteenth century. Between 1804 and 1809 they reduced successively the Hausa states of Gobir, Zamfara, Zaria, Katsena, Kebbi, and Kano, establishing a ruling Fulani emir in each. Moving eastward, they carved out new emirates in Bauchi and Adamawa at the expense of various more backward peoples, and to the south they set up conquest states among, *inter alia,* the Nupe and the northern Yoruba. These conquests markedly changed the indigenous political systems of the Hausa, the Nupe, and the Ilorin Yoruba; and they introduced complex patterns of administrative organization for the first time to the previously stateless inhabitants of Adamawa and Bauchi.

The second major historical development was the progressive establishment of British colonial government, which introduced all the remaining politically undeveloped societies to the complexities of a formal administrative system. Because of the policy of "indirect rule," however, it left relatively undisturbed the preexisting structures of the societies with more elaborate political systems. Indeed, it probably operated on the whole to "freeze" these structures and to render them temporarily impervious to the normal processes of change.

The third major development has been the emergence of new social and economic classes to whom political power has increasingly accrued. Recruited for the most part from outside the groups in control of the traditional political systems, the new elite consists of those who have profited by the economic and educational advantages made available under the British colonial regime. Acquiring new technological skills, experience in the lower administrative ranks, wealth through economic enterprise, and education along European lines, these people have gradually achieved a dominant role on the political scene. They form the principal elements in the political parties that have sought and gained independence. As others have pointed out, they constitute the dynamic element in the political situation today.

The task of classifying the Nigerian peoples according to their culture-historical backgrounds is formidable. Well over 300 separate tribes with distinct names have been recognized in the territory now comprising the state of Nigeria, although some of these 300, of course, extend across the political borders of Nigeria. By combining contiguous tribes characterized by essentially similar cultures and social institutions, this number can be reduced to 122 tribal groupings, which I have separately listed and mapped in an earlier study.[3] These 122 groups of tribes, who speak languages of four distinct linguistic subfamilies—roughly comparable, for example, to Celtic, Germanic, Italic, and Slavic in Europe—can be further reduced, on the basis of linguistic and cultural relationships, to yield the six major ethnic provinces into which Nigeria is most conveniently divided. These and their component societies are identified below.

(1) *Northeastern or Bornu Province.* This province, with a total population of approximately 1.5 million, embraces four tribal groups of the independent Kanuric or Central Saharan

[3] Murdock, *op. cit.*

linguistic family—the Beriberi, Kanuri, Koyam, and Manga—together with the intrusive Shuwa, an Arab people speaking a language of the Semitic subfamily of the Hamitic or Afroasiatic linguistic family. The great Kanuri nation, comprising four-fifths of the population of the province, has been politically dominant in Bornu since 1380, when it established there a powerful conquest state that survived into the modern period. The Kanuri are linguistically akin to the Teda nation of the east central Sahara and probably rose to power through control of the caravan trade across the Sahara with Libya and Tripolitania.

(2) *Northern or Hausa Province.* This province has a total population of approximately seven million, of whom at least five million belong to the great Hausa nation. The Hausa, with the kindred Auyokawa and Maguzawa, belong to the Chadic subfamily of the Hamitic or Afroasiatic linguistic family. Their complex civilization and mercantile proclivities apparently owe their origin to millennia of involvement in the caravan trade across the Sahara with ancient Carthage and modern Tunisia. Since the early nineteenth century, however, they have been politically subordinate to the Fulani, who speak a language of the Atlantic subfamily of the Nigritic or Niger-Congo linguistic family and are especially well represented in Sokoto, Bauchi, and Adamawa. Three minor tribes are located along the northwestern border of Nigeria: the Dendi, Busa, and Tienga. The Dendi are a branch of the Songhai of the middle Niger and speak a language of the independent Songhaic family. The Busa and Tienga belong to the Mande or Mandingo subfamily of the Nigritic or Niger-Congo linguistic subfamily.

(3) *Southwestern or Kwa Province.* This province, with a population of nearly twelve million, is inhabited exclusively by peoples speaking languages of the Nigritic or Niger-Congo family and, with one exception, of the Kwa subfamily thereof. The exception is the Ijaw tribe, whose language is classed by itself as an independent subfamily. Differences in the level of indigenous political organization within the province make it advisable to

classify the Kwa peoples (other than the Ijaw) in five distinct
clusters, as follows:

> Yoruba cluster—Bunu, Egba, Ekiti, Ife, Ijebu, Itsekiri, and
> Yoruba. (Total population about five million.)
> Nupe cluster—Gbari, Igbira, Koro, Nge, and Nupe. (Total
> population nearly one million.)
> Edo cluster—Edo, Isoko, and Kukuruku. (Total population
> in excess of one million.)
> Ibo cluster—the various subtribes of the Ibo nation. (Total
> population nearly four million.)
> Idoma cluster—Afo, Arago, Egede, Gili, Idoma, Igala, and
> Iyala. (Total population about six hundred thousand.)

(4) *Central or Bantoid Province.* This province, with a total
population of perhaps 3.5 million, comprises no fewer than 39 distinct tribal groups. All speak languages of the Bantoid or Central
subfamily of the Nigritic or Niger-Congo linguistic family. With
the exception of the Ibibio and Tiv, who number approximately
one million and 800,000 respectively, all the Bantoid peoples are
limited in size, exceeding 100,000 in only a very few instances.
They are listed below.

Afusare	Ekoi	Katab	Orri
Anyang	Gure	Kentu	Reshe
Basa	Ibibio	Kurama	Tigon
Batu	Jarawa	Mada	Tiv
Birom	Jerawa	Mama	Yako
Boki	Jibu	Mambila	Yergum
Borrom	Jukun	Mbembe	Yeskwa
Butawa	Kadara	Mbula	Zuande
Chawai	Kamberi	Ndoro	Zumper
Dakakari	Kamuku	Ododop	

(5) *Eastern or Chadic Province.* The great bulk of the 1.5
million inhabitants of this province speak languages of the Chadic
subfamily of the Hamitic or Afroasiatic linguistic family. Though
related linguistically to the Hausa, they exhibit, for the most part,

distinctive and much simpler cultures and political organizations. The twenty-four Chadic tribes of the province are listed below.

Angas	Gerawa	Margi
Bachama	Gude	Mober
Bata	Gwandara	Ngizim
Bede	Hona	Tangale
Bolewa	Kapsiki	Tera
Buduma	Karekare	Wakura
Bura	Kotoko	Warjawa
Dera	Mandara	Wurkum

Interspersed among the Chadic tribes and the neighboring Bantoid peoples are eight tribes speaking languages of the eastern subfamily of the Nigritic or Niger-Congo linguistic family. The Chamba, Daka, Jen, Kam, Longuda, Mumuye, Vere, and Yungur should be treated as a separate sub-unit, which we shall call the Adamawa cluster, since they affiliate in many respects more closely with their Bantoid than with their Chadic neighbors. In numbers they comprise barely 10 per cent of the total population of the province.

(6) *Southeastern or Cameroon Province.* In the former British Cameroons, in the extreme southeast, are found thirteen tribes that speak not merely Bantoid but strictly Bantu languages. It was from this region that the Bantu peoples who now inhabit the Congo basin and much of eastern and southern Africa appear to have migrated about two thousand years ago. The impetus for the expansion seems to have been the borrowing of several important food crops of Southeast Asian origin—notably bananas, taro, and yams—which enabled them for the first time to extend agriculture into the tropical forest, previously inhabited only by Pygmies with a hunting and gathering economy. The Bantu of the Cameroon Province number nearly seven hundred thousand and comprise the following tribal groups: Fungom, Fut, Kom, Kossi, Kpe, Kundu, Li, Mum, Ndob, Nsaw, Nsungli, Widekum, and Wum.

II

The indigenous political systems of Nigeria can be divided broadly into three categories—large states, small states, and politically autonomous communities that lack the essential features of true states. Although I shall discuss at some length the last two categories, it is not necessary that the large states be described in detail since their structure and characteristics are familiar to most Africanists already; moreover, they differ little in essential features from the small states that are described below. I shall therefore only locate and identify these large states with reference to the classification of ethnic or cultural provinces and then proceed to a more detailed examination of the small states and the autonomous communities.

(1) *Large states.* The entire Northeastern or Bornu province was long dominated by one great state, that of the Kanuri, which even resisted successfully the Fulani conquests. A second great state, the dual Fulani empire of Gwandu and Sokoto, has similarly controlled the Northern or Hausa Province ever since Osman dan Fodio overcame the earlier indigenous Hausa states in the first decade of the nineteenth century. In the Southwestern or Kwa Province, the tribes of the Yoruba cluster have long been organized in a number of large states and some lesser ones constructed on the same model; the Nupe cluster has been dominated since about 1400 by the great state of the Nupe; and the great state of Benin had already established hegemony over the Edo cluster for several centuries prior to the first visit of the Portuguese in 1485. If a large state is defined as one of more than two hundred thousand population, large states are confined to these three regions. In the eastern clusters of the Kwa Province, as well as throughout the Central or Bantoid, the Eastern or Chadic, and the Southeastern or Cameroon Provinces, one finds only smaller states or stateless societies.

The two and one-half provinces within which large states predominate embrace more than 15 million of the 25 or 26 million inhabitants of Nigeria (this population estimate is derived from ethnographic sources, not from census figures). They include two of the three major foci of political power in modern Nigeria—the Fulani-Hausa in the north and the Yoruba in the southwest. The third focus—the southeast under Ibo leadership—lies in the region of lesser socio-political systems with some ten million inhabitants.

(2) *Small states.* A small state may be defined for present purposes as one which organizes by formal political means a population ranging from a maximum of about two hundred thousand to a minimum that may on occasion barely exceed one thousand. Of the ten million Nigerians who were traditionally organized in "lesser socio-political systems," i.e., who lacked large states, approximately a quarter were organized in small states structured on a similar model. Small states characterized an appreciable majority of the inhabitants of the Eastern or Chadic Province and of the Southeastern or Cameroon Province but less than 10 per cent of the inhabitants of the Central or Bantoid Province, the Adamawa cluster of the Eastern Province, and the three eastern clusters (Ibo, Idoma, and Ijaw) of the Southwestern or Kwa Province.

I shall describe briefly the structure of four of these states, one from each of the provinces where they occur. These descriptions will serve incidentally to characterize the larger traditional states of other parts of Nigeria, which differ essentially only in the greater size of the populations governed.

The Igala tribe of the Idoma cluster of the Southwestern or Kwa Province was formerly politically organized under a divine king, who resided in a capital town. Here he was served by palace officials and favorites, many of them eunuchs, and early accounts suggest a Queen-Mother of elevated status. A territorial bureaucracy of hereditary titled officials administered the country and collected taxes and tribute. The highest among them formed a supreme executive and judicial council, which advised the king and chose his successor from among the royal lineages that filled the office in rotation. The ruler was hedged in by a multitude of taboos and was believed neither to eat nor to sleep. Human sacrifices attended his death.

The Jukun, almost alone among the tribes of the Central or Bantoid Province, were organized in a unified state until their conquest by the Fulani in the early nineteenth century. An administrative hierarchy of district chiefs and provincial governors collected tribute in game and agricultural produce. The governors, who belonged to the royal family, also served as ministers of state at the capital and formed a privy council headed by a prime minister. In theory the king had absolute power and could appropriate any property and take any woman as a wife. He was served by specialized palace officials, including a chief steward, a chief chamberlain, and a chief groom. Prominent at the court were two female figures whom even the king treated with respect: a Queen-Mother, the favorite wife of the previous king, and a Queen-Sister, a sister of the former king with authority over all the women at court. The ruler was regarded as divine, the representative and mediator of the gods, and his person was sacred; his feet could not touch the ground, and he communicated with his subjects from behind a screen. His primary function was the supernatural control of the forces of nature. If he failed, or in any other way showed evidence of the loss of divine power, e.g., by falling ill, suffering an accident, or even by sneezing, he was put to death. The role of executioner fell to one of the ministers, the Abun Achuwo, who also had the authority to select the ruler's successor.

The Bolewa were one of a number of societies in the Eastern or Chadic Province characterized by small states. Here, too, the ruler had some of the characteristics of a divine king. Associated with him were numerous titled officials: ministers, palace attendants, a Queen-Mother, and a Queen-Consort of elevated status, who was not permitted to bear sons. The prime minister and head of the administrative organization had to be a commoner. The eldest son of the monarch, though a minister, could not succeed directly to the throne, since succession alternated between two branches of the royal lineage.

The Mum tribe of the Southeastern or Cameroon Province was organized in an integrated political system under an absolute monarch with many of the characteristics of a divine king. The ruler resided in a capital town, maintained an elaborate court with a highly respected Queen-Mother and differentiated officials, ruled with the assistance of a privy council of seven ministers, and administered his country through a hierarchy of vassal chiefs and appointive district heads. He was succeeded by a son, though not necessarily the eldest.

(3) *Autonomous communities.* Simple political systems that integrate only very small populations—either a single local community or at most a small cluster of contiguous settlements—are found in many parts of the primitive world and must have been universal before man's advance from a hunting and gathering economy to an economy based on food production. Although kinship and other social relations may be maintained over a considerably broader territory, the area of political relationships remains very limited in these "primitive democracies."

The so-called Neolithic Revolution, which first occurred in the Near East about ten thousand years ago, paved the way to the development of more complex and comprehensive political systems to which the term "state" can be appropriately applied. It did not, however, assure their appearance, for more than agriculture and animal husbandry are necessary to produce complex political institutions. Irrigated agriculture in semi-arid regions is doubtless one such sufficient cause, since it can give rise to urban aggregations too large for informal mechanisms of social control to be effective, and especially because the construction and maintenance of large-scale irrigation systems require a tight organization with coercive powers to organize the labor force and regulate the equitable distribution of water. States can arise through conquest under other geographical conditions, but this is unlikely to occur until a sufficiently high level of technological development has been reached to make conquest and the exploitation of subjugated peoples an obviously profitable enterprise. It is not my purpose here to write a dissertation on the origin of the state, but merely to indicate that societies can remain stateless even after they achieve agriculture and domestic animals if certain other social and technological conditions are not present.

Nearly a third of Nigeria's inhabitants fall into this category, for they have not, in the past, been politically organized in states, either large or small. For the most part they have lived in autonomous local communities—villages or clusters of small hamlets —without formal political bonds with other comparable units. Leadership in local affairs is normally assumed by a headman, whose office is often hereditary within the senior lineage of the community but is rarely associated with any coercive authority. He may share his functions and responsibilities with a ritual specialist or titled assistants, but decisions are reached only in consultation with a council of elders or family heads and on the basis of general consensus. Relations with neighboring communities are sometimes warlike; headhunting and even cannibalism were formerly not uncommon in some of the more backward areas. More often such relations are friendly, but they are based on bonds of kinship and marriage, of peaceful intergroup trade, or of common religious observances rather than on formal political ties. A few examples will reveal some of the ways in which groups of contiguous communities relate themselves to one another short of sacrificing their autonomy through the formation of even a petty state.

Among the Widekum of the Southeastern or Cameroon Province, although each local community enjoys independence under the leadership of a headman and a council of lineage heads, all the communities of a subtribe consider their members to be related by common descent and, in recognition thereof, acknowledge one local headman as senior to the rest. Though he exercises no political authority outside his own community, he has the special function of sacrificing to the ancestral spirits and the earth gods in behalf of the entire subtribe.

The Yungur of the Adamawa cluster of the Eastern Province lack any true political integration beyond the level of the local community with a hereditary headman, whose functions are largely ritual in character and who is assisted by a council of elders. All the communities of a district, however, acknowledge the ritual supremacy of one headman, whose person is sacred and whose rainmaking powers earn for him recognition as priest-chief of the district as a whole. One hereditary rainmaker formerly enjoyed a comparable repute throughout the neighboring Longuda tribe. In case of a prolonged drought he was beheaded. Perhaps we can glimpse here the roots of the divine kingship as it has developed in many of the larger states.

In the Idoma tribe of the Southwestern or Kwa Province the most vital political unit is the local community—an aggregation of settlements inhabited by the members of one patrilineal clan, who rarely number as many as two thousand people. The clan head, called "owner of the land," serves as local headman and is assisted by a council of elders or by a popular assembly. Related clans, if they occupy a contiguous district, are loosely federated into a larger unit on the basis of assumed kinship and the observance of common totemic taboos. A chief of the district is selected in rotation from the component clans, but his position is in no respect comparable to that of the paramount chief of a small state.

The Tiv tribe of the Central or Bantoid Province is organized on the basis of a segmentary lineage system without stable leadership or recognized offices at either the local or the district level. The heads of larger lineage segments are able to mobilize their members in opposition to other comparable segments, but jealousy and even sorcery prevent their attainment of effective control over the rival smaller segments of their own group.

Among the Ibibio, the largest tribe of the same province, each of the component wards or hamlets of a community, which typically are localized patrilineal lineages, has both a secular and a ritual head, usually the oldest man and the head of the resident lineage respectively. The community as a whole has a headman and a council of lineage heads, but the principal political influence is commonly exercised by the members of secret societies with graded titles. The Leopard Society, with five grades and a leader for each, is particularly influential, and the leader of its ranking grade often holds the office of headman. Groups of villages are united into districts by common rituals, a tradition of kinship, and sometimes also by a ritual and secular chief and a council of elders, but each community nevertheless remains to a large extent politically autonomous.

The villages of the neighboring Ibo of the Southwestern or Kwa Province tend similarly toward local autonomy, despite their aggregation into districts with a common market place and ritual center. Even the village commonly lacks a recognized headman, being governed by a council of lineage heads with the head of the senior lineage as presiding officer.

Among the Afikpo Ibo in the east, integration is achieved through a complex system of age-sets and age-grades. At intervals of about three years the young men who have come of age in each village are organized in an age-set, of which there may to from five to nine at any given time. Some of these sets serve as village policemen and executors of the decisions of the village elders. At intervals of eight or nine years, the three oldest of these sets in all the villages of a subtribe are promoted to the lowest of three senior age-grades, whose previous members are advanced to the intermediate senior age-grade. The members of the first senior grade serve as warriors. Those of the intermediate senior grade, which comprises six age-sets, constitute the council of elders in their respective communities. The members of the third senior grade enjoy great prestige but exercise no actual authority. This rests exclusively with the men of the intermediate senior age-grade, for there are no local headmen. Brawls occur between communities of the same subtribe, but killing is strictly forbidden; the vanquished, at the most, suffer only a beating. True warfare, involving the taking of heads as trophies, occurs only between communities of different subtribes.

III

Predictions about the future of the new states of Africa are always dangerous, but I share with other Africanists the conviction that Nigeria's prospect of making a successful transition to full membership in the international community of free nations is better than that of most other new sub-Saharan states. Nigeria might well set a pattern that could be followed by the rest of Negro Africa.

While the future political and economic progress of Nigeria undoubtedly will depend to a great extent upon "modern" ideas and institutions, as succeeding chapters will suggest, we should not ignore the possibility that traditional factors will continue to influence the course of twentieth-century development. Social scientists at this time would be hard pressed to suggest a positive relationship between the traditional social orders surveyed in this introductory chapter and the nature of the future political development of Nigeria; however, several questions are apparent and seem worthy of our attention in the years ahead. Though by no means exhausting the list, I shall conclude by suggesting several of these. If there are common elements in the experience of peoples living under democratic regimes, whether they be simple or complex, may it not be that certain traditional groups of the Nigerian peoples, habituated to a primitive type of democracy, will find complex democratic institutions more congenial than authoritarian ones? If this should prove true, will not modern democratic ideas be best received by the Ibo and their stateless neighbors, who have already shown evidence of successful adaptation to other introductions from the West? Will the general tone of Nigerian political development be set by these groups? On the other hand, should the tone of Nigerian development be set by the more numerous inhabitants of northern and northwestern Nigeria, is it possible that these groups, more habituated to absolutist and bureaucratic states, may gravitate toward more authoritarian forms of government? In the north it seems possible that the Hausa, subordinated to the Fulani minority for more than a century and a half, will desire to alter their present political position. If this assumption is valid, what will this mean in terms of the development of Northern Nigeria in particular and of the Federation in general?

While these and other questions may not be answered until some time in the distant future, it behooves Africanists of all disciplines to pay especially close attention to coming events in the new state of Nigeria.

2

The Evolution of British Policy
Toward Nigeria

W. B. Hamilton

The story of British policy toward Nigeria [1] covers a short period in the world's annals. The acquisition of territory began a
hundred years ago (Lagos) and was not completed until 1914;
fully half of it was taken over in the present century.[2] The very
name of the country was suggested by Flora Shaw (Lady Lugard)
only in 1897; moreover, the area to which she gave a name did
not have a unified administration until 1914, and that constituted
a mere personal union under Sir Frederick (later Lord) Lugard,
as a sort of emperor over two large areas of many native governments. Yet on October 1, 1960, the British departed, hopefully
leaving behind a federal state. Within the very brief period here
surveyed events occurred at two entirely different speeds: in the
years before 1945, except for brief straining bursts of hurry in
1884 and 1897–98, there seemed to be ample leisure in which to
contemplate slow evolution, but in the few years after World
War II what before seemed incredible happened with lightning
speed.

The British first came to Nigeria, that is to the Bights of Benin
and Biafra, to trade in men, an enterprise in which they soon took
the lead.[3] After Parliament, in an act jammed through by Lord

---

[1] The author has chosen to exclude from consideration the Cameroons Mandate,
attached to Nigeria for administrative purposes by Order in Council, June 26, 1923.
[2] On September 16, 1914, Egbaland or Abeokuta, not far from Lagos, became
the last area acquired. Most of the present Eastern Region was not occupied until
1903–9.
[3] The Introduction to Vol. II of Elizabeth Donnan, ed., *Documents Illustrative
of the Slave Trade to America* (4 vols.; Washington, 1930–35), relates the organ-

Grenville in the expiring days of his administration (approved March 25, 1807), made it a crime for an Englishman to engage in the slave trade, they expended a great amount of money and energy in fighting that trade. No amount of emphasis on other motives of that people in its expansion can dull the luster of the nineteenth-century crusade against the slave trade, a crusade in which not only reformers but also the Foreign and Colonial offices and the Navy were heavily engaged.[4] Hampered by the refusal of other European nationals—despite repeated bribes by the British Government to persuade them to prohibit the trade effectively— and by the unco-operative attitude of the United States, British cruisers were not able to stamp out the slave trade in West Africa until slavery was abolished in the western hemisphere. With all their cost to the British in men and money, the squadrons cap-tured only about 10 per cent of the shipping involved in the trade. But in rough figures, between 1810 and 1864, this noble work returned 150,000 potential slaves to West Africa.[5]

In the Niger delta the proscription of slaving posed problems for the British traders and for the African middlemen who sup-plied the slaves. Fortunately there was arising another staple, palm oil, and the demand for it was increasing. The alleged new cleanliness of the English and the undoubted increase of the machines of the industrial revolution created a market for soap and lubricants. The Africans, good traders, took over this trade, with some revolutionary adjustments, in return for the same goods as in the old—guns and "trade spirits," the latter being cheap gin and rum from Holland and Hamburg. The middlemen battened on producer and merchant alike, and, if they were chiefs, got an additional tribute in presents or "comey," which was an export or trading charge.

---

ization of the British slave trade. See also Gomer Williams, *History of the Liver-pool Privateers and Letters of Marque With an Account of the Liverpool Slave Trade* (London, 1897); and A. Mackenzie-Grieve, *The Last Years of the English Slave Trade, Liverpool, 1750–1807* (London, 1941).

  [4] Sir R. Coupland, *The British Anti-Slavery Movement* (2nd ed., London, 1939); C. Lloyd, *The Navy and the Slave Trade: the Suppression of the African Slave Trade in the Nineteenth Century* (London, 1949); and W. L. Mathieson, *Great Britain and the Slave Trade, 1839–1865* (London, 1929) will give an introduc-tion to the subject and to the voluminous literature.

  [5] Lloyd, *op. cit.*, pp. 275–76.

The reformers at home likewise saw profit in the new trade. The theory arose that "legitimate," or non-slave trade, would drive out the trade in human beings, and, if it were so pushed as to convert the Africans to it, stop the slave raiding and even pacify and civilize the natives. Thomas Fowell Buxton, for example, in *The African Slave Trade and the Remedy*, 1839, argued that the gospel and the plow were needed. Thus did trade, the preoccupation of a trading people, take on the aura of beneficence, providing it were "legitimate." The merchants joined in the attack on the slave trade because it went to rivals and diverted the channels of the middlemen. In sum, the energies of all the Englishmen on the Niger Coast were devoted to attacking the slave trade and positively supporting the legitimate traders. A British naval squadron patrolled the coasts under orders to promote these twin ends. Inevitably, either aim, and certainly the two combined, would involve the Navy in intervention in the politics of the "city-states" of the Oil Rivers. One of the earlier instances was the overthrow in 1837, under the guns of English boats, of the regent of Bonny, Alali, closely allied with the slave traders, and his replacement with the young king, William Dappa Pepple, who promptly made a treaty favorable to the English merchants.[6]

To Dr. K. O. Dike, the Bonny affair signalized the triumph of the British and of legitimate trade, and the arrival of gunboat diplomacy. The British naval officers entered upon a period of treaty-making, and, in some instances, king-making. Most of the treaties tried to bribe the kings to stop the slave trade by promising annual subventions for a term, at the expense of the British taxpayer.[7] (It will be remembered that Castlereagh and others had offered monetary payments to European powers for the same purpose.) Naval diplomacy, however, had its shortcomings. The officers were birds of passage, a fact not conducive to continuity. The treaties they signed were not always ratified, and they might, indeed, disappear within the strange disarray of departments in

[6] K. Onwuka Dike, *Trade and Politics in the Niger Delta, 1830–1885: An Introduction to the Economic and Political History of Nigeria* (Oxford, 1956), pp. 69–77.
[7] *Ibid.*, pp. 77–86. Chap. v is entitled "The Slave-Trade Treaties."

the English government that dealt with the Oil Rivers. The Foreign Office was the most important of these departments, but there were also the Admiralty and the Board of Trade, and above all the Treasury, a very difficult body. Too, the naval officers (gentlemen) sometimes cooled about supporting the rascally traders; Palmerston had in 1848 to order them to resume interference in the African states.[8]

Lord Palmerston was an activist, an interventionist, an expansionist, and a fanatical foe of the slave trade. Perceiving the unsatisfactory vagueness in British policy and conduct on the Niger Coast, as well as the existing anarchy, he appointed a consul, over the opposition of the Colonial Office. So decisive was this step that before too long the English consul was *de facto* governor of the Bights of Benin and Biafra.[9] It cannot be claimed that consular government, with which the British extemporized in the Oil Rivers throughout the century, was very effective, or at least it might be argued that its effects were sporadic.[10]

The next step, the forcible reduction of Lagos and the extension thence of consular rule, perfectly illustrates the complexity of motives and forces operating upon British policy. By the end of the 1840's missionaries, notably Henry Townsend of the Church Missionary Society, had established themselves inland at Abeokuta, town of the Egbas. Abeokuta needed support against the King of Dahomey, and British sympathies were easily aroused because that king was an unregenerate slaver. The Egbas (and the missionaries) also needed to trade through Lagos, where the slave-trading Kosoko had deposed his uncle, Akitoye, a man disposed toward "legitimate," rather than the slave, trade. In 1849 the CMS put heavy pressure on Palmerston for support of Abeokuta and for the stationing of a gunboat at Lagos.[11] With his predilections, such incitements as Consul John Beecroft's statement that "it is easy to discern that Lagos is the focus of the Slave Trade in the Bight of Benin . . ." were unnecessary to cause Palm-

[8] *Ibid.*, pp. 86, 91.
[9] *Ibid.*, pp. 93, 128. John Beecroft, an able and informed man, was appointed first consul on June 30, 1849.
[10] See, for example, Sir William Neville M. Geary, *Nigeria under British Rule* (London, 1927), chap. iv.
[11] Saburi O. Biobaku, *The Egba and Their Neighbours, 1842–1872* (Oxford, 1957), p. 36.

erston to command Beecroft to negotiate with Lagos to stop the trade. He furnished the consul with a good Palmerstonian argument: ". . . the British Government is resolved to put an end to the African Slave Trade, and has the means and power to do so." Furthermore, Kosoko was to be threatened with support of his rival.[12] Early in 1851 Beecroft made a visit to Abeokuta, where, it is clear, he fell into the hands of chiefs, missionaries, and supporters of Akitoye, all of whom were opposed to Kosoko in Lagos. He urged attack.[13] In brief, Palmerston in September ordered a blockade of the Dahomey Coast and the expulsion of Kosoko, if it could be accomplished without too much risk; after an abortive effort the British captured Lagos, December 24–28; Akitoye, restored as king, signed a treaty with the British January 1, 1852.[14] There were of course many dissatisfactions with the British consuls, with Dosunmu [15] (who had succeeded his father as king of Lagos), and with the general political situation in Yorubaland, where wars were endemic. Whatever the motives, John Brand, the Consul at Lagos, recommended to the Foreign Secretary, Lord John Russell, the occupation of Lagos, giving as reasons the absence of effective government, inadequate protection of property, irregular administration of justice, and an unsatisfactory mode of collecting debts. A year later, Lord John ordered the occupation, giving as *his* reasons the desires to complete the suppression of the slave trade in the Bight, to aid and support the development of lawful commerce, and to "check the aggressive spirit of the King of Dahomey." [16] Accordingly, on August 6, 1861,

[12] Beecroft, from Clarence, Fernando Po, to Palmerston, Dec. 5, 1850 (not received until March 15, 1851); Palmerston to Beecroft, Feb. 20, 1851, in Great Britain, House of Commons, *Sessional Papers, 1852,* LIV, 221 ff., "Papers relative to The Reduction of Lagos by Her Majesty's Forces on the West Coast of Africa" (No. 1455), pp. 83, 86.

[13] Report by Beecroft from Fernando Po on his visit, Feb. 21, 1851 (received June 10), *ibid.,* pp. 91 ff. The missionaries, as these documents show, were making similar suggestions to Commodore Fanshawe, of the patrol squadron, and to others.

[14] Palmerston to Lords Commissioners of the Admiralty, Sept. 27, 1851, *ibid.,* pp. 135–36; Biobaku, *op. cit.,* pp. 40–46; Sir Alan Burns, *History of Nigeria* (5th ed.; London, 1955), chap. x.

[15] The author follows Dr. Biobaku's spelling of this name. In most works it is "Docemo"; in Burns, "Dosumu."

[16] Brand, from Lagos, to Russell, April 9, 1860; Russell to Consul H. G. Foote, June 22, 1861, in Great Britain, House of Commons, *Sessional Papers, 1862,* LXI, 339 ff., "Papers Relating to the Occupation of Lagos," (No. 2982), pp. 4–5. See also *ibid.,* pp. 365 ff., "Additional Papers Relating to the Occupation of Lagos" (No. 3003).

Dosunmu signed away his sovereignty, retaining his title, and was pensioned off. In 1862 Lagos became a crown colony; the Colonial Office had an unwelcome gift from the Foreign Office, to the annexation of which they had however, Dr. C. W. Newbury points out, agreed in June of 1861; and the Treasury for some years had the privilege of contributing to the cost of administration of Lagos.

Even on such a brief and oversimplified summary as the narrative just concluded, it is possible to perceive that British policy in West Africa was significantly influenced by the involvement of missionaries, and some consuls, in the politics of the Africans, in this case principally those of the Egbas. This fact was well-understood by the resident Britons.[17] How much it was grasped by the higher officials in Whitehall, it is hard to say, although they certainly had the documents before them. There is some truth in the witticism in a new, much-discussed book that "Ignorant of realities and intoxicated with the exuberance of their own generosity, the British [at home] conceived tropical African issues as problems of ethical behaviour—a habit which has endured." [18] The Palmerstons and the Russells had their own attitudes through which they filtered the reports from the Bights, and they were not ignoble ones. They occupied and then annexed Lagos because it was represented to them that it would conduce to the welfare of the Africans, the reduction of the trade in slaves, and the glory of

[17] It therefore seems a bit extraordinary to see involvement announced as new and revisionist doctrine in J. D. Hargreaves, "Towards a History of the Partition of Africa," *Journal of African History*, I (1960), 97–109. When we say Britons understood they were involved in Egba and other Yoruba politics, we do not mean to imply they possessed the sociological and anthropological information to understand *what* they were involved in—that is, the political and social structures of these peoples. See, for example, Margery Perham, *Lugard: The Years of Authority, 1898–1945* (London, 1960), pp. 438–56. Lord Passfield, Jan. 27, 1931, underlined the obvious when he wrote of the disturbances in the East in 1929 that they made evident the necessity of further inquiry into the social organization of the inhabitants. Lugard's blindness was remarked upon: "It will be remembered that when Sir Frederick (now Lord) Lugard recommended the termination of the appointment of Mr. Northcote Thomas, the anthropologist who was at work in Southern Nigeria from 1909 to 1913, he expressed the view that researches into native law and custom were best conducted by Political Officers. . . ." Great Britain, *Parliamentary Papers, 1930–31*, XXIII, "Despatch from the Secretary of State for the Colonies to the Officer Administering Nigeria regarding the Report of the Commission of Inquiry into the Disturbances at Aba and other places in South-East Nigeria in November and December, 1929" (Cmd. 3784).

[18] Ronald Robinson and John Gallagher, with Alice Denny [Robinson], *Africa and the Victorians: The Climax of Imperialism in the Dark Continent* (London and New York, 1961), p. 27.

God to do so. They were not under pressure from merchants in this case. Indeed, especially when the unpopularity of the annexation among the Africans to the north and a purely coincidental increase in civil war among the Yorubas diminished the trade of Lagos, the merchants regarded annexation as a grievance.[19] They always knew, as well, that trade had to pay the costs of administration of a British colony. Russell's salute to trade in explaining his reasons was partly the habitual genuflection of a nineteenth-century Englishman (not that he did not mean it; he had lively hopes for cotton cultivation, for example), along with the reformer's salute to "legitimate" trade as the enemy of the slave traffic.

In any event, the British were now installed on the coast of Nigeria. There they intended to remain. As far as Nigeria goes, the discussion by historians of a general policy of withdrawal, economy, and lack of interest in colonies in the 1860's is inapplicable. The atmosphere is typified by the report of a committee of the House of Commons in 1865 on West Africa, a committee dominated by its chairman, C. B. Adderley, an economizing anti-humanitarian.[20] Its members' questions hammered away skeptically at the supposed benefits of British rule. Its recommendations called for economy in colonial government, preparation of the Africans for self-rule, eventual withdrawal from all West African possessions except Sierra Leone, an end to expansion, and an end to domestic slavery in Lagos. But it also concluded that it was not possible, wholly or immediately, to withdraw the British government "from any settlements or engagements on the West African Coast." [21] And as Dr. Dike points out, there was no abatement in British expansion, in the peculiar manner of the times, in Nigeria. The committee of Commons, as he says, was creating confusion by oversimplified thinking: that whereas occupation entailed expense, free trade was free. This was an oversimplification, for free trade demanded expense and involvement.[22]

---

[19] As shown by their testimony before the Adderley committee. See Great Britain, House of Commons, *Sessional Papers, 1865*, V, "Report from the Select Committee on Africa (Western Coast) together with Proceedings of the Committee, Minutes of Evidence, and Appendix."

[20] *Ibid.* Also see Sir C. B. Adderley, *Review of "The Colonial Policy of Lord J. Russell's Administration," and of Subsequent Colonial History* (London, 1869).

[21] "Report from the Select Committee on Africa . . . ," p. iii.

[22] Dike, *Trade and Politics,* p. 166.

Lord Kimberley, Colonial Secretary in the Liberal cabinet, in 1873 ordered Lagos held, by force if necessary; [23] and his Tory successor in the next year, Lord Carnarvon, decided that the civilizing influence of trade and Britain's obligations to "friendly tribes" dictated remaining on the Gold Coast. However, presumably to save money, there would continue an amalgamation of governments: [24] Lagos was administered by the governor at Sierra Leone from 1866 to 1874, and from the Gold Coast from that year to 1886. In 1872 the judicial and governing duties of the consuls in the Bights were increased by an order in Council placing Englishmen there under the consuls' jurisdiction.[25]

The English were curious to know what lay behind this coast of creeks and swamps where they had so long traded. They had made a beginning at exploration with the celebrated journey of Mungo Park in 1795–97, and continued with a long, romantic roll [26] that includes Park again in 1805; Denham, Clapperton, and Oudney, 1822–24; Clapperton and his servant Richard Lander, 1826–27; Barth, 1850–54. Most of these adventurers traveled in the North, and all left journals comprising many volumes. It remained for Lander, with his brother John, to make the descent 'n 1830 that showed that the Oil Rivers were the mouths of the ˙iger, and thus that a highway lay into the interior. It is remarkable for the purposes of this paper to point out that while the first journey of Mungo Park was financed by the African Association, men of scientific and philanthropic interests, almost all the rest were subsidized, and indeed organized, by the British government, likewise men of scientific and humanitarian interests, but also of a passion for trade.

After 1830 the great aim was to break through the reef of the African middlemen, who had controlled the trade for centuries, and deal directly with the "producers" of palm oil. This the middlemen strongly resisted, aided by those merchants who had

[23] Biobaku, *op. cit.*, p. 94.
[24] E. A. Benian, *et al.*, eds., *The Cambridge History of the British Empire* (9 vols.; Cambridge, 1929–59), III, 43. (Hereinafter cited as *CHBE*.)
[25] Dike, *Trade and Politics*, p. 201. This same order likewise recognized the mixed African and trader courts of equity that had long been in operation.
[26] Summary account, and short-title bibliography, in Burns, *op. cit.*, 5th ed., pp. 74–98.

established profitable connections with them; much African history hangs on the conflict that ensued.[27] Again, the British government participated in the breakthrough. In 1841 it organized an expedition that was to instal missions and a model farm at Lokoja. The whole scheme was freighted with the hopes of such reformers as Buxton, who never recovered from its collapse.[28] The Government likewise subsidized, or contracted for, the later voyages up the Niger of the steamers of Macgregor Laird (d. 1861), who dominated the scene for nearly thirty years. Indeed it was a government ship, contracted by Laird, which in 1854, under the command of W. B. Baikie, demonstrated the secret of up-river trade by Europeans: quinine. In 1857 the Government entered into an agreement with Laird to subsidize five annual expeditions up the river.[29] One of Government's motives was deliberately to assist in the process by which Laird's steamships were breaking the monopoly of the middlemen and the old supercargoes,[30] and another "was to strike the slave trade at its roots." [31]

In 1860, as samples of governmental policy on the up-river trade: (1) The Foreign Office, on recommendation from the Board of Trade that the trading interests receive protection, appointed John Washington, Hydrographer to the Admiralty, to examine the problem. He rather thought cannon balls a poor foundation for trade, but Palmerston minuted on his report for armed protection and for the occupation of Lagos. (2) Lord John Russell recommended subsidizing a "chosen" firm, and the Treasury, after grumbling that using public money for exploration was one thing, but subsidizing commercial ventures was quite another, reluctantly agreed. After a long fight, the Liverpool coastal

---

[27] The authority on this story is Dike, *Trade and Politics.*

[28] According to the sketch of him in the Eleventh Edition of the *Encyclopaedia Britannica.* Story in Burns, *op. cit.* (2nd ed.; London, 1936), pp. 103–4.

[29] Testimony of James A. Tobin, a Liverpool merchant, before the Adderley Committee of 1865 ("Report from the Select Committee on Africa . . . ," pp. 214 ff.) was that the amount of the subsidy was £8000, decreasing by £500 a year to £6000, and that Laird was to return one-half of the profits over 6 per cent on his investment.

[30] Robinson, Gallagher, and Denny, *op. cit.,* pp. 36–37.

[31] According to W. Wylde, Superintendent of the Slave Trade Department of the Foreign Office, testimony before the Adderley Committee of 1865 ("Report from the Select Committee on Africa . . . ," pp. 108 ff.), Wylde was referring specifically to the tenuous settlement maintained by Baikie at Lokoja, 1859–64.

merchants defeated the scheme. (3) The Admiralty ordered convoying up the river; the local Navymen demurred.[32]

From 1866 to 1869 a consulate was maintained at Lokoja,[33] but the difficulties of its defense proved too great; and to rid themselves of the expense of even one gunboat expedition a year the British sent W. H. Simpson in 1871 to get Masaba, the Emir of Nupe, to take over the protection of the trade. He agreed, his price being the establishment of the middlemen system up the river, with his Nupe trade at Egga having a monopoly.[34] This could not be satisfactory for long, but there seemed little choice. Government was averse to administration costs, to annexation, and yet an increasing trade in the Niger[35] was assuredly to involve them again and again in the affairs of the region. Their hand was soon forced by a Manxman and the French.

Sir George Goldie,[36] a young man who had shown no promise of any sort before he was in 1876 put in charge of a small family interest in the Niger trade, was one of the geniuses who drive straight toward a logical ideal. No free trader really believes in free trade—he wishes to crush his competitor. Goldie conceived that the remedy for the troubles of the Niger trade was monopoly, and he set about single-mindedly to achieve it. By 1879 he had combined most of the firms trading on the river into the United African Company. Dr. Flint, in his book on Goldie, makes a neat point about the theory of imperialism after looking at the organizer and directors of UAC. He quotes J. A. Hobson's celebrated dictum on *Imperialism* (1902) that "the dominant and directive motive was the demand for markets and for profitable investment by the exporting and financial classes." Flint avers that these motives fit no shareholder of Goldie's company. They exported other people's firearms and European spirits to swap for oil for soap and other factories not owned by them; they were not "exporters."

[32] Burns, *op. cit.*, 2nd ed., p. 107; Dike, *Trade and Politics*, pp. 174–80.
[33] Burns, *op. cit.*, 2nd ed., p. 150.
[34] John E. Flint, *Sir George Goldie and the Making of Nigeria* (London, 1960), pp. 24–25.
[35] Jack Simmons, in *CHBE*, III, 66, 74–75. Detailed accounts are Allan McPhee, *The Economic Revolution in British West Africa* (London, 1926); and A. N. Cook, *British Enterprise in Nigeria* (Philadelphia, 1943).
[36] George Dashwood Goldie Taubman until 1887.

They were not financiers looking for a place to invest; they had scarcely any capital.[37] The question of Goldie's motivations in building an empire in Africa remains unanswered. Money will not quite do; Goldie drove hard for a profit, but a profit had some further satisfaction for him than mere money. Power, obviously; Goldie was an imperious autocrat, if not a very showy one. Patriotism, empire building? Doubtless later on, after he had acquired a taste for international diplomacy, but probably not at first.[38]

Goldie had no sooner formed his combine than French traders moved in and, with the help of mutineers against the Emir of Nupe, broke his monopoly. He then concluded that the solution lay in a charter from the government, a view in which he was confirmed by the chartering of the North Borneo Company in 1881. Rounding up some directors with prestige and political connections, Goldie laid siege to a government that was beginning to have its own qualms about the French, now very active around and behind the English spheres in West Africa, and about the Germans. Consul Edward Hewett suggested a colony, a protectorate, or a chartered company for the Oil Rivers. The Foreign Office began to grope around, meeting with hostility in the Colonial Office, where the Secretary, Lord Kimberley, was especially averse to a colony. Increasing French pressure moderated the do-nothing attitude of the latter office, but it still vetoed the idea of a colony, so that Granville at the Foreign Office was left with a protectorate as a mere expedient, a casual solution that set the pattern for British governmental operations in Africa. In November of 1883 the Cabinet agreed on a protectorate over the Cameroons, Oil Rivers, and Niger mouths on the cheapest possible basis—no government, no recurrent expense to imperial funds. There followed a six-months' search for the means of financing a protectorate. Goldie "helped" by offering his manager, David McIntosh, as vice-consul on the Niger; the Foreign Office scraped up, after agonizing economies, £5,790, and Hewett, with the

[37] Flint, *op. cit.*, pp. 30–33.
[38] It is amusing that the new biography by an Englishman gives a hard-bitten impression of Goldie in his early stages, while Dike, who has made us see an economic motive in all the British enterprise in Africa, attributes to him patriotic empire-building aims.

necessary backing, began to make treaties (spring of 1884) with
the Oil River chiefs. McIntosh, for his part, secured the states on
both sides of the Niger up to the confluence with the Benue in
treaties that ceded sovereignty to the *company*! [39]

The hour was five minutes to twelve: the Berlin Conference
on West Africa was at hand, France was demanding an international commission on the Niger, and Bismarck was supporting
her to make the British come to heel. Goldie put everything he
had into buying up the French companies and concluded his
amalgamation of them two weeks before the Conference opened.
Three days before that event, the Colonial Committee of the
Cabinet gave the National African Company the right to hoist
the Union Jack over areas where they held "independent title."
So at the Conference Britain fended off an international commission and was left with the Nigerian Coast and the lower Niger,
on conditions that included free navigation on the river. [40] On
June 5, 1885, Great Britain proclaimed a protectorate over the
coast between Lagos and the Rio del Rey, from the banks of the
Niger to its confluence with the Benue, and from the banks of the
Benue northward through Ibi.

It was the government of Gladstone acting in this imperial
manner. There needs to be a re-examination of the impression
left by writers able to make easy generalizations about imperialism that the Liberals were against expansion and the Tories, especially after Disraeli, were for it. In the microcosm of Nigeria we
have seen Palmerston and Russell taking Lagos and establishing
consular power on the Bights. The extension of the latter in 1872
was in an administration of Gladstone. The same Gladstonian
regime that claimed Nigeria in the scramble for Africa took Egypt
and chartered the North Borneo Company, and, having really
settled Goldie on the Niger, came back into office in time to grant
him the charter that he so strongly desired (1886). [41]

The chartering of Goldie's company was, like the protectorate
scheme, merely the easiest expedient to avoid governmental re-

[39] Flint, *op. cit.*, pp. 47–55. The delay over a few pennies had cost Great Britain
the Cameroons.
[40] *Ibid.*, pp. 64–70.
[41] It passed the Great Seal July 10.

sponsibility and expense. It was not a positive measure to forward English trade, but a sort of negative action, *faute de mieux*. The company was to exercise the Queen's jurisdiction over subjects and foreigners under the Foreign Jurisdiction Act; the Foreign Office was to have a veto over transfers of cessions or rights under treaties of the company, relations with foreign powers, and policy concerning local peoples; and the company was to discourage and as far as possible abolish slavery.

That was not very far. In 1897, freeing Kabba from Nupe, Goldie proclaimed that slavery was abolished there, and after his victory over the Emir of Nupe he issued a proclamation abolishing the legal status of slavery—a meaningless gesture designed to appeal to opinion in Britain.[42] He did inveigh with real feeling against the horrors and socially disruptive effects of slave raiding, which he thought would have to be put down by police action. He had not the money or the force to do so. Lugard did have them, and probably extirpated the worst of the slave raiding. His basic law forbade the practice, renewed the declaration that slavery had no legal status, and said children born after April 1, 1901, were free. This policy, together with right of a slave to appeal to the courts for manumission if he could prove mistreatment, was extended to the south, and resulted in a gradual emancipation of slaves.[43]

Goldie actually administered very little territory. His empire was the river. Behind its banks he "ruled," if at all, indirectly, perforce; he could not afford administrative machinery. Of this necessity, Goldie stated the policy as early as 1886, and in 1897 laid the theoretical groundwork for what subsequently became dogma.[44]

Wherein lay Goldie's contribution to Nigeria? It was simply and grandly this, that his merely being there, his policy of jealously monopolistic exclusion, and his treaties with the emirs saved Northern Nigeria for England (and for Nigeria) at a time when the country was too stingy and too preoccupied with other areas

[42] Flint, *op. cit.*, pp. 250, 257.
[43] Perham, *op. cit.*, II, 40–42, 171–72, 457–58; Burns, *op. cit.*, 2nd ed., pp. 207–11.
[44] Flint, *op. cit.*, pp. 94–95, 258–59.

to contest the area. Not commerce, but strategy, guided the government of Salisbury in the late 1880's and early 1890's. Their preoccupation with East Africa, because of their obsession with India and the Near East, was so excessive that they were, before Chamberlain, quite willing to yield in West Africa to secure the Nile. Only Goldie's work prevented more concession than was made.[45] His company was chartered to retain the area cheaply, and Sir Percy Anderson in the Foreign Office viewed it as the function of Goldie to push on north to combat the French. Anderson, in briefing Rosebery when he became Secretary in 1892, admitted that the company was a monopoly but pointed out that it secured possession for Great Britain of a large area of Africa.[46] The French rivalry, brewing for so many years, became more serious toward the mid-nineties and came to a showdown in 1896–97, with an actual race for occupation in the west-central areas of the present Nigeria. The tale is far too long to tell here; we shall merely introduce Captain Frederick Lugard to West Africa. In 1894 Goldie engaged him to lead a treaty-making expedition to the towns of Borgu to forestall the French.[47] As the crisis worsened with the French, who were sending troops into the area, Joseph Chamberlain at last turned his attention, hitherto distracted by Rhodes and Jameson and the Colonial Conference, to West Africa. He sent Lugard out to organize and command a West African Frontier Force. The British Government was at last going to act on its own to hold territory, it was going to use force, and it was going to spend some money.[48] The necessity for the Company was therefore at an end, although Goldie tried to demonstrate his usefulness by leading a brilliant attack on Nupe and Ilorin. As it would be with the Fashoda incident, the battle between the British and the French was transferred to the conference table, where the Colonial Secretary took charge of diplomacy and in the summer

[45] Robinson, Gallagher, and Denny, *op. cit.,* pp. 390–93.
[46] *Ibid.,* pp. 100, 190–91.
[47] *Ibid.,* pp. 220 ff.; Perham, *op. cit.,* I, 532–42.
[48] Chamberlain of course dramatized the active, the aggressive, elements in policy at the higher London points of policy-making. But it must be noted that to give him sole credit for official action in occupying and garrisoning Nigeria is to overlook the occupation and garrisoning by local officials of the interior of Yorubaland, begun in 1892 by Governor (of Lagos) Sir Gilbert Carter and continued by his successor in the 1890's. Geary, *op. cit.,* pp. 50–51; Burns, *op. cit.,* 5th ed., pp. 204–7.

of 1898 forced the French into a favorable settlement—approximately the present western and northern boundaries of Nigeria.[49] In the following year the charter of the Royal Niger Company was revoked; it was paid £865,000.[50] The North was now a protectorate of the Crown.

Thus, on the neat date of January 1, 1900, Britain had three Nigerian possessions: the new Protectorate of Northern Nigeria, placed under Lugard as high commissioner; the Protectorate of Southern Nigeria—which was the old Oil Rivers Protectorate of 1885 extended and renamed the Niger Coast Protectorate in 1893 —now handed over from the Foreign to the Colonial Office; and the Colony of Lagos, to which time had added much of the southwest, or Yorubaland. An Order in Council of 1887 had provided for the exercise in "adjacent areas" of British jurisdiction in the "Protectorate of Lagos," but the legal basis, if any, for British jurisdiction in much of the southwest was quite vague.[51] However, an Order in Council, July 24, 1901, declared all the territory bounded by the French territories and the Northern and Southern protectorates to constitute "the Lagos Protectorate," without prejudice to rights secured to natives by treaties or agreements with Great Britain.[52] The fact seems to be that unless one simply accepts British power over all Nigeria as something that did exist, *de facto,* one is thrown back for legal sanction onto the Foreign Jurisdiction Acts of Parliament at Westminster, especially that of 1890; treaties with Yoruba towns; and clauses in certain international agreements, such as the Berlin Act of 1885, the Brussels Act of 1890, and the Convention of Saint-Germain, 1919. Parliament (Westminster) has never legislated on the assumption of power in Nigeria.[53]

Not to follow all the boundary changes and changes in name,

[49] Perham, *op. cit.,* I, chaps. xxix–xxxi; Flint, *op. cit.,* chaps. 10–12.
[50] Flint, *op. cit.,* p. 307.
[51] See Perham, *op. cit.,* II, 432–36, on this last point only. Lugard wanted a clear declaration of sovereignty over the Yoruba states such as he laid down in the North. He did not get it. From certain actions, in the 1890's principally, it seems that the British could have claimed much of the southwest by right of conquest, but it does not appear that this basis was ever put forward.
[52] Geary, *op. cit.,* p. 52.
[53] B. J. Walker, "The Birth of Federalism in Nigeria," in L. Brett, ed., *Constitutional Problems of Federalism in Nigeria* (Lagos, 1961). See also *CHBE,* III, 681; and, in general, M. F. Lindley, *The Acquisition and Government of Backward Territory in International Law* (London, 1926).

the union of Nigeria under a single administration—that of Lugard, by the Colonial Office and Lugard, January 1, 1914 [54]—affords an opportunity for some elementary observations. There was a governor-general, in Lugard's case an autocrat, but the component divisions of the country remained clear: the Colony, with an administrator; the Northern and Southern provinces, the latter of which was later divided into Western and Eastern. The purpose was not to try to make a unitary state; the North and the South would of necessity have different treatment. The chief reasons for the union were financial; the South produced a surplus in revenue, while the North was poverty-stricken and required annual subventions from Britain. Together, the South could help pay for the North, and development costs could be spread around on an equalization or distribution principle. In addition, communications and transportation, especially a unified administration of the railways, required union.[55] The unifying effect of Lugard's scheme, with its single name and central governor, its administration of policy by a single pair of hands, is not to be discounted. Still, it may be seen in retrospect that the unifying influences that were more important were the southern penetration of the Muslim Fulani-Hausa in the early nineteenth century, the south-north tie of the railroads and roads, the fact that northern trade perforce must run to the south and through it to the ports, and the nationalist aspirations of some of the southern patriots.

Much of Lugard's action ran counter to these forces. Indirect rule—which was elevated into a dogma so absurd that it led to the artificial effort to *make* chiefs in Iboland in order that there would be chiefs through whom to govern—while a necessity, was also a divisive force. So was his protection of the North from the forces of the twentieth century. (It is a strange fact that the British administrators almost to a man were much in sympathy with the reactionary emirs.) Lugard did not like the South, or its people. He never felt at home there, as he did with the people

[54] The name was the Colony and Protectorate of Nigeria.
[55] Great Britain, *Parliamentary Papers, 1919, Accounts and Papers*, Vol. XXXVI, "Report by Sir F. D. Lugard on the Amalgamation of Northern and Southern Nigeria, and Administration, 1912–1919," (Cmd. 468), p. 7; K. O. Dike, "The Making of Nigeria," *Latitude*, Summer, 1960, p. 26. This is apparently a reprint from some literature of the Federal Information Office prior to the 1957 constitution.

he had conquered and remade in the Northern Protectorate, 1900–06. He heartily disliked the educated Africans in the South and excluded them from government, even wiping out the little embryonic legislative council in the Colony that was characteristic of the ninetenth-century crown colony, with its handful of "unofficial" members. This exclusion of course perversely made nationalists of them, and indirect rule set them against the chiefs.[56] Both Lugard and Miss Perham (in 1936) thought Africans ought to be worked into the lower levels of government, not the "superstructure," as the latter, said Miss Perham, must eventually be demolished. Thus, inconsistently, in the thirties some prospect of ultimate control was held out to Africans, while the more politically minded of them were prevented from gaining experience in government.[57] In 1922 Sir Hugh Clifford, perhaps as the result of agitation by the West African National Congress (1920) of J. C. Hayford, re-established the Nigerian Legislative Council, consisting of twenty-seven officials and nineteen Africans. Four of the latter were elective for the first time in Nigerian history; three were drawn from Lagos and one from Calabar. This Council legislated for the Colony and Southern provinces only.[58]

An aspect of Lugard's (and British) policy that has had profound effects is that on land tenure. Except for some coastal areas, European ownership (and in the North any private ownership) of land has been forbidden, and the various types of tribal control have retained the land in the hands of Nigerians, with relatively little private ownership. This policy, along with the mosquito, has kept down European settlement and much European vested interest and thus made independence easier to obtain. The plantation system likewise was excluded; Lever Brothers was rebuffed in 1907 and subsequent efforts by others likewise. The Secretary of State, Lewis Harcourt, said in 1913:

The soap-boilers of the world are tumbling over one another to acquire the raw material of their industry. But I am the officially constituted

[56] James S. Coleman, *Nigeria: Background to Nationalism* (Berkeley and Los Angeles, 1958), p. 156; Perham, *op. cit.*, II, 389–90.
[57] Coleman, *op. cit.*, pp. 160–61.
[58] Joan Wheare, *The Nigerian Legislative Council* (London, 1950); Dike, "The Making of Nigeria," p. 29; Burns, *op. cit.*, 2nd ed., pp. 250–51.

protector of the natives in our own colonies, and it is my duty to see that they are not as far as I can prevent it, unduly damaged by this foreign competition.

Ordinances promulgated in 1945 nationalized minerals and public lands.[59]

The policies on land tenure and plantations accord with the constantly restated intention of Britain as a colonial power to attend to the welfare of the subject peoples—the better half of Lugard's *Dual Mandate*. But the old theory of financial relations was the same as that held by medieval England about the king —a colony was to live of its own. The fact had been something else again: Nigeria had cost the British a great deal before the end of the nineteenth century. We may recall from the meager data [60] permitted by the scope of this paper that the British maintained the naval squadron in Nigerian waters for two generations; financed the explorations; subsidized Laird's expeditions up the Niger; and bore the deficit in the administration of Lagos, 1861– 65. When Joseph Chamberlain came to the Colonial Office in 1895, he turned his frustrated Radical domestic energies into "imperialism," and a revolutionary new attitude was adopted toward the colonies: they were to be regarded as undeveloped estates, the government's duty being to develop them for both native and imperial posterity, and look after their welfare.[61] Soon there would be imperially assisted research in tropical agriculture and medicine. More immediately, the pocketbook of Whitehall was opened for troops in Nigeria, for buying out the Royal Niger Company, and for loans.[62] The railways began to be built: by the opening of the century to Ibadan; by 1911, to Kano. With the acquisition of

[59] Quotation from *CHBE*, III, 469. See also *ibid.*, III, 392–93; Coleman, *op. cit.*, pp. 58–60, 282 ff.; Perham, *op. cit.*, II, 579; Burns, *op. cit.*, 2nd ed., pp. 267, 304; T. O. Elias, *Nigerian Land Law and Custom* (London, 1951); C. K. Meek, *Land Tenure and Land Administration in Nigeria and the Cameroons* (London, 1957).

[60] Sir William Geary, who was unable to make a book out of his material, nonetheless was diligent about gathering figures from the parliamentary papers, and his *Nigeria under British Rule* abounds in them.

[61] Geary dedicated his book to Chamberlain, "whose statesmanship developed West Africa for the benefit of its native inhabitants, for British trade, and for the increase of the empire." The latest statement of this oft-repeated shift in policy is in Robinson, Gallagher, and Denny, *op. cit.*, pp. 395 ff.

[62] See *Colonial Loans Act of 1899, 62 and 63 Victoria*, chap. 36.

the North and the military reduction of the emirates by Lugard, the British Government was at last committeed to administration on a large scale. By 1918 the grants-in-aid required by the North came to at least £4,261,000.[63]

The 1920's saw the inception of the welfare principle on a more extensive scale. In 1926 the Empire Marketing Board was established, which made grants for research in various fields, including control of the tsetse fly; the board expired in 1933–34. A more ambitious scheme was the establishment of the Colonial Advisory Committee in 1929, designed both to develop the colonies and to support the British economy, struck by the depression. Since Nigeria was in a fairly good economic position, the colony did not profit extensively from the largesse of these schemes. East Africa and the poverty-stricken West Indies got the lion's share. By the *Ninth Annual Report* of the Committee in 1938, Nigeria had received a total of only £321,953.[64] These gestures were but prelude to the real breakthrough of the Colonial Development and Welfare Act of 1940, and its successors in 1945, 1949, 1950, 1955. These acts provided millions of pounds for Nigeria; her own government poured in millions more, and social services, education, and economic development leapt forward at an unprecedented pace.[65]

Simultaneously there was an explosive rush toward self-government and a hectic rash of constitution-making: 1945–46, 1951, 1954, 1957–58, climaxing in the independence of a federated Nigeria, October 1, 1960. The most interesting question is not why

[63] This is the figure given by Lugard in "Report . . . on the Amalgamation . . . ," p. 46. To this must be added the £865,000 paid Goldie. The latter amount was supposed to be repaid from receipts from territories that had been administered by the Company. It was difficult to tell what these territories were, and the Company had expended only £50,000 a year on administration. Nigeria, however, made substantial contributions toward the cost of the war, and by 1935 had borne deficits in the Cameroons of more than £733,082. In April, 1937, Nigeria made a defense gift of £75,000 to H. M. Government. A bill was therefore brought in at Westminster to quash the liability for the purchase cost. These facts recited in Great Britain, *Parliamentary Papers*, Vol. XX, "Nigeria, Remission of Payments to the Exchequer under the Royal Niger Company Act, 1899. Memorandum on the Financial Resolution" (Cmd. 5488).

[64] See the following *Reports* of the Colonial Advisory Committee: Cmds. 3540 (1929), 4079 (1931–32), 4634 (1933–34), 5789 (1938).

[65] Summary in *The U. K. Development and Welfare Acts* (London: British Information Services, I.D. 892 [Revised], March, 1960).

Britain went along with this abrupt development, but how it was possible for the Nigerians to go along with each other. For the purposes of this paper, the question ought to be phrased: Did England help develop a federal Nigeria on democratic lines as an act of conscious policy? Obviously, until the papers and memoirs of recent politicians and officials in both countries are open, we can merely guess and deduce.

As to the question of independence in some form or other, the British were of course obliged to let go. It was a long-settled policy. The pressures of the educated elite were reinforced tenfold by the profound influences of the war.[66] The Labour Government were quite as much prisoners of their own propaganda for freedom as were the nationalist agitators. The times were changed. Even British elements as reactionary on colonial matters as Sir Winston Churchill had neither the stomach nor the resources to fight it out against determined nationalists. In Burma and in India the policy was simply to run, whether the mutineers were to scuttle the ship or not.

In Nigeria, on the other hand, there was no large-scale disposition by the nationalists to use force—or at least no large amount of arms was available to them. Ironically, a major threat of the use of force came from the North, which muttered darkly about resuming its drive to the south if Britain left. Accordingly, there was some time, not as much as Britain thought, but some, in which to make an effort to tidy up the internal situation before leaving. The manner in which British and Nigerian leaders brought about the degree of tidiness that existed at independence is not really explained by accounts now available. It is assuredly a credit to both groups. More than that, it is miraculous.

There seems to be some evidence that the creation of a federal Nigeria, and a democratic one, was a conscious, settled policy of the postwar Colonial Office. As for the genesis of the federal solution, it would be interesting to have a precise history of its

[66] There is no need to restate this familiar story here. See the excellent brief analyses in Coleman, *op. cit.*, pp. 230–37, 409 ff., as well as *passim*. Among the Nigerian accounts published since his bibliography was assembled are Kalu Ezera, *Constitutional Developments in Nigeria* (Cambridge, 1960), and *Awo: the Autobiography of Chief Obafemi Awolowo* (Cambridge, 1960).

Nigerian application in the minds of the Office, but it is not necessary to strain at it: the British empire has swarmed with federations, and a plan to apply the federal solution to an India with mixed governments held together by the British raj had been embodied in the Act of 1935. It is therefore with no difficulty that we can accept as sincere the British statements that they favored a federal Nigeria. Still the insulation of the North, which British policy had encouraged, and the Richards constitution of 1946 seem at first blush a strange way to encourage unity. This scheme, which in the view of Dike [67] and others "reversed the trend toward unification," set up regional assemblies in three regions, undemocratically chosen and almost powerless. (But it did inject Northern members into the old legislative council,[68] and the regional idea embodied a solution by Sir Bernard Bourdillon of the embarrassment of enlarging greatly the legislative council with northern members not at home in the language—English— or the thought of the Southerners.) [69] Richards' proposal declared that the purpose of it "was to 'promote the unity of Nigeria,' on the assumption that regional political integration was a necessary first step to national political integration." Coleman's judgment is that "in the balance, it is clear that British policy has been directed toward the development of a federal system based upon regions as the constituent units." [70]

The end of the war and Richards' constitution propelled the militant nationalist agitation of Nnamdi Azikiwe and his National Council of Nigeria and the Cameroons (NCNC) to its height, and thus the hurry, the urgency, increased. Change was facilitated in 1947 and 1948 by the facts that Arthur Creech Jones, a Fabian Afrophile, was Secretary of State, and a very tactful new governor, Sir John Macpherson, had succeeded Richards. Macpherson announced a speed-up in the schedule for revision of the Con-

---

[67] Dike, "The Making of Nigeria," p. 30.
[68] *Proposals for the Revision of the Constitution of Nigeria* (London, [1945], Cmd. 6599).
[69] Ezera, *op. cit.*, pp. 64 ff.
[70] Coleman, *op. cit.*, pp. 322–24. Ezera, *op. cit.* pp. 120–21, quotes the Secretary of State to the Governor, July 15, 1950, as saying: "One of the great advantages of encouraging the regions to develop each along its own characteristic lines will be that by that very process the unity of Nigeria will be strengthened."

stitution, initiated social fraternization with the African elite, declared that Nigerianization of the senior civil service and promotion of higher education would proceed at a faster rate, and began to democratize the native authorities.[71] Here we speed toward independence and democracy, and there can be little doubt it was consciously directed policy from the Colonial Office. In Dr. Kalu Ezera's view the old tendency of the Office to let local governors set policy, only approving or modifying it, was abandoned after the war in favor of an activist policy, involving policy studies and reports as a basis for guidance of the men in the field.[72]

The devolution, the regionalization, of power and political organization grew more marked in the early 1950's, when a Yoruba political party, the Action Group (AG), and a conservative Northern party, the Northern Peoples' Congress (NPC), were formed and two constitutions strengthened regionalism. The Constitution of 1954 gave effective control over their departments to regional ministers (who were Nigerian, with a Nigerian premier at their head). Democracy was evidenced in direct election of the Western and Eastern members of the Federal House.[73] Regional though it was in emphasis—it promised internal full self-government shortly to Regions wishing it—this Constitution was worked out finally in Lagos by a conference at which the Secretary of State, Oliver Lyttelton, held together the embittered factions with some skill. And in an interim in the writing of the document, Lyttelton answered wild threats by Awolowo with a declaration that force would be resisted, and "any attempt to secure the secession of the Western Region from the Federation would be regarded as the use of force."[74] The British seemed to be sticking to their policy of unity through disparateness.

The passage of time, brief as it was, was enabling the North to catch up with events sufficiently so that she would not feel at an utter disadvantage with the southerners in an independent

[71] Coleman, *op. cit.*, p. 309, and chap. xiv, *passim.*
[72] Ezera, *op. cit.*, p. 83 n. 2.
[73] *Report by the Conference on the Nigerian Constitution Held in London in July and August, 1953* (London [1953], Cmd. 8934); and *Report by the Resumed Conference on the Nigerian Constitution Held in Lagos in January and February, 1954* (London [1954], Cmd. 9059).
[74] Ezera, *op. cit.*, pp. 187–88.

government. As Ghana celebrated her independence, the northern leaders joined the southern ones in demanding that a date be fixed for freedom. This action gave a psychological unity to the Nigerian picture that was quite encouraging. In this atmosphere the constitutional conference of 1957 made some further advances on the road to a scheme under which an independent Nigeria could operate.[75] Of the divisive forces loosed by both the political scrapping of the 1950's and the imminent departure of the British raj, none was more shrill in tone than the real and alleged fears of minorities, with a demand for creating new states out of portions of the Regions. The 1957 conference agreed upon a commission to study this problem. The commission recommended against new states, as encouraging tribal disunity at the expense of an effective nationalism.[76] This report then was a final unifying measure of the British. It cleared the way for a resumed conference in 1958, which shaped the Constitution for independence, and set October 1, 1960, as the day for its accomplishment.[77] Imperial proconsuls and independent premiers parted with protestations of mutual esteem, and Nigeria remains in the Commonwealth.

Summary

The British came to Nigeria to trade (and to explore, for mixed motives). With the rise of the evangelical movement in the eighteenth century, they developed strong humanitarian and religious motives. Government had to assist, first in the latter endeavors

[75] W. B. Hamilton, "The Nigerian Constitutional Conference of 1957," *South Atlantic Quarterly*, LVII (Autumn, 1958), 491–507; *Report by the Nigeria Constitutional Conference Held in London in May and June, 1957* (London, 1957, Cmnd. 207).

[76] Commission appointed to enquire into the fears of minorities and the means of allaying them, *Nigeria* (London, 1958, Cmnd. 505). This report made a number of significant recommendations, including a Bill of Rights for the new Constitution, and the maintenance of federal, versus regional, control of the police force.

[77] *Report by the Resumed Nigeria Constitutional Conference Held in London in September and October, 1958* (London, Cmnd. 569). For a review and commentary upon the 1960 Constitution, see R. Taylor Cole, "The Independence Constitution of Federal Nigeria," *South Atlantic Quarterly*, LX (Winter, 1961), 1–18, and *infra*, chap. iv.

and then in the former. Thus the British Government was inevitably drawn on both counts into governing in Nigeria and into local politics, and having installed herself on the coast, expanded inland to protect both trade and philanthropic interests and to put down disorders on the borders of her governmental activity. Expansion was vastly quickened by foreign competition in the scramble for Africa.

Great Britain governed as little (and as cheaply) as she could, and hence established her sway over territories by vague non-governing protectorates or by turning over the job to private individuals under charter. Such a policy served the Treasury, but not the other interests of the British. It was impractical. The proconsul Lugard in particular changed the former attitude because he was an autocrat who loved one-man planning and administering and, further, loved to tidy up. He turned a necessity of cheap and practical governing into a theory of indirect rule as a positive good, which grew into a dogma slavishly followed by his successors, and held out as a pattern for the slow development of all the "backward" empire. Before it could be installed on thorough lines, indirect rule was out of date.

New pressures of nationalists, combined with ancient aims languidly intended to be applied to Nigeria at some distant tomorrow, propelled the colonies toward self-government. The British, with new conscience, responded to this demand by busying themselves with its realization, and sought to accompany it with a program to promote the welfare and development of the emerging peoples, a program growing out of Joseph Chamberlain's ideas, the depression, and twentieth-century trends in government in England. In Nigeria, having bolted the area together with ties of government and communication, they even got interested in maintaining the country intact, and they actively pursued this end, using the divisions created by history and by rough tribal groupings, to help the Nigerians create a federation, with democratic institutions. They were of course too slow in occupying, too slow in governing, too slow in welfare and developmental activity, too slow in training for independence; but, when they faced up to this last, they were perhaps superb in their timing.

Historically, except for moments of rigidity such as 1770–80, British colonial policy has responded to pressures from the men on the spot. This is true in Nigeria not only of the Africans, be they Egba chiefs or western-trained "radicals," but also of the instances in which governmental action has been shaped by the Townsends, the Harry Johnstons,[78] the Goldies, and the Lugards. Policy has been shaped likewise by pressure groups in England— merchants, philanthropic societies, and religious groups. National strategy and external events shaped colonial policy, particularly the actions of other countries, and also the shifting commercial theories or psychological outlooks of the time—the prevailing set of attitudes.

In the nineteenth century, at least, colonial policy was made, when there was any, by the interaction of those forces and a large number of officials in the Foreign Office, the Colonial Office, the Treasury, the Admiralty, the Board of Trade, and the War Office. The machinery was clumsy, but even so there was still scope for the influence of strong cabinet official and strong permanent official alike. How little Parliament had to do with it! It is true that in a negative way that institution exercised influence, for the officials who took the action, who shaped the policy, would go to any length to prevent parliamentary debate and hence avoided any action requiring a parliamentary appropriation.[79]

[78] See the tale of the fall of Ja Ja in Roland Oliver, *Sir Harry Johnston & the Scramble for Africa* (London, 1957), pp. 107–19. Also see documents appended to Geary, *op. cit.*

[79] The earlier portions of this paper would have profited from the use of C. W. Newbury's *The Western Slave Coast and Its Rulers: European Trade and Administration Among the Yoruba and Adja-Speaking Peoples of Southwestern Nigeria, Southern Dahomey and Togo* (Oxford, Clarendon Press, 1961), but the author did not see the book before the paper was in proof.

Part Two

Politics and Government

3

Emergent Federalism in Nigeria [1]

Taylor Cole

Since the months preceding the independence of the Federation of Nigeria (October 1, 1960), considerable printer's ink has been spilled in appraising the nature of Nigerian nationhood and in predicting the future of Nigerian federalism. Some of this writing reflects the serious doubts, also evident among prominent Nigerian leaders during the period 1946–51, concerning the existence of a Nigerian nation [2] and the future stability of a federal system. Sir Alan Burns, both a recognized historian and past colonial administrator in Nigeria, observed in 1954 that "there is no Nigerian nation, no Nigerian language . . . and no Nigerian tradition. The very name of Nigeria was invented by the British to describe a country inhabited by a medley of formerly warring tribes with no common culture, and united only in so far as they are governed by a single Power." [3] Lord Milverton maintained in 1955 that Nigeria "is still more of a geographic expression than a nation." [4] To these reflections may be added the more recent views of an American social scientist who, after surveying the growth of separatist movements and tribal appeals following 1947, con-

[1] This essay, in somewhat different form, appeared originally in L. Brett, ed., *Constitutional Problems of Federalism in Nigeria* (Lagos, 1961), pp. 1–11. The Duke University Press is indebted to the Nigeria Bar Association for permission to reprint it in the present volume.

[2] See James S. Coleman, *Nigeria: Background to Nationalism* (Berkeley, 1958), esp. p. 320.

[3] "The Movement toward Self-Government in British Colonial Territories," *Optima*, IV (June, 1954), 9; cf. Godwin A. Odenigwe, "The Constitutional Development of Nigeria; The Origins of Federalism, 1862–1954" (unpublished Ph.D. dissertation, Clark University, 1957), pp. 335–36.

[4] "Thoughts on Nationalism in Africa," *Corona*, VII (Dec., 1955), 447.

cluded that "the chances for a viable, united Nigerian nation-state are rather slim indeed." [5]

It is not our purpose to outline in detail the arguments leading to these conclusions, but passing mention may be made of some of the facts that often creep into the writings. The first is that Nigeria is a recent creation and came into being as a result of the fiat of a colonial power. The official "birth" of Nigeria can be dated back to January 1, 1900, when the Protectorates of Northern and Southern Nigeria were created. Indeed, the name "Nigeria" had first appeared in print only three years earlier, in 1897.[6] The subsequent history of Nigeria has included, after the developments of 1906, the amalgamation of these administrations into the Colony and Protectorate of Nigeria in 1914, and constitutional changes in the decades since that time. The division into three groupings of provinces and the Colony of Lagos was formally recognized in the controversial Richards Constitution of 1946,[7] which solidified previously existing territorial divisions. Various modifications were made in the constitutions of 1951 and 1954, the latter of which incorporated provisions for federalism as well as for parliamentary government. It was under the Constitution of 1954, as amended in accordance with the recommendations of subsequent Nigerian Constitutional Conferences,[8] that the Western and Eastern Regions were granted internal "self-government" in August, 1957, and the Northern Region in March, 1959. Thus, legal diversity was substituted for the unified political structure that existed prior to World War II.

The distribution of powers between the central and regional

[5] Martin L. Kilson, "The Rise of Nationalist Organisations and Parties in British West Africa," in *Africa Seen by American Negroes* (Paris, 1958), pp. 62–63.

[6] C. K. Meek, "The Niger and the Classics: the History of a Name," *Journal of African History*, I (1960), 1.

[7] R. E. Wraith, in a recent review, commends Dr. Kalu Ezera on his treatment of the Milverton (Richards) "myth." "The myth, widely held among Nigerian intelligentsia," says Wraith, "holds that God created a united country called Nigeria, in which all men lived at peace; until one day there came a wicked man called Richards, who set out subtly to destroy this unity, this peace, by dividing the country into Regions in order that the British could go on ruling it forever." Review of Kalu Ezera, *Constitutional Developments in Nigeria* (Cambridge, 1960), in *Journal of the Historical Society of Nigeria*, II (Dec., 1960), 166–67.

[8] The Southern Cameroons, which in the past has been a British trust territory administered by Nigeria with the Governor-General serving as High Commissioner and which opted, following Nigerian independence, to join the Cameroon Republic to form the Federal Republic of Cameroon, has been omitted from consideration in this chapter.

governments, so the analysis goes, has undergone changes since the Constitution of 1946—chiefly in 1951 and 1954—but they have served more to restrict than to augment the powers at the center. The amendments to the Constitution of 1954 and the adjustments in the Independence Constitution of 1960 have slightly altered, but have not fundamentally changed, the distribution made in 1954. The controversy shortly after independence over the power of the Federal Government to dissolve regional legislatures during emergencies brought from leaders of the Western Region a strong "states rights" appraisal of the distribution of powers. "All the Governments of the Federation are coordinate and not in any way subordinate to each other," said Premier S. L. Akintola on this occasion.[9] "Nigeria is not yet a nation as Britain or America is," editorialized the *Daily Express*. "We chose the Federal system of government because we realized that this is the only way to keep the diverse elements together." [10] Despite the demands of a coalition government, the NCNC newspaper *West African Pilot* took offense at remarks attributed to Sir Ahmadu Bello, the Premier of the Northern Region, while on a tour of Moslem states in Asia. "Foreign Affairs is the exclusive preserve of the Federal Government and the Prime Minister," it editorialized; "the Sardauna has no right to discuss the establishment of diplomatic ties with foreign heads of State." [11]

The Senate of the Federation, embodying equal representation from each of the Regions, has more limited powers than the House of Representatives. Holding its first meetings in 1960, the Senate is still an unproved body. In the Lower House of the Federal Legislature, the House of Representatives, roughly one-half of the members are elected from the Northern Region, a fact that underscores the relative disparity of this Region in population and size. The Supreme Court, with original jurisdiction over disputes between the Federation and Regions and between Regions, and with original and appellate jurisdiction in constitutional ques-

---

[9] *Daily Express* (Lagos), Oct. 13, 1960, p. 1.
[10] *Ibid.*, Oct. 15, 1960, p. 4.
[11] July 6, 1961, p. 4. However, the NCNC party through a spokesman later dissociated "itself completely from these unwarranted attacks" by those who alleged that the Sardauna favored the creation of a "Commonwealth or Confederation of Moslem States," and in particular from the editorial comment referred to above. *Ibid.*, July 12, 1961, p. 1.

tions involving regional and federal legislation, is still not a fully tested constitutional arbiter.[12] The Minorities Commission in 1958 concluded that the Federal Government, in comparison with the regional governments, occupies "a secondary place in the estimation of most Nigerians." [13] And Robin Hallett expressed the layman's point of view when he said, "The relations of the Regions one with another are haunted by fear and suspicion: the North apprehensive of the South, hurries forward its policy of Northernization; the South is half-afraid, half-contemptuous, and almost wholly ignorant of the North. Then look how weak the Federal Government is. . . ." [14]

Certain features of Nigerian society are considered by these skeptics to be obstacles to Nigerian unification. With a high percentage of illiteracy, the country's economy continues to be based on the agriculture, fishing, animal husbandry, and forestry of the rural areas. During the period 1950–57 more than three-fifths of the gross domestic product and more than three-fourths of the gainful employment could be attributed to these activities. While the tempo of development is accelerating, industry is still a minor factor in the country's national income; among the estimated population of over 35 million the average per capita real income is about £30.[15] Furthermore, the per capita income is unevenly distributed: gaps are evident between the Western Region and the other two Regions.[16] In other respects the statistical gap

[12] The Supreme Court was created in 1954. The changes in its jurisdiction, powers, and procedure since that date were embodied in the Federal Supreme Court Ordinance, 1960. It is to be noted that the Chief Justices of the High Courts of the Regions are *ex officio* members of the Supreme Court. Up to July, 1961, there had been only one minor instance when the Supreme Court had declared one provision of a regional legislative enactment to be unconstitutional. See *In re: S. S. Olawayin v. Commissioner of Police,* F.S.C. 73/1961. In October, 1961, certain sections of a federal act were invalidated in the "National Bank" case. *West Africa,* Nov. 4, 1961, pp. 1209–10, 1227. Appeals in limited number are taken to the Privy Council. During the three-year period 1957–59, some fourteen appeals in both civil and criminal cases were taken from Nigeria. Appeals in the future may be expected in cases involving the civil rights guarantees of the present Constitution.
[13] Commission appointed to enquire into the fears of minorities and the means of allaying them, *Nigeria* (London, 1958, Cmnd. 505), p. 5.
[14] "Unity, Double-Think and the University," *Ibadan,* No. 6 (1959), p. 4.
[15] See National Economic Council, *Economic Survey of Nigeria, 1959* (Lagos, 1959), esp. pp. 1–11; Royal Institute of International Affairs, *Nigeria: The Political and Economic Background* (Oxford, 1960).
[16] According to an unpublished study on national income by E. F. Jackson and

between the North and the South is also marked, particularly in school attendance and in the extent of the development of the market economy. In addition, in the North the impact of the ideas of Nigerian nationalism has been later and more limited. These differences affect the flow of ideas and breed distrust.[17]

The ties of most of these inhabitants are with their family or village and rarely extend beyond the tribe. The urban drift—encouraged by an opportunity to earn a steady money income, the effects of improving educational facilities, and the attractions of urban life—has caught many tribesmen from the villages in its fold. But they still look back to their original homes as their permanent abodes and refuges in times of adversity. It is true that economic development has served to link the village closer to the urban areas, and to increase somewhat the social mobility, particularly in the South, but this development has as yet been a modest one. Various types of interest groups, such as trade unions, may play some unifying role in the future; however, these are still in the infant stage of development and are so weak that they provide little cohesive force in Nigeria today. In short, it is the local affiliations and tribal patterns that continue to dominate the life of the average Nigerian.

To summarize, it is contended that the trend of the last decade and a half has been toward separation rather than unity; that there has been no real emergence of symbols that would attract the loyalties, or even the attention, of the illiterate and impoverished masses; that increasing urbanization, economic development, and social mobility have not as yet resulted in a new social setting on which a national consciousness can be grounded; that political parties and other groups fail to accept the common interests on which ties of national unity can rest; and that without the existence of such ties of unity a central government in a Nigerian federal system must either remain as a weak party or disappear entirely.

Although this point of view may be widely accepted, it is my

Pius Okigbo, to be issued by the Federal Office of Statistics, the "gross domestic product per head" in 1957–58 at 1957 prices was about £21.6 in the Northern Region, £21.7 in the Eastern Region, and £30.9 in the Western Region.

[17] Ayo Ogunsheye, "Nigeria's Political Prospects," *Ibadan,* No. 11 (1961), p. 6.

opinion that it does not adequately take into account certain forces and developments that are resulting in greater social and political integration and that are thereby providing support for the growing strength and role of the central government. References could be made to the use of the English language as a lingua franca (the second language for the increasing percentage of educated Nigerians) and to the adoption of the essential forms of British parliamentary government. Though the impact of the English law has produced its stresses and strains, it has been a unifying force and has almost superseded customary law in such areas as the law of evidence and procedure. "It is clear enough," contends T. O. Elias, "that . . . a body of statutory common law has developed which, although clearly inspired by or modeled on English law, has been applied to Hausa, Ibo and Yoruba, to Ibibio, Efik and Bini, to Moslem, Christian and so-called Pagan alike—without the least murmur or protest on the part of any minority group in Nigeria."[18] The acceptance of common legal standards has been evidenced most recently by the criminal law reform in the North.[19] Though the progress of "Nigerianization" of the public services has varied from government to government, a substantial but rapidly declining percentage of the permanent secretaries in the Northern and Eastern Regions were expatriate officers in July, 1961.[20] These officials still play an important part in decision-making in their ministries. And while they may reflect disagreement between their respective governments on other

[18] *The Impact of English Law on Nigerian Customary Law* (Lagos, 1958), pp. 30–31.

[19] See J. N. D. Anderson, "Conflict of Laws in Nigeria: A New Start," *International and Comparative Law Quarterly*, VIII (July, 1959), 441–56. The significance of these developments in providing for the wider acceptance and application of common legal principles has been stressed to the author by members of the judiciary in both the Federation and the Northern Region. During 1960 national legislation was enacted to make the general legal principles operative in the Region applicable to federal offenses, to designate those matters that were exclusively federal, and to authorize the courts of the Northern Region to assume jurisdiction. See explanation in *Senate Debates* (Daily Parts), May 3, 1960, pp. 513–15. There were objections raised by some members in the Senate to the enactment of the national legislation on the grounds that it would have a "disunifying" effect in Nigeria. *Ibid.* (Daily Parts), May 3, 1960, pp. 515 ff.

[20] Shortly after independence the Western Region Government abruptly replaced all remaining expatriate permanent secretaries with Nigerian ones. Nigerianization in the upper echelons of the public service is least advanced in the Northern Region.

matters, they are usually in accord in their acceptance of recent British policy, which has been to unite Nigeria and to keep it united. In addition, the history of other federations, including Canada and Australia in the Commonwealth, point up the effects over a period of time of centripetal pressures.

But there are other factors and forces operative in Nigeria that, it is believed, are serving to integrate Nigerian society and to point to the growing role of the central government in the federal system. The most important of these is the impact of certain economic developments, which have necessarily underscored the key position of the government at the center. First of all, the central government provides the channel through which the bulk of the revenue for the operation of the regional governments is made available. The basis for allocation to the Regions of revenues raised by the Federation has been the subject of several reports by commissions and personages in 1947, 1951, 1954, and most recently in 1958.[21] Various criteria for such allocations have been applied in the past, but the Report of 1958, as now implemented, places the emphasis upon the maintenance of the essential services by the regional governments, the population of the Regions, and the "balanced development" of the Federation. The most important sources of revenue of the Federation for all purposes are the import and export duties, and these could hardly be collected directly by the Regions. Some 70 per cent of the general import revenue from specified sources is retained by the Federal Government, and 30 per cent is put in a pool for distribution to the Regions; all of the export revenues now go to the Regions on the basis of derivation. The Estimates for 1960–61 stipulated that out of a total anticipated revenue of over £95,000,000, some £42,200,000, or approximately 44 per cent of the total, would pass to the Regions under the revenue allocation system.[22] Well

---

[21] Nigeria, *Report of the Fiscal Commission* (Cmnd. 481, 1958).

[22] Speech by the Minister of Finance on the Appropriations (1960–61) Bill, *House of Representatives Debates* (Daily Parts), April 4, 1960, pp. 585–86. The total amount of "statutory and non-statutory appropriations" to the Regions increased slightly in 1961–62, but the percentage of the total of over £105,000,000 of anticipated federal revenue declined because of a drop in the export revenue, particularly on cocoa. *Estimates of the Government of the Federation of Nigeria 1961–62 [Memorandum]* (Lagos, 1961), p. 3.

over three-fifths of the regional revenue is thus derived from federal "grants and allocations" to the Regions.[23]

Other economic considerations might be mentioned. The Federal Government, through the Nigerian Railway Corporation, operates the railways, and it also has the responsibility for the main highways. The railways are of primary and the highways of secondary importance as transportation channels.[24] As in the case of the main rail routes, the pattern of trade in Nigeria runs primarily in a north-south direction, with the railways originating in the north and terminating at the coastal ports of the south. The products of all Regions designed for export find their main outlets through the coastal ports, primarily Lagos and Port Harcourt. Furthermore, most towns and cities in Nigeria have grown up as a result of the availability of these transportation facilities, and there is considerable indirect evidence of their effects on the growth of markets and the division of labor.[25] In short, the ties provided by the main transportation routes, now largely under the jurisdiction of federal authorities, serve to emphasize central control of the transport system and, at the same time, accentuate the growing economic interdependence of the Regions of the country.

The National Economic Council—organized in 1955 and composed of the Prime Minister, as chairman, and four ministers drawn from the federal Council of Ministers and four from each regional Executive Council, together with the Economic Advisor

[23] Over two-thirds of the revenue of the Regions in 1956 was derived from these sources. *Nigeria: Handbook of Commerce and Industry* (Lagos, 1957), pp. 126, 128. For the anticipated statutory payments from the Federal Government to the Eastern Region for the fiscal year 1961–62, see statement of the Minister of Finance in Eastern House of Chiefs, *Parliamentary Debates*, Second Session, 1960–61, April 25, 1960, p. 31. The implementation of the recommendations of the Fiscal (Raisman) Commission of 1958 has meant an increase in the percentage of total federal revenue allocated to the Regions from about 39 per cent in 1958–59 to well over 40 per cent today. Note comments of the Federal Minister of Finance on the effects of this trend, in *House of Representatives Debates* (Daily Parts), Jan. 18, 1960, pp. 3–6.

[24] The International Bank estimated that in ton miles in 1952–53, rail accounted for 61 per cent, road 30 per cent, and river 9 per cent of the total. E. K. Hawkins, *Road Transport in Nigeria* (London, 1957), p. 3. There is evidence that the importance of road as a transportation channel has increased sharply since 1952–53. The present researches of V. W. Hogg and the forthcoming report to the Government of the Stanford Research Institute will throw additional light on these changes.

[25] *Ibid.*, p. 23.

to the Federal Government—has served as an important forum for considering economic problems and encouraging the co-operation of all governments in the development of a national economic policy. Basic disagreements are frequently ventilated, such as those involving a common transportation policy, the development of the Niger River, or the location of a new steel mill. Established under its aegis after 1958 was the Joint Planning Committee, which today is composed of eight permanent officials (two from the Federal and two from each of the Regional Governments), and is chaired by the Economic Advisor. Various reports, including the *Economic Survey of Nigeria, 1959,* have been issued by the Committee. Sub-committees of the Joint Planning Committee, such as those on Agricultural Policy and on Statistics, have been set up to prepare specialized studies. A less-publicized body is the Loans Advisory Council. Consisting of the Ministers and Permanent Secretaries of Finance in all of the governments, it is the consultative agency to consider the apportionment for federal and regional purposes of money raised by loan, and particularly of foreign loan money, all of which has to be raised by the Federal Government.[26] As their reserves are being rapidly exhausted, the need for increasing amounts of foreign loan funds for development purposes in each of the Regions will make the work of the Loans Advisory Council more difficult in the period ahead. In this and other economic activities, the role of the Central Bank of Nigeria is becoming increasingly important.

Obviously there are centrifugal pressures exerted by certain economic forces, especially in a country marked by the uneven economic progress of the Regions, and it is a bit too early to speak of national economic planning.[27] However, the Ministry of Economic Development, itself in its formative stage of development, has set up an Economic Planning Unit, which is staffed by Ameri-

[26] See Federation of Nigeria, *The Economic Programme of the Government of the Federation of Nigeria 1955–60, Sessional Paper No. 2 of 1956* (Lagos, 1956), p. 9; see also the Minister of Finance in *House of Representatives Debates* (Daily Parts), April 4, 1960, pp. 557–58, 575–76, and *ibid.* (Daily Parts), April 6, 1961, pp. 931–32.
[27] Cf. the comments and proposals of the Leader of the Opposition, Chief Awolowo, in *House of Representatives Debates* (Daily Parts), April 22, 1960, pp. 1611–18, and *ibid.* (Daily Parts), April 12, 1961, p. 1352.

can and Nigerian economists and which has worked in consultation with corresponding officials in the regional governments to
evaluate economic trends and to prepare the recently submitted
"Federal Government Development Program 1962–68." To the
present, the Ministry has suffered from frequent ministerial
changes and has not acquired the needed personnel or status in
Cabinet deliberations to make it an effective planning agency.
On balance, however, the developments that have been mentioned provide a growing awareness of the interdependence of
all governments, regional and federal, as well as an increasing
recognition of the role of the central government in the economic
growth of Nigeria. As one parliamentarian has observed, "the
economies of the Regions of this country are so related that it is
a fallacy to speak of the development of the East or the West or
the North without thinking of the development of the Federation
of Nigeria as a whole. . . . You cannot develop any fractions;
you must always develop *in toto.*" [28]

Trade unions in Nigeria are in the formative stage of development and evidence many organizational weaknesses and considerable internal disunity.[29] However, certain older unions, including the Nigeria Association of Teachers, have their headquarters
in Lagos and serve to provide a meeting ground for the discussion
of common occupational problems. An Employers' Consultative
Association, consisting of the chief employers in private industry
and trade in Nigeria, in 1960 established a permanent secretary
in Lagos to deal with questions of concern to employers. Other
organizations, including the schools and the churches, have
played a part in bringing groups together. In the "Joint Pastoral
Letter" of 1960, the Nigerian Hierarchy of the Catholic Church
observed:

Fortunately recent years have seen a steady growth in an over-all
Nigerian nationalism that has cut across ethnic divisions and that has
drawn our people together. The citizens have become conscious of

[28] *Ibid.* (Daily Parts), Jan. 19, 1960, p. 22.
[29] See W. A. Warmington, *A West Africa Trade Union* (Oxford, 1960), pp. 1 ff.
A forthcoming volume now in press by T. M. Yesufu of the federal Ministry of
Labour dealing with industrial relations in Nigeria contains considerable information on Nigerian trade unions.

themselves as a people who possess a unity that vastly outweighs differences. . . . We insist that no Catholic can with good conscience indulge in a policy that sets one section of the state against another—"tribalism" as the attitude is usually called.[30]

Minority groups in each of the Regions look to the Federation for protection against the feared excesses of dominant political groups.[31] Each Region has a government resting primarily on the political support of certain tribal groups, the Hausa-Fulani in the North, the Yoruba in the West, and the Ibo in the East. The minority groups, broadly defined but consisting primarily of ethnic and religious units, constitute about one-third of the population in each Region. Many voiced their plaints to the Commission appointed "to enquire into the fears of minorities and the means for allaying them," which published a comprehensive report in 1958.[32] Most Ibos are critical of Yoruba rule in the West; many of the Ibibios and Ijaws in the East are concerned over alleged discrimination at the hands of the Ibos in educational matters and economic policies; Pagans, Christians, and Yorubas in the Northern Region have charged political discrimination, unfairness in the administration of justice, and the use of locally controlled native authority police for oppressive purposes. For these reasons, most of the minorities would prefer to circumscribe the powers of the Regions rather than those of the Federal Government. Some of them have demanded the incorporation of guarantees in the Constitution to provide added protection for human rights, and some have gone so far as to propose the creation of new states and political subdivisions. The most vocal of these minority groups strongly opposed earlier moves of the governments of the Northern and Western Regions to "regionalize" the police force. They were comforted by arrangements that, while making provision for police commissioners in each Region, left effective control of the "Nigeria Police" in the hands of the Governor-General prior to 1960. The creation of new states, particularly of a Mid-West state, for which there has been continuing

---

[30] *The Catholic Church in an Independent Nigeria* (n. p., 1960), p. 8.
[31] For a discussion of the tribal composition of Nigeria, see Murdock, *supra*, chap. i.
[32] *Op. cit.*

agitation and party support, might serve to place some of the minorities within political boundaries more to their liking. The creation of new states would also serve to reduce in part the degree of control that any one regional political party might exert in the federal Parliament since the new states would be accorded equal representation with the present Regions in the Senate.[33]

The early development of a new political elite and its significance in the emergence of Nigerian nationalism has been most fully discussed in James S. Coleman, *Nigeria: Background to Nationalism*.[34] Actually there is no single political elite in Nigeria, and distinctions have to be drawn particularly between elites of the North and those of the South. A typical leader in the South would be a self-made man (though occasionally one of the old elite) between the ages of 35 and 55, with the equivalent of a secondary education in a missionary-operated school (or perhaps in a Nigerian government school), and possibly with a degree from some foreign educational institution.[35] The past and present premiers of the Western Region, Chief Awolowo and Chief Akintola, and those of the Eastern Region, Dr. Azikiwe and Dr. Okpara, could be cited as examples. It is this new type of Western-educated leader who looks askance at many of the tribal obligations. It is his desire to remove the barriers to national economic development as rapidly as possible. In the North, the retention of Islamic culture and traditional social and economic patterns has left its political heritage. If the new currents that have been felt in Nigeria have not as yet undermined the position of the traditional authorities, nevertheless, the impact of educational innovations, economic pressures, and demands of minorities are beginning to be felt. One cannot yet say that the existing political

[33] The complicated procedures for the creation of new states under provisions of the present Constitution offer difficult barriers. The amendment to admit the Mid-West State as a fourth Region has been the subject of continuing partisan debate in Parliament. See, as of this writing, *House of Representative Debates* (Daily Parts), March 30, 1962, pp. 569 ff. Considerable uncertainty lies in whether the required 60 per cent majority approval will be forthcoming in the area that would be included in the projected Region. *West Africa*, July 1, 1961, p. 723.
[34] *Op. cit.*, esp. pp. 353 ff., 378–84.
[35] Hugh H. Smythe and Mabel M. Smythe, *The New Nigerian Elite* (Stanford, 1960), esp. chap. xi; Gabriel A. Almond and James S. Coleman, eds., *The Politics of the Developing Areas* (Princeton, 1960), pp. 341–45.

elites in either the North or South will be able to command both the respect of the masses and the support of the economically favored and traditionally rooted elements in the society over a long period of time,[36] but, unlike the situation of a few years ago, there is no *serious* talk of the dismemberment of Nigeria, or of secession, coming from these responsible leaders in any of the Regions today. The new political elites assume the continuance of a united Nigeria.

It is the changed attitude of certain of these political leaders toward participation in the government at the center that marks a major change during the past decade. As late as the first elections to the federal House of Representatives under the 1954 Constitution, there was uncertainty as to the attractiveness and future prestige of federal office-holding, whether in Parliament or in the public service. Indeed, despite recent changes, less than one per cent of the senior civil servants in the federal public service come from Northern Nigeria.[37] However, it may be that educational considerations are as responsible for this situation as are personal preferences. With due allowance for the special position of the Sardauna of Sokoto, the parliamentary election campaign of 1959 pointed toward the future participation in the central government in Lagos for the leaders of each of the political parties—the Northern Peoples Congress (NPC) with its strength in the North, the Action Group (AG), which has a clear majority in the West, and the National Council of Nigeria and the Cameroons (NCNC), which is dominant in the East. As of May, 1962, Sir Abubakar, the deputy leader of the NPC, is the Prime Minister of a government based on a coalition of the NPC and the NCNC; Dr. Azikiwe of the NCNC was President of the Senate and is now Governor-General of the Federation; and Chief Awo-

---

[36] On the North, note particularly the prophecies in the outstanding work by M. G. Smith, *Government in Zazzau* (London, 1960), pp. 292–95; see also in general Smythe and Smythe, *op. cit.*, pp. 166 ff., and, particularly, references to lack of identification with the masses. Forthcoming studies by Richard Sklar and Kenneth Post dealing with aspects of Nigerian political parties and elections will be worth consulting.

[37] On March 4, 1960, only 29 out of 4,398 "officers in C scale and above" designated the Northern Region as their "Region of origin." The Parliamentary Secretary to the Minister of Pensions in *House of Representatives Debates*, April 20, 1960, p. 1453. Cf. *ibid.* (Daily Parts), April 4, 1962, pp. 815–17.

lowo, the leader of the Action Group, is the Leader of the Opposition in the federal House of Representatives. Viewing the national election of 1959 and the Northern election of May, 1961, it is apparent that the pull of political gravity is still quite high from Kaduna, the capital of the Northern Region, but the center of power has certainly moved somewhat in the direction of Lagos, the federal capital. Consequently, it is no longer true to say that one of the major weaknesses of "federalism" in Nigeria has been the failure of the major party leaders to leave their regional confines and to stake their political careers on their records of participation in the central Parliament or Council of Ministers.[38]

Various adjustments have been worked out for increasing the co-operation between the federal and regional governments. In these arrangements, the initiative has usually been taken by the permanent officials of a federal ministry or agency of Lagos, which has also provided the staff. In addition to consultation between ministries, there are periodic conferences to consider specific matters, such as fisheries, agriculture, civil aviation, etc.[39] Mention has previously been made of the National Economic Council and the Loans Advisory Council. To cite other illustrations, conferences of the Ministers of Labor are held periodically; regular meetings of the members of Public Service Commissions take place annually. The early hopes that the National Council of Establishments would play a leading part in the formulation of uniform public service policies have not been realized. Its Secretary serves today chiefly as an infrequently used mailbox for communications between the respective ministers and officials. Nevertheless, the general organization and the salary structure of the four services are fairly similar,[40] and transfers of personnel among them are possible and occasionally arranged.

Special mention might be made of the developments in the field

---

[38] Cf. Ezera, *op. cit.*, chap. x, esp. p. 201.

[39] *The Economic Programme of the Government of the Federation of Nigeria, 1955–60*, p. 10.

[40] The failure in 1959 of the Western Region to participate in the "Commission appointed by the Governments of the Federation, the Northern Region, the Eastern Region and the Southern Cameroons" to review and make recommendations on salaries and wages indicates the continuing difficulties in securing joint action and agreement. See Federation of Nigeria, *Review of Salaries and Wages* (Lagos, 1959).

of education. The report of the Ashby Commission in 1960 on the needs of Nigeria at the post-certificate and higher educational levels was examined carefully by various groups and agencies in the Federation and Regions. The report was accepted "in principle" by all of the regional ministries, and with some amendments by the Federal Government which has, to use its own language, "raised the targets." [41] Various new co-ordinating agencies have been projected by the Federal Government, some, but not all, of which were recommended by the Ashby Commission. These include a National Universities Commission, an Inter-Regional Manpower-Board, and an All-Nigeria Academic Council. The present avenues for co-ordination through meetings of ministers, permanent secretaries, and other educational officials will be continued, but some additional agencies to channel applications for foreign aid and to supervise technical assistance schemes are envisaged.

Regional, rather than "federal," pressures will explain the "regional representation" apparent in various public corporations. In some cases this is provided by law—for example, the Electricity Corporation of Nigeria, the Nigerian Broadcasting Corporation, the Nigerian Ports Authority, and the Nigerian Railway Corporation. In other cases—for example the Nigerian Coal Corporation—regional representation is practiced though there is no legal basis for it. The Police Council of the Federation includes a regional Minister from each Region. Certain advisory bodies, such as the Posts and Telegraphs Advisory Council, the Federal Labor Advisory Council, and the Federal Scholarships Advisory Board, which were set up solely under the authority of the federal ministers, do in fact have members who reflect regional points of view. There is strong sentiment in some quarters that regional representation, at least on the statutory corporation, is objectionable on several counts and should be abolished. But, whatever the merits of this viewpoint, the boards of the statutory

[41] Federation of Nigeria, *Educational Development 1960–70*, Sessional Paper No. 3 of 1961 (Lagos, 1961). The report of the Ashby Commission, or the Commission on Post-School Certificate and Higher Education in Nigeria, has been published by the Federal Ministry of Education under the title, *Investment in Education* (Lagos and London, 1960).

corporations and the consultative bodies on which "regional representatives" have been included do provide additional forums where an exchange of regional and other specialized views can take place under the aegis of a national body in search of agreement on issues of national concern.

Since achieving independence on October 1, 1960, Nigeria has had full responsibility, in name as well as in fact, for the maintenance of national defense and for the conduct of foreign relations. The control of defense matters was transferred early in 1960 from the Office of the Governor-General to the Office of the Prime Minister in anticipation of independence (with the Governor-General retaining the right to use his reserve powers until that time), while the control of foreign relations rested in fact in the Prime Minister's Office before independence was actually achieved. A Ministry of Foreign Affairs and Commonwealth Relations, and a Ministry of Defense have been established. By the summer of 1961 a substantial number of selected Nigerians had received some training for the foreign service in several foreign countries, primarily in British Embassies and Consulates, and at least twelve missions had been established. The appeal of foreign service posts has been high, and all governments, including that of the Northern Region, have "seconded" selected officials for these posts. Among these officials, as among many of the political leaders, there is a tendency to minimize the pretensions of the leaders in other African countries and to believe that Nigeria has the potentiality to make *her* the political leader in Africa.[42] The future conduct of Nigerian foreign policy and defense matters thus focuses a strong psychological spotlight on the central government. As a unifying factor, it may act as a partial substitute in the future for the unifying effect of the present-day charges of "colonial domination" and the continued clamor for rapid Nigerianization of the public services.

In the meantime certain writers are beginning to argue that there are more cultural affinities than differences among Nigerians. Despite the marked cultural variations among tribal groups, there is an inclination to recognize both material and non-

[42] Also see L. Gray Cowan, *infra*, chap vi.

material similarities among the "Negro, Arab and Western European cultures." "Nigeria is not an accident," argued Okoi Arikpo. "It is not an artificial creation nor an arbitrary block of land chipped off the surface of tropical Africa. On the contrary, in Nigeria we are dealing with a cultural melting-pot where cultural influences from all directions have met to produce a most virile cultural complex." [43] Mention might also be made of the growing number of popular writings dealing with the "projection of the Nigerian personality." [44] These and other appraisals may properly be subjected to careful scrutiny, but the essence of the matter is the growing belief that a Nigerian "nation" does exist. A noticeable change in the attitude of members of the political elites is evidenced in their increasing, if somewhat hesitant, willingness to refer to themselves as Nigerians, rather than as Yorubas, Ibos, or Hausas.

Whatever be the conflicting views today regarding the existence of a Nigerian nation, or the nature of Nigerian "nationhood" or of the "Nigerian personality," it is recognized that in the beginning Nigeria was created by the fiat of a foreign power. Its boundaries and even its name are of recent vintage. New factors and forces within the past decade have added their weight to the English language and the legal and parliamentary institutions, which reflect the British heritage, to provide the basis of a growing unity and support for an expanded role of the central government. In assaying these factors and forces, it must be remembered that Nigeria was politically unified under British rule for several decades after 1914. The unifying forces which have been discussed have consequently been those that provided certain checks to the post-World War II trends, particularly between 1946 and 1957, when Nigerian demands for regional self-government and the appeals of tribal nationalism were at their peak. Today, despite continu-

[43] "Is there a Nigerian Nation," *West Africa Review*, XXXI (Feb., 1960), 53–54; cf. Nduka Igbodo, "Conditions that will make Nigeria fit to Lead Africa," *Daily Times* (Lagos), Feb. 23, 1960, p. 5, and I. A. Akingogbin, "Who Are the Nigerians," *ibid.*, July 11, 1960, p. 5.
[44] Oluwole Kolawole, "That Personality: Who's projecting it?," *Daily Express* (Lagos), June 16, 1961, p. 4. In general, the term "African personality" expresses the aspirations implicit in the term "Negritude" as used in French-speaking West Africa.

ing dangers, contended the Leader of the Opposition, Chief Awolowo, in the Federal House of Representatives in April, 1960, "the unity of the country is assured, assured in the sense that it is a heritage which is being handed over to us by the British Government on their departure from this country, and secondly because all the leaders of opinion in this country are determined that Nigeria should remain united." [45] Most skeptics of federal arrangements in Nigeria will be inclined to agree with the Premier of the Eastern Region, Dr. Okpara, who said: "The federal structure has many drawbacks. It is a costly and weak form of government. . . . But I submit, Sir, it were better to have a unified country with a federal system of government than to disintegrate." [46] And, in the view of a competent observer, Alhaji Sir Abubakar Balewa "puts national unity above all else." To quote the Prime Minister himself, "as the Prime Minister of the Federation I regard myself as a Nigerian and I am working for the interest of the country as a whole. . . . We are all—the opposition and the Government—working sincerely for the unity of the country." [47]

The viability of any federal system of government depends upon the shifting balance of centrifugal and centripetal forces in a society. Federalism is the process by which adjustment is made between those forces making for disunity and those making for unity. It has been my contention that unifying pressures in Nigeria are increasing in their impact. As a consequence, one who is accustomed to stress the factors and developments making for closer political union in American federalism from the Articles of Confederation to the ratified Constitution in 1789 is justified in taking a similar approach in appraising the development of Nigerian federalism during the period between its Constitution of 1954 and the Independence Constitution of 1960.

[45] *House of Representatives Debates* (Daily Parts), April 1, 1960, p. 1; Obafemi Awolowo, *Awo: The Autobiography of Chief Obafemi Awolowo* (Cambridge, 1960), p. 300. Note, however, the remarks of Chief Awolowo regarding the "continued unity of the Federation" on the assumption that "no one state should be so large and so powerful as to override the wishes of the other states put together." *House of Representatives Debates* (Daily Parts), April 4, 1961, p. 789.
[46] *Daily Times* (Lagos), March 25, 1960, p. 1.
[47] *House of Representatives Debates* (Daily Parts), March 30, 1961, pp. 697–98.

4

The Independence Constitution
of Federal Nigeria [1]

Taylor Cole

I

On October 1 of 1960 the Federation of Nigeria became the
sixteenth African state to achieve independence in that year.
During this period of rapid political and social change in Africa,
the constitutional history and the main features of the evolving
political system of Nigeria have received particular attention.
Some of this attention has understandably been focused on the
Independence Constitution, and the present discussion too will
be centered on an examination of it. This essay will be particularly concerned with its history and interpretation (Section
II) and with certain constitutional problems viewed in the light
of discussions going on at the time of independence (Section
III). A penultimate section outlining several of the major constitutional developments during the first year of independence
will permit a post mortem on these discussions.

II

The Constitution of Nigeria has recent roots, as the previous
chapters have indicated.[2] Britain established a unitary political

[1] An early version of this essay appeared in *The South Atlantic Quarterly,* LX
(Winter, 1961), 1–18.
[2] See *supra,* chaps. ii and iii.

system for the whole of Nigeria following the final unification in 1914 of the Protectorates of Southern and Northern Nigeria, created in 1900, and the Colony and Protectorate of Lagos. The groupings of provinces into three main regional divisions in the 1930's were solidified in the Constitution of 1946. The period 1946–54, a period that saw three constitutions (1946, 1951, and 1954), was marked by the acceptance of federal arrangements, which were a response to the pressures for separation and regional autonomy, and by the continued evolution of responsible parliamentary government. The autonomy of the Regions was given added recognition when internal "self-government" was granted to the Eastern and Western Regions in 1957 and to the Northern Region in 1959. To incorporate these and other changes, the Constitution of 1954 was liberally amended during the years 1954–60 [3] in accordance with the recommendations of various constitutional conferences and meetings, the last two of which were held in London in May, 1960, and in Lagos in July, 1960. In each succeeding constitutional conference and meeting, the role and influence of the British representatives, designated by the Secretary of State for the Colonies, had been progressively reduced, until at the last meetings in 1960 they played largely the part of advisers and observers while final details for the Constitution [4] were being hammered out by the Nigerian participants.

The Independence Constitution was issued, as was the Constitution of 1954, by the Queen-in-Council on the basis of powers vested in her by the Foreign Jurisdiction Act, 1890, "or otherwise" possessed by her. Its provisions were the result of agreements over a long period of time, or of a "bundle of compromises," to borrow from Farrand's characterization of the work of the Con-

[3] *The Nigeria (Constitution) Order in Council, 1954,* commonly referred to as the Constitution of 1954, and other "Constitutional Instruments," as amended through March, 1960, have been published as a Supplement to the Government Gazette. See Federation of Nigeria, *Official Gazette,* XLVII, 20 (April 14, 1960), Part D. This Constitution, with the attached Schedules, was a lengthy document of some 153 pages.
[4] The Independence Constitution of the Federation of Nigeria is included in the "Second Schedule" of the *Nigeria (Constitution) Order in Council, 1960.* The constitutions of the Northern, Western, and Eastern Regions comprise the Third, Fourth, and Fifth Schedules, respectively, of this document, which was laid before Parliament on September 16, 1960. These four Schedules cover nearly 170 pages.

stitutional Convention that met in Philadelphia in 1787. During the years from 1946 to 1954, the compromises represented not only adjustments between the points of view of the British Colonial Office and the nationalist leaders of various Nigerian movements, organizations, and emerging political parties, but also those among the Nigerian leaders and spokesmen themselves. The chief compromises were between those who favored a strong central government, perhaps one modeled on the unitary government in Nigeria after 1914, and those who advocated the maximum degree of autonomy for the Regions. In particular, sharp differences over the allocation of tax revenues between the Federation and the Regions under a federal system had to be reconciled. There were also differences between those favoring added guarantees for the protection of minority rights, including the creation of new states, and those who felt that such guarantees would be, at worst, restrictive on the Regions and objectionable to Native Authorities and, at best, useless.

The legitimacy of the Constitution is to be found not in the work of a popularly elected constitutional convention, or in ratification by legislative bodies or the electorate, but in two other sources. The one is the approval given by the elected representatives from the governments of the Federation and all of the Regions through their participation in the drafting of the provisions of the Constitution. The participants at the last meetings in 1960 included not only members from political parties that supported the coalition Government of the Federation, but also members of the Action Group, the opposition party in Parliament.[5] The other source is the formal action of the Queen-in-Council, acting under parliamentary authorization and the prerogative.

The provisions of the new Constitution embody in a more systematic organization and in more lucid phraseology the main contents of the Constitution of 1954, together with subsequent amendments and changes that had been agreed upon during 1960. Instead of one document for the Federation and Regions,

---

[5] The account of the participation of the present Leader of the Opposition in Parliament in these constitutional conferences may be found in Obafemi Awolowo, *Awo: The Autobiography of Chief Obafemi Awolowo* (Cambridge, 1960).

there are now separate constitutions for each of the four political units. The Nigeria Independence Act, 1960, which included the essential provisions of the Statute of Westminster, was enacted in 1960 by the United Kingdom Parliament following an official request from the Nigerian Federal Legislature (now called "Parliament" under the new Constitution). In keeping with the unwritten and adopted practices followed in the admission of new members, the governments of the other member countries indicated their willingness to accept Nigeria as a member of the Commonwealth after independence. To implement her part of this decision, the United Kingdom Government appointed a High Commissioner for the Federation and a Deputy High Commissioner to each regional capital. Appointments of new officials to the posts of governors and Governor-General have been made by the Queen at the request of the responsible Nigerian governments. Nigeria had previously indicated her intention of continuing to permit appeals to the Judicial Committee of the Privy Council.

On October 1, after Lord Head had been received by the Prime Minister as the first United Kingdom High Commissioner to the Federation of Nigeria, there was an exchange of highly significant and controversial letters between Sir Abubakar and the High Commissioner. In accordance with these letters, the Government of the Federation of Nigeria assumed all rights and obligations stipulated in the international agreements entered into "on their behalf by the Government of the United Kingdom before independence," and these agreements were to continue in force "until such time as the Government of Nigeria can consider whether they require modification or re-negotiation in any respect."[6] The Parliament of Nigeria provided the sequel to these developments in 1961 by the passage of an act to provide for the alteration of the Royal Style and Titles. The "assent of the Legislature of the Federation of Nigeria" was thereby granted to Her Majesty "for use in the Federation of Nigeria" of the following style and titles:

[6] The texts of the letters were not available to the author, and the quotations are from a mimeographed Nigerian Ministry of Information Release of Oct. 1, 1960. Note *House of Representatives Debates* (Daily Parts), April 9, 1962, pp. 1161 ff.

"Elizabeth the Second, Queen of Nigeria, and of Her other Realms and Territories, Head of the Commonwealth."[7]

The boundaries of Nigeria have been affected since independence by the admission of the Northern Cameroons into Nigeria as a province of the Northern Region[8] and by the action of the Southern Cameroons in opting in 1961 to join the Republic of the Cameroons. The trusteeship of the Northern Cameroons had been exercised under the responsibility of the Northern Regional Government, whereas that of the Southern Cameroons, until independence, had been exercised on behalf of the United Kingdom under the authority of the Governor-General of Nigeria. In fact, the "withdrawal" through a plebiscite of the Southern Cameroons removed an area that had been heavily integrated, both economically and politically, into the Federation of Nigeria, an area that most Nigerians had expected to become one of the Regions in the Federation. Its "severance" has posed some continuing problems in working out the new economic and political relationships between this area and the Federation, especially following the final withdrawal of British troops and Nigerian police after October 1, 1961.

III

During the last stages of the formal "transfer of power," a Seminar on Constitutional Problems of Federalism in Nigeria met in Lagos during the period August 8–15, 1960. Convened under the auspices of a committee representing the Supreme Court and the Nigeria Bar Association and made possible by a substantial grant from the Ford Foundation, the seminar included among its participants the chief justices and members of the Supreme Court, the

[7] No. 7 of 1961, in Federation of Nigeria, *Official Gazette*, XLVIII, No. 39 (June 1, 1961), p. A21. Note the reference to this bill by the Minister of Justice and Attorney General Elias, in *House of Representatives Debates* (Daily Parts), April 11, 1961, pp. 1312–14. For a comparison of the form of title used in other Commonwealth countries, see Central Office of Information, *The Monarchy and the Commonwealth* (London, 1961), Appendix.

[8] Government Notice No. 1109, in Federation of Nigeria, *Official Gazette*, XLVIII, 40 (June 1, 1961), 745.

High Courts of the Regions, and the High Court of Lagos, the at-
torneys-general of the Federation and Regions, as well as a number of officials and members of the bar. Foreign guests included
prominent judges, legal officials, and academicians from the
United States, the United Kingdom, Canada, Australia, and
Ghana.[9] An address by the Prime Minister of the Federation, Sir
Abubakar, opened the meetings. The purpose of the seminar was
to examine the provisions of the Nigerian Constitution, and, in
the light of the experiences of other federations, to consider the
major constitutional problems that Nigeria will face in the future.[10] No effort was made to agree on any recommendations or
to provide any final answers to questions that only Nigeria could
discover for herself. The following analysis of the Independence
Constitution, while representing strictly a personal appraisal,
will necessarily draw heavily on seminar discussions.[11]

The provisions of the Independence Constitution are little
known in Nigeria except to those officials and political leaders
who participated in its drafting at various stages and who are
responsible for its implementation. Its phraseology owes much
to the English-trained lawyer, whether Nigerian or expatriate. In
particular this is true of those written provisions that clearly recognize the acceptance of the English rule of law. The chapter

[9] Among these guests were Sir Kenneth Bailey, Solicitor General of the Commonwealth of Australia; Lord Denning, Lord of Appeal in Ordinary in the United
Kingdom; Professor Erwin N. Griswold, Dean of the Law School of Harvard Uni-
versity; Professor Philip C. Jessup, then of the School of Law of Columbia Uni-
versity; Judge Stanley F. Reed, retired Justice of the Supreme Court of the United
States; Judge Charles E. Wyzanski, Jr., Judge of the United States District Court,
Massachusetts; Judge D. C. Wells, Justice of the Supreme Court of Ontario, Can-
ada; A. McNulty, Secretary, Commission on Human Rights, Council of Europe;
Sir Kenneth Diplock, Judge of the High Court of England and Wales; A. Casely-
Hayford, President of the Ghana Bar Association; and B. J. da Rocha, Assistant
Secretary, Ghana Bar Association.

[10] The seminar was compelled to discuss the constitutional problems in the light
of the Constitution of 1954, as amended to 1960, and the pertinent constitutional
instruments, rather than on the basis of the new Independence Constitution. However, it was recognized that few changes in substance had been made in the former Constitution, and the members of the seminar were informed of changes that
were pertinent to the discussions. Furthermore, a substantial number of the actual
participants in the last constitutional meeting in Lagos, which agreed on the
final phraseology of the Independence Constitution, were participants in the
seminar.

[11] The formal papers and a summary of the discussions of the seminar have
been published by the Nigeria Bar Association. See L. Brett, ed., *Constitutional
Problems of Federalism in Nigeria* (Lagos, 1961).

on the courts,[12] despite its unique features, gives special evidence of indebtedness to well-established English precedents. The chief problems have been those involving criminal law and procedure in the Northern Region, where native courts have applied Muslim law. But in 1959–60 there was a reform of this criminal law and procedure that, despite modifications in 1961, served to bring it more into line with the common law; moreover, the detailed guarantees of "Fundamental Rights" in the Constitution [13] provide at least some procedural "due process of law" and judicial protection against such abuses as discriminatory, and cruel and inhuman, treatment. This, however, is not to imply that the spirit of the constitutional provisions may not, under existing conditions, be evaded or violated in their implementation.

The provisions for responsible parliamentary government are included in the sections of the Constitution dealing with the Governor-General, Parliament, and Executive Powers.[14] The reserved powers possessed by the Governor-General under the Constitution of 1954, it was noted, have been removed under the Independence Constitution. Much that would be considered to be "conventions of the constitution" in the United Kingdom have been spelled out in written provisions in Nigeria. This is particularly true of the position of the ministers, their selection, and their relationship to Parliament. However, we can search in vain here, as in most other Commonwealth countries, for a mention of political parties in the document. The provisions regarding the upper houses, both in the Federation and in the Regions, recognize the secondary position of these recently created second chambers to the lower houses; indeed, analogies to the House of Lords are occasionally drawn. To illustrate, the powers of the Senate in the Federation follow somewhat the pattern set by the Parliament Acts of 1911 and 1949 in the United Kingdom; and the maximum number of ministers who can come from the Senate is rigidly limited. The upper house, or House of Chiefs, in each of the Regions is designed to graft into the political structure at the regional capital both the traditional and the recently established

[12] Constitution, chap. viii.
[13] Constitution, chap. iii.
[14] Constitution, chaps. iv–vi.

and recognized native authorities and local leaders. These upper chambers participate in the selection of the members of the Senate.

Fear of the misuse of the power of appointment and removal is witnessed in provisions dealing with the public service, and those covering the composition and responsibility of such executive bodies as the Judicial Service Commission,[15] Police Service Commission,[16] and Public Service Commission.[17] The primary objective of these agencies is to remove the higher bureaucracy, the police, and the judiciary as far as possible from the pressures of extended families and political groups for patronage, privilege, and preference. The reasons for the establishment of the Public Service Commission, to select it for mention, are reminiscent of those that led to the creation of the first Civil Service Commissions in the United States and Canada.

There are two ways of guaranteeing the fundamentality of the Nigerian Constitution, that is, in recognizing its supremacy over ordinary legislative enactments. The one is by judicial review and the other is by the process of amendment. With respect to judicial review, the power of the Supreme Court of the Federation extends, as under the Constitution of 1954, not only to disputes between the Federation and the Regions and between Regions, but also to the constitutionality of acts of both the regional and federal legislative bodies. Appeals will continue to lie to the Judicial Committee of the Privy Council,[18] though some members of the seminar expressed skepticism of these arrangements for independent Nigeria. The majority opinion stressed the continued advantage of appeal to an outside and impartial body, though suggesting the desirability of broadening the membership of the Judicial Committee to include distinguished African judges who would be cognizant of local conditions and of the nuances of customary law. But, to repeat, the discussion was at least for the time an academic one, for the Independence Constitution recognizes the Judicial Committee as the final court of appeal from the Nigerian Supreme Court.

[15] Sections 120–21.
[16] Sections 102–3.
[17] Sections 140–43.
[18] Section 114.

The interpretation of the Constitution, or the "approaches" to its interpretation, provoked the sharpest differences of opinion at the seminar. American discussants, with their considerable respect for the roles of the Marshalls, the Holmeses, and the Brandeises as "constitutional statesmen," maintained that a constitution should be viewed as something more than the provision of an "insurance policy" and that it should be interpreted by judges who are cognizant of sociological change and aware of "durable public opinion." The assumption here was that the courts provide one of the chief avenues for constitutional development, and perhaps the most important one in a rapidly developing and changing country whose constitution incorporates a difficult process of amendment. The other position, reflecting perhaps the heritage of historical and analytical legal training in Britain, placed stress upon the need to confine interpretations to the written word, to the phraseology as it would be viewed by a reasonable man who was concerned with its "pith and substance." Changes in the Constitution should not and could not be made by the courts, acting as constitutional legislators, but only by the legislatures as participants in the formal process of amendment. This point of view was generally defended by the participants in the seminar from the Commonwealth countries. The choice before the Nigerian judge was frequently referred to as that between a "liberal" or "flexible" versus the "strict" and "rigid" interpretation.

The Constitution of 1954 contained no provisions for amendment, and all changes in it were necessarily made by Order in Council. The Independence Constitution, in contrast, contains provisions for formal amendment, which were framed after considerable discussion. The "entrenched" provisions of the Constitution (i.e., those dealing with the judiciary, fundamental rights, amendment, etc.) can be changed only by a two-thirds majority of all of the members of both houses of the Federal Parliament followed by the approval of the legislative houses in two of the Regions.[19] The nearest analogy would appear to be one of the

---

[19] Section 4. The amendment of "entrenched" provisions of the regional constitutions also requires the approval, by appropriate resolution, of both houses of the Federal Parliament. Section 5.

methods of initiating and ratifying amendments to the Constitution of the United States.

Under the Constitution of 1954, the Governor-General was given broad reserved powers that permitted him to suspend certain guarantees and provisions in the Constitution in order to deal with emergency situations. Under the Independence Constitution, various provisions of the Constitution can be suspended under such conditions, but only with the approval of the Parliament. Excepting one recommendation that emergency powers be strictly construed, surprisingly little attention in seminar discussions was devoted to a consideration of emergencies. In the light of the experience of other modern states with martial law, state of siege, and constitutional dictatorship, it appears that the discussion of these would have been deserving of more attention. In the final analysis, the real meaning and significance of the Constitution can be measured by the ease with which it can be suspended, or, as one participant observed, what can be done "when it hurts."

The federal system of Nigeria, as previously indicated, is the product of several decades of incubation. Various unifying forces have served to check the separatist and autonomist pressures in the Federation as a whole and to provide a basis on which the growth of the powers of the central government could be predicated. A careful comparison of the provisions of the Independence Constitution with those of the 1954 Constitution, as subsequently amended, will indicate that the powers of the central government were slightly augmented in several respects (i.e., in the fields of commerce, taxation, and foreign affairs). Today, the federal features of the government of the Federation are evidenced in (1) the institutional arrangements by which the position of the Regions is recognized in the constitutional organs of the Federation, and (2) the division of powers between the Federation and the Regions.

To provide a bill of particulars as to the institutional arrangements, the Regions are allowed equal representation in the Senate of the Federation, with provision for twelve members from each of the Regions who constitute most of the membership of the upper house. The Supreme Court of the Federation, with its powers of judicial review, includes in its ex officio membership the chief justices of the High Courts of the Regions. The part played by the Regions in the amending procedure has been mentioned. The Regions are represented on such constitutional bodies as the Police Council and Judicial Service Commission. There is also representation provided by statute on the boards of several public corporations, i.e., the Electricity Corporation of Nigeria, the Nigerian Ports Authority, the Nigerian Railway Corporation, and the Nigerian Broadcasting Corporation. The National Economic Council, which is concerned with evolving common policies on economic problems, and its subsidiary National Planning Committee, include in their membership corresponding federal and regional officials. The Loans Advisory Council, which is responsible for raising foreign and internal loan money for all governments, and the National Council of Establishments, which deals with public service questions, are similarly constituted. In short, there are many institutional arrangements, some recognized and others permitted under the Constitution, through which the Regions are "represented." They provide a part of the web of relationships by which federal and regional officials are brought into contact and through which their points of view are exchanged. But the seminar did not concern itself to any appreciable extent with these arrangements, or with the general development and problems of administrative federalism.

It was rather to the division of powers that it devoted its major attention, both in the prepared papers and in the discussions. For this emphasis there were possibly three reasons. One was the belief that the interpretation of the provisions dealing with the allocation of powers would occupy the attention of the judges and legal officials in an acute way during the early months after October 1. Another has been the tendency in most Commonwealth countries to conceive of the essence of federalism in strictly legal terms. Finally, there was need for some arbitrary division of labor, and the discussion of the legal division of powers certainly made adequate demands on the time of the laborers in the vineyard.

By and large, the division of powers in Nigeria follows Australian and American precedents, at least to the extent that most delegated powers are vested in the central government and reserved powers are left to the Regions. There are two variations that need mention. First, there are certain powers (i.e., to establish a regional bank) that are delegated to the Regions. Second, the "concurrent powers" of the Federation and Regions are specifically recognized in separate sections of the Constitution. Their designation is more reminiscent of some provisions to be found in the Indian Constitution or the West German *Grundgesetz* than of those in the Australian or American constitutions. Be that as it may, the authors of the papers and the Nigerian participants in the seminar were principally concerned with Australian and American, and to a lesser extent with Canadian, legal decisions, precedents, and practices as of future interest for Nigerian constitutional interpreters.

As specified in the Independence Constitution, the Federal Government is granted exclusive jurisdiction over banking (with the exception noted), external affairs, basic communications, defense, citizenship, emigration and immigration, public debt, and the affairs of Lagos. It shares with the Regions concurrent powers over labor, public safety and public order, industrial development, roads, prisons, and public works. Reserved to the Regions are the major fields of health, agriculture, and education (except higher education). The Regions are empowered to exercise powers on the concurrent list subject to the federal priority, when federal and regional enactments conflict or are inconsistent. Members of the seminar recognized that, in other federations, the Federal Government has not usually been hesitant to seek to "cover the field" of the concurrent powers.

Special attention was devoted by the seminar to three areas where the jurisdictional boundaries between the Federation and Regions will certainly raise difficult questions. They are: (1) taxation, (2) trade and commerce, and (3) implementation of international agreements. There is no concurrent power of taxation recognized in the Nigerian Constitution. On the basis of the recommendations of a series of commissions in the past, the taxing powers have been divided in the Constitution between the

Federation and the Regions. Indeed, one of the major discussion points at the last constitutional meetings in 1960 involved the power to tax incomes, collected by the Federation and formerly distributed to the Regions on the basis of origin.[20] The income from the important import taxes, collected by the Federation, is in part retained by the Federal Government and in part distributed to the Regions according to specified criteria, whereas the proceeds of the export taxes, also collected by the Federation, are distributed in their entirety to the Regions on the basis of their derivation. The result has been that over 44 per cent of the total anticipated revenue collected by the Federal Government in 1960–61 was returned to the Regions and that nearly two-thirds of the total revenue of the Regions during that fiscal year was derived from federal grants and allocations.

Much attention was given by the seminar to the taxation of governmental instrumentalities in other federations. Consistent with what appear to be the converging opinions of American and Australian courts, it was believed that, while income taxes can be levied on the salaries of civil servants, "one constituent entity of the Nigerian Federation cannot tax the government of another constituent entity nor can it use its powers to tax the civil servants of another constituent entity in order to force upon the other entity a particular policy." [21] Just how far the taxing power can be used for regulatory purposes and how far the wide and somewhat irregular contours provided by American judicial precedent may excite the imagination of the Nigerian judge remains to be seen. In any event, the cases with which the Nigerian judge will continue to be faced will present him with instances where taxing laws, so defined by legislative statement, will certainly have the "incidental effect" of regulation of matters not otherwise within the legislators' competence.

Perhaps the most difficult problems of interpretation would arise, it was felt, in delineating the powers of the Federation over "trade and commerce." Again the gamut of foreign experiences was a wide one and ranged from the sharply restrictive interpre-

[20] Cf. Section 7 of the Constitution of 1954 and Section 70 of the Constitution of 1960.
[21] Mr. Justice Charles, in Brett, *op. cit.*, p. 81.

tation of the trade and commerce powers of the Dominion Government of Canada to the broad interpretation of the commerce powers of the Federal Government of the United States. In Nigeria, the powers, over what the courts in the United States would call "commerce," have been spelled out in some detail in the exclusive and concurrent powers of the Federal Government. The powers include those over "aviation," "railways," "trunk roads," "maritime shipping and navigation," "posts, telegraphs, and telephones," "wireless, broadcasting, and television" (except as provided by regional governments), and "trade and commerce between Nigeria and other countries" and "among the territories." It might be said that there was only limited opposition from the Regions to vesting most of these powers in the Federal Government in 1954, in part because there was limited interregional trade at the time and also because "the familiar conflict between the industrial regions and the agricultural regions, or between regions whose prosperity depends on export and those who depend upon home markets, was absent." [22] But these conditions are changing, and regional dissatisfaction with exclusive federal control over interregional trade and commerce and maritime shipping has been growing. Nevertheless, the Independence Constitution has strengthened rather than weakened the Federation's powers by removing one important provision, Section 58A, which was inserted in the 1954 Constitution by way of amendment in 1959. This section provided that "no restriction shall be imposed upon trade or commerce among the Regions . . . by or in pursuance of any law enacted by any legislature in Nigeria." The significance of the removal of this restrictive provision is at the moment a subject of sharp controversy and one that will require future judicial attention.

These broad powers in the field of trade and commerce, when coupled with those possessed by the Federation over taxation, defense, control of electricity and patents, labor, scientific and industrial research, water power, and statistics should be sufficient to remove some doubts as to the adequacy of its powers to undergird legally a comprehensive plan for the economic development

[22] Chief H. O. Davies, Q. C., in *ibid.*, p. 94.

of Nigeria. And, in particular, a "liberal" interpretation of the powers of the Federation over trade and commerce should at least lower the remaining barriers resulting from regional control over health, agriculture, education, and local government affairs.

The consideration by the seminar of international agreements was centered on two questions: (1) Which of the international agreements of the United Kingdom, applicable to Nigeria, would be binding on Nigeria after October 1, 1960? and (2) How would these international agreements be implemented under the Nigerian federal system? Certain Nigerian participants felt that Nigeria should be free to decide after independence as to which of the more than three hundred applicable international agreements would be binding on her, since as a "colony" she had had no part in their negotiations. However, it was generally recognized in the seminar that the rules of international law governing state succession should and would be followed. If there were doubts as to the existence and applicability of precedent in the case of some of the treaties and agreements, certainly there were clearly recognized and accepted principles of international law to cover many of the others. Regarding the implementation of treaties, the unresolved limits of legislative powers in the United States and in Australia received the respectful attention of the members of the seminar. The Nigerian constitutional provisions do not follow the principles of the decisions in *Missouri v. Holland* and of the *Curtiss-Wright Export Corporation* cases, but rather those of the Canadian International Labour Office Conventions cases decided by the Judicial Committee of the Privy Council in 1937. On the crucial issue, the Federal Parliament can clearly pass legislation for the implementation of international agreements involving the exercise of powers falling under the exclusive and concurrent lists; it clearly cannot implement treaties and agreements through legislation which involves the exercise of powers otherwise reserved to the Regions, that is, without some appropriate form of regional approval or acquiescence in the federal action.[23] The treaty-making power cannot, conse-

[23] Constitution, Section 69.

quently, be utilized in Nigeria to expand the competence of the Federal Parliament.

IV

The major constitutional questions that have emerged in Nigeria since independence have been those that have been debated in the political sectors and that have not as yet involved consideration by the judiciary. As a background for a mention of several of these questions, it is necessary to remember that the present Government, headed by Alhaji Sir Abubakar Tafawa Balewa, has found its support since the national election on December 12, 1959, in a tenuous coalition of the Hausa-Fulani-dominated Northern Peoples Congress (NPC), with its substantial plurality in the House of Representatives elected from the Northern Region, and the National Council of Nigeria and the Cameroons (NCNC), the main strength of which lies among the Ibos in the Eastern Region. The opposition in the House of Representatives has been furnished by the Action Group (AG), which in 1962 was beset by sharp internal dissension among its leaders, has its fulcrum among the Yorubas of the Western Region. On the whole, the coalition has followed a moderate evolutionary course in internal matters. It has placed a stress on economic development internally and a policy of "non-identification with any bloc or group" in external affairs.[24] The control of the regional governments by the NPC in the North, the AG in the West, and the NCNC in the East has been reaffirmed in regional elections held during a two-year period since the national election in 1959. The NPC victory in the Northern regional election in May, 1961, was particularly decisive and resulted in the almost complete elimination of legislative representation by opposition parties. Since the Northern Region contains a majority of the population of Nigeria, the results of this regional election have at a minimum increased the political reassurance of the NPC leaders at both the

[24] See speech (of the Governor-General) from the Throne, *House of Representatives Debates* (Daily Parts), March 29, 1961, p. 598; cf. L. Gray Cowan, "Nigerian Foreign Policy," *infra*, chap. vi.

regional and federal levels. In short, the trend has been toward the greater one-party dominance in each Region, and the increasing role of the NPC on the national scene.

At the same time, previous developments culminating in this NPC regional election victory have increased the concerns of the opposition party in Nigeria as to the future constitutional evolution in the country. These concerns are intensified by the justified belief that a strong dislike of Southerners led to a willingness on the part of the Northerners to "close ranks" behind the NPC. In addition, the use of effective tactics against parties that had Southern leaders or even strong Southern ties contributed to this election victory in a Region where there is a marked identification of administrative and social authority and where the pressures of communal voting are strong. Not only the AG but also the Northern Elements Progressive Union (NEPU), which had Northern leadership but Southern affiliation with the NCNC, were swamped in the election. The elimination for the time of any effective legislative opposition in the North has been coupled with expressed fears of the possibility of a revival of a Hausa-Fulani empire in Nigeria, perhaps as a part of a Muslim Commonwealth, with its alleged authoritarian orientation. On the basis of these fears, whether actual or fanciful, AG leaders on the national scene have looked with particular concern at an alleged program to reduce the AG as a political party to ineffectiveness and the Western Region to impotence.

Developments since independence, several of which may involve constitutional questions, have added in varying degrees to these concerns. One has been moves to expand the area of the Federal Territory of Lagos, which would necessarily reduce the size of the Western Region; a second has been the fear that the federal appropriations and perhaps the power to allocate foreign loans might be used after necessary constitutional changes to provide educational and social services on a national minimum basis at the expense of the higher standards of the Western Region; a third has been the general unwillingness on the part of the NPC and NCNC to create new Regions (i.e., the Middle Belt and COR States) out of territories which would be carved from the Northern and Eastern Regions, despite initial agreement of all major political parties including the AG to create a Mid-West State out of territory of the Western Region; a fourth has been the charges that the civil rights of members of the AG are violated frequently, and that Yorubas in the federal public service suffer from discriminations; and, finally, there has been the series of legal controversies arising out of the efforts of the Government in 1961 to investigate the National Bank.

These circumstances, coupled with his deep disappointments at the results of the national election in 1959 and his search for some future political following among the discontented, may help explain the course of action followed by Chief Awolowo, the Leader of the Opposition, in his proposals for a sudden reorientation in foreign policy [25] and his sensitivity to certain actions by the Government during the year. A major illustration was the controversy over the interpretation of Section 65 of the Constitution, dealing with special powers of Parliament in relation to emergencies,[26] which arose shortly after independence. In sharp exchanges in the press and in the House of Representatives, Action Group leaders differed strongly with interpretations allegedly placed on Section 65 by the Federal Minister of Justice and Attorney General Elias and by Premier Okpara of the Eastern Region, regarding the power of the Federal Government to dissolve a Regional Legislature. Chief S. L. Akintola, Premier of the West-

[25] His most marked departure was his advocacy of Nigeria's joining the Ghana-Guinea-Mali Union after a surprise trip to Ghana in the summer of 1961. See *Daily Express* (Lagos), June 14, 1961, pp. 1–2; *ibid.*, June 29, 1961, p. 7. Cf. his views as expressed in Obafemi Awolowo, *op. cit.*, pp. 310–12.

[26] The pertinent provisions of Section 65 are:

"1) Parliament may at any time make such laws for Nigeria or any part thereof with respect to matters not included in the Legislative Lists as may appear to Parliament to be necessary or expedient for the purpose of maintaining or securing peace, order and good government during any period of emergency.

. . . .

"3) In this section 'period of emergency' means any period during which—
a) the Federation is at war
b) there is in force a resolution passed by each House of Parliament declaring that a state of public emergency exists; or
c) there is in force a resolution of each House of Parliament supported by the votes of not less than two-thirds of all the members of the House declaring that democratic institutions in Nigeria are threatened by subversion."

ern Region,[27] and Chief Awolowo[28] disagreed in strong words with these views of Elias and Okpara. The matter was quietly dropped after Sir Abubakar, the Federal Prime Minister, had publicly stated that "all of the Governments of the Federation were autonomous, each with . . . clearly defined functions, and that 'none could dissolve the other.'"[29]

In the light of this brief, but bitter, controversy, it is somewhat surprising that little opposition was offered to the final passage of the Emergency Powers Act, which was finally enacted by Parliament in the spring of 1961.[30] In effect, this Act empowered the Government to make regulations during the legally defined emergency periods for the arrest, detention, and deportation of persons, the "entering and search of premises," and the "requisition of property or undertakings" during these periods. Such regulations were to be subject to revocation by parliamentary resolution. The authority to pass these "regulations, orders or rules" will in the future be exercised under parliamentary authorization rather than, as in the past, under the powers of the Governor-General as granted by the Emergency Powers Orders in Council of the United Kingdom, 1939–59. This Act provides the legislative answer to the passing queries about emergency powers in the seminar on constitutional problems of federalism.

Two leading cases, involving similar questions of interpretation of provisions of the Independence Constitution, have arisen under the human rights sections of the Constitution. The able Counsel for the Defense in both cases was Chief F. R. A. Williams, the former Attorney General of the Western Region, whose name has been identified with the advocacy of the enforcement of the guarantees in the human rights sections of the Constitution. In one of these cases, *Queen v. Amalgamated Press (of Nigeria) Ltd., and Assoc.*,[31] the Amalgamated Press as the publisher of the *Sun-*

---

[27] *Daily Express* (Lagos), Oct. 13, 1960, p. 1.
[28] *Ibid.*, Nov. 30, 1960, p. 1.
[29] *Daily Times* (Lagos), Nov. 7, 1960, p. 1.
[30] *House of Representatives Debates* (Daily Parts), March 30, 1961, pp. 610–12. It might be added that no use had been made in the past of the emergency powers except in wartime.
[31] The author has had access to a typed copy of this case, which was kindly furnished by Mr. Justice G. B. A. Coker of the High Court of Lagos.

day Express had been charged with printing seditious matter and of disseminating false news with intent to alarm the public contrary to Sections 51 and 59 of the Criminal Code. The question of the constitutionality of Sections 51 and 59 of the Criminal Code was referred to the Supreme Court by the High Court of Lagos, before which the case was heard, and the Supreme Court held that these Sections had not been "invalidated" by Sections 1 and 24 of the Constitution and were therefore enforceable.[32] A similar conclusion had been reached on a much publicized case involving Dr. Chike Obi, former member of the House of Representatives, in the course of which the Supreme Court examined at considerable length the legal meaning of sedition.[33] While the Supreme Court held in both instances the provisions of the existing Criminal Code to be constitutional, the last word has not been said on the legal questions involved.[34] More recently, in the case of *Chief Doherty v. Sir Abubakar Tafawa Balewa and others,* the Supreme Court invalidated specified sections of the Commissions and Tribunals Enquiry Act, in part because these sections violated certain of the fundamental human rights guarantees of the Constitution.[35] It is clear that these cases are the forerunners of others which will require interpretation by the Supreme Court of the civil rights guarantees in the Constitution. This development is in keeping with predictions that were made in the seminar about the future role of the Supreme Court.

Other types of questions involving constitutional interpretation may be presented to the Supreme Court in the near future. So far no case involving the constitutionality of a treaty has been referred to it. But there are many uncertainties that lie ahead. At the present time, there is disposition in some official Nigerian quarters (as there was in the seminar) to question the extent to which Nigeria is bound, as well as the extent to which she ought

[32] *Queen v. Amalgamated Press (of Nigeria) Limited and Assoc.,* F.S.C. 99/1961.
[33] *Director of Public Prosecutions v. Chike Obi,* F.S.C. 56/1961.
[34] The motion by the Defense Counsel for leave to appeal the case to the Judicial Committee of the Privy Council was granted. In the hearing, the Director of Prosecutions had argued that the "decision of the court on constitutional matters was final." *Daily Times* (Lagos), July 4, 1961, p. 1.
[35] *West Africa,* Nov. 4, 1961, pp. 1209–10, 1227. The Nigerian Government's application for appeal to the Privy Council has been granted. *Ibid.,* Nov. 25, 1961, p. 1311.

to be bound, by the pertinent letters exchanged between the United Kingdom and Nigeria on October 1, 1960.[36] A newly created Division in the Ministry of Justice is now engaged in the arduous task of trying to collect and classify the more than three hundred (the number is uncertain) pertinent bilateral and multilateral treaties and conventions, a task that is being carried out under difficult circumstances since the texts of certain ones are not as yet available in the newly organized Ministry of Foreign Affairs and Commonwealth Relations. In the meantime, certain legal questions have already been raised. For example, did the severance of diplomatic relations with France in 1961 in protest against French atomic bomb experimentation in the Sahara violate France's rights, and hence Nigeria's commitments, under a convention of 1923, to which the United Kingdom was a signatory, regarding the use of Nigerian ports and airfields? But, to repeat, there have been no questions regarding treaty implementation which have as yet been referred to the courts.

Despite predictions to the contrary, no cases involving the commerce power of the Federal Government came before the Supreme Court during the first year of independence. The effect of the repeal of Section 58A therefore remains judicially untested. Likewise, there have been no cases involving the interpretation of the federal and regional taxing powers, though the payment of the regional tax on petrol used in vehicles of the Federal Government in one instance might have involved an interpretation regarding regional taxation of federal instrumentalities, had the question been pushed at this time. Does a contract between a regional government and a foreign contractor, under which a down payment is made on completed work and subsequent payments are continued over a period of years, violate the provisions of the constitution granting exclusive powers to the Federal Government for the "borrowings of moneys outside Nigeria for the purposes of the Federation or of any Region . . ."?[37] To the present, these questions have not been presented to the court. All of

[36] See above, p. 66. In view of the contents of these letters, one legal official has suggested that a resort to *rebus sic stantibus* might be made in order to rectify the "original mistake."
[37] Constitution, Item 5 of the "Exclusive Legislative List" in the Schedule.

this means that during its first year neither the Supreme Court of Nigeria nor the Judicial Committee of the Privy Council has played a significant role in the development of the Independence Constitution.

V

The Constitution of the United States, framed by the Philadelphia Convention in 1787, was once termed the greatest work that had ever been "struck off" by mortal man. Comparable language had been used on official occasions to refer to the Independence Constitution of Nigeria. In truth, the final phraseology of the latter document, like the former, was the work over a period of time of practical men who were drawing upon past experience. Both constitutions embodied provisions for the institutions of representative government and various legal principles and practices which were part of the English heritage as it had been modified in the local environments. As of the date of their inception, both of these constitutions exhibited the desire to provide checks on the possible exercise of arbitrary and unrestrained power. This desire helps explain such institutions and arrangements as judicial review of legislative enactments (whether implied as in the United States, or specified as in Nigeria), written guarantees of human rights, and federalism. In both instances there was present among the framers a considerable faith in the courts and a belief that a written document could embody the fundamental law.

It is understandable why Nigerian judges and political leaders are looking today with continuing interest at the other federations in the Commonwealth, whether kingdoms as in the case of Canada and Australia, or republics as in the case of India. The provisions for the distribution of powers and equal representation in the upper chambers in the Nigerian Constitution show certain similarities not only to the American but also to the Australian Constitution. The responsible cabinet government, the retention of appeals to the Privy Council, and the relationship of the regional governments to the Crown also suggest some further Australian analogies. These circumstances will both explain and justify the frequent references by writers and discussants of seminar papers to Australian legal precedents. It would appear that, at least during the early years after independence, the highest courts in Nigeria may glance first of all to Australia, and next to the United States and Canada, and possibly India, when they look outside British experience for judicial guidance.

In viewing the federal relationships that are grounded in the Constitution, one must remember that Nigeria was recently created by the fiat of a foreign power and that she operated under a unitary system of government for several decades after 1914. The separatist and autonomist moves after 1946, which culminated in the "self-government" of the three regions, have been checked within the past few years. To the unifying force of the English heritage—the system of law, responsible parliamentary government, and a common language—there have been added other centripetal pressures. Some of these are economic, involving the role of the central government as a channel of transmission of tax revenues to the regions and of its control over the major channels of communication; some are based upon the fears of minorities who desire federal protection and guarantees against dominant political groups in the Regions; some result from the advantages of co-operation between Federal and Regional Governments in administrative and other agencies, including statutory corporations; some are psychological, as evidenced by the widespread demands for rapid "Nigerianization" of the upper echelons of the public services and by the common pride in Nigerian control of her foreign relations and defense matters; and some reflect the faith and belief of the party leaders, who now hold offices in the government at the center, that the positions of greatest prestige for the future are in Lagos.[38] The Nigerian participants in the seminar appeared to approve as desirable and to accept as inevitable this trend, which has been shifting the balance of the scales, previously tilted on the side of regional autonomy. And, if

---

[38] See *supra*, chap. iii, "Emergent Federalism in Nigeria."

one views the several last changes agreed upon after the constitutional meetings in 1960, they appear to be more empowering than restrictive of the powers of the government of the Federation.

If a comparison were made, not with the federations that have been mentioned, but with other developing countries that are in a roughly comparable stage of economic development, several observations might be made. In the case of Nigeria, there would be lacking a strong army, a unified church, and well-established trade unions and employer organizations. There would also be lacking any charismatic leader with a *nation-wide* appeal or the extended experience of a largely illiterate populace with such forms of political participation as voting and officeholding. Though secondary interest groups are few in number and generally ineffective, there would be present such well-organized ones as the Nigeria Bar Association, Nigeria Teachers Association, and the Market Women's organizations.[39] There would also be in evidence the deeply entrenched tribal and traditional groups whose views are reflected in many ways in the political process; the emergent political parties, which are beginning to appeal more than formerly in national terms but which still have their political roots in tribal groupings in the separate Regions; and the bureaucracies of the Federation and Regions, composed almost entirely of Nigerians at the middle and lower echelons, and of expatriates and a rapidly increasing percentage of Nigerians at the highest echelons. Today, basic political decisions on the national level are largely the resultants of the conflicts and compromises between these major groups on the Nigerian stage. And, today, these decisions are most basically affected by widely held attitudes toward anti-colonialism, by tribalism, and by the urge for rapid technological change and economic development. Here one must search for the sinews of the "living constitution"; here one will find the elements of the "unwritten constitution."

There are many unanswered questions that will have a bearing on the solutions provided for the "constitutional problems of federalism in Nigeria." After all, federalism is the process of draw-

[39] Though little research on interest groups in Nigeria has been projected in the past, two studies of the Market Women's organizations are now being prepared.

ing the shifting balance line between the centripetal forces making for unity and the centrifugal pressures making for disunity. Will the present leadership of the governments and of the political parties, which came into control during the pre-independence period, weather the pressures from Nigerian aspirants for power during the post-independence period? What will be the impact of regional educational developments on the composition of the political elites, and of the rapidly growing number of unemployed school leavers on the orientation and stability of the political system? What effects will the rapid strides toward Nigerianization have on the stability and efficiency of the higher bureaucracy, especially during a period of accelerated economic development? Can the movement toward "Northernization" of the public services in the Northern Region be reconciled with Nigerianization at the federal level and thus not prove to be a disunifying factor in the years ahead? [40] Does Nigeria, with her substantial assets for an "economic take-off," have the constitutional framework, political machinery, and trained manpower available to encourage and facilitate national economic planning? What will be the effect upon the unity of Nigeria of a continuing economic development more rapid in the Western than that in the other two Regions? Will the political parties, the recent offspring of tribal groupings, tend to speak more in national rather than in regional terms and thus increasingly serve, along with other institutions, as forces for political and social integration? Will the trend toward a solidifying of the "one-party" system in each of the Regions provide effective buffers against a "one-party" system in the Federation? Will the transportation and communication routes running from north to south provide the unifying role in Nigeria that the railroad routes running from east to west once played in Canada? What will be the effects of the increasing social mobility and growth of urbanization on the development of interests and viewpoints not bound by locality and tribal obligation? Will the impact of the East-West conflict, already witnessed in the internal struggles in the trade unions affiliated with rival trade union federations, have serious internal repercussions

[40] See *infra*, chap. v, "Bureaucracy in Transition."

in Nigeria? Will the development of Pan-Africanism of various hues and of neutralism of differing interpretations prove to be internally disruptive? Will fears of a revival of a Hausa-Fulani Empire and of the establishment of a Commonwealth of Moslem states lead to an increase in a common uncertainty in the South?

The mere listing of these questions suggests the barriers to the attainment of some ideal goals in Nigeria. It was Spencer who spoke of the murder of the beautiful ideal by a gang of brutal facts; it was the able Nigerian Prime Minister, Sir Abubakar, who, in his address at the opening of the seminar in August, 1960, remarked that the best may be the enemy of the good. The good, to Sir Abubakar, probably consisted of the final transition from a dependent to an independent status with a political system that was basically democratic; in having a respected and accepted written constitution that provides for enforceable restraints upon the exercise of arbitrary powers; in witnessing the continued process of federalism whereby, at least for the present, the unifying and integrating forces are in increasing evidence; and in the development of a viable economy that may provide a slowly rising real income for the growing population and that might furnish the economic foundation for a stable constitutional government. The obstacles to the attainment of these goals are formidable. But more than any other country south of the Sahara, Nigeria offered then, and offers today, the possibility of attaining them.

5

Bureaucracy in Transition [1]

Taylor Cole

The federal system in Nigeria, which has evolved over a long period of time, is anchored in the Independence Constitution of 1960, but as suggested in the preceding chapters, the bureaucracy of the Federation has played a large part in making basic political decisions at the national level. Indeed, a political history of the Nigerian Federation could well be centered on the evolution of its bureaucracy which has from the colonial period to the present occupied a central position of prestige and power.[2] For this reason, I propose to examine the bureaucracy, giving particular attention to some aspects of its organization and to certain of its major problems. The emphasis here is placed upon the technical and formal aspects of organization, with a realization that such matters as changes in the social composition, the relationships of age groups in the bureaucracy, and the modification of the bureaucrat's conception of his role should receive an independent examination in the future.

I. Organization and Control

As the following chart will show, outside the agricultural sector over 60 per cent of those listed by the Federal Office of Statistics

[1] The original version of this essay was published in *Public Administration*, XXXVIII (Winter, 1960), 321–37. The Duke University Press is indebted to the publisher for permission to reprint portions of the original paper.
[2] Reference might be made to the thoughtful paper of Victor C. Ferkiss, "The Role of the Public Services in Nigeria and Ghana," presented at the American Political Science Association Meeting, St. Louis, September, 1961.

as employed in Nigeria are public employees. With due allowance for the inadequacies of the statistics, the total "public employment" (including employees of the Federal Government, Regional Governments, local governments, and public corporations) in September, 1958, was 302,200, as against 176,100 in private, commercial, industrial, and "other" employment.

Distribution of Non-Agricultural Employment [3]

Employer	Number of employees	Percentage of total
Federal government	47,500	9.9
Regional governments	72,100	15.1
Local governments and other	87,000	18.2
Public corporations	95,600	20.0
Total public employees	302,200	63.2
Private, commercial, and other	176,100	36.9
Total	478,300	100.1 *

* Percentages are rounded off to the first decimal place.

These figures give a rough picture of the relative importance of the public, as compared to the private, commercial, and industrial sectors. They also indicate the much smaller percentage of employees of the Federal Government in comparison with that of the three regional governments and the public corporations.

The bureaucracy of the Federal Government, comprising today some 50,000 employees,[4] has evolved its own organs of control, which can be listed on three levels. At the top, the Governor-

[3] The main sources consulted were publications of the Federal Office of Statistics, especially the *Report on Employment and Earnings Enquiry* (Lagos, 1958). Use was also made of reports and information from the Public Service Commission, Nigerianization Office, etc. The Federal Office of Statistics recognizes that its coverage of "commercial and other" employees is inadequate, but it considers the figures for "public employment" to be reasonably complete.

[4] A recent compilation of the "Staff of the Federal Service," which does not include daily-rated employees, indicates that on Aug. 1, 1959, there were 41,318 employees in all salary grades. See Federation of Nigeria, "Analysis of Staff of the Federal Service," *Official Gazette*, XLVI (Aug. 27, 1959), 1154–55. The Mbanefo Commission estimated that, in the "third quarter of 1959," there were 10,400 "general and special labourers" of the Federal Government. Federation of Nigeria, *Review of Salaries and Wages* (Lagos, 1959), p. 34. If there has been no duplication in any of the figures, there was a total of 51,718 federal employees in the third quarter of 1959. This figure corresponds closely to the 47,500 listed in the preceding chart.

General, as the representative of the Secretary of State for the Colonies, "controlled" in a formal sense the public services until independence, as the power to make appointments and removals was legally vested in him until that time. In fact, this "control" had largely passed to the Prime Minister and the Council of Ministers prior to independence. Today, final decisions on the most basic matters are referred to the Prime Minister [5] through the Secretary to the Prime Minister, who might be called the co-ordinator and "unofficial head of the civil service." The proposals of the Council of Ministers for appropriations or other legislation must, of course, be referred to Parliament for its consideration and enactment. Much of the pertinent discussion in Parliament involving the public service centers around either individual complaints or such broad policy questions as Nigerianization. In short, the agencies of control at the apex are the Prime Minister and the Cabinet, and their respective secretaries. Their mutual relationships are affected by the exigencies of coalition government under a parliamentary political system.

At the second level are several agencies that deal with the civil service as a whole within the framework of the policy decisions made by the Government. These agencies include the Ministry of Finance, the recently formed Ministry of Establishments (for-

[5] The terms and conditions of service were in the past covered in the "Colonial Regulations for the time being in force . . . and the current General Orders, Regulations and Instructions of the Federation of Nigeria." There was no single codification of the scattered provisions, though some moves had been made in 1960 by the Federal Establishment Office to provide one. A step in this direction had previously been taken in the preparation of the *Establishment Handbook, 1958* [Circular A 33/1958].

A new issue of the General Orders has been announced by the Ministry of Establishments, but it had not appeared as of July, 1961. The existing Orders remain in effect until the appearance of the new General Orders, with certain qualifications, i.e., (1) the Prime Minister, and not the Governor-General or "Governor," is the authority for the service conditions, privileges, and rights recognized in the General Orders; (2) the Colonial Regulations will no longer be in effect, though provisions which are identical with the Colonial Regulations, as quoted in the General Orders, will remain for the time in force, but they will be used on the authority of the Prime Minister, and not the Secretary of State for the Colonies; (3) petitions regarding appointments, promotions, and disciplinary matters should be directed to the Public Service Commission, while petitions on other subjects should be addressed to the Prime Minister; and (4) powers vested under the General Orders in the "Head of Department" will in the future be exercised by the Permanent Secretary in those Ministries where the departments have been "integrated." See in this connection, *Nigeria Journal* [official journal of the Association of Senior Civil Servants], LXV (May, 1961), 41.

merly the Ministry of Pensions, Establishments, and Nigerianisation, and commonly referred to as the Ministry of Pensions), and the Public Service Commission. Each of these has experienced a period of change since the application of the Constitution of 1954. The Public Service Commission, an independent body composed of five members (appointed by the Governor-General on the advice of the Prime Minister), has the legal responsibility under the Constitution for appointments, promotions, and discipline in the service;[6] the Federal Establishment Office in the Ministry of Establishments has charge of any staff proposals involving annual or additional expenditures, gradings, Whitley Council matters, conditions of service, salaries and wages, and pensions. At best, the relations between these agencies are complicated. On paper, the Federal Establishment Office of the Ministry of Establishments approves the need for the establishment of a new post; the Permanent Secretary of the Ministry of Finance, acting for the Minister, decides whether funds are available for the post; and the Public Service Commission recommends the person for appointment after the Nigerianization Officer of the Ministry of Establishments has determined whether a qualified Nigerian is available. But, in actual fact, there is lack of clarity in the shifting relationships between the agencies,[7] and their functioning depends heavily upon personal contacts and extra-legal arrangements.

At the third level, that is, within the ministries themselves, there are the Permanent Secretaries and their immediate subordinates, particularly those officials in the Administrative and Establishment Divisions, who deal with civil service questions. Much of the negotiation involving the selection for entry and promotion of personnel is handled in the ministries by committees on which the Public Service Commission is represented and whose recommendations are subject to the final approval of the Public Service Commission. Administrative and executive officers are "posted" to the ministries, the former by a committee that includes in its

[6] Constitution, chap. x.
[7] One attempt to "spell out" the "division of functions" between the Public Service Commission and the Federal Establishment Office of the Ministry of Establishments was made early in 1960 in Federal Establishment Office Circular 7/1960.

membership the Secretary to the Prime Minister, and the latter by the Permanent Secretary of the Ministry of Establishments. A large number of the final decisions on personnel questions are the product of informal handling between the Permanent Secretaries, the Federal Establishment Office, the Ministry of Finance, the Public Service Commission, and the Prime Minister's Office, and defy formal explanation.

Although one cannot accept *in toto* the statement of a highly placed official that the whole system of personnel direction is a "headless" one which "flaps in all directions," it is safe to argue that any co-ordination results largely from the many informal understandings that exist. In 1960 several steps, perhaps motivated by the desire to accelerate Nigerianization, and, according to official explanations, to prevent the burgeoning of the size of the establishments, indicated a willingness on the part of the Council of Ministers to exercise greater supervision over appointments and promotions.[8] It is also pertinent to note the recommendation of the Parliamentary Committee on Nigerianisation of the Federal Public Service that the post of "Head of the Public Service" be created to direct and co-ordinate the work of the Public Service Commission, the Federal Establishment Office, and other agencies.[9]

The pattern of gradations in the public service, both of the Federal and Regional Governments, follows the British model, except where modifications have been made to meet local conditions. This pattern is based today primarily upon the recommendations of the Gorsuch Commission,[10] which dealt with the "structure of remuneration of the public service," following the constitutional changes in 1954.[11] The gradations of the civil service in-

[8] Circular 13/1960, on the "General Level of Establishment in Federal Public Service," stipulated that "no new posts should be created in the future without the approval of the Council of Ministers" and that "there should be no recruitment to posts which have remained vacant for more than two years." Federation of Nigeria, *Official Gazette*, XLVII (March 24, 1960), 370–71. Earlier, the Council of Ministers dealt with the "level of establishments" only when considering the *Estimates*.

[9] *Final Report*, Sessional Paper No. 6 of 1959 (Lagos, 1959), p. 72.

[10] Federation of Nigeria, *Report of the Commission on the Public Services of the Governments in the Federation of Nigeria, 1954–55* (Lagos, 1955).

[11] After the dissolution of the former unitary service and the split into federal and regional public services, arrangements were made for the allocation of senior personnel on the basis of personal preferences where possible. Today, transfers

clude the Administrative and Professional Classes, the Executive and Higher Technical Classes, the Clerical and Technical Classes, the Subclerical and Minor Technical Classes, etc. Omitting from consideration the supernumerary posts, two different avenues are open to secure an appointment in the Administrative Class. The one is by promotion from the Executive Class or from certain other eligible groups; the second, for qualified degree holders, is through direct entry after examination. The Executive Class is a recent and rather artificial creation, which resulted from the belief of the Gorsuch Commission that the senior officials were necessarily devoting too much of their time to routine work.[12] Originally the Executive Class was filled largely by the promotion of former clerical officers at the bottom, while its more qualified recruits were being rapidly siphoned off at the top to the Administrative Class. Younger eligibles, often with degrees but little experience, are now rapidly replacing the older employees. As yet, they have evidenced little *esprit de corps*. Plans for the formation of the Executive Class were too long delayed and in the beginning were badly implemented; its future role will remain uncertain unless active steps are taken to develop more expertise.

II. Civil Service Trade Unions

The guarantee and protection of the rights of the civil servants have also received considerable attention. The various rights of the four different types of employees[13] are covered in several legal sources.[14] Brief comment may be made regarding certain features which have occasioned much agitation among groups of employees. First, there is a wide gap between the top salaries of

without loss of duly acquired rights are possible between the services, and officers are occasionally "seconded" for periods of time from one service to the other—most frequently, it might be added, from the regional to the federal service.

[12] In April, 1960, the Executive Class, controlled by the then Minister of Pensions, comprised 526 posts, with ranks ranging from Assistant Executive Officer to Senior Executive Officer. Some 428 of these posts were filled. See the Minister of Pensions in *House of Representatives Debates* (Daily Parts), April 11, 1960, p. 1021.

[13] Pensionable officer, contract officer, non-pensionable appointee, and trainee or learner.

[14] See *supra*, p. 91 n. 5.

the superscale posts, which ranged up to £3,600 per annum prior to the modest increases in 1960, and those of the lowest scale for the established staff;[15] at the same time, the average "cash earnings" for all federal employees (established staff as of September, 1958) was £17.95 per month.[16] Second, whatever their justifications, there are some remaining disparities between the employment conditions for expatriate and indigenous officers. Third, the required number of hours of work per week (thirty-four hours for office workers), when coupled with extremely generous leave provisions and liberally interpreted and widely utilized arrangements for maternity and sick leave, results in an average number of work hours per year for the employee in the lower ranks of the service that is below that of any Western European country.[17] Finally, with the exception of a few critical services, such as defense, police, and prisons, the civil servant possesses the same right to strike as does the private employee.

For the protection of his rights and the furtherance of his interests, the Nigerian civil servant is often inclined to look to some member of his extended family in Parliament or in a position of authority in one of the ministries. General belief is that this type of personal influence is increasing. The group efforts are exerted by the various employee associations and unions. Most of these are registered as trade unions for negotiating purposes with the Ministry of Internal Affairs. Three of the oldest and most active of the associations composed solely of civil servants are the Association of Senior Civil Servants (still largely an expatriate group), the Nigeria Civil Service Union (made up almost exclusively of Nigerian clerical employees), and the Nigeria Union of Teachers (the largest and most effectively organized of the unions, which is composed primarily of teachers employed by the regional and

[15] See *Staff List, Revised to 1st April 1960* (Lagos, 1960), p. v. Consult Federation of Nigeria, *Review of Salaries and Wages* (Lagos, 1959), for the new salary and wage scales, which went into effect in 1960; the salary of the top superscale post, Group I, was raised to £3,900 per annum, and somewhat larger percentage increases were made in the salaries at the lower levels.

[16] *Report on Employment and Earnings Enquiry*, pp. 2–3. This figure may be compared with the average of £7.21 (approximately $20.00) for local government employees.

[17] Only scattered data are available, but there is agreement on this point by a number of responsible officials.

local authorities under regional control). Most of the unions of industrial and technical workers were as of July, 1961, affiliated with the Trades Union Congress of Nigeria (TUCN),[18] which, in turn, maintained a recently concluded affiliation with the International Confederation of Free Trade Unions (ICFTU); others were affiliated with the Nigeria Trades Union Congress (NTUC), a splinter group of unions that broke away in 1960 after a period of bitter controversy. The effects on the NTUC and the TUCN of the unity moves, including the establishment in the fall of 1961 of a United Labor Congress, remain to be seen, but they did not appear up to May, 1962, to be promising.

There is considerable skepticism regarding the effectiveness of the machinery for negotiation in the public services, including the Whitley Council system. Among the reasons offered is the weakness of the unions themselves. With the exception of those previously mentioned and a few others, such as the Nigeria Nurses Association, most of the unions are of recent origin and evidence the effects of poor organization, inadequate finances, and, too often, of irresponsible leadership.[19] The serious efforts to federate the unions have resulted in some progress, but the ideological leanings of some union leaders, together with conflicting personal ambitions, have led in the past to the various separatist moves by dissident elements and to the establishment of competing splinter organizations.

In this atmosphere the Whitley Council system, transplanted to Nigeria,[20] has so far failed to generate enthusiasm among most organized public employees. The Association of Senior Civil Servants, which provides the Staff Side of one of the three Whitley Councils (Whitley Council I), has repeatedly insisted that there

[18] Of the non-industrial unions and associations, neither the Nigeria Civil Service Union, nor the Association of Senior Civil Servants, nor the Nigeria Union of Teachers has been affiliated with the TUCN.
[19] Cf. W. A. Warmington, *A West African Trade Union* (Oxford, 1960), pp. 1 ff.; cf. the speech by T. E. A. Salubi, Federal Commissioner of Labor, at ILO Conference, Geneva, June, 1961.
[20] See "Constitutions" of Whitley Councils I, II, and III (mimeographed). The Whitley Councils have no statutory basis, and rest upon voluntary agreements between the parties. On all three Councils, the Chairman of the Official Side is the Permanent Secretary of the Ministry of Establishments and the Secretary of the Official Side is the Senior Assistant Secretary and Head of the Staff Relations Section of the Ministry of Establishments.

was no real "negotiation" with the Official Side, and that such agreements as were reached were either not implemented or were acted on only after long delays.[21] Whitley Council II, for which the Nigeria Civil Service Association provides the Staff Side, has apparently done better in the eyes of both its Official and Staff Side members. Whitley Council III, the "industrial Whitley Council," has proved to be almost completely ineffective, if not inoperative at times. This was due in part to the sharp differences among the numerous trade unions that provide the membership of the Staff Side. In any event, the Whitley Council system has benefited neither from its early history nor from its later years of experience in Nigeria. Despite some cautious optimism expressed on the Official Side, its functioning must be characterized as largely ineffective.[22]

No mention has been made of the right of the Staff Side to declare a labor dispute under the Labor Ordinance and, subsequently, to resort to arbitration. There have been only a few references to arbitration during the past decade. However, there have been frequent threats of strikes and an occasional resort to them. Post and telegraph workers went on strike in both 1947 and 1958, but each time the results were unfavorable for them. Railway employees went on strike in 1951–52 and threatened to strike again in the spring of 1960.[23] There is little evidence that any of these strikes have achieved their major objectives. Moreover, their failures have left a continued heritage of bitterness on the part of those participants who, as in 1947, were dismissed from their jobs

[21] See *Nigerian Journal*, XLIII (Sept.–Nov., 1957), 69; XLIV (June–July, 1958), 38–39; and XLIV (July–Sept., 1959), 44–45, where the Federal Chairman of the Association commented as follows: "It is now apparent that Government only uses Whitley machinery to suit itself." Finally, as a result of these and some personal considerations, the Staff Side of Whitley Council I "walked out" of the Council in the summer of 1960 and, despite conciliatory moves, had not returned by the late summer of 1961. *Ibid.*, XLV (June–July, 1960), 7, 12.

[22] Instead of Whitley Councils, the major statutory corporations have set up joint industrial councils, which, with considerable variations, follow some of the main outlines of the Whitley Council systems. Their record ranges from the unhappy one of the Nigerian Railway Corporation to the more satisfactory one of the Nigerian Ports Authority. In general, they have functioned more effectively than has Whitley Council III.

[23] See comments of Prime Minister Balewa in *House of Representatives Debates*, *1959–60*, I, 105–6; see also those of the Minister of Transport in *ibid.* (Daily Parts), April 11, 1960, pp. 1006–7.

and lost their previously acquired pension rights after re-engagement. It is evident that the record to date of the employee unions as instruments for guaranteeing and furthering the interests of their members is a poor one.

III. Effect of Administrative Changes

Various types of administrative changes and adjustments during the past few years have had their effect upon the status of major segments of public employees. One has been the creation of the four major public utility corporations, the Electricity Corporation of Nigeria, the Nigerian Railway Corporation, the Nigerian Coal Corporation, and the Nigerian Ports Authority. Together with certain other public corporations, such as the National Broadcasting Corporation, they account for approximately one-fifth of those listed as employed in all public agencies and in private commerce and industry.[24]

Several features deserve mention in considering these public utility corporations as employers. Unlike Britain, where the public corporations usually took over from municipal or private control, these were created out of previously existing government departments, and, at the time of their establishment, guaranteed to the employees in the civil service a status that would not be disadvantageous compared with their previous positions. In the absence of certain guarantees of security of tenure, etc., given in the regular government service, the employees have been granted slightly more advantageous salaries for comparable work, their salaries averaging perhaps 10 per cent higher than those in the federal service. In the competition for certain categories of scarce personnel, the corporations can frequently "outbid" their competitors in the government departments. This fact adds to the rivalry that has been growing between the Regional Governments, the Federal Government, the public corporations, and private industry. One finds this especially true under the pressure of de-

[24] The largest employer is the Nigerian Railway Corporation with over 32,000 employees in 1960.

mands for rapid Nigerianization, where the number of trained Nigerians in certain professional and technical fields is limited. While the formation of the corporations has permitted greater managerial freedom in other respects, there has not been the anticipated flexibility and discretion in personnel policies.[25] Certainly, many acute personnel problems remain unsolved, as in the case of the Nigerian Railway Corporation and the Nigerian Coal Corporation, which have been seriously affected by technological and other economic changes.

These considerations have contributed their share to the causes that led in 1957 to the appointment by the Federal Council of Ministers of a committee to study the relations between the public corporations and the Government, the Federal Legislature, and the public. The report of the committee was examined in 1958 by the National Economic Council and Joint Planning Committee and, according to an official statement, "a large measure of agreement" had been reached through these media by the Federal and Regional Governments.[26] A Commission of Inquiry, headed by Dr. T. O. Elias, was subsequently appointed by the Prime Minister to inquire into the affairs of the Nigerian Railway Corporation, and this committee made a number of recommendations that dealt among other matters with the general responsibility of statutory corporations to Parliament.[27] The services of Professor W. A. Robson were then procured, and Professor Robson in 1961 prepared a confidential report on statutory corporations that contained recommendations reportedly different in important respects from those included in the Elias Committee report. The delays in the acceptance of the report by the Council of Ministers indicate the difficulties in securing the requisite agreement on the pressing issues that have been raised and are also suggestive of the pressures that exist to maintain the present uncertain and un-

[25] A. H. Hanson, "Public Enterprise in Nigeria: I, Federal Public Utilities," *Public Administration*, XXXVI (Winter, 1958), 370.
[26] *Statement by the Government of the Federation of Nigeria on the Report of the Elias Commission of Inquiry*, Sessional Paper No. 7 of 1960 (Lagos, 1960), p. 5.
[27] Federation of Nigeria, *Report of the Elias Commission of Inquiry into the Administration, Economics and Industrial Relations of the Nigerian Railway Corporation* (Lagos, 1960), p. 63.

satisfactory status quo. Though there are no major moves to abolish or "reconvert" to government departments or ministries, it is still too early to say that in the long run some of them will escape the fate of public utility corporations in certain other developing countries.[28]

The problem of administrative reorganization has been ever-present in Nigeria, at least since 1950. The Governor-General then served as the head of a unified service, with a Chief Secretary and Secretariat in Lagos, and Chief Commissioners in the East, West, and North under whom the Residents of the provinces operated. Following the constitutional changes in 1951 and 1954, there evolved at the center a parallel system of ministries with responsibility over certain groups of subjects and with staffs who reported to the Minister through a Secretary, and of unifunctional departments with heads who reported directly to the Minister. In terms of allocation of responsibility, the result was confusing and in some ways comparable to that found in certain American states before the halcyon period of state administrative reorganization. Prefaced by measures taken in the Regions, the Council of Ministers of the Federation appointed a committee composed of high-ranking civil servants, which in 1959 submitted a report, *The Integration of Departments with Ministries.*[29] In essence, the committeee recommended that an organizational pattern, based in most respects on British precedents, be adopted. Ministries and departments were to be "integrated"; Permanent Secretaries of the ministries were to act as the official liaison between the Minister and the heads of divisions, which in most cases were to replace departments, as well as to serve as the general administrative heads of the ministries. There were some differences in the types of organization recommended for specific ministries. To take one example, the Ministry of Communications and Aviation was to incorporate several previously existing departments, which were to be reorganized and grouped into four divisions. Changes were proposed for the internal structure of ministries, with new

---

[28] Hanson, *op. cit.*, p. 381.
[29] (Lagos, 1959); cf. this report with *White Paper on the Reorganization of Ministries*, Sessional Paper No. 2 of 1959 of the Western Region of Nigeria (Ibadan, 1959).

posts of deputy Permanent Secretary or the equivalent to be set up in certain ones (later used to help expedite the Nigerianization program), and with the formation of divisions responsible for finance and establishments.

One of the most important effects of this integration, where it has been completed, has been to provide a new set of relationships between the Permanent Secretaries of the ministries and the former heads of the departments, who were often professionally trained doctors, engineers, etc. Certain of the departmental heads have become "directors" of divisions (as in the Ministries of Works and Surveys, and Communications) and others have been given the titles of "advisors" (as in the Ministries of Education and Health). Some of the integration has occurred more on paper than in practice, with divisions that have replaced former departments (i.e., in the Ministries of Works and Surveys and of Communications) continuing at least for the time to occupy a largely autonomous status within their ministries. But the trend toward integration continues, and much of this autonomy in these and other departments has begun to disappear.

In most ministries the changes have been accepted as desirable and, perhaps, as inevitable. But the many critics can present telling evidence that integration has produced unhappy personal relationships to the detriment of the service and, basing their case upon comparisons of the Annual Federal Estimates "before and after," that it has resulted in increased costs through the upgrading of posts and the establishment of additional ones for the performance of the same tasks. In addition, it has been charged that integration has retarded Nigerianization.[30] The last word has not been said on whether ambitious reorganization plans based upon experience in the United Kingdom can be applied without some modification to the developing countries. At least, with integration being of recent vintage and as yet not fully achieved, one cannot generalize on the basis of Nigerian experience at either the federal or regional levels.

One other type of administrative adjustment might be men-

[30] Federation of Nigeria, *Final Report of the Parliamentary Committee on the Nigerianisation of the Federal Public Service*, Sessional Paper No. 6 of 1959 (Lagos, 1959), p. 76.

tioned. There has also been the reorganization of some of the ministries and the creation of a number of new ones, following the reconstitution of the government after the national election in December, 1959. Prior to independence, there was created the Ministry of Pensions (now Establishments), which represented a marriage of political convenience of several agencies, including the Federal Establishment Office, the Pension Division, and the Nigerianization Office, all of which were taken from the Prime Minister's Office. A Ministry of Economic Development was also set up, composed likewise of several divisions, which in skeleton form had been previously located in other ministries. As previously indicated,[31] this agency has been faced with the formidable task of recruiting staff, particularly trained economists, to deal with the planning of future economic development.

Additional ministries have been established either on the eve of or following independence. The transfer in early 1960 of the responsibility for defense from the Governor-General's Office to the Office of the Prime Minister was followed later by the removal of defense matters from the Office of the Prime Minister to a separate Ministry of Defense, which was no longer headed by the Prime Minister. A Ministry of State for the Navy was appointed. Although the Office of the Governor-General retained certain reserved powers in this field, the "External Affairs Division" of the Prime Minister's Office had in fact before independence assumed the major responsibility for the conduct of foreign relations. A Ministry of Foreign Affairs and Commonwealth Relations was subsequently established, and it was headed by the Prime Minister until July, 1961. Another creation of the Independence Constitution has been the Ministry of Justice, which has been in the process of development under direction of the Minister of Justice and Attorney General, Dr. T. O. Elias, since October, 1960.[32] Much of the work of this Ministry, as well as of that of the Ministry of Foreign Affairs and Commonwealth Relations and the Ministry of Defense, involved responsibilities formerly handled by the Governor-General and the Colonial Office. Re-

[31] See *supra*, chap. iii, pp. 53–54.
[32] *House of Representatives Debates* (Daily Parts), April 11, 1962, pp. 1354 ff.

organizations involving such Ministries as Education, Establishments, and Transport and Aviation are under discussion, and new ministries may be created out of other existing ones that have not been mentioned. The creation and reorganization of some of these new Ministries have been by-products of the period of post-independence administrative adjustment and have in some cases evidenced the present inclination to temporize with piecemeal steps. So far there has been no indication of a willingness to face the vital task of comprehensive administrative reorganization—perhaps one based upon an investigation and report by some future Nigerian "Hoover Commission." [33] In the meantime, the lack of administrative direction becomes more and more evident, as those Ministries that are headed by politically potent Ministers tend to acquire a semi-independent status. Coalition government has been one, but only one, of the factors contributing to the growing "atomization" of the administration, and so far there is no evidence that a strong direction will be furnished by the Council of Ministers. But perhaps the accent on needed unity has been overstressed, for the administrative organization has at least struggled through the period of the transfer of power and of the year following independence without signs of collapse.

IV. Nigerianization

The most explosive issues, and certainly the most controversial ones, faced by Nigeria during her transitional period to independence involved the Nigerianization, "Expatriatization," and Northernization of the public services. The history of Nigerianization, which means essentially the accelerated replacement of ex-

[33] Regarding economic planning, the future relationship of the Ministry of Economic Development to such bodies as the National Economic Council and its subordinate Joint Planning Committee, the Central Bank of Nigeria, the Federal Ministry of Finance, as well as to other ministries and agencies that are involved at the federal and regional levels, would constitute one of the problems deserving the special attention of such a commission. Note the discussion by the Leader of the Opposition, Chief Awolowo, in *House of Representatives Debates* (Daily Parts), April 22, 1960, pp. 1611–18.

patriate officials in the higher-level posts by Nigerians, can be read in the comparative light of the experience of other British Commonwealth areas in replacing expatriate with indigenous personnel, both before and after independence. In the case of Nigeria the move to speed the process of replacement dates back to the period of the eve of World War II, when a modest scholarship scheme was started to train a few Nigerians for senior posts. After certain intervening developments, a commission was appointed by the Council of Ministers in 1952 to study the Nigerianization policy, and its report in 1953 recommended a number of steps to limit the appointment and promotion of non-Nigerians and, correspondingly, to encourage the placement of Nigerians when qualified ones were available.[34] After some preliminary steps, a Nigerianisation Officer was appointed with the primary objective of pushing the training and recruitment of Nigerians for the public service.[35] Popular pressures and demands in Parliament led to the appointment of a special committee of the House of Representatives in March, 1958, to study the progress that had been made and methods to accelerate the pace. In its final report in 1959,[36] this committee commented adversely on previous plans to train Nigerians, on the unwarranted concessions that were being granted to expatriate officers, and on the lack of progress in placing Nigerians in senior posts. It pointed out that of 73 superscale posts in the administrative service, only 10 were held by Nigerians or other West Africans, while 63 were held by expatriate officers; that Nigerians held only 1 of 14 posts of Permanent Secretary, 2 of 20 posts of Deputy Permanent Secretary, and 6 of 34 posts of Senior Assistant Secretary.[37] Citing the experience of Malaya, the committee vigorously demanded that all higher posts, including all permanent secretarial posts, must be filled by Nigerians at the time of independence, or very soon after—even if the requisite

[34] Sir Sydney Phillipson and S. O. Adebo, *The Nigerianisation of the Civil Service, Review of Policy and Machinery* (Lagos, 1954).
[35] See Federation of Nigeria, *Annual Report of the Nigerianisation Officer for the Year 1957* (Lagos, 1958).
[36] *Final Report of the Parliamentary Committee on the Nigerianisation of Federal Public Service.*
[37] Cf. Federation of Nigeria, *Staff List, Revised to 1st April 1960* (Lagos, 1960). Note the report of the Parliamentary Secretary to the Ministry of Pensions in *House of Representatives Debates* (Daily Parts), April 13, 1960, p. 1140.

steps to secure "flexibility" involved some deterioration of standards. In 1958 the Government issued a sharply worded rebuttal to the interim report of this committee,[38] and a tentative, carefully phrased statement on the final report of the committee was issued informally in December, 1959.[39]

The sequel to this historical account may be read in the latest report of the Public Service Commission.[40] "It is apparent," said the Commission, "that by the end of 1961 Nigerianization of the Federal Service will have ceased to be a major problem." This statement was based upon the rapidity with which the services had been Nigerianized in 1960. During that year six Nigerians were promoted to the position of Permanent Secretary to make a total of seven, and by the end of 1961, 64 per cent of the "posts in the senior service," with the exception of Police and Judiciary, would be occupied by African officers. Certain Ministries, particularly Foreign Affairs and Commonwealth Relations, are completely Nigerianized and others are moving rapidly in that direction. The down-grading in fact of the Nigerianisation Office in the Ministry of Establishments was further evidence that the main objectives had been realized, though most officials in Nigeria have insisted that much work remained, particularly in the improvement of the educational and technical qualifications of Nigerians eligible to fill the remaining posts in the senior service. Nevertheless, a majority of the politicians still view the problem as a major one and advocate the need for even more rapid action.

The corollary aspect of the staffing problems raised by Nigerianization is that of "Expatriatization," to coin a word for the retention of expatriates and the filling of new posts by expatriates in the public service in Nigeria. The status of the expatriate officer today hardly raises any considerations that have not been found in some degree by other parts of the British Commonwealth during the period of transfer of power, notably, in Ghana, Sudan, and

[38] Federation of Nigeria, *Views of the Government of the Federation on the Interim Report of the Committee on Nigerianisation,* Sessional Paper No. 7 of 1958 (Lagos, 1958).

[39] "Government Comments on Nigerianisation Report," *Daily Times* (Lagos), Dec. 4, 1959, p. 3. In 1960 the Government issued the white paper, *Matters Arising out of the Final Report of the Nigerianisation Committee* (Lagos, 1960).

[40] Federation of Nigeria, *Fourth Annual Report of the Federal Public Service for the Period 1st January to 31st December,* 1960 (Lagos, 1961), p. 8.

Malaya. In Nigeria, as in some of these areas, many of the most capable and energetic of the expatriate officers left at an early date. Those who remain [41] have been concerned with five major considerations: (1) the guarantee of security in the face of political uncertainties; (2) the nature of the inducements offered to retain them; (3) their status, in the light of previous responsibilities and attachments, and of the current views of the political leaders; (4) the alternatives which are open to them elsewhere; and (5) in many cases an interest in their work and respect for various personal commitments made during previous years.

For several years the Colonial Office had apparently assumed that, while most expatriate officers would eventually be replaced in Nigeria, the change might occur without disrupting the government or without serious inconvenience to the officers involved. It was also recognized that the Secretary of State for the Colonies retained at least some responsibility for officials who had been employed by the Colonial Office directly or with its sanction, not only before but even after independence. In consequence, a sequence of policy statements and proposals were made from 1954–58 [42] designed to reconcile the differing and somewhat conflicting demands and fears of the indigenous political leaders, the wishes and complaints of the expatriate officers, and the responsibilities of the Colonial Office. Two types of lists of expatriate officials were devised. The first, the Special List, later known as List A, failed to offer attractive possibilities to a large majority of expatriate officials. A second Special List, List B, introduced later in 1958, added some new inducements, including immediate ad-

[41] Expatriate officers are normally classed either as "pensionable officers" or "contract officers," the latter being employed for definite terms and without guaranteed pension rights. With rare exceptions, expatriate officers newly employed are on contract basis. As of March 1, 1960, the total number of "Overseas Officers" of all types was 1,812, which included 1,724 "officers in C Scale and above." Parliamentary Secretary to the Ministry of Pensions in *House of Representatives Debates* (Daily Parts), April 20, 1960, p. 1453.

[42] For 1954, see Colonial No. 306 of 1954; for 1958, "Statement of Policy Regarding Overseas Officers Serving in Nigeria," Cmnd. 497 of July, 1958. For a discussion of the schemes based on the principles of Colonial No. 306, and put in force in the Federation of Malaya and Singapore, see T. E. Smith, "The Effect of Recent Constitutional Changes on the Public Service in the Federation of Malaya and Singapore," *Public Administration*, XXXVII (Autumn, 1959), 267–73; and, Robert O. Tilman, "The Nationalization of the Colonial Services in Malaya," *South Atlantic Quarterly* (Spring, 1962), pp. 183–96.

vances in compensation after independence, or against future entitlement, and other concessions.[43] It was felt that these would meet some of the expectations of expatriate officers, and thereby discourage wholesale retirements and resignations. Sharp controversy has raged from the beginning, especially among the Nigerians, over the purpose and justification for List B. The Parliamentary Committee on Nigerianisation was caustically critical of the "concessions" thereby made to foreign officers still in policy-determining positions, while the Nigerian "Government" stressed that its legitimate purpose was to retain the services of needed expatriate officers.[44]

The sequel to these developments has been the departure from Nigeria of expatriate officers at a rate more rapid than had been expected by the Government, even on the eve of independence, but less rapid than had occurred in certain other countries, such as Sudan and Malaya. According to the Public Service Commission, of 688 "pensionable overseas officers" on the rolls as of October 1, 1960, some 266, or 39 per cent, will have left by the end of 1961.[45] Of this latter number, 236 officers were on List B. Some of these departures were hastened by two considerations. The one has been the series of decisions of the Committee of the Council of Ministers, the so-called Committee on Freezing, which has power to act upon the applications of overseas officers who have requested that their lump sum compensation be "frozen" (in effect, the applications of those expatriate officers, usually over the age of forty and in senior posts, who have expressed a desire to prolong their tenure in Nigeria under the existing financial arrangements). The other was the failure of the "Macleod proposals" to secure the approval of the Nigerian Government.

[43] The best discussion of these developments is Part I of Kenneth Younger, *Public Service in New States: A Study in Some Trained Manpower Problems* (London, 1960), a study that was based upon a survey he made in the summer of 1959.

[44] "It certainly would not help against the possibility of an exodus of the senior officers of the Administrative Service in 1960 if the Government were to take active steps to remove them all before then; this would merely insure an emergency of a more acute kind." *Views of the Government of the Federation on the Interim Report of the Committee on Nigerianisation*, p. 3.

[45] *Fourth Annual Report of the Federal Public Service . . .* , p. 9. Some 521 pensionable overseas officers remained on the rolls in April, 1962. *House of Representatives Debates* (Daily Parts), April 5, 1962, p. 990.

This scheme had been announced by the Secretary of State for the Colonies in 1960 to furnish certain financial inducements, paid by the United Kingdom, to overseas officers in order to make possible a prolongation of their service. The "Macleod proposals" were rejected by the Nigerian Government as involving inappropriate ties between an independent country and the Colonial Office and as meaning a continuation of undesirable distinctions between indigenous and expatriate officers.[46] It is clear that the present trend will continue until the persistent pressures for Nigerianization have run their course. In the meantime there is the occasional voice raised in official quarters by those who appreciate the "growing difficulty" in recruiting certain types of needed overseas replacements on contract, and of "finding sufficient manpower to carry out the big development programme of the Federal Government." [47]

A third current which has affected the employment situation in Nigeria has brought from the Muslim North demands for "Northernization." In 1957, the Public Service Commission of the Northern Region stated: "It is the policy of the Regional Government to Northernise the Public Service: if a qualified Northerner is available, he is given priority in recruitment; if no Northerner is available, an Expatriate may be recruited or a non-Northerner on contract terms." [48] Since that date, the insistence upon the employment of only Northerners, even at the expense of interpreting generously the minimum qualifications, has been increasing year by year. In its actual application Northernization has been directed much more vigorously against Southern Nigerians than against Expatriates, and it is clear that few Southerners will be allowed to remain long in any conspicuous positions in the service of the Northern Regional Government.[49] A special Northernisation Committee was set up in 1959 under the

[46] Minister of Establishments in *House of Representatives Debates* (Daily Parts), April 8, 1961, pp. 1049–50; *Nigerian Journal*, XLV (May, 1961), 37–38.
[47] *Fourth Annual Report of the Federal Public Service* . . . , p. 8.
[48] Northern Region of Nigeria, Public Service Commission, *Report on the Public Service Commission for the Period 1st November 1954 to 31st December 1957* (Kaduna, 1958), p. 7.
[49] A typical headline in the newspaper reflecting the views of the Western Regional Government: "Northernisation: More Southerners Sacked." *Daily Service* (Lagos), Feb. 17, 1960, p. 2.

Chairmanship of the Northern Regional Minister of Education [50] to speed up the program. Despite this step and belated efforts to improve the retarded elementary educational system and to provide scholarships for training, few indigenous public servants had reached the upper echelons of the public service hierarchy by the summer of 1960. Indeed, there was no Nigerian Permanent Secretary prior to the appointment of one in August, 1960. Since that date additional appointments have been made.

Though Northernization is of less concern at the federal than at the regional level, a coalition Federal Government that received over 60 per cent of its parliamentary support from adherents of the Northern Peoples Congress would be expected to, and in fact does, temper its pressures for Nigerianization at a time when less than 1 per cent of the higher posts in the Federal Service are filled by Northerners,[51] and when, in consequence, the posts vacated by Expatriates would almost certainly be filled by Southerners.[52]

To remedy this situation, quota systems have been evolved for the recruitment of officers of the army.[53] And it is an open secret that the Public Service Commission gives preference to applicants from the North when the minimum of qualifications are offered. In addition, pressures have occasionally been brought on officials in the North to accept positions in Lagos. In consequence some slight increase in the number of Northerners holding posts in the federal service has been evident since 1961, especially in

[50] Northern Regional Legislature, House of Chiefs, *Debates, Official Report,* March 9–12, 1959, pp. 2–3.
[51] Federation of Nigeria, *Annual Report of the Nigerianisation Officer for the Year 1957* (Lagos, 1958), p. 7. On March 1, 1960, only 29 of 4,398 "officers in C Scale and above" listed the Northern Region as their "Region of origin." The Parliamentary Secretary to the Ministry of Pensions in *House of Representatives Debates* (Daily Parts), April 20, 1960, p. 1453. In April, 1961, some 13 of 236 *Nigerian* officers in the police forces came from the Northern Region. There were 225 non-Nigerian officers. *Ibid.* (Daily Parts), April 14, 1961, Appendix, p. 33. By November, 1961, one person of "northern origin" held the grade of Permanent Secretary in the Federation. *Ibid.* (Daily Parts), Nov. 15, 1961, p. 3.
[52] Said an NCNC member, Dr. Kalu Ezera, in reference to the filling of the post of Secretary to the Prime Minister: "If the Prime Minister feels that Nigerianisation means Southernisation, then let him Hausanise it." *House of Representatives Debates* (Daily Parts), April 4, 1960, p. 640.
[53] Those going to military school are recruited on the basis of 50 per cent from the Northern Region, 25 per cent from the Eastern, and 25 per cent from the Western. Minister of Defense in *House of Representatives Debates* (Daily Parts), April 13, 1961, p. 1516. Note comments of Ferkiss, *op. cit.,* p. 16.

certain selected sectors.[54] Nevertheless, one can see why the ruling powers in the Northern Region are not as passionately committed to the encouragement of Nigerianization in the Federation as are those from the Eastern and Western Regions.

V. Immediate Problems

Implicit in all the discussions on Nigerianization and Northernization is the lack of adequately trained and experienced Nigerians to fill the posts now occupied by expatriates and to meet the needs of an expanded service during the next decade. Unfortunately, at the present time, there are no criteria by which the needs of the service can be adequately measured. In the absence of any effective organizations and methods investigations, of any general manpower survey, or of any over-all study of the federal administration, statistics now available on the large number of existing vacancies tell very little. Evaluation for general classes of the service must, furthermore, be made in terms of the questionable justification of the comparatively limited hours of service that the average employee is required to contribute per annum. In addition, there is valid room for suspicion that overstaffing in some divisions, primarily in the middle segments of the service (between the Assistant Chief Clerk and Executive Officer Grades), may be the rule rather than the exception in terms of job requirements.

However, the shortages in certain categories, administrative and professional, are real, whether occasioned by resignations, absence of qualified recruits, or lack of experience and training.[55] The situation has been variously characterized as "critical" or "threatening" by realists who stop short of prophesying the "breakdown of the service." Two pioneering reports, which followed ear-

[54] *House of Representatives Debates* (Daily Parts), April 4, 1962, pp. 815–18.
[55] A large, but inadequate, number of Nigerians were studying abroad on government scholarships or private arrangements, the largest number being in the United Kingdom. Various types of specialized training abroad for senior civil servants are being provided by such agencies as the former International Cooperation Administration (now AID) of the United States. Little use has yet been made of the United Nations instrumentalities for training purposes.

lier ones touching on this matter, have analyzed the inadequacies and needs in training and have proposed some remedial measures. In a thoughtful account, prepared in 1958 under the auspices of the Ford Foundation, J. Donald Kingsley made a number of specific proposals regarding staff development.[56] Some of the steps advocated were marked by the stamps of urgency and emergency. Certain of his recommendations, regarding both formal and organized on-the-job training, have been in fact implemented in the Western and Eastern Regions. If they were also accepted more widely at the federal level, they would both complement and give new orientation to the various training centers of certain ministries and other agencies, including the statutory corporations. Frederick Harbison, in an able report in 1960 on "High-Level Manpower for Nigeria's Future," prepared for the Ashby Commission, stressed the need for training programs that would permit the more effective and more rapid use of *employed manpower*. These would include the creation of additional institutes of public administration for training purposes, both at the regional and national levels. Steps are being seriously considered to implement these and other proposals that have been made.[57] It may be added that all of these investigators find a continuing need for the expatriate to contribute his share of experience in such activities during the next few years.

The next five years will be the critical period. Assuming a continuance of the present rate of economic development, some

[56] This unpublished report, "Staffing, Organizational and Training Problems in the Public Service of the Western Region," was made to the Premier of the Western Region. Subsequent unpublished reports in later years have been made to the governments of the other Regions by Dr. Kingsley. The most recent was prepared in conjunction with Sir Arthur Nevil Rucker. Completed in January, 1961, this report was entitled "Staffing and Development of the Public Service of Northern Nigeria."

[57] Mention might be made of the divisions of the University that the Ashby Commission recommended be created in Lagos. The training programs of the Institute of Administration in Zaria are being considerably expanded and developed through assistance from the Ford Foundation and the former International Cooperation Administration. The change in 1961 in the syllabus for the B.Sc. (Econ.) degree at University College, Ibadan, indicates a recognition that most of its recipients will go into the public service and that some changes were necessary to equip them better to serve that purpose. The new syllabus places a greater emphasis than the old upon the acquisition of certain administrative skills, and the "social relevance and utility" of the work now required under part II of that syllabus.

reasonable demand-supply ratio for trained administrative officials may have been reached by the end of that time. Certainly, by then, the stage will have been passed when the emphasis would be put as heavily as it is today upon the search for the general degree-holder in the public service. At the same time, to judge by the experience of other developing countries, the need for professional and scientific personnel will continue to be acute, even if there is a rapid increase in the output of educational institutions. Indeed, a special type of unemployed intellectual with a yearning for a high-level administrative post may have appeared.[58] This type of unemployment will accentuate the acute danger of rapidly increasing numbers of unemployed and frustrated "school leavers" who are in search of any type of position in the public service.[59]

There are many other immediate problems which would merit additional attention, but mention will be made of only one—that is, the problem of corruption in the public service. It has long been recognized that various forms of corruption are in evidence in developing countries as they move away from their tribal moorings of an agricultural society into the twilight period marked by the steps toward industrialization. One explanation lies in the "extent to which the manifest goals of bureaucracies in underdeveloped countries are challenged by their welfare imperatives."[60] Nigeria has been no exception in this respect, though the evidence so far would indicate that she has avoided some of the excesses which have been in evidence in a number of other developing countries. At the same time, the Nigerians themselves recognize the growing seriousness of the various types of corrup-

[58] See the pertinent letter of W. Arthur Lewis dealing with the relationship between educational and economic development, in *Economist*, CXC (Jan. 10, 1959), 118, and the comments of the Advisory Committee on Education in the Colonies, *A.C.E.C.* (59), 22.

[59] See Archibald Callaway, "School Leavers and the Developing Economy of Nigeria," *infra*, chap. ix.

[60] Robert V. Presthus, "Weberian v. Welfare Bureaucracy in Traditional Society," *Administrative Service Quarterly*, VI (June, 1961), 2. The problem of "neutrality" in the public services in the less-developed areas where much of the development is a function of the public sector has been considered in several of the papers prepared for a Conference on Bureaucracy and Political Development, held at Palo Alto, California, Jan. 29–Feb. 2, 1962, under the auspices of the Committee on Comparative Politics of the Social Science Research Council.

tion and of their effects on the functioning of the public service. Debates in Parliament [61] and reports of commissions [62] have referred in detail to manifestations of this "career worm" which has "eaten into high places, in low places in the country." [63] Even an official committee has reported to the cabinet on "bribery and corruption" in recruitment in the public service. [64] Whether the rapid increase in corruption will reach those limits where it will completely impair the effective functioning of the public service, with its pretensions to impartiality and nonpartisanship, remains to be seen. Already its spreading virus has increased the skepticism of a significant percentage of Nigerians as to the possible efficacy of democratic, parliamentary government, at least as it is understood in the light of the British model by independent Nigeria.

In addition, the bureaucracy of the independent Federation has inherited many other technical and organizational problems, some of which press for early attention. Among these are: the future relationships of the Ministry of Establishments to the Ministry of Finance and Public Service Commission; the continued integration of ministries and departments, the merits of which have already been the object of unpublicized official inquiry; the responsibility of the statutory corporations and the rights of their employees, who seek additional civil servant privileges while retaining their special perquisites; the recruitment and retention of certain categories of scarce personnel, such as pharmacists, engineers, and architects; the training of employed manpower, with a special eye on the members of the Executive Class; the search for some adjustment between the pressures for Northernization, Expatriatization, and Nigerianization; and special manpower needs and organization required for the implementation of any projected industrial development programs and national economic plans.

[61] Debate on "Anti-Bribery Movement," in *House of Representatives Debates* (Daily Parts), April 11, 1961, pp. 1197 ff.
[62] See chap. v on "Corruption in Railway," in *Report of the Elias Commission of Inquiry* . . . , pp. 44–46.
[63] Dr. Kalu Ezera in *House of Representatives Debates* (Daily Parts), April 11, 1961, p. 1207; cf. Ferkiss, *op. cit.*, pp. 6, 9.
[64] Note references in editorial in *Daily Express* (Lagos), July 6, 1961, p. 4.

VI. Conclusion

During the final period of transition to independent status, Nigeria benefited from the astute leadership of the Governor-General, Sir James Robertson, and the Prime Minister, Alhaji Sir Abubakar Tafawa Balewa, as well as others. Above all, steps were taken to avoid crises that might endanger the future unity of Nigeria. The degree of final agreement on the provisions of the new Constitution was one evidence of their success. The orderly functioning of the government during the first years of independence has been another.

But there are lingering questions that call for continuing consideration in independent Nigeria. Two or three of these as raised by a thoughtful observer of the Nigerian bureaucracy may be posed by way of conclusion. How can the bureaucratic organization be modified and the bureaucracy be utilized to encourage the process of political unification, essential to a viable federal system, and of political democratization, given the existing scarcities of trained top-level administrators, of public educational facilities of quality, and of an appreciable number of interest groups with a sense of national community? How can one correlate or synthesize the attitudes toward loyalty and duty of an official, which are inherent in the tribal cultures, with those toward the role and status of the civil servants, which were bequeathed by the British colonial administrators, with the end of developing a sense of private integrity and of public responsibility? To what extent is political development in a broad sense dependent upon the "progress" in public administration and economic growth?[65] These queries raise considerations to which attention is given in other chapters of this volume. On their answers will depend the role of the bureaucracy in the future social integration of Nigeria and its effectiveness in the political democratization of that country.

[65] A query raised by Fred Riggs in an unpublished paper, "Bureaucrats and Political Development: A Paradoxical View." Professor Riggs concludes that there is no necessary compatibility.

6

Nigerian Foreign Policy

L. Gray Cowan

Independence came for Nigeria at a most critical juncture in the history of West Africa. The present Federal Government took office at the moment when the focus of West African interest was shifting from the colonial relationship to the relations of the independent states of Africa to each other and to the rest of the world. Nigeria also took her seat in the United Nations at a point when African issues were of supreme importance in the world organization. As Africa's most populous state she was expected to assume a public posture on questions which involved not only the future of Africa but ultimately, perhaps, the peace of the world. On some of these questions—Algeria, and racial discrimination in the Union of South Africa—Nigeria's stand was already clear, but on others, such as the Congo, the expression of Nigeria's views by the Prime Minister was eagerly awaited by the Great Powers as well as by the other African states. The policy principles enunciated by Sir Abubakar Tafawa Balewa in his speech at the United Nations in October, 1960 (largely a reaffirmation of the stand which he had taken publicly at the independence ceremonies a few days before), were shortly translated into action when a Nigerian delegate became the head of the Congo Conciliation Commission. Nigerian representatives were clearly prepared to accept their full share of responsibility for the settlement of African problems within the framework of decisions taken by the United Nations.

Beginning with the day of independence, Nigeria has been under severe pressure from several sources in the making of her foreign policy. With the entry of the cold war into Africa by way of the Congo, the Nigerian Government's support of the West has been under increasing attack from the East, from other African states, and from segments of public opinion within Nigeria which favor an all-out neutralist stand. Some of the surrounding independent states of West Africa have also brought pressure for an open declaration of support for Pan-Africanism. Shortly after the beginning of the new year, there were signs that another pressure would soon be felt from the north. The apparent victory of Colonel Nasser at the Casablanca Conference was an indication of the efforts being made by Egypt to block Israeli plans for technical aid to the African countries. Because of the growing strength of Islam in Nigeria and the close cultural relationships of the Northerners with Egypt, Nigerian policy-makers are peculiarly vulnerable to Egyptian influences.

Nigeria's introduction to the battles of world politics has been sudden and rude. With a minimum of trained personnel both for the foreign office at home and for representation abroad, she has been expected to assume a decisive role in African politics—a role which the world seems to have taken for granted because of her size and population. While there is no doubt that Nigeria's present and future place is of vital importance in the political development of a community of African states—particularly in view of the fact that one in every four Africans south of the Sahara is a Nigerian—the tendency to expect too much immediately of Nigeria's influence in Africa must be avoided. If the West looks on Nigeria as a counterbalance to African inclinations to support certain policies espoused by the East, there is bound to be disappointment. For all the capacities of her leaders, Nigeria is still inexperienced in foreign relations and she still possesses only one vote in the United Nations.

The present paper is concerned with the basic considerations that play a part in foreign policy making in Nigeria today and with the principal positions adopted thus far by Nigeria on foreign issues. Finally, an attempt is made to find out to what extent these positions are reflections of the foreign policy platforms of the three major parties and of press and public opinion on external relations.

I. Pre-Independence Preparation of Nigerians in Foreign Relations

Nigerian independence was foreseen sufficiently far in advance to permit at least the making of plans for the opening of a Ministry of Foreign Affairs and for some training of Nigerians in representation of their country abroad. While it is generally acknowledged that, because of a shortage of qualified personnel, the pre-independence training program was inadequate, it nevertheless was more extensive than that for any of the other West African states prior to independence. The External Affairs division of the Prime Minister's Office gave opportunity after 1958 for the training of a few Nigerians in the procedures of operating a foreign office but very little in the way of substantive decision could be put in Nigerian hands.

The basic plan for training Nigerians in overseas representation was laid down in 1956.[1] In the Sessional Paper it was stated that, in principle, training was required for three main classes of staff to deal with external affairs: diplomatic representatives, consular and trade representatives abroad, and the staff of a ministry within the home government concerned with foreign affairs. Because of the high standards required, training for prospective holders of representational posts should be begun well in advance of the planned independence date. The Sessional Paper pointed out, however, that representation in every country where Nigerian interests were involved would be prohibitively expensive and that therefore Nigeria, as was the case with other newer members of the Commonwealth, would have to intrust her representation in less important countries to the British diplomatic representatives stationed there.

[1] Federation of Nigeria, *The Training of Nigerians for the Representation of Their Country Overseas, a Statement of Policy by the Government of the Federation of Nigeria*, Sessional Paper No. 11 of 1956 (Lagos, 1956).

The Federal Government, in whose hands the Constitution placed exclusive control over foreign affairs, had proceeded, prior to 1956, to establish Nigerian representation in certain key spots within the framework of the British diplomatic service. A student liaison office was set up in Washington which was also charged with arranging visits to the United States of Nigerian ministers. The large number of pilgrims going annually from Nigeria to the Holy Places of Islam in Saudi Arabia necessitated the establishment of Pilgrim Offices in Khartoum and Jedda to safeguard their interests. In accordance with the terms of the Labor Agreement with the Government of the Spanish Territories of the Gulf of Guinea, and with the French Government for Gabon, Nigerian Vice-Consuls and Labor Department Representatives were appointed to Santa Isabel and Libreville to insure that the interests of Nigerian contract labor in these two territories were looked after. Nigeria also had a special representative of the Federal Government at the Trusteeship Council meetings at the United Nations to advise on British Cameroons affairs. Finally, there was a Commissioner for the Federation at the Nigeria Office in London, as well as Commissioners for the three Regions. These Commissioners had no formal diplomatic functions, but were concerned with student welfare, the improvement of trade relations, and general publicity for Nigeria in the United Kingdom. Within Nigeria the External Affairs Branch of the Chief Secretary's office dealt with the issuing of passports and visas and relations with the consular representatives of foreign countries resident in Lagos.

In the plans for the training of diplomatic representatives it was assumed that Nigeria would wish to establish, immediately upon independence, High Commissioner's offices in London and Accra; embassies in Washington, Khartoum, and one West European capital; a delegation to the United Nations; and consular offices in Jedda, Fernando Po, and Libreville. In order not to rob existing ministries in Lagos of present or potential personnel for the staffing of embassies and a Foreign Ministry, it was decided not to set up a special school for the young diplomats but to use the existing offices for training by placing in them a few carefully selected young officers who would thus gain the practical experience necessary to become assistant and principal secretaries and, eventually, heads of mission. It was expected that the expatriate holders of the chief posts in the Nigerian offices abroad would give particular attention to the training of these young men. Recruits for the potential Nigerian Foreign Service were to be drawn both from the ranks of civil servants already occupying administrative posts in federal and regional ministries and from new entrants to the public service who were considered to be particularly suited to foreign service work.

In the main the principles laid down in the Sessional Paper of 1956 were adhered to over the four years intervening before independence. In the *Federal Estimates* for 1957–58 a vote of £20,000 was asked for the expenses of posting the recruits to the overseas offices and the incidental expenses of special training, particularly in languages. By April, 1960, fifty-five officers had been trained or were in training. It would appear that the early fears expressed in Parliament and elsewhere that the shortage of trained Northerners would confine Nigerian representation abroad to Southerners were groundless. The senior Nigerian diplomat occupying the post of High Commissioner in London is Alhaji Abdulmaliki and the Permanent Representative to the United Nations is Alhaji Muhammadu Ngileruma, a former Pilgrims Officer in Khartoum and, at an earlier period, Waziri of the Bornu Native Administration. Northerners occupy the ambassadorships at Khartoum and Yaounde and one of the Prime Minister's advisers on African affairs in Lagos is Mallam Isa Wali, formerly a trainee in the Nigerian Liaison Office in Washington.

Because of the expected influence of Nigeria in West African affairs the Federal Government was under great pressure to expand its representation abroad, particularly in Moscow and in Eastern Europe, and to receive ambassadors from the Eastern bloc. Sir Abubakar pointed out, however, that the possibilities of increased representation were severely limited by finances (the Nigerian diplomatic service, with eleven ambassadors and high commissioners, costs the Federation over £2,000,000 annually) and by a shortage of personnel. At independence the Soviet Government pressed strongly for the immediate exchange of representatives but Sir Abubakar is reported to have told Mr. Malik, "We will not be bullied. Protocol must be followed and we will consider an application in the proper form." Agreement was finally reached in June, 1961, on an exchange of representatives at the ambassadorial level. Nigerians are well aware that, for the sake of showing their own independence, relations with the Soviet bloc must be established but they are to be on Nigerian, not Soviet, terms.

II. Principles of Nigerian Foreign Policy

The Prime Minister, who has retained at least temporarily the portfolio of Foreign Minister, has taken the opportunity on at least two major occasions to state the general principles which his government regards as the cornerstones of Nigerian foreign policy. He outlined these principles in a foreign policy speech to the House of Representatives in Lagos on August 27, 1960, and reiterated and amplified them in his address to the General Assembly of the United Nations on October 7. He pointed with pride to the fact that Nigeria had been accepted as a member of the Commonwealth but in speaking to the legislature he was careful to emphasize that "we shall nevertheless have a free hand to select those policies which we consider to be most advantageous for Nigeria."

Despite his implied commitment to the West—"we shall never forget our old friends"—Sir Abubakar has made it clear that Nigeria will not under his government be prepared to associate itself "as a matter of routine" with any of the power blocs. He is far from agreeing with the concept of power blocs within the United Nations: "I hate the very idea of blocs existing at all in the United Nations; it seems to me to be a contradiction in terms." The Prime Minister's statement left him open to criticism from some sections of the Nigerian press for what appeared to be a somewhat lukewarm attitude toward full co-operation with the other African and Asian states, but there seems little doubt that he meant his views on blocs to be taken at full face value. He has repeatedly warned of the urgency of preventing the ideological cold war from coming to Africa and in his speech before the United Nations, after praising technical assistance schemes, he went on to add pointedly:

I do not seriously suggest that it is in the best interests of world peace for assistance from elsewhere to be given only to those countries which, although still underdeveloped, are politically stable and have a properly constituted government which is capable of understanding the risks of accepting aid from another country. I certainly deprecate direct assistance being given by individual powers to countries which are not yet able to stand on their own feet or are politically unstable because such aid will only give rise to suspicions and in the end the receiving country may find itself involved in the ideological war.

Presumably Sir Abubakar feels that Nigeria is sufficiently stable politically to understand the risks of accepting aid from any outside source, although his personal preference would be for Western aid.

In both major policy statements he went out of his way to emphasize to Nigeria's African neighbors that, despite its size and population, his country has absolutely no expansionist intentions. Although African boundaries were artificial creations of the European powers, nevertheless, "those boundaries should be respected and, in the interests of peace, must remain the recognized boundaries until such time as the peoples concerned decide of their own free will to merge into one unit. We shall discourage any attempt to influence such communities by force. . . ." Despite the declarations of the Prime Minister, however, possible Nigerian expansionist tendencies cannot be entirely overlooked by her immediate neighbors. To the north there are close ethnic ties between the peoples of Niger and the Hausa and Fulani of Northern Nigeria. The Sardauna of Sokoto, the Northern Prime Minister, has remarked publicly that parts of Niger were once part of the old Fulani empire and there are signs that M. Hamani Diori, the President of Niger, is not entirely comfortable with the idea of an independent Nigeria along the seven hundred miles of his southern frontier. Along much of the border with Dahomey, both in the north and at the coast, there are similar tribal groups on both sides; in addition, there is a strong economic pull toward Nigeria since her ports and rail lines could be a major means of evacuation of the products of Niger and northern Dahomey.[2] The same attraction exists to the east for the Republic of Chad. To the southeast the decision of the southern part of the former British Cameroons to become part of the Republic of the Cameroon leaves open the possibility of future friction along this border. Finally, a case can be made for the eventual absorption by Nigeria of Fernando Po when the Spanish colonial regime ends, considering the long-standing labor exchange between that island and Eastern Nigeria. Whatever may be the immediate attitude of the Nigerian Government on the question of border readjustment, it may well be that political and economic forces in Africa may force a reconsideration of whether Nigeria's interests may not be served best in the long run by an expansion of her present boundaries.

On the all-important question of Pan-Africanism, Sir Abubakar has taken a clear and firm stand that is almost directly opposed to the conception of Pan-Africanism held by Dr. Nkrumah. The Nigerian leader appears to share M. Houphouet-Boigny's vision of an African union arising out of closer economic and cultural relations between the member states. He has stated flatly that Nigeria is determined to encourage as far as possible the development of co-operation first at these levels. A major policy aim of his government is to secure agreement on a plan for improvement of inter-African communications and transport facilities, pooling of resources for higher education and scientific research, and an expansion of trade and travel. It is, however, in his view, premature even to think in terms of an African Common Market. The Nigerian Government hopes for joint consultations with other African states on *non-political* matters but on the question of a possible political union, Sir Abubakar left no doubt as to his views:

I must say that I do not think myself that ideas of political union are practicable in the immediate future. I do not rule out the possibility of eventual union but for the present it is unrealistic to expect countries to

[2] On this point, see the series of articles on Dahomey by John West in the *Daily Service* (Lagos), March 11–14, 1960. The writer strongly advocated that Dahomey should join Nigeria after both became independent.

give up the sovereignty which they have so recently acquired and I am quite sure that it is wrong to imagine that political union could of itself bring countries together: on the contrary it will follow as the natural consequence of co-operation in other fields.

In an implied warning to Ghana and Guinea, he went on to add:

I wish to state that I think it will be the greatest threat to peace in Africa if any country sets out to undermine the authority of the properly chosen leaders of another state, with a view to imposing political union. That way there can only be trouble. In the fulness of time, as political relations develop, and there is more and more consultation between the states of a regional grouping, then political union may well be the natural result but it would be wrong either to impose it or to seek to hasten the process unduly.

It is on this issue of Pan-Africanism perhaps more than any other foreign policy question that Sir Abubakar may run into serious difficulties at home. His views on the future of political union are shared by his own party but many prominent members of the NCNC and the Action Group are in strong disagreement. In placing economic co-operation ahead of political union he has run head-on into an articulate group of young NCNC back-benchers who are ardent exponents of the Nkrumah thesis, "Seek ye first the political kingdom."

The Monrovia Conference in May, 1961, gave Sir Abubakar an opportunity to present to a purely African audience an expansion of his views on the future direction of political development in Africa. It has been widely reported that the Nigerian leader made a strong impression on his fellow delegates and the final resolutions of the Conference reflected much of his point of view. The resolution on African unity stated in part that "the unity that is aimed to be achieved at the moment is not the political integration of African states but unity of aspiration and action." To implement this principle, technical committees met during the summer in Dakar to discuss details of economic, educational, and technical co-operation and to lay plans for the proposed "inter-African and Malagasy Advisory Organization," one of whose commissions will be designed to deal with the peaceful settlement of African disputes. The Monrovia Conference was a decided step forward in Nigeria's leadership in West Africa (the follow-up conference was to meet in Lagos later in the year), but it remains to be seen whether it will be possible to arrive at a compromise between the kind of African unity envisaged at Monrovia and the much closer union advocated by the Ghana-Guinea-Mali group which was absent from the Monrovia conference table.

On the issue of the Congo, Sir Abubakar went into considerable detail regarding the Nigerian position in his speech to the United Nations. To prevent Africa from becoming a battleground for ideological warfare he maintained that the Congo issue must be settled by the African states alone. He suggested a fact-finding commission composed primarily of African states—in any case, none of the Great Powers should be included in it "because however honest their intentions it would be inevitable that they would be regarded as having a particular interest in the problem." The fact that the UN Congo Conciliation Commission was led by the Honorable Jaja Wachuku indicates that the Prime Minister was prepared to take active steps to see that his suggestion was implemented. He advocated holding new elections in the Congo, so that properly authorized leaders could emerge to deal with the United Nations; once they had been chosen, they must be supported even if "they may seem to some of us to be far from perfect and to some even objectionable." The Congo was a sovereign, independent state and could not remain under UN administration, but it was, he believed, the duty of the UN to provide those conditions under which the Congolese could freely choose the most generally acceptable form of government—whether confederation or federation. In view of the minority problems present in Nigeria and the demand for the formation of new states to be carved from the present regions, it is perhaps not surprising that Sir Abubakar failed to condemn strongly M. Tshombe's separatist claims. As a final point in Nigeria's program for the Congo, he suggested that other African states join with Nigeria in offering Congolese boys places in African secondary and technical schools and in sending short-term missions to the Congo. The Monrovia Conference resolution on the Congo which stated that African countries should refrain from favoring rival groups within the Congo serves as a further reinforcement of Nigeria's general position.

Of necessity, Nigerian statements on foreign policy have thus far been couched largely in terms of generalizations and principles, which now must be further interpreted by day-to-day policy decisions. But already there is evidence that regional interests and party commitments within Nigeria are providing the basis for disagreement not only on the application of the principles but on the principles themselves.

III. The Nigerian Parties and Foreign Policy

With the federal elections of December, 1959, foreign policy issues came to a much larger place in the platforms of Nigeria's political parties. During the election campaign the major differences on foreign policy between the two Southern parties became clear-cut and were well publicized. The Northern Peoples Congress, on the other hand, made less effort to acquaint the voters with its foreign policy platform, presumably because it felt that the bulk of Northerners were more concerned with internal than with external issues.

The basic stand on foreign policy of Dr. Azikiwe's party, the NCNC, was stated in its election manifesto. The party, it was claimed, stood for a policy of non-alignment with any particular axis of geopolitics, Eastern or Western, so as to permit Nigeria the greatest freedom of action to choose those policies which would best suit her national interests. The NCNC favored membership in the Commonwealth, but was opposed to Nigeria's involvement in any kind of military pact, although it was added, somewhat inconsistently, that "whether a position of neutrality in military matters will be in the National Interest of Nigeria or not will be decided after relevant factors have been taken into consideration upon the attainment of independence." Non-alignment, the manifesto made clear, was not to be confused with neutrality on foreign policy questions:

We will choose to be independent in our attitude because it will leave the initiative with us. We will spike neutrality because it is defeatist and lacks moral conviction. We shall be opposed to partisanship be-

cause it is an exhibition of prejudice. . . . We shall, therefore, be just
and upright and steer a middle course by relying upon our native grit
and national integrity to pull us through.

Within Africa the party believed in developing friendly relations
with all states who believed in "fundamental human rights" but
the manifesto itself was curiously silent on the subject of Pan-
Africanism. In the course of the campaign, however, it was made
clear that the NCNC favored the idea of a Federation of West
African States but with certain reservations: "We realize that, in
view of the onerous difficulties involved in the implementation of
any such federation the issue should remain a long term one pend-
ing the attainment of independence by all, or at least a majority,
of countries that comprise the geographical stretch of West Africa." Since the election and the independence of the French-
speaking states the NCNC appears to be veering toward a policy
of stronger support for West African union, under pressure from
some of the young, militant Zikist groups and the Pan African
Youths Movement which are allied to the party. It remains to be
seen how long the senior leaders of the party, who are restrained
by the responsibilities of maintaining the coalition with the NPC,
will be able to resist the younger men who find Nkrumah's brand
of Pan-Africanism very appealing.

As was to be expected, the foreign policy planks of the Northern Peoples Congress platform followed the generally conservative line of its domestic policy. The Congress favored membership in the Commonwealth and the creation of close ties with
England and with the United States. Within Africa it advocated
maintaining friendly relations and close ties of co-operation with
all states, but no mention was made of any possible Nigerian membership in a West African union. Shortly after the election, Sir
Ahmadu Bello, the Premier of the Region, made his position on
Pan-Africanism clear in a press conference when he pointed out
that he had not discussed the subject with Dr. Nkrumah while
visiting Accra because "it is premature to start thinking of that
as our own homes are not yet consolidated." The NPC has consistently favored an anti-neutralist and pro-Western line; the
Sardauna believes that no nation can stand alone today and there-

fore neutrality is out of the question. He refused even to consider the possibility of accepting Russian loans at very favorable interest rates as some other independent states of Africa had done: "That is not our policy. We must work with those we are accustomed to. . . . If they [the loans] were to bring in Soviet technicians, we do not know how they would get along with the Nigerian people." There are indications that the strongly pro-Western position of the NPC is being eroded to some degree by the pressure for neutralism being exerted on the Prime Minister in Lagos, but the party appears to be no more favorable to Pan-Africanism now than it was before independence. The party's election declaration made it clear, however, that a pro-Western orientation did not exclude contacts with the Arab countries; the North, it was stated, had long had friendly cultural relations with Egypt and many Northerners had been to Mecca. Within a matter of months this Northern attitude threatened to involve Nigeria in the Arab-Israeli dispute and was to become one of the major foreign policy issues prior to independence.

The only other important Northern party, the Northern Elements Progressive Union, under Mallam Aminu Kano's leadership, took foreign policy positions which coincided almost completely with those of its southern ally, the NCNC. NEPU favored Pan-African union and the creation of an African mutual defense pact rather than Nigerian participation in any Eastern or Western military alliance. NEPU delegations took part in the All-African Peoples Conference in Tunis in January, 1960, and in the Emergency Conference held in Accra in April of that year. However, in its foreign policy stand NEPU probably represents today only a small minority of the Northern voters. Support for its views is concentrated in a younger, educated group who are beginning to feel that NPC has failed to identify itself closely enough with the new role which they expect Nigeria and the African states to play in world affairs. Mallam Aminu's stand on Pan-Africanism has received somewhat less publicity since his assumption of the office of chief government whip in the House, but it became clear that his point of view has not changed when his party expressed public agreement in June, 1961, with the leader of the Action

Group, whose changing views on Pan-Africanism will be mentioned later.

In its role as the official opposition the Action Group has lost no opportunity to attack the governing coalition on questions of foreign policy. The NCNC and the Action Group were clearly divided initially on the fundamental issues of Pan-Africanism and neutrality; they agreed on membership in the Commonwealth and on certain aspects of Nigerian foreign economic policy. In the federal election campaign the Action Group announced its approval of alignment with the Western democracies and its opposition to any form of political union among the West African states. Chief Awolowo, the party's leader, explained his position in some detail in his recently published autobiography; many of his comments on foreign policy published there are reproduced almost verbatim from speeches he made during the election campaign.[3] He pointed out that although the West still discriminated against the black man and perpetrated injustices in parts of Africa, these evils were diminishing and were the subject of strong criticism in the Western countries. But only in the West could a man freely exercise the right to express any opinion he desired; for this reason he believed Nigeria should remain in the Western camp. Neutralism in African foreign policy he branded as "an unmitigated disservice to humanity," and concluded that such a policy was "no more and no less than the projection, conscious or unconscious, of the deepseated prejudices which these nations have had towards some of the countries of the Western democracies." He saw no objection to Nigeria's seeking aid from any source but he condemned in the strongest terms the playing off of two opposing forces against one another—it never paid off in the end and by it honor and dignity were forever lost.

The Action Group leader was completely opposed to the notion of a union of African states:

I am firmly of the opinion that it is visionary now and for many years to come to labor for the emergence of a United States of Africa. . . . It is unrealistic in the extreme to expect that African nations which

[3] Obafemi Awolowo, *Awo: The Autobiography of Chief Obafemi Awolowo* (Cambridge, 1960).

have only recently won their independence from foreign rule would be willing to surrender or even diminish their sovereignty in the pursuit of what is quite plainly an *ignis fatuus*. Apart from the impracticableness of the proposition, any serious attempt to bring about political union among the states of Africa is sure to engender suspicion, distrust and disharmony among these states. Economic and cultural association among the states of Africa . . . is no less fanciful than political union.

Despite these broad assertions of the impracticability of a United States of Africa, Chief Awolowo favored co-operation between the states of West Africa on a restricted, non-political scale. He emphasized that Pan-Africanism should aim at seeking the complete liberation of Africa and the elimination of racial prejudice: "if the aims and objects of Pan-Africanism are limited in this way, and are not extended to the pursuit of a Pan-African government . . . , Nigeria should give to it her fullest possible backing."

Chief Awolowo held strong views on the place of Egypt in African politics. Although Egypt was physically in Africa, there had never been any cultural affinity between her and the black races of Africa: "The United Arab Republic, the pet creature of Nasser, which has one foot in Africa and another in the Middle East, is the very antithesis of a workable African community." Because of Nasser's territorial ambitions in Africa, Awolowo insisted that "effective cooperation with Nasser . . . would be possible only if the black races of Africa were prepared to remain as satellites of Egypt's orbit, as Syria now is." In his effort to exclude Nasser from Negro Africa, Chief Awolowo chose to ignore the cultural origins of many of his fellow Nigerians in the North; even if one grants the validity of much of the argument he set forth, it would seem to do little good to the cause of national unity to imply that those Nigerians who maintained cultural bonds with the Arab world are not true "black Africans."

The Action Group's stand on foreign policy was subjected to violent criticism during the 1959 campaign by the NCNC leadership. Dr. Azikiwe and other NCNC leaders claimed that, in its desire to align Nigeria with the Western Powers, the Action Group was betraying the African nationalist struggle because these were the same colonial powers (except for the United States) which had so long held Africans in bondage. They argued, too, that the Action Group stand against neutrality would deprive Nigeria of a valuable diplomatic bargaining point and might unnecessarily antagonize states "which might not have malicious designs on Nigeria." From time to time also in the House of Representatives the Action Group's position was deprecated as being contrary to Nigeria's national interests in that it would prevent the use of Nigeria's influence on both sides in the cold war to introduce some "rationality and sanity into contemporary diplomacy."

There is no doubt that some of the positions on foreign policy taken by the parties during the campaign were designed with an eye toward voter appeal, but the principles enunciated in the party platforms appear to have represented fairly accurately the lines adopted by all parties up to mid-1961. However, a highly significant change of attitude on the part of Chief Awolowo and his party appears to have taken place as a result of a five-day visit he paid to Ghana early in June, 1961. Accompanied by the leader of the opposition in the East, Mr. S. G. Ikoku, the Northern opposition leader, Alhaji Ibrahim Imam, and Mr. Alfred Rewano, Chairman of the Western Region Development Commission, Chief Awolowo undertook a "fact-finding" mission to Accra where he received a friendly welcome from Dr. Nkrumah. On his arrival he restated his position that a black African community must be formed without the North African leaders (including Nasser) since they were Pan-Arabist in sentiment. He also emphasized that a timetable should be set up for full African freedom and that all African countries should sever defensive alliances with foreign powers to insure full African sovereignty.

Chief Awolowo seems clearly to have been influenced by President Nkrumah's views in the course of his stay. Upon his return to Lagos he issued a statement in which he advocated that Nigeria should forthwith join the Ghana-Guinea-Mali Union (which he maintained would shortly be strengthened by the addition of Upper Volta and Gambia). Nigeria, he insisted, had failed to take a strong enough stand on African nationalism and had further weakened the confidence of genuine African nationalists in her position by attending the Monrovia Conference and by maintaining a foreign military alliance. He joined President Nkrumah in condemning the entire Monrovia Conference because it "was convened through the financial backing of certain Western powers."

Chief Awolowo's statement brought down upon his head a barrage of criticism from both outside and inside Nigeria. President Tubman lost no time in pointing out that the costs of the Monrovia Conference, amounting to over $300,000, had been borne entirely by the Liberian Government. At home the Federal Government reiterated its stand that a political union of African states would at the moment be inexpedient and emphasized that the Monrovia resolutions would be implemented shortly at the Lagos meeting. The NCNC, in a lengthy declaration, concluded that, while the party admired Chief Awolowo's intelligence, it could not concede that his entry into African politics had been "impressive."

It is not yet clear whether Chief Awolowo's change of views will have an effect on the direction of Nigerian foreign policy. He has been consistently opposed to any kind of military alliance between European and African states and he had been increasingly critical, even before his Ghanaian visit, of racial discrimination in the West. Because of his previous highly critical view of President Nkrumah's statements that Ghanaian sovereignty should be sacrificed to a wider African union, it is difficult to understand his present advocacy of Nigerian membership in a union which would eventually mean the loss of Nigerian sovereignty. The Action Group leader's new stance represents in all probability a genuine shift in his personal viewpoint combined with an element of political expediency. There would appear to be little doubt that he regarded the Defense Pact with Britain as an infringement on Nigeria's newly won sovereignty and resented what he felt was an insult to the dignity of the leaders of a free nation. But the fact cannot be ignored that Chief Awolowo is a highly skilled and experienced politician. The issues of Pan-Africanism and of Nigeria's role in West African politics are extremely controversial, and as leader of the opposition he is quick to sense that they provide abundant political capital. It is clear that the NCNC in its present alliance with the NPC cannot take as firm a stand in favor of Pan-Africanism as it might, were it not forced to consider the more conservative views of the NPC. Chief Awolowo is in the enviable position of being able to champion a cause which not only acutely embarrasses the government but at the same time adds to the political strength of his own party since it enlists the support of those youth elements, which, regardless of party, feel that Nigeria's present position is out of step with that of the "genuine" African nationalists such as President Nkrumah. The fact that Chief Awolowo went to Ghana accompanied by the Action Group leaders of the East and the North seems to indicate that the point of view expressed on his return was designed to become a part of the Action Group's national appeal.

IV. Nigerian Press and Public Opinion on Foreign Policy Issues

Real Nigerian public awareness of foreign policy issues can be said to date only from late 1959. Up to that point the literate portion of the Nigerian public was too preoccupied with internal issues arising out of the independence struggle and the creation of a federal framework to turn much of its attention to external questions. While Nigeria was still a colony foreign relations remained under the control of the United Kingdom Government and on only a few issues was the Nigerian legislature called upon to express any opinion at all. As a result, the future position of Nigeria in the international community received only the barest of press coverage. Beginning, however, with the federal election campaign in September, 1959, foreign policy questions have been receiving steadily increasing space in the daily papers and several series of feature articles have been published on the situation in other African countries and on the international situation in general. Discussion of purely local issues has given way to some extent to news stories on international events. The activities of Nigerian officials at the United Nations and of ministers on official missions abroad have received full and critical attention. But the process of creating an educated public opinion on foreign policy is a slow one, and it cannot yet be said that the average Nigerian outside the large urban areas has any very clear notion of the significance of the debates on foreign policy in the legislature.

The Nigerian papers are in the main the mouthpiece for the major parties and as such faithfully reflect their foreign policy positions. Only three papers approach anything like a national circulation, the *Daily Express* (formerly the *Daily Service*), which is the Action Group paper, the *West African Pilot*, Dr. Azikiwe's paper, and the *Daily Times*, controlled by an English publisher, which lists itself as independent but tends to follow a pro-government line. If the average Nigerian reader were to follow his own party paper he would hear only one side of most foreign policy issues; even the news stories in the two major party papers often appear to be slanted toward specific editorial viewpoints. The papers are influential in forming public opinion on internal questions, but there is some doubt that, at the moment at least, they have a great deal of effect on opinion on foreign affairs. Public knowledge in this field is still too limited to be very critical; a man is likely to follow the party line on foreign affairs simply because he agrees with the party on local and national issues.

Thus far relatively few major foreign policy decisions have aroused public interest. The continuing question of a neutralist vs. a pro-Western policy has occasioned a good deal of debate, focused largely upon the opposing stands taken by the *Pilot* and the *Express*. The *Pilot* has tended to hammer on the theme of a qualified non-alignment within a Commonwealth framework, taking its cue from the public speeches of NCNC party officials. Lengthy feature articles by local lawyers and academic specialists explaining the advantages of non-alignment appear with fair regularity, along with letters to the editor favoring the party viewpoint. The former *Daily Service* took issue with the *Pilot* frequently, expounding editorially and in its letters column the views of prominent Action Group supporters of a Western alignment.

Pan-Africanism has, of course, been a source of much comment. The *Pilot* strongly favors a policy of West African co-operation without, however, consistently coming out for the close type of political union favored by Dr. Nkrumah. In the spring of 1959 the paper published a series of articles stressing the view that all of Africa's present ills could be attributed to the arbitrary frontiers established by the imperialists and suggesting that Pan-Africanism was the only hope for African survival in a nuclear age. The *Daily Service*, on the other hand, consistently attacked the concept of political union in West Africa, particularly through its columnist John West. The paper made much of the visit of President Tubman to Nigeria in 1960 as an expression of the bond of friendship between the two countries and of the identity of his views on Pan-Africanism with those of the Action Group:

President Tubman seems to share the same views with most of Nigeria's leaders on the question of African unity and Pan-Africanism.[4] He does not appear to believe either in a political federation of the African states or in the theory that a messiah of African freedom has in fact arisen in Accra. He has advocated the policy of cooperation on Ministerial and official levels between the African states in economic, educational and cultural fields. And this is the policy which is generally in line with the thinking of Nigerian leaders and which should prove acceptable to them.[5]

The reference to a "messiah" growing up in Accra gives a clue to the Action Group's views on President Nkrumah and on the Ghanaian Government in general at that time. The *Daily Service* before independence was violently opposed to what it believed to be irredentist ambitions on the part of President Nkrumah and to his desire to be the spokesman for an independent West Africa. The paper bitterly attacked the Osagyefo's speeches on the occasion of Togolese independence:

We believe that African unity and African nationalism would be mere empty vaporings . . . unless the freedom of the individual African state is guaranteed without any reservation whatever. . . . The *Daily Service* concedes to Dr. Nkrumah the right to be known as the Messiah (or is it the Fuehrer?) of Africa. But all reasonable men recognize that territorial ambitions run counter to the ideal of unity. Nor is it in the interest of that unity or even of a projected West African union for an African country to intervene in the internal affairs of another. . . . Already this dictatorial ambition is known to have strained relations between Ghana and Guinea. . . . The only hope for African unity,

---

[4] The *Daily Service* line was that NCNC leaders espousing Pan-Africanism were "irresponsible."
[5] *Daily Service* (Lagos), June 28, 1960 (editorial).

therefore, is that such countries as Nigeria should guarantee the independence of smaller African states.

Nigerian relations with Ghana have been cool for some time and the question of rivalry over the leadership of West Africa is never very far below the surface. The Action Group accused the NCNC of importing thugs from Ghana during the federal election campaign, which brought forth bitter protests from some Ghanaians that this was part of a concerted campaign to undermine Nigerian public faith in the disinterested role that Ghana sought to play in the Pan-Africanist movement. The recent abrupt change in Chief Awolowo's attitude toward Ghana may leave the party paper in some embarrassment, but fortunately the public's memory of editorial positions is no longer in Nigeria than it is elsewhere in the world.

One specific issue of Nigeria's relations with foreign countries gave rise to acrimonious public discussion. In June, 1960, the news became public that the Federal Government had entered into an agreement with the Government of Israel for a substantial technical assistance loan and for export credits. The Principal Organizing Secretary for the NPC immediately issued a statement condemning the agreement and this was followed by an official release from the Northern Regional Government dissociating itself from the agreement entirely and refusing to accept any of the Israeli aid when it became available. The reason advanced was that such aid would mean the involvement of Nigeria in the Arab-Israeli dispute. Both the Action Group and the NCNC severely criticized the action of the NPC, pointing out that Nigeria could not afford to do without any aid that was offered and accepting Israeli aid would involve Nigeria in the Arab-Israeli question only if aid from the UAR were refused at some future date. The Action Group paper added fuel to the fire by remarking parenthetically that it did not expect UAR aid anyway, since Egypt had nothing to offer Nigeria. In addition to embarrassing the Federal Government in its negotiations, the Northern Region's statement posed the nice constitutional question of whether a Region had the right to dissociate itself from an agreement entered into for the whole of Nigeria by the Federal Government. When questioned about the agreement, the Prime Minister admitted that his party took full responsibility for the NPC statement (with which he did not personally agree), warned against letting religion affect Nigerian political decisions, and immediately left for Kaduna to pour oil on troubled waters there.

On three foreign issues, all dealing with Africa, the parties, and therefore the press, have been in complete agreement. No other African problem aroused such widespread public indignation as the South African Government's actions at Sharpeville. The three major parties vied with each other in their condemnation of the Union and the demand was repeatedly made that after independence Nigeria should insist on the expulsion of the Union from the Commonwealth or withdraw herself. There was substantial agreement also on the Nigerian attitude toward French atomic experiments in the Sahara. It was felt in some areas that during the first series of experiments in the spring of 1960 the Prime Minister was less firm than he might have been in condemning France and that he had too easily accepted the opinion of British scientists that there was no public danger from fallout. However, the action of the independent government in breaking relations with France clearly indicates the solid opposition of all shades of Nigerian political opinion to the French use of the Sahara for this purpose.

From the beginning of the disturbances in Angola there was unanimous condemnation of Portuguese actions in the press. The Security Council debates were fully reported, and there was editorial comment on the failure of Great Britain to vote for the Afro-Asian motion calling on Portugal to end "repressive measures." The United States was praised for its favorable vote: "But for the American vote in favor of the motion it would be difficult to challenge the growing feeling that the all-white North Atlantic Treaty Organization is now a counterpoise to the United Nations organization in which Afro-Asian solidarity is being regarded as an irritating threat to certain European interests in many parts of the world." [6] Issues of direct African concern centering about residual colonialism can be expected to arouse the liveliest public reac-

[6] *Daily Times* (Lagos), June 12, 1961.

tion; the more abstract issues of the cold war do not yet play a major role in the general consciousness of foreign relations.

Relations between the former administering power and Nigeria will doubtless continue to supply fuel for foreign policy debate for some years to come. The liveliest foreign policy controversy after independence arose around the question of the Nigerian defense agreement with the United Kingdom Government. The principles of this agreement, based on the constitutional talks of May, 1960, were published and laid before the House of Representatives for ratification in November. The agreement seemed on the surface harmless enough. It provided for mutual assistance on military matters, for the training of Nigerian forces by the United Kingdom, and for assistance in equipping them. In return, Britain received military overflying rights and staging facilities. The agreement in its final form did not mention the possibility of a British military base in Northern Nigeria, although this had apparently been requested and had been turned down by the Nigerian delegation at the London talks. The publication of the agreement was the signal for one of the most severe outbursts of public indignation seen in Lagos for many years. Students from the University at Ibadan marched on the House in Lagos and manhandled some of the ministers. The debate in the House took the form of a violent criticism of the government, the opposition demanding that the agreement be abrogated immediately because it was a limitation on Nigerian sovereignty. Although the agreement was finally ratified, the controversy continued. The Action Group seized on the Defense Pact as a political club with which to belabor the coalition government as inadequate and fumbling. The defense question appears to have been the beginning of Mr. Awolowo's move away from his former resolutely pro-Western stand. He afterward publicly accused Britain of seeking to reimpose imperial control in the guise of diplomatic and administrative relations. In the debate in the House on foreign policy early in December, 1960, the chief opposition foreign policy specialist, Chief Anthony Enahoro, demanded that trade with the Iron Curtain countries be increased, that more Nigerians be educated in the East, and that the government set a five-year time limit for decolonization in Africa.

The storm which arose over the Defense Pact derives from extreme sensitivity to any suspicion of continuing British domination of an independent Nigeria. As some observers have pointed out, the Pact can be unilaterally abrogated, and under it there is very little likelihood of Nigeria being involved in a war against her will. The military assistance offered is in fact no greater than that at present being offered to Ghana. Apart from its utility as a point of attack for the opposition, the Defense Pact debate did, however, focus attention on Nigeria's desire to prove that she is capable of a genuinely independent leadership of the West African states and that she is prepared to forego if necessary an advantageous arrangement for her own defense to demonstrate her freedom from obligation to any of the great power centers.

Outside the political parties there is little evidence of organized pressure groups designed solely to influence government action on foreign policy. There are, however, groups whose major purpose is to bring about certain internal reforms in Nigeria who have expressed their views on external policy from time to time in the press. The Zikist National Vanguard protested strongly the continued employment after independence of an expatriate as private secretary to the Prime Minister and joined the more recently organized Pan-African Youths Movement in a number of public meetings at which the government was urged to espouse more closely the Ghanaian concepts of Pan-Africanism. Although both these groups maintain only a loose affiliation with the NCNC, their views are from time to time embarrassing to the party in its role as a member of the government coalition.

A somewhat more important pressure group which directed its attention to foreign policy from time to time during 1960 was the Nigerian Socialist Group. The Group, based in Enugu in the Eastern Region, denied that it had any connection to a political party, claiming that it was a "discussion group drawn from the existing parties and outside. . . . All members have common socialist beliefs." Its appeal was largely to the younger militant groups such as those who made up the Pan-African Youths Movement. The assertion that it was without party affiliation was borne out by the fact that among its major spokesmen were the Minister of Information in the Eastern Region, Mr. B. C. Okwu, and the head of the opposition in the Eastern House, the Action Group leader, Mr. Ikoku. Mr. Okwu made a number of speeches to youth groups on Nigerian foreign policy; and in a talk in the Enugu sports stadium in March, 1960, as part of the "Nigeria Week" organized by the Group, he laid down the principles upon which the Group believed Nigerian policy should be based. The Socialist Group favored a militant form of Pan-Africanism and believed that the fight against Western imperialism could be won in the end only by a united effort of all African states. Imperialism was blamed for the debasement of the African, and in view of this Mr. Okwu maintained that "it borders on insanity for anyone to suggest for Nigeria a policy of alignment with the West. The Western bloc is responsible for all present and future suffering of the African." Russia, on the other hand, was not responsible for the detention of Jomo Kenyatta, nor of Hastings Banda, and, therefore, "Nigeria's doors should be thrown open to the East and West without discrimination." The influence of the Socialist Group was limited, but the fact that high officials of both parties in the Eastern Region were prepared to take a public stand in support of its program made it of more than casual importance. Mr. Okwu's statements were given broad press coverage both in the *Pilot* and in the official government news releases in the Eastern Region. It is clear that his appeal to youth was far from falling on deaf ears, and the response the Socialist Group elicited may well have been a factor in the later changes in the policy of the Action Group in particular.

Organized labor has from time to time spoken out upon foreign policy issues, but unfortunately labor comment appears to be couched frequently in terms of the interests of one or another faction of the labor movement, rather than in terms of over-all Nigerian national interest. From the so-called Imoudu faction of the Trades Union Congress Mr. Okwu received warm support for his views on Pan-Africanism. This same faction petitioned the Prime Minister urging a neutralist foreign policy and support

of Mr. Nkrumah's effort to form a union of West African states.
The opposing faction of the Congress, led by Mr. L. L. Borha,
accused the Imoudu faction of taking a leftist line by its support of the Ghanaian initiative to form an All-African Trade
Union Federation. The Borha faction did not improve Ghanaian-
Nigerian relations by blaming the Ghana Trades Union Congress
for being "a positive source of Communist infiltration into the
workers of this country." The basis for this suspicion appears to
have been the attendance by the Imoudu faction at the meeting in Accra looking toward the formation of the All-African
Trade Union Federation; from this the Borha faction deduced
that the Ghanaian TUC (and therefore the CPP) was trying to
split the Nigerian labor movement (which was already hope-
lessly split) and, by implication, to undermine Nigerian independence.

The Casablanca Conference in June, 1961, which established
the All-African Trade Union Federation, did little to heal the
breach between the Nigerian and Ghanaian labor federations.
Representatives of one wing of the Nigerian labor movement attended the meeting and voted for the controversial resolution
disaffiliating the AATUF from the ICFTU, but the Acting General Secretary of the opposing Nigerian faction, Mr. Eric Hen-
shaw, branded the Conference a complete failure because the decisions were taken by representatives of splinter groups and "hired
hooligans," who represented nobody but themselves. Potentially
the labor movement in Nigeria might well play an important role
in the shaping of public opinion on foreign policy, but the force
of labor's views cannot impress the government until labor speaks
with one voice.

V. The Future of Nigerian Foreign Policy

After only a few months of independence Nigeria is still grop-
ing for a foreign policy upon which the major parties can at least
agree in principle. The precise boundaries of Nigerian influence
in African politics are by no means clear as yet although the

Monrovia Conference went a long way toward indicating the kind of role Nigeria may be expected to play in future. The dispatch of Nigerian troops to the Congo created a new public awareness at home of the fact that Nigeria now has a place in world affairs as well as on the African scene. The widespread popular interest in African problems indicates that Nigerian influence will continue for the immediate future to be directed primarily toward the liberation of the remaining colonial areas from European control.

There appears to be a growing realization that a united front at home on the major issues of foreign policy is necessary if Nigeria is going to assume a decisive role in African politics. On the question of non-alignment or neutrality the parties are drawing closer although the specific meaning of the terms is yet to be fully agreed upon. The apparent modification in the position of the Opposition on non-alignment stems directly from the controversy over the Defense Pact, but it is also quite possible that the Action Group is responding to a gradual shift in Nigerian public opinion. The Defense Pact issue points up the tendency in Nigeria, as in other West African states, to equate the demonstration of real independence with the adoption of an anti-Western line. The Action Group is under a certain pressure to prove to the public that it is no less favorable to a strong assertion of Nigerian independence than is the NCNC. Foreshadowing Chief Awolowo's recent statements was an editorial in the *Daily Express* of November, 1960, posing the question of Action Group policy directly:

The Prime Minister has said that his government will not align with any bloc as a matter of routine, a policy with which very few will disagree. But does this mean also nonalignment on the economic, technical, cultural and military fronts as well as on the ideological front? . . . The Opposition spokesmen . . . must make clear that alignment with the West on an ideological basis is possible without military pacts with the Western democracies; and that an open door policy on the economic, technical and cultural front cannot put into jeopardy the ideological ideals which the country believes in.[7]

The Soviet Government is, of course, anxious to prove that there are positive benefits for Nigeria in a non-alignment policy. Despite Sir Abubakar's obvious deliberation in establishing diplo-

[7] *Daily Express* (Lagos), Nov. 24, 1960.

matic relations, the Soviets apparently felt that Nigeria was sufficiently important to submit willingly to his condition that they wait in line and take their turn with everyone else in making their request for exchange of representatives. The Soviet press did not give a great deal of attention to Nigerian independence, and there are only a handful of Nigerian students studying in Moscow. Soviet interest might rapidly increase, however, if Nigeria were to give any sign whatever of receptivity to Soviet advances. So long as Nigeria maintains her present posture of lukewarm interest in Pan-Africanism the Soviet Union's hands are in some degree fettered. The Russians undoubtedly find the Ghanaian and Guinean commitment to Pan-Africanism much more congenial than the Nigerian attitude, and they are tempted to side with these smaller countries. At the same time they are aware of Nigeria's greater potentialities as an influential factor in West African politics. Too great a display of interest in either Ghana or Nigeria may well alienate one of the two; the Soviets therefore must be content to await a further evaluation of Nigeria's role before making a decision to favor one side or the other.

For purely practical reasons Nigeria's ties with the West will remain quite strong for the foreseeable future. Her entire educational system is British-based and Western-oriented, and Nigeria will be dependent for some years on the West for continued assistance in the expansion of her educational system, particularly in the form of short-term teaching personnel. Her economy is still geared to the trade pattern developed during the period of colonial relationship, and even if the government desires to change the present pattern, it will take some years before new markets and new sources of imports can be developed. Continued financial aid from Britain is expected, although Chief Awolowo took umbrage at the fact that the United Kingdom Government lumped Nigeria with the British dependent territories in making financial arrangements to retain the services of some expatriate officers for a further period of years. With the cutting off of Colonial Development and Welfare Funds at independence, Nigeria had to seek some replacement for this source of aid, and her first inclination was to turn to Britain and the United States.

The basic dilemma—centering about the psychological need to assert full political independence and sovereignty while being forced to submit to a continuing state of economic dependence— will continue to plague Nigeria's foreign policy makers for some time. While the basically pro-Western orientation of Nigeria's present generation of leaders is clear, the West, and particularly the United States, cannot afford to take this point of view for granted. There are pressures building up inside and outside Nigeria which may bring about a radical change in the Nigerian position; the West should not be surprised if non-alignment shortly begins to become a much more prominent theme in Nigerian foreign policy than it has been in the past. The rising generation of younger Nigerian leaders may well be prepared to sacrifice a continuing relationship to the West if this relationship appears likely to threaten Nigeria's potential position of leadership in African politics.

Part Three

Problems of Economic Development

7

Population Movements and Economic Development in Nigeria

Joseph J. Spengler

Sometimes the sagacity of a superior mind can even anticipate the results of experience.

A. A. Cournot, in *Mathematical Principles of the Theory of Wealth*, chap. i

The future is big with every possibility of achievement and of tragedy.

A. N. Whitehead, in *Modes of Thought*, chap. ix

Among the main determinants of economic development are population movements. This essay has to do with the manner in which these movements may affect the progress of economic development in Nigeria. Analysis will be conducted in terms of the impact of such movements upon conventionally measured income per capita, it being assumed that income per capita is the best single indicator of improvement in the average lot of a population. Analysis will be carried on at two levels, the theoretical and the empirical, both because the available data are incomplete and because they yield considerable meaning only when fed into appropriate models. The first portion of this paper has to do with theoretical aspects of the subject, and the second, with its empirical dimensions.

I. Population Movements and Their Effects: Theoretical

Both population movements and their effects may be dealt with in theoretical terms. The population movements of principal concern are natural growth and migration, each of which conditions a population's size and may modify its composition and its distribution in space. These movements, together with their impact upon population composition and distribution, condition the magnitude of a population's per capita income, the rate of change in this magnitude, and possibly the manner in which aggregate income is distributed.

(1) *Natural Growth: Demographic and Economic Effects*

Natural growth, together with its impact upon the composition and the spatial distribution of a population, is the product of mortality and fertility. A population's longer-run rate of growth depends, as does its age composition, upon the behavior of both its mortality and fertility. Otherwise the composition of population depends wholly (e.g., genetic) or in part (e.g., tribal, educational, occupational) upon the extent to which fertility, mortality, and (hence) natural increase vary from one component group to another. Similarly, a population's distribution in space may be conditioned by interregional differences in the rate of natural increase. Age composition and so-called tribal [1] composition are of considerable economic significance, as is a population's spatial distribution. Genetic composition may or may not be significant. Changes in population composition may be important even though they are not primarily the result of intergroup differences in nat-

[1] A tribe is conceived of as a culture-bearing social unit; its numbers may therefore be affected by intertribal movement as well as by natural increase. There is considerable disagreement among Africanists respecting what constitutes a tribe, and to what extent various elements of Nigeria's present population are describable as tribes. My concern is with cultural elements of tribal origin which retard economic development. For a description of the tribal composition of Nigeria's population, see G. P. Murdock, "The Traditional Socio-Political Systems of Nigeria: An Introductory Survey," *supra*, chap. i; also see Murdock, *Africa, Its Peoples and Their Culture History* (New York, 1959).

ural increase and intergroup shifts of population. My discussion will be confined to age, tribal, and spatial composition.

(a) *Natural growth: demographic effects.* The behavior of natural increase, depending as it does upon the behavior of age-specific mortality and age-specific fertility, may be examined in terms of a stable-population model of the sort summarized in Table 1.[2] Use of this sort of model enables one to avoid restrictions imposed by the use of stationary populations.[3] It also enables one to rule out the impact of transitional influences,[4] given that one's concern is with the long run instead of with shorter periods and associated short-run problems that are significantly affected by these transitional influences. Finally, it enables us to indicate the dimenisons of the population problem and something of the population prospect, even though data are sparse and defective.

Returning to Table 1 and reading horizontally, one notes that, given an unchanging gross reproduction rate of 3 (which implies a crude birth rate of between 43 and 48), the crude rate of natural increase in the stable population (produced by this gross reproduction rate and the postulated set of age-specific death rates) steadily rises as mortality declines and expectation of life at birth increases. With life expectancies at birth of 50–64 years we find associated very high rates of natural increase (i.e., 3–3.4 per cent per year), and even with a life expectancy of so little as 40 we find correlated a rate of increase of 2.3 per cent. These figures are significant inasmuch as gross reproduction, while on rare occasions as high as 4 (implying birth rates of 53–64 and natural increase rates of 11–49 per 1000), seldom rises much above 3 even when fertility is subject to little or no control through use of contraceptives. Should gross reproduction be as low as 2.5, but

[2] See p. 150.
[3] A stationary population is but one member of the species stable population. For example, see "The Cause of the Aging of Populations: Declining Mortality or Declining Fertility," *Population Bulletin of the United Nations*, No. 4 (Dec., 1954), pp. 30–38.
[4] For example, see F. Lorimer, "Dynamics of Age Structure in a Population with Initially High Fertility and Mortality," *ibid.*, No. 1 (Dec., 1951), pp. 31–41, and "Some Quantitative Aspects of the Aging of Western Populations," *ibid.*, pp. 42–57.

Table 1. *Population Growth under Stable Population Conditions* *

G.R.R.†	E = 30				E = 40				E = 50				E = 60.4				E = 70.2			
	P.	B.R.	D.R.	N.I.	P.	B.R.	D.R.	N.I.	P.	B.R.	D.R.	N.I.	P.	B.R.	D.R.	N.I.	P.	B.R.	D.R.	N.I.
3.0	54.5	47.7	33.7	14.0	52.5	46.0	23.3	22.7	50.9	44.9	15.8	29.1	49.6	43.8	9.6	34.2	48.4	42.9	4.8	38.1
2.5	57.6	40.6	33.2	7.4	55.6	39.3	23.2	16.1	53.9	38.4	16.0	22.4	52.6	37.7	10.1	27.6	51.4	37.0	5.5	31.5
2.0	60.9	32.7	33.6	-0.9	55.8	31.7	23.7	8.0	57.2	31.1	16.8	14.3	55.8	30.6	11.1	19.5	54.7	30.1	6.8	23.3
1.5	63.8	23.8	35.0	-11.2	61.6	23.1	25.6	-2.5	60.0	22.7	18.8	3.9	58.7	22.5	13.5	9.0	57.7	22.3	9.4	12.9
1.0	65.0	14.0	39.9	-25.9	62.6	13.6	30.9	-17.3	60.7	13.4	24.3	-10.9	59.4	13.3	19.0	-5.7	58.6	13.3	15.1	-1.8

* This table derives from United Nations Organization, *The Aging of Population and Its Economic and Social Implications* (New York, 1956), p. 27.
† Abbreviations used are as follows: G.R.R.—Gross Reproduction Rate; E—Expectation of life at birth; P—percentage of stable population aged 15–59; B.R.—Births per 1000 inhabitants; D.R.—Deaths per 1000 inhabitants; N.I.—Excess of births over deaths per 1000 inhabitants. .

with life expectancy ranging from 40 to 70, the rate of natural increase would fall within the range 1.6–3.2 per cent per year. Given that gross reproduction approximates 2.5–3.0 and that life expectancy falls within the range 40–50 years, the rate of natural increase falls within the range 1.6–2.9 per cent per year. This rate will exceed 1 per cent even if life expectancy falls somewhat short of 40. The limited information available respecting population growth in Nigeria, when interpreted in terms of Table 1, suggests, as we note later, that the rate of population growth, though high (i.e., probably about 2 per cent) already, is still susceptible of being greatly increased through mortality reduction.

When one reads Table 1 vertically, several facts stand out. With a life expectancy of below 40, a gross reproduction rate of close to 2 is essential to a population's longer-run replacement. This circumstance helps to explain why peoples living in relatively backward economies tend to infuse a fertility-fostering bias into their reproduction-oriented institutions,[5] even though the drive of sex is imperious enough under most circumstances to outweigh, if only slightly, the forces making for death.[6] With a life expectancy of 50 and over, however, quite high rates of natural increase are produced by gross reproduction rates that little more than sustained populations so long as mortality remained high (i.e., with life expectancy in or below the 30's, as was true of most of the world's population 175 years ago). Yet, because these high gross reproduction rates remain underpinned by fertility-fostering social arrangements as well as by an imperious sexual drive, it is difficult to reduce them even when the need for high fertility rates is past. Herein lies the origin of the Malthusian trap discussed below, in which many backward populations are caught, with the result that improvements in capacity to produce goods tend to be swamped by increases in population consequent upon such improvements.[7]

[5] While such bias may have been inspired in part by rational considerations, it is also the product of favorable accident and social selection. E.g., see G. P. Murdock, *Social Structure* (New York, 1949), pp. 4, 9–12.
[6] The imperiousness of this drive is inferable from the universal effort of society to regulate it. On such regulation see *ibid.*, chap. ix.
[7] For example, see Harvey Leibenstein, *Economic Backwardness and Economic Growth* (New York, 1957), chaps. iii, viii, x.

Examination of the columns headed P indicates that, *with life expectancy given*, decline in gross reproduction is accompanied by increase in the percentage of the population found in the age-group 15–59. This percentage constitutes a rough index of a population's *potential* productive power per capita under *ceteris paribus* conditions. It indicates, for example, that, given a gross reproduction rate of 1.5, potential productive power per capita is 17–19 per cent greater than given a gross reproduction rate of 3. Of course, *ceteris paribus* conditions may not rule. There may be significant differences in technology, in a population's stock of productive factors complementary to labor, in the relative importance of the agricultural sector, in hours worked per man, in the extent to which women as well as males under 15 or above 59 participate in the labor force, in the correlation of age with both productivity per worker and the participation of males aged 15–59 in the labor force, and so on.[8] Furthermore, should life expectancy rise as gross reproduction falls, much of the improvement consequent upon fertility reduction might be canceled; thus a combination of G.R.R. = 2.5 with E = 30 gives practically the same fraction aged 15–59 as does a combination of G.R.R. = 1.5 with E = 70.2. Nonetheless, under similar mortality conditions, the fraction of the population of working age will be decidedly larger (say one-sixth) when gross reproduction is relatively low, and the average individual will therefore have more goods and/or more leisure at his disposal. Furthermore, it will then be much easier to educate the young, for with high fertility about twice as large a fraction of the labor force would be required to educate those of school age.[9]

[8] For example, see John Durand, "Population Structure as a Factor in Manpower and Dependency Problems of Under-developed Countries," *Population Bulletin of the United Nations*, No. 3 (Oct., 1953), pp. 1–16; also United Nations Organization, *The Aging of Populations*, Part III. (Hereinafter, when appearing as the author in notes, United Nations Organization will be abbreviated UNO.)

[9] For example, with high fertility, 55 of each 100 thousands of population might fall in the age-group 15–64 and 42 thousands in the age-group 0–14; whereas, in a low-fertility population, the corresponding figures would be in the neighborhood of 65 and 25 thousands. Then, with a given pupil-teacher ratio, and with the age-groups 0–14 and 15–64 assumed to reflect the demand for and the supply of teachers, the fraction of those aged 15–64 required to teach those aged 0–14 would be twice as high in the high-fertility as in the low-fertility population (i.e., [42/55] ÷ [25/65] approximates 2).

(b) *Natural growth: economic effects.* The economic effects of the variations in natural growth described in the preceding section may be examined under three headings: (i) those associated with changes in age composition; (ii) those associated with population growth as such; and (iii) those associated with increase in the ratio of a population to its habitat.

(i) It need only be observed that when a population is growing 2–3 per cent per year and therefore includes a relatively small number of persons of productive age, its *potential* productive power per capita will be 10–15 per cent below what it could be if its rate of growth were very low. It may also be observed that its capacity to educate its youth will be lower. As will be indicated below, both these unfavorable effects are associated with the age composition of the population of Nigeria.

(ii) When a population is growing, a part of the capital that it forms by adding to its stock of reproducible physical and personal assets must be devoted to equipping the resulting increments to the population. In consequence the amount of reproducible physical assets available per person or per worker will be lower than it otherwise would have been and per capita productive power will therefore be lower. While it is not possible to measure this adverse effect of population growth with precision, its order of magnitude may be suggested. If a population is growing 2–3 per cent per year, it must increase its stock of wealth 2–3 per cent per year merely to maintain its wealth-population ratio at a constant level. If the wealth-income ratio falls within the range of 3–5, a saving ratio of 3–5 per cent of the national income is required to offset a 1 per cent per year rate of population growth, and a saving ratio of 6–15 per cent to offset a 2–3 per cent per year rate of growth.[10] These figures need to be adjusted upward, say to 8–17 per cent, to provide for the use of manpower and resources in education not otherwise allowed for. While it is quite possible, because of improvements in technology, for per capita income to rise even though the ratio of conventionally measured wealth to population remains unchanged, it needs to

[10] See UNO, ECAFE, *Economic Bulletin for Asia and the Far East,* X, 1 (June, 1959), 28–42. The whole of this number treats of Asian population problems, which resemble those of Africa in a number of respects.

be noted that the rapidity with which technological improvements can be introduced and diffused usually depends upon the rate of capital formation per capita.

How much faster per capita income would grow if the rate of population growth were low instead of high depends upon the extent to which the productive power diverted from equipping increments to a population is utilized instead to increase wealth per capita and upon the forms that this additional wealth assumes. If, with a population growing 3 per cent per year and capital being formed at a rate of 10–12 per cent, per capita income is rising at a rate of x per cent per year, the value of x will probably be below 1 per cent. If, however, this same population were growing less than 0.5 per cent per year and relevant conditions were otherwise similar, per capita income would be rising at a rate of $x + 1$ or more per cent, particularly if the newly formed capital were utilized to introduce improved methods of production which greatly elevated productivity.

It may be noted parenthetically that in practice it probably is easier to keep the composition of a nation's assets up to date when numbers are growing slowly than when they are advancing rapidly, since then a larger fraction of the newly formed capital may readily be used to support the introduction and extension of the most advanced methods of production. Of course, if a heightened rate of population growth gives rise to a heightened rate of capital formation, and most of this increase is incorporated in relatively advanced productive equipment, the composition of a nation's assets will be transformed at a heightened rate. This outcome may be reinforced if the young people being added to the labor force at a heightened rate are adept at learning how to operate the advanced equipment.[11]

Population growth may be the source of certain beneficial effects, however, given that the necessary side conditions are present. An economy whose population is growing may prove

[11] If both the rate of population growth and therefore the rate of capital formation were accelerating, the rate at which the stock of physical assets was augmented would rise, but probably not enough to generate a capital-transformation rate in excess of rates easily attainable if the population were growing slowly under otherwise similar conditions. It is transformation of producers' capital that counts, not that of consumers' capital.

more flexible than one whose numbers are not growing, provided that capital is being formed at a sufficiently high rate and that individuals readily find employment upon their attainment of working age. Insofar as young people are capable of adopting advanced methods decidedly faster than older people, it may prove easier to modernize a population that is growing rapidly, given the necessary teachers and physical assets.[12] These and other beneficial effects consequent upon population growth are much less likely to be realized in an underdeveloped than in a developed country, particularly when the underdeveloped country is one in which population already is dense (at least in its easily cultivable areas) and per capita income, capital formation, and educational attainments are very low. Nigeria, it will be seen, does not appear to be a country in which a high rate of population growth is likely to be accompanied by significant beneficial effects even though over-all population density there is much below Asia's.

(iii) Under (ii) attention was concentrated upon effects associated with augmenting reproductive assets faster than population. Hereunder attention will be concentrated upon effects associated with a population's being larger instead of smaller and with increases in the ratio of a population to those of its natural resources which are fixed in supply (e.g., land, hydroelectric potential) or depletable (e.g., fossil-fuel resources, metallic reserves). Increase in a population's size tends to be accompanied (within limits) by increase in internal division of labor and other changes making for economies of scale or increasing returns; it may compel or facilitate reorganization of an economy; it may improve a population's environment (e.g., if increase in over-all density makes for the elimination of various diseases); and so on. Increase in the ratio of population to agricultural land or other natural resources eventually tends to be accompanied by decrease in physical output per unit of labor input unless improvements in methods and increase in capital more than offset this tendency.

Population growth, when coupled with shortage of land and/or

[12] Concerning some of these conditions, see my "The Population Problem: Yesterday, Today, Tomorrow," *Southern Economic Journal,* XXVII (Jan., 1961), 194–208.

of other natural resources, usually is a greater deterrent to the rise of per capita income in an underdeveloped country such as Nigeria than in an advanced one. This may be illustrated with the help of Arnold Harberger's formulation of the Malthusian problem, an illustration which I have used elsewhere.[13] Let R represent the annual rate of growth of national output when the labor force is stationary; L, the annual rate of growth of the labor force; F, the fraction of output imputable to the labor force; and Y, the annual rate of growth of national output, expressed in percentages as are R and L. Then $Y = FL + R$; and since per capita income will remain stationary so long as $Y = L = R/(1 - F)$, the highest rate of population growth compatible with the non-reduction of living standards is $R/(1 - F)$. $R = IP + T$, when I represents the annual rate of net investment; P, the rate of productivity of new investment, I; and T, the rate of increase in income per year attributable to the elements or changes included under "technological progress." Accordingly, if in underdeveloped countries I approximates 5 per cent, P approximates 0.15–0.2, and T approximates 1 per cent, R will approximate 1.75–2.0 per cent, whereas in advanced countries it might approximate 2–4 per cent. In underdeveloped countries, therefore, under the conditions assumed and with F approximating 0.5 or 0.6, population could grow 3–4 per cent per year and yet not outstrip Y and thereby depress per capita income. Of course, if the population grew only 0.5 per cent, per capita income would rise roughly between 2 and 3 per cent. The value of R depends upon an underdeveloped country's joint capacity to form capital, to educate its population appropriately, to introduce improved methods of production, and to utilize these methods and available capital with optimum effectiveness; and this capacity in turn tends to be associated negatively with population growth and positively with natural-resource plenty.

Let us now suppose that Nigeria's population were approximately stationary instead of growing about 2 per cent per year.

[13] His model is employed in his "Variations on a Theme by Malthus," in R. G. Francis, ed., *The Population Ahead* (Minneapolis, 1958), pp. 108–24. I used his statement in my essay in Spengler, ed., *Natural Resources and Economic Growth* (Baltimore, 1961), pp. 300–1.

On the assumption that labor-force-participation rates by age remained unchanged, output per capita would be about 10 per cent higher. There would also be the equivalent of 6–8 per cent of national income available for increasing assets per head. The pressure of numbers upon natural resources would not be increasing. In sum, the average individual would dispose of about one-sixth more income, or its equivalent, which might be invested or devoted to consumption and leisure.

A country may be described as being caught in a Malthusian trap when improvements in productive power and hence in income are small and succeeded by increases in population, with the result that total income increases little (if any) more rapidly than population. Most of the world answered to this description prior to the eighteenth century and much of it apparently still does. Prior to the eighteenth century population grew very slowly (e.g., about ⅓ per cent per year in Europe and Asia in 1650–1750), but apparently so did aggregate income in most countries. At present, aggregate income usually increases, but this increase is often very nearly offset by population increase, which now often approximates 2–3 per cent or more per year. Escape consists initially in making aggregate income increase enough faster than little regulated population, or in regulating numbers and reducing the rate of population growth appreciably below that of aggregate income; for then per capita income can rise fast enough to augment the average propensity to save and enable capital to increase continuously and more rapidly than population. When this happens, per capita income should continue to rise, particularly if innovation reinforces the income-increasing effect of a rising capital-population ratio and if, as is likely, socio-economic changes associated with income increase make for greater recourse to contraceptive measures or for more effective use of them.[14] Presumably escape is possible today if population does not grow more than 2 per cent per year, and it may even be possible if population grows somewhat more rapidly; but escape

[14] For example, see R. R. Nelson, "Growth Models and the Escape from the Low-Level Equilibrium Trap: The Case of Japan," *Economic Development and Cultural Change*, VIII, 1 (July, 1960), 378–88. See also on Japan and Taiwan, *Economic Bulletin for Asia and the Far East*, pp. 37–40.

is much more likely, and per capita income can progress much more rapidly, if fertility is controlled and the rate of population growth is held below 1 per cent.[15]

(2) *Migration, Mobility, Composition: Their Economic Effects*

A disposition to migrate to places where economic opportunity is greater is essential to economic development, just as is a disposition to change employment when individual output (income) is thereby increased. Given enough mobility and a sufficiently strong disposition on the part of workers to migrate, an economy will remain flexible and the population will achieve a roughly optimal distribution of labor and other agents of production in geographic and economic space (i.e., among industries, occupations, etc.).

Table 2.

	Attributes	
Occupation	Relevant	Irrelevant
A	abcdef	ghij
B	abcde	ghi
C	abcd	gh
D	abc	g
E	ab	—
F	a	—

What has been said may be illustrated. Suppose the labor force is distributed among six occupations A–F. Suppose, further, that one must have attributes *abcdef* to be technically qualified to fill occupation A, and fewer attributes to fill occupations B–F (as shown in columns 1 and 2 in Table 2). Then, as illustrated in Table 3, in the absence of artificial barriers, an equilibrium situation would come into being. At equilibrium wage w_a the supply S_a of persons qualified for occupation A would be roughly in bal-

---

[15] The contribution that decrease in fertility can make to increase of per capita income is admirably demonstrated in respect of India and Mexico by A. J. Coale and E. M. Hoover, in *Population Growth and Economic Development in Low-Income Countries* (Princeton, 1958).

ance with the demand D_a for such persons, and the relative number of these involuntarily unemployed, u_a, would be quite small. Of course, if schedule S_a intersected D_a at $w_a < w_b$ individuals would tend to move out of employment A into employment B until w_a approximated w_b. In general, so long as individuals stood to better their rates of remuneration by moving and were free to do so, they would tend to change occupations. Such movement would give rise to an optimum distribution of workers among occupations, though whether an optimum optimorum were reached would depend on whether other conditions essential to such optimum were operative. Unlike most economic universes, of course, the universe envisaged in Tables 2 and 3 normally implies movement in but one direction, namely, downward.

Table 3.

Equilibrium		Disequilibrium	
$S_a = D_a$ at w_a	$u_a \sim 0$ *	$w'_a > w_a$	$u'_a > U_a$
$S_b = D_b$ at w_b	$u_b \sim 0$	$w'_b > w_b$	$u'_b > U_b$
$S_c = D_c$ at w_c	$u_c \sim 0$	$w'_c > w_c$	$u'_c > U_c$
$S_d = D_d$ at w_d	$u_d \sim 0$	$w'_d > w_d$	$u'_d > U_d$
$S_e = D_e$ at w_e	$u_e \sim 0$	$w'_e < w_e$	$u'_e \sim U_e$
$S_f = D_f$ at w_f	$u_f \sim 0$	$w'_f < w_f$	$u'_f \sim U_f$

* $\sim$ signifies "approximates"

A less satisfactory distribution of workers among occupations results if possession of irrelevant attributes is also insisted upon. For example, it might be stipulated that an individual could engage in occupation A only if he possessed both relevant attributes *abcdef* and irrelevant attributes *ghij*. The effect of this condition would be to restrict the number of individuals able to qualify, since only some, but not all, of those with relevant attributes *abcdef* would also possess irrelevant attributes *ghij*. In consequence, as illustrated in Table 3 (columns 4–5), the wage resulting would be $w'_a > w_a$, there would be greater unemployment among those technically qualified for A (i.e., $u'_a > u_a$), and some of these unemployed persons would move from A to B unless also barred from B by the non-possession of all the required irrelevant attributes *ghi.* At what point such movement would stop would depend upon the pattern of irrelevant attributes operative. In Table 3, however, it is suggested that under the disequilibrium conditions associated with the presence of the designated irrelevant attributes (see last column of Table 2), fewer persons would be employed in occupations *A–C* than under the equilibrium conditions obtaining when only demand schedules and relevant attributes were controlling; and that more persons would be employed in occupations *D–F*.

Aggregate output will be greater when only relevant attributes govern the supply of labor available to particular occupations than when irrelevant attributes also condition this supply. How much greater aggregate output will be (given essentially static technological conditions) depends upon both the occupational distribution of the persons employed and the extent to which members of the labor force are unemployed. It is supposed that the values assumed by u_a–u_f are positive, but small. The values u'_a–u'_c and possibly also u'_d would be greater than corresponding values u_a–u_d; but values u'_e and u'_f would not differ greatly from u_e and u_f, given that complementary inputs were available and that D_e and D_f were sufficiently large to absorb technically competent persons denied access to occupations *A–D.* While a part of the resulting loss of output will be incident on persons technically qualified to fill occupations *A–C* but denied access thereto, some of the loss will be incident also upon those qualified only to fill occupations *D–F*, and some will fall upon possessors of complementary agents of production which consequently are utilized at lower rates.[16] Given dynamic conditions, the loss of output occasioned by the introduction of irrelevant qualifications would be even greater. For, since some of those denied access to occupations *A–D* would have relatively high propensities to save or to innovate, capital formation and the income-increasing effects of innovation would be less than they otherwise would have been.

In Nigeria, as in many African states, emphasis upon irrelevant qualifications is likely to flow from cultural residues associated

---

[16] Concerning the economic effects and the incidence of discrimination see Gary S. Becker, *The Economics of Discrimination* (Chicago, 1957).

with the past or the present tribal composition of the population; for, as shown later, tribal distinctions of the sort that disappeared from Western Europe many centuries ago often remain operative. In general, economic development is retarded insofar as membership in a given tribe (or cluster of culturally similar tribes), or some guild-like or other (e.g., age-set) component thereof, is made a qualification for access to employment in a given occupation at a given place. Accordingly, whatever facilitates the dissipation of such insistence and of the value orientations [17] upon which it rests is conducive (*ceteris paribus*) to economic development. In Africa in general and in Nigeria in particular urbanization, nationalism, federationist movements, and perhaps universal religions (e.g., Christianity, Islam) may be included among these salutary dissipative forces.[18] For these processes gradually eventuate in an individual's turning from tribal to other institutions for the satisfaction of his needs. Thus removal to town entails replacement of memberships in tribal associations by memberships in urban economic, political, and religious associations; [19] but it does not sever the individual's connections with the traditional society into which he was born, nor is he likely to do so until this type of society has been superseded by a "modern"

[17] See Talcott Parsons' analysis of the underlying value orientations in his *The Social System* (Glencoe, Ill., 1951), pp. 101–14; also, M. J. Levy, Jr., *The Structure of Society* (Princeton, 1952), pp. 421–43. See S. N. Eisenstadt's analysis of the allocative role of age-sets, in "African Age Groups," *Africa*, XXIV (April, 1954), 100–10; also International Labour Office, *African Labour Survey* (Geneva, 1958), p. 66.

[18] On the role of nationalism, see Rupert Emerson, *From Empire to Nation* (Cambridge, Mass., 1960), and Bert F. Hoselitz, "Nationalism, Economic Development and Democracy," in Hoselitz, ed., *Agrarian Societies in Transition* (*Annals of the American Academy of Political and Social Science, CCCV* [May, 1956]) pp. 1–11. On the role of urbanism, see James S. Coleman, "The Politics of Sub-Saharan Africa," in Gabriel A. Almond and Coleman, eds., *The Politics of the Developing Areas* (Princeton, 1960), pp. 270–74; R. Redfield and M. B. Singer, "The Cultural Role of Cities," *Economic Development and Cultural Change*, III, 1 (Oct., 1954), 53–73, esp. pp. 63 ff. As Hoselitz points out, however, the agglomeration of diverse cultural groups in a city may not eventuate in sufficient cultural homogeneity and may even swamp those elements whose values are most favorable to economic development. See his *Sociological Aspects of Economic Growth* (Glencoe, Ill. 1960), pp. 203 ff. His argument probably fits some Asian situations better than those encountered in Africa. On federationist movements see M. J. Herskovits, *Africa* (A Study Prepared at the Request of the Committee on Foreign Relations of the United States Senate [Pursuant to S. Res. 336, 85th Cong., and S. Res. 31, 86th Cong.], Oct. 23, 1959), pp. 27 ff.

[19] E.g., see Michael Banton, "Adaptation and Integration in the Social System of Temne Immigrants in Freetown," *Africa*, XXVI (Oct., 1956), 354 ff.

type.[20] Under *ceteris paribus* conditions, of course, "moderniza-tion" can proceed more rapidly when, as in Nigeria, race member-ship as such is not a barrier to employment in high-level occupa-tions.

Adverse effects consequent upon the interference of tribal alle-giance with economic mobility may be accentuated if such allegiance makes unduly difficult achievement of the degree of consensus requisite for the formulation and administration of de-velopment-oriented policies, or prevents control of the apparatus of state by groups willing and able to carry out such policies even in the absence of consensus.[21] It is not yet clear whether the di-verse ethnic groups and subgroups composing the population of Nigeria (or that of any other African state) have been able to achieve a persisting consensus. Undoubtedly, some small sense of unity was generated by the fact that these diverse elements were under the rule of a colonial administration responsible for the entire politically created country of Nigeria. The governing elite that has emerged in this state resembles that which has emerged in various other African states; its outlook is national, rather than tribal or local, only about a third having come from old ruling families, and only some of these having filled traditional leadership roles; [22] and it apparently commands the support of much of the populace, in part because it possessed the skills needed to do away with colonial rule and to supply a national ad-

---

[20] For example, see Kenneth Little, "Structural Change in the Sierra Leone Pro-tectorate," *Africa*, XXV (July, 1955), 217–33. Even though the Western indoctrina-tion associated with education makes the educated African "ambitious for personal success in the new careers and occupations opened up to him by contact with the outside world," its culture is still "alien" and not a substitute for that of his tradi-tional society. *Ibid.*, pp. 231–32. See also H. H. Smythe and Mabel M. Smythe. *The New Nigerian Elite* (Stanford, 1960).

[21] For example, on how ethnic differences have accentuated regionalism, see J. R. V. Prescott, "Nigeria's Regional Boundary Problems," *Geographical Review*, XLIX (Oct., 1959), 485–505. Tribalism may not be wholly without beneficial effects. Some salutary intertribal emulation and competition may be generated. Furthermore, where mores and loyalties are pluralistic and diverse, extreme cul-tural homogeneity is avoided and the variance required for progress is conserved. On this point see Claire Russell and W. M. S. Russell, "An Approach to Human Ethnology," *Behavioral Science*, II (July, 1957), 197.

[22] For example, see Smythe, and Smythe, *op. cit.;* Coleman, *op. cit.*, pp. 283 ff., 324 ff.; F. X. Sutton, "Representation and the Nature of Political Systems," *Com-parative Studies in Society and History*, II (Oct., 1959), 1–10.

ministration. Moreover, the expectations of various elements in the population have increased, and more and more individuals count upon the government for help in realizing the expectations and the aspirations that come in the wake of spreading education. Charismatic leadership of the sort associated with Nkrumah also tends to strengthen national ties at the expense of local loyalties. Nonetheless, despite the consensus-producing influences enumerated, the threat of disunity is not wholly past. Disunity will not, however, be averted through a benevolent dictatorship, asserts Herskovits. Instead he anticipates "states with one-party systems, based on wide popular support, having strong executives and weak legislative bodies, and political maneuvering within the party rather than between constituted majority and minority groupings." [23] Such popular support will not continue to be forthcoming, however, if the bureaucracy is greatly overpaid, governmental revenues are wasted on unproductive buildings, and there is consequently but little capital remaining for true economic growth.

II. Population Movements: Economic Development

Having outlined an apparatus of analysis in Part I and indicated its main implications, we may examine the population movements that have taken place in Nigeria, project the movements in prospect, note how the population is distributed in space and among social and tribal categories, indicate the main features of the Nigerian economy, and finally infer how various population factors may affect the course of economic development in Nigeria. These circumstances will be examined in turn; but their examination will entail considerable conjecture, since the data available are quite incomplete.

[23] *Africa*, p. 27. This prospective trend is in line with that outlined by Z. Brzezinski in "The Politics of Underdevelopment," *World Politics*, IX (Oct., 1956), 55–75. See also Coleman, *op. cit.*, pp. 295 ff., on reasons for the emergence of one-party-dominant systems.

(1) *Past and Prospective Population Growth*

The bare facts of Nigeria's purported current population, population density, and supposed rate of growth are reported in Table 4.[24] The population of the Federation—now perhaps close

Table 4. *Population Growth and Density, by Region* †

Region	Area (Km²)	Population per Km²	Midyear population (in thousands) 1953	Midyear population (in thousands) 1958	Annual rate of increase, 1953–58 (%)
Eastern	76,364	104	7,229	7,927	1.9
Northern	684,490	26	16,454	18,043	1.9
Western	117,524	57	6,144	6,736	1.9
Lagos	70	4,942	277	346	4.5
All	878,447	38	30,104	33,052	1.9

† This table derives from United Nations Organization, *Demographic Yearbook, 1959* (New York, 1959), pp. 112, 127.

to 35 millions and comprising about one-fifth of the population of tropical and southern Africa and about one-seventh of the population of the whole of Africa—exceeds that of any other primary political entity situated in that continent. Nigeria's over-all population density as well as the ratio of its population to "usable" land is much greater than that of Africa (which approximated 8 per km.² in 1958) and somewhat greater than that of any other of the larger African political entities. While its rate of growth (supposedly) is about the same as that reported for the continent as a whole, it is well to recall that information regarding growth rates is inadequate for most parts of Africa.[25]

[24] See UNO, *Demographic Yearbook, 1959* (New York, 1959), pp. 112, 127 for data on Africa. The Nigerian data are based upon a census taken in 1952–53 and referred to below. R. M. Prothero endorses the view that this census count was not off more than 3 per cent. See his "The Population Census of Northern Nigeria, 1952: Problems and Results," *Population Studies,* X (Nov., 1956), 181.
[25] The rate of growth reported for Nigeria is subject to error in excess of 5 per 1000; that for some other parts of Africa is subject to even greater error than is Nigeria's. On the state of demographic information regarding Africa, see Frank Lorimer, *Demographic Information on Tropical Africa* (Boston, 1961); Union Internationale pour L'Étude Scientific de la Population, *Problems in African Demography* (Paris, 1960). On African population pressure, see R. W. Stephens, *Population Pressures in Africa South of the Sahara* (Washington, 1958). Con-

One cannot, of course, infer much from growth rates based upon a limited and recent experience, nor can one count much on pre-1950 reports. Until the 1940's the rate of growth was very low. R. R. Kuczynski, in his monumental demographic survey of the British Colonial Empire, concluded his detailed examination of the quite incomplete data relating to mortality, fertility, and population growth in Nigeria, with these words:

It is hardly necessary to add anything concerning Nigeria as a whole. I am inclined to think that the population increased very little, if at all, in the first quarter of the present century, and that it increased somewhat but probably less than 10 per cent in the following 15 years.[26]

Mortality was sufficiently high, as a rule, to counterbalance a fairly high fertility completely or nearly so. In recent years, however, the population has increased somewhat faster, though how much faster is unclear, given the inadequacy of the census of 1931.[27] According to a United Nations projection, Nigeria's population will number some 42 millions by 1975, and, given an unanticipated decline in mortality, could number some 90 millions

cerning the shortcomings of statistical data relating to Nigeria and other parts of Subsaharan Africa, see W. O. Jones, *Manioc in Africa* (Stanford, 1959), pp. 289–94; Helen Farnsworth, "Defects, Uses, and Abuses of Natural Consumption Data," *Food Research Institute Studies*, II (Nov., 1961), 179–202.

[26] *Demographic Survey of the British Colonial Empire*, Vol. I, *West Africa* (London, 1948), p. 762. Pages 524–774 relate to Nigeria and the Cameroons. Mortality long was high even among the Europeans. See *ibid.*, pp. 763 ff. The rate Kuczynski gives for 1925–40, about 7/12 of 1 per cent per year, would double the population in about 140 years. Population estimates for Africa, though of doubtful validity, indicate that the population of Africa did not increase and may have decreased between 1650 and 1850. Apparently, growth did not get under way until peace and order were introduced in the second half of the nineteenth century. For example, see UNO, *The Determinants and Consequences of Population Trends* (New York, 1953), pp. 10–11. Kuczynski's account of mortality in Nigeria (*op. cit.*, pp. 691–759) reminds one of Malthus' account of check-ridden African populations. See *Essay on Population*, 6th ed., Bk. I, chap. viii.

[27] See Kuczynski, *op. cit.*, pp. 570 ff., 596 ff.; also Prothero, *op. cit.*, p. 181, who puts the error of the 1931 census at about 10 per cent. Given a population of 21–22 million as of 1931 and a population of 31.5 million as of 1952–53, population grew at least 43 per cent, or about 1.75 per cent per year. The rate of growth of the population of Middle Africa in 1925–50, which is supposed to typify that of Nigeria, is put at about 1.25 per cent per year in UNO, *The Future Growth of World Population* (New York, 1958), p. 53. The International Bank Commission estimated Nigeria's rate of population growth since the early 1930's at about 1.5 per cent per year. See *The Economic Development of Nigeria* (Baltimore, 1955), p. 11. As of December, 1961, the rate of population growth in tropical and southern Africa in 1950–60 was put at 2.1 per cent per year. See Dorothy Good, "Preliminary Results of 1960 and 1961 Population Censuses," *Population Index*, XXVIII (Jan., 1962), 11.

by the year 2000.[28] Under the circumstances the non-African population, numbering about 17 thousands in 1953 and constituting only about ½₀ of one per cent of the total population would remain insignificant. Nigeria will really be, in Ibn Battúta's phrase, a Negroland.[29]

The use of seemingly concrete and precise figures in respect of the population prospect of Nigeria and Middle Africa is a bit misleading, given the deficiencies in the data. Though gross reproduction varies considerably with people or place, it is below the attainable maximum of about 4—its over-all rate supposedly being in the neighborhood of 3 in Nigeria and in Middle Africa generally.[30] Mortality apparently remains very high. Thus, according to a United Nations study, "expectation of life in Middle Africa may approach 30 years, but it is not very likely to rise much above this figure within the near future." [31] Combination of these fertility and mortality estimates (see Table 1) suggests a rate of natural increase in the neighborhood of 1.5 per cent per year (since the age composition of the population is approximately stable). Accordingly, it is questionable whether the actual rate is as high as the 1.9 per cent reported in Table 4, though it could be if mortality has fallen significantly.

It is probable that the rate of natural increase will rise rather than fall in the immediate future. A decline in fertility is not immediately in prospect; prevailing fertility differences, though pronounced, do not foretoken a decline, nor are the occupational and the educational structures of the population yet of a sort to conduce to such decline. In fact, fertility may increase initially as health and economic conditions improve. Even so, the course of growth will depend predominantly upon the course of mortality. Should the rate of growth rise, it will be because disease is being increasingly throttled rather more than because fertility has risen.

[28] *The Future Growth of World Population*, pp. 70, 72; see also p. 13.
[29] See Hamilton A. R. Gibb, trans., *Travels of Ibn Battúta* (London, 1957), chap. xiv. Ibn Battúta visited Nigeria in 1352. On the Negroes of the Sahara and the Sudan fringe in Battúta's day, see Murdock, *Africa*, chaps. xvi–xvii; also E. W. Bovill, *The Golden Trade of the Moors* (London, 1958).
[30] *The Future Growth of World Population*, pp. 5, 53–54, and UNO, *Report on the World Social Situation* (New York, 1957), pp. 6–7; Frank Lorimer et al., *Culture and Human Fertility* (Paris, 1954), pp. 76, 316–17, 322, 326–27, 332. See also Frank Lorimer and Mark Karp, *Population in Africa* (Boston, 1960), pp. 4–5.
[31] *The Future Growth of World Population*, p. 3.

That disease may be increasingly curbed in Nigeria is plain, given modern methods of disease and death control and the character of the diseases common in that country. For not only is the incidence of some controllable non-localized diseases (e.g., tuberculosis, venereal diseases) high; there is also a great deal of disease of the sort found in countries with low standards of living and hygiene (e.g., fevers, dysentery, meningitis, smallpox, plague, rickettsial disease, leprosy, worm infestation), or that thrives in a warm and humid tropical environment (e.g., malaria, sleeping sickness, yellow fever, yaws, disease due to parasitic worms). Some of these diseases kill quickly; some kill slowly; and some (especially when accompanied by malnutrition, which is common) shorten life, largely by weakening the body and reducing the productive powers of the population; and some also reduce fertility.[32] There is much scope, therefore, for increasing population growth through the control and prevention of many of the diseases now incident. A combined attack on the medical, agricultural, educational, social-service, and public-health fronts is indicated. The task may be rendered more difficult in the immediate future if the diffusion of disease is accentuated by the high mobility of the population and its increasing concentration in towns and cities. Moreover, because of shortages of requisite personnel and resources, together with obstacles interposed by the ignorance, suspicion, etc., of the masses, the assault on disease will probably continue to proceed slowly for several or more decades.[33] In such event Nigeria's population may not grow much more than 1.5

[32] On disease in Nigeria, see K. M. Buchanan and J. C. Pugh, *Land and People in Nigeria* (London, 1955), pp. 41–57. See also G. H. T. Kimble, *Tropical Africa* (New York, 1960), II, 33–51; J. H. Wellington, "Possibilities of Settlement in Africa," in I. Bowman, ed., *Limits of Land Settlement* (New York, 1937), pp. 237–42, 246–48; N. S. Scrimshaw and M. Béhar, "Protein Malnutrition in Young Children," *Science*, CXXXIII (June 30, 1961), 2039–47; Kuczynski, *op. cit.*, pp. 691–759, esp. pp. 696–98, on famines, which occurred so late as the 1920's. The ill effects of malnutrition in childhood cannot be wholly corrected by satisfactory diet in adolescence or adulthood, experience indicates. See L. D. Stamp, *Our Developing World* (London, 1960), p. 58. The high mortality characteristic of their children caused the Yoruba to believe children belong to the Eleru, a race of spirit children, and are not usually destined to remain long. See *African Abstracts*, X (1959), item 213; also see *ibid.*, XII (1961), item 211 on difficulty of teaching the Hausa to control sleeping sickness.
[33] For example, see Kimble, *op. cit.*, II, chap. xvii, also chaps. xvi, xviii; see also *Report on the World Social Situation*, chap. iii. The experience of Ceylon and other underdeveloped countries suggests, however, that mortality can be reduced very rapidly.

per cent per year even though fertility remains at current levels. This rate, nonetheless, would permit Nigeria's numbers to double every forty-seven years.

If mortality and fertility remain comparatively stable, the age composition of Nigeria's population will not change much in the immediate future. Something like 55 per cent of the population will fall within the age group 15–59 and something like 41 per cent will be less than 15. According to the imperfect age data gathered in the census of 1953, 44.3 per cent of the population fell in the age group 0–14, and 47.7 per cent in the age group 15–49.[34] These imperfect data suggest that the actual distribution does not differ markedly from that of a stable population based upon a gross reproduction rate of 3 and a life expectancy of about 30.

It was implied earlier that the growth potential in Nigeria, as in Subsaharan Africa generally, is quite high because, while mortality is susceptible of considerable reduction, fertility is not likely to decline much in the near future. Fertility is affected by a variety of conditions which, even in a people among whom contraceptive practices are little known, prevent the number of live births from being nearly as high as it might, given a population's age and sex structure.[35] Various of these conditions appear to be present in Nigeria as in other parts of Subsaharan Africa. For while there is little knowledge of contraception, spacing of children is customary and there is some knowledge of abortifacients as well as some practice of abortion and infanticide, though opinion differs regarding how great and widespread are attempts to control population growth.[36] Today (as a result of the progress of

[34] Data are not given in a form to permit estimation of the fraction aged 15–59, but it probably approximates 54 per cent. In East Africa only about 41 per cent of the African population is estimated to be under 15 years of age.

[35] See Kingsley Davis and Judith Blake, "Social Structure and Fertility: An Analytic Framework," *Economic Development and Cultural Change*, IV, 3 (April, 1956), 211–35, and literature therein cited; also Frank Lorimer *et al.*, *Culture and Human Fertility*, *passim*; and L. Henry, "Some Data on Natural Fertility," *Eugenics Quarterly*, VIII (June, 1961), 81–91.

[36] See Ardener *et al.*, *op. cit.*, pp. 304–8; Lorimer *et al.*, *op. cit.*, pp. 87–88, 93–94, 102–3, 125–26, 265–358, 367, 390, 393; Kuczynski, *op. cit.*, pp. 677–79, 682–83. For evidence of the regulation of numbers in Africa see *African Abstracts*, VI (1955), items 75 and 383; VII (1957), items 359–80; VIII (1957), items 321 and 537; IX (1958), item 182; X (1959), items 369, 419, 420. See also *ibid.*, XI (1960), item 364, for summary of an account of the Ila, a Northern-Rhodesian

urbanization) perhaps even more than in the past venereal disease makes for infertility.[37] Prolongation of lactation, together with abstinence, is found among some peoples.[38] Polygamy is common, especially among Moslems; it is less favorable to fertility than is monogamy, serving to reduce coitus per wife and sperm emission per coitus, to prolong the period of post-conceptual abstinence, and to increase the divorce rate.[39] In general, variation in fertility by region and people reflects the unevenness with which social and health conditions relatively inimical to fertility are distributed.[40] Fertility-favoring conditions, of course, also are present, but they are less powerful than in parts of Asia and neighboring islands.[41] Thus emphasis upon kinship is widespread as is a

---

tribe numbering about 22,000, which had to bring in slaves to keep up its numbers since abortion and infanticide were so common. According to A. Romaniuk's paper prepared for the world population conference (New York, Sept., 1961) abortion and venereal disease were largely responsible for the lowness of fertility found in parts of the Belgian Congo.

[37] Lorimer *et al.*, *op. cit.*, pp. 248, 300–1, 347–48; also Kuczynski, *op. cit.*, pp. 663, 679, 684–86, 688–89, 691. Poor diet also has had an adverse effect upon fertility. *Ibid.*, pp. 682–83; Lorimer *et al*, *op. cit.*, pp. 22, 127.

[38] Kuczynski, *op. cit.*, pp. 229, 231, 682; Lorimer *et al.*, *op. cit.*, pp. 16, 86–88, 103, 123. Prolongation of lactation, C. Tietze reports in a paper prepared for the world population conference (New York, Sept., 1961), does not afford protection against pregnancy for more than ten months after confinement; thereafter it is of significance only if accompanied by at least a partial tabu on intercourse. Mungo Park, observing that few Mandingo (i.e., Mande) women "have more than five or six children," attributed this to the fact that "three years nursing is not uncommon, and during this period the husband devotes his attention to other wives." See his *Travels in the Interior Districts of Africa* (New York, 1800), chap. xx, p. 263.

[39] See V. R. Dorjahn, "Fertility, Polygyny, and Their Interrelations in Temne Society," *American Anthropologist*, LX (Oct., 1958), 838–60; H. V. Musham, "Fertility of Polygamous Marriages," *Population Studies*, X (July, 1956), 3–16; Kuczynski, *op. cit.*, p. 678. Cairo propaganda holds otherwise. In a recent tract issued in a number of African languages, it is said: "Christian missionaries preach one wife to you in order to make your race diminish. Islam permits four wives." See *Time*, Feb. 3, 1961, p. 25.

[40] For example, see Prothero, *op. cit.*, p. 182; Kuczynski, *op. cit.*, pp. 675, 677, 679–83. C. A. L. Myburgh finds considerable variation in mortality and fertility in Subsaharan Africa; he attributes some of the variation in fertility to "variations in the incidence of venereal and other diseases and variations in marriage customs including the incidence of polygamy." See "Estimating the Fertility and Mortality of African Populations from the Total Number of Children Ever Born and the Number of These Still Living," *Population Studies*, X (Nov., 1956), 206. The number of children aged 0–6 years per 1000 females aged 15–49 varies about as much by province in the Western and Eastern Regions as in the Northern Region. See Federation of Nigeria, Department of Statistics, *Population Census of Nigeria, 1952–53* (Lagos, n.d.), summary table on ages. The ratios by region are: Northern, 1081; Western, 1206; Eastern, 1099.

[41] For example, in the Cocos Islands gross reproduction has approximated 4 and the crude birth rate has been in the middle 50's, even above that of Taiwan and

strong desire for children, and this usually conduces to high fertility by making woman's social position hinge largely upon her
child-bearing capacity.[42] Women tend to marry early (though
less early than they might), doing so even in cities where men
marry much later; and the presence of the extended family facilitates marriage and the associated role of producing children, as
sometimes also does an "apathetic acceptance of circumstances." [43]

How long it will take slowly progressing Nigerian and African
urbanization and industrialization to weaken traditional props of
fertility, to disorganize traditional society and destabilize "mari-
tal" connections, and to introduce goals and accentuate practices
inimical to fertility, is not presently predictable, but the period
probably will be a long one. As urbanization and industrialization
progress, however, it is to be expected that kinship ties will be
weakened, that the extended family (the presence of which is
highly correlated with the pursuit of agriculture) will gradually
be superseded, that the age at which women marry will advance,
and that wants will keep abreast of disposable income and may
even expand more rapidly. In the very immediate future, nonetheless, fertility could rise, given a decline in venereal disease

Singapore Chinese women. The earliness with which the Cocos Islands women
marry is largely responsible for height of the gross reproduction rates recorded; a
girl marrying at or below 16 will have had 9.5–10 births by the ages 40–45; whereas
one not marrying until 20 or 21 will have had only 6.25–6.5 births by the ages
40–45. See T. E. Smith, "The Cocos-Keeling Islands: A Demographic Laboratory,"
Population Studies, XIV (Nov., 1960), 102, 107–12.

[42] "Corporate unilateral kinship groups and the related emphasis on mother
rights or father rights in social organization tend to generate strong motivations
for high fertility. These motivations spring from the ethnocentric character of
the interest formed in lineage relations. . . . Corporate kinship groups generate
strong motives for high fertility, and . . . this particular sort of motivation is
specific to societies in which such groups play a significant role." See Lorimer
et al., op. cit., p. 90, also pp. 78, 81, 247–48, 367; also *ibid.*, p. 83, on male children
as a source of power and female children as media wherewith to obtain cattle.
On kinship and fertility, see also *African Abstracts*, XI (Jan., 1960), item 75.

[43] Lorimer *et al., op. cit.*, pp. 247–48, 378–80, 388–89. Unfortunately relevant
data on age at marriage are too insufficient and uncertain to permit generalization.
See UNO, *Special Study on Social Conditions in Non-Self-Governing Territories*
(New York, 1958), chap. iii. The available evidence does, however, indicate early
marriage. See C. J. Martin, "Some Estimates of the General Age Distribution, Fertility and Rate of Natural Increase of the African Population of British East Africa,"
Population Studies, VII (Nov., 1953), 192–95; Lorimer *et al., op. cit.*, pp. 283,
297, 348, 372–73, 384–85; Kenneth Little, "Some Urban Patterns of Marriage and
Domesticity in West Africa," in Little, ed., *Urbanism in West Africa* (appearing
as *Sociological Review*, VII [July, 1959]), 70–75; Tanya Baker and Mary Bird,
"Urbanisation and the Position of Women," *ibid.*, pp. 99–121; Kuczynski, *op. cit.*,
p. 611; *African Abstracts*, IX (1958), item 168.

and in the force of sexual tabus and improvement in health and living conditions.[44]

(2) Population Composition

In this subsection we examine the educational, the occupational, the rural-urban, and the tribal and racial composition of the Nigerian population and inquire into the manner in which variation along each of these four social dimensions is associated with economic development. Unlike age composition, which is a purely demographic phenomenon, each of these modes of composition is primarily a social phenomenon. For changes in educational, occupational, and rural-urban composition are in large measure the product of essentially socio-economic change; and the socio-economic significance of changes in racial and tribal composition (which, insofar as they have a genetic basis, are the result of reproductive selection) depends largely upon prevailing non-demographic, socio-economic and cultural circumstances.

This subsection somewhat overlaps in content the one that follows. In (3) I shall deal in greater detail with migration that is affected not only by the spatial distribution of resources and economic opportunity but also by elements discussed here under (2) and by circumstances underlying these elements. The impact of sexually selective migration upon sex composition will also be noticed in (3).[45]

[44] See Lorimer *et al., op. cit.,* pp. 247–51; J. L. Comhaire, "Economic Change and the Extended Family," in Hoselitz, ed., *op. cit.,* pp. 45–52; Pius Okigbo, "Social Consequences of Economic Development in West Africa," *ibid.,* pp. 127–31; M. F. Nimkoff and Russell Middleton, "Types of Family and Types of Economy," *American Journal of Sociology,* LXVI (Nov., 1960), pp. 215–25. Urbanization facilitates intertribal marriage, delays male marriage, and improves the position of women generally. See papers by Little and by Baker and Bird cited in the previous note. On the emergence of the nuclear family in urban settings and on changes in the roles of women, see also *Special Study on Social Conditions in Non-Self-Governing Territories,* chap. iii. Romaniuk, *op. cit.,* reports that in some Congolese urban centers fertility seems to have risen in recent years, whereas L. T. Badenhorst and B. Unterhalter find that among the urban Bantu fertility is declining very slowly. See "A Study of Fertility in an Urban Community," *Population Studies,* XV (July, 1961), 78–85.

[45] Reported sex ratios vary considerably by age and place. The ratio of males to females, 0.96 for Nigeria as a whole, is slightly above 1.0 among those aged under 15, about 0.88 among those aged 15–49, and slightly lower among those 50

(a) *Education composition.* Educational composition is of great economic significance for a number of reasons. First, economic productivity depends upon applied science (and hence upon man's mastering and learning to apply modern natural and social science) in even greater measure than upon the rate of physical capital formation. Second, continuing economic progress is possible only insofar as the elite component of a population is large, has a modern and highly scientific bent, and is capable of supplying aggressive and effective leadership. Third, continuing educational progress appears to be essential to continuing economic progress. Unless a sufficiently large fraction of a population is somewhat educated, it will not acquire, or comply with, "the behaviors appropriate to an industrial way of life" sufficiently to insure sustained economic progress,[46] and it may not modify its habits of consumption rapidly enough to keep the elasticity of demand for income in terms of effort at an adequate level. Moreover, it will not be able to communicate and act on information with sufficient skill. Finally, unless enough of a population is effectively literate (say, 80–90 per cent), it is unlikely to bring its fertility under effective control. Popular education is thus as essential as advanced education. In fact, in the absence of widespread popular education and literacy, advanced education, being quite uncommon, tends to become a symbol of status and prestige rather than an instrument making for economic progress, and even elementary education may generate useless or unrealizable aspirations. Elite and popular education thus are necessary complements rather than substitutes.

Supplying education absorbs labor, capital, and other inputs that have alternate uses. Furthermore, increments in productiv-

and over. The ratio ranges, by province, from 0.79 to 0.98 among those aged 15–49. Variation in sex ratio, sometimes partially attributable to sexually selective mortality, is affected principally by sexually selective migration, at least in times of peace.

[46] On what is involved in committing a population to the norms and actions animating a modern labor force, see essay by A. S. Feldman and W. F. Moore in Moore and Feldman, eds., *Labor Commitment and Social Change in Developing Areas* (New York, 1960), chap. i–v. Much of this inquiry relates to Africa. On the general question of the demand for "high-level manpower," see Frederick Harbison, "Human Resources and Economic Development in Nigeria," *infra*, chap. viii. On the problem of underemployment due to a large number of undereducated "school leavers," see Archibald Callaway, "School Leavers and the Developing Economy of Nigeria," *infra*, chap. ix.

ity consequent upon education may not begin to be available for 1–16 (or more) years after the investment in education has been made. These prospective increments should therefore be discounted to the points in time at which the amounts of inputs to be invested in education are being determined in the light of the alternatives available. The applicable discount rates will be high in Nigeria because capital is very scarce. Considerable care must be exercised, therefore, so that investment in education, together with its allocation to diverse purposes, is economically determined along with other forms of investment, and emphasis is put upon productivity-increasing rather than upon resource-wasting types of education. Exercise of such care should make apparent also the need to reduce fertility and thereby make available more education-producing inputs per individual undergoing education.[47]

The educational attainments of Nigeria's population fall far short of the minimal requirements for industrial development, with competent personnel constituting less than 1 per cent (i.e., about ¾ per cent) of the population. In the 1952–53 census only 12 per cent of the population were reported as literate, a figure much below that found in a number of African lands. This percentage approximated 16 in the Eastern and Western regions, but only 7.4 in the Northern region, in the Moslem parts of which the European educational tradition had not been established. It is, of course, not certain that all reported as literate were effectively literate. At that time about one-third of those aged 7–14 were in primary school, whereas by 1957 about 2.45 million, or a number equal to nearly half of those aged 7–14, were reported as enrolled. The present goal, however, is at least 85 per cent literacy by 1970. It is planned to provide primary schooling for all children in the Eastern and Western regions by 1970, of whom 70 per 1000 will continue through secondary school; of this 70 about 16 will undergo additional training, with 5–6 going to a university. In the Northern region only about 25 per cent will

[47] On economic aspects of investment in education, see H. S. Houthaker, "Education and Income," *Review of Economics and Statistics*, XLI (Feb., 1959), 24–28; T. W. Schultz, "Investment in Man: An Economist's View," *Social Service Review*, XXXIII (June, 1959), 109–17; Carl S. Shoup, *The Fiscal System of Venezuela* (Baltimore, 1959), chap. xv and *passim*.

complete primary school, but of each 1000 primary graduates 100 will enter secondary school, of whom 28 will undergo advanced training, 8–12 in a university. It is hoped that by 1970 this program will supply Nigeria, relatively few of whose teachers are presently competent, with a minimal African elite, that is, with about 36 thousand (or three times the current supply) senior managerial, professional, administrative, and graduate-teacher personnel and about 55,000 (or about 4½ times the present supply) intermediate technical and supervisory personnel and non-graduate teachers.[48] Of course, if Nigeria's population were stationary, the amount of skilled personnel made available per capita by this program would be about one-fifth greater by 1970 than it will be, given the current rate of population growth.

(b) *Occupational composition.* Nigeria's labor force is that of a very underdeveloped country. For while a large fraction of its indigenous population (54.4 per cent of the males and 41.7 per cent of the females) [49] is reported in the labor force, only 4–5 per cent of its economically active population are described as wage-earners. This reported fraction, though possibly too low, is not much below that reported for various other African economies.[50]

---

[48] See Federation of Nigeria, Federal Ministry of Education, *Investment in Education* (Lagos and London, 1960), esp. Part I, secs. 2–6, Part II, chap. i. For recent and current data see also UNO, *Report on the World Social Situation*, chap. v; International Bank, *op. cit.*, pp. 69–75, 560–601; UNO, *Statistical Yearbook 1959*, p. 553. In 1958 per capita newspaper circulation in Nigeria was one-third that in Ghana and one-fourth that in Algeria. See *ibid.*, p. 578, also p. 576 on per capita newsprint consumption.

[49] These percentages are based upon the 1952–53 census. See International Labour Office, *Yearbook, 1959* (Geneva, 1959), p. 7.

[50] For the percentages see International Labour Office, *African Labour Survey* (Geneva, 1958), p. 666; "The Influence of International Labour Conventions on Nigerian Labour Legislation," *International Labour Review*, LXXXII (July, 1960), 27. "It is estimated that in Ghana and Nigeria, where nearly three-quarters of African males (over 15 years of age) are engaged outside the subsistence economy in money-earning activities, wages amount to only 8 and 10 per cent respectively of the money income earned by them." See "Interracial Wage Structure in Certain Parts of Africa," *ibid.*, LXXVIII (July, 1958), 37, under Table IX. Since labor turnover is usually high in Africa, the absolute number of persons serving as wage-earners for at least a part of a year is a number of times as large as the man-years worked by the labor force in that year. See UNO, *Economic Survey of Africa since 1950* (New York, 1959), p. 43. In Nigeria as elsewhere in Africa people have not become disposed to be fulltime and skilled wage-earners, and a shortage of voluntary labor caused recourse to forced labor so late as 1926 to carry on road and railroad construction. However, while tribal, attitudinal, and other conditions continue to disincline individuals to become wage-earners, their number is growing faster

Something like four-fifths of this labor force is engaged in agriculture, much of it under traditional, subsistence conditions. Of the males over 15 engaged in agriculture, around 1950 close to three-fifths (about 57 per cent) were engaged in subsistence pro-

Table 5. *Nigerian African Males, by Occupation and Region, 1952–53* *

	Region					
	North		*West*		*East*	
Occupation	*Number (000)*	*Per cent*	*Number (000)*	*Per cent*	*Number (000)*	*Per cent*
Agriculture, fishing	3,786	47.1	1,154	38.5	1,306	37.4
Craftsmen	291	3.5	119	4.0	75	2.2
Trading, clerical	151	1.8	145	4.8	148	4.2
Administrative, professional, technical	104	1.3	54	1.8	50	1.4
Other occupations	245	3.0	125	4.2	142	4.1
Other males not working	3,562	43.3	1,404	46.8	1,767	50.7
All males	8,229	100.0	3,001	100.0	3,488	100.0

* This table derives from Federation of Nigeria, Department of Statistics, *Population Census of Nigeria, 1952–53* (Lagos, n.d.).

duction. The remainder were involved in commercial production, but most of these were within the indigenous economy, and only about 4 per cent of the male agriculturalists could be described as wage-earners.[51] This situation is reflected in the fact that the

than the population and the labor force, in part because individuals feel the need of more income and are becoming familiar with wage employment, and also presumably because the stock of capital and other factors co-operant with labor is increasing and making it possible to employ more workers. On the plentitude of labor and its skills see *ibid.*, pp. 41–43; *African Abstracts*, VIII (1957), item 439; P. T. Bauer, *West African Trade* (London, 1954), pp. 18–21. On trends, see "The Development of Wage-Earning Employment in Tropical Africa," *International Labour Review*, LXXIV (Sept., 1956), 239–58; also UNO, *Review of Economic Conditions in Africa* (Supplement to *World Report, 1949–50*) (New York, 1951), p. 76.

[51] See International Bank, *op. cit.*, p. 192; UNO, *Enlargement of the Exchange Economy in Tropical Africa* (New York, 1954), p. 17. Data relating to agricultural employment are misleading in that a considerable fraction of the labor time of those described as agriculturalists is devoted to trade, handicrafts, and other non-agricultural activities. Moreover, what is called subsistence agriculture often falls short of being purely subsistence agriculture. For example, see Bauer, *op. cit.*, chap. ii; UNO, *Economic Survey of Africa since 1950*, p. 43.

African population is predominantly rural and that agriculture was the source of about two-thirds of the gross domestic product in many countries in the early 1950's.[52] It is reflected also in the figures reported in Table 5, which indicate that of all the economically active males the fraction in agriculture ranges from about 72 per cent in the Western region to 83 per cent in the Northern Region.[53] With the occupational structure favorable to fertility and with the population growth in prospect, therefore, together with the prevailing shortage of capital and skilled manpower, it may take 3–5 or more decades to reduce the size of the agricultural labor force below that now prevailing. This inference is reinforced by several observations: African males, of whom only some engage in agriculture, "retire" early; there is little "surplus" labor, or unutilized but exploitable labor time, to be found at present in agriculture, the conduct of which absorbs much of the time of women and children.

(c) *Rural-urban composition.* The city is the instrument through which man usually is transformed and modernized. Even in the modern world city air is free air in that it dissipates ancient traditional ties that are incompatible with effective industrial development. Furthermore, urbanization renders an economy more competitive, enlarges the scope given to the economic principle and rational economic behavior, and thereby makes economic activity more efficient. Finally, the agglomeration of population in cities permits economies of scale in the use of transport and of some forms of socio-economic overhead capital, in the employment of labor time, and in the provision of such productivity-increasing services as education, health, training, etc. Against these economies, of course, there may have to be charged a higher input of resources per capita in the form of housing, sanitation facilities, etc.; but on balance it is probable that under the conditions encountered in Nigeria this higher input is more than off-

[52] *Ibid.*, pp. 14, 16.
[53] About 78 per cent of the economically active females are reported in agriculture. Of the 324,000 wage-earners, agriculture and forestry accounted for 54,000; mining and quarrying, 50,000; building and construction, 54,000; and government services, 52,000. Manufacturing engaged 16,000; transport, 37,000; commerce, 36,000; and domestic and other services, 25,000. ILO, *African Labour Survey*, p. 667.

set by the advantages resulting. In fact, in Nigeria "the essential conditions for the development of manufacturing industry are still not normally found outside urban areas." [54]

Regarding Nigeria, two aspects of urbanization need to be heeded. First, as will be noted, how large a fraction of the population is describable as living in urban communities is even more a matter of definition in Nigeria (with its Yoruban rural "cities") than in many countries. Second, insofar as the term urbanization is conceived of as summarily describing the mentality-transforming and economy-producing forces and processes already referred to, allowance must be made for the fact that the strength of these forces and processes is a function not only of the relative number of persons situated in "urban" places but also of the socio-economic character of particular cities and of the spatial distribution of the cities encountered in a country.

The concentration of population in urban centers has increased in recent years, but still varies greatly by region. According to the census of 1952–53, 18 per cent of the population lived in towns with population of 5,000 or more, with the percentage ranging from 9 in the Northern Region through 14 in the Eastern Region (including the Southern Cameroons) to 46 in the Western Region (excluding Lagos with a population of about 267,000). Of greater significance, the percentage living in cities of 20,000 and over ranged from 3.6 in the North through 6.3 in the East to 29 in the West. (In Nigeria as a whole the figure is 10 per cent.) The number of towns with 20,000 or more inhabitants numbered 47 in 1952–53 as compared with 16 in 1921, when about 5 per cent of the population lived in communities of this size. While the progress of urbanization will be affected somewhat by cultural factors, among them those associated with religious beliefs,[55] it will be

---

[54] J. Heads, "Urbanization and Economic Progress in Nigeria," *South African Journal of Economics*, XXVII (Sept., 1959), 235.

[55] According to the census of 1952–53 Nigeria's population was 44 per cent Moslem, 22 per cent Christian, and 34 per cent "others" (i.e., mostly Pagan, Animist, etc.). The corresponding percentages, by region, were: Northern, 73, 2.7, and 34; Western, 32.4, 36.2, and 31.4; Eastern, 0.3, 50.1, and 49.6; Southern Cameroons, 3.5, 40.5, and 56; and Lagos, 42.1, 54.5, and 3.4. These and other census data are reported in the summary tables in Federation of Nigeria, Department of Statistics, *Population Census of Nigeria, 1952–53* (Lagos, n.d.). Also see *infra*, n. 57.

dominated by the pattern of consumption and by advances in productivity per worker. Inasmuch as gradual improvement in agricultural efficiency is to be expected and since the demand for domestically produced foodstuffs will remain below unity (perhaps about 0.65) while that for the products of secondary and tertiary activity (which can best be carried on in towns) will continue to exceed unity, the relative importance of agriculture and rural communities will decline while that of town-centered activities and urban communities will increase.[56]

The presence in the Western Region of 4.3 of the country's 5.1 million Yoruba, together with the preindustrial character of Yoruba towns and cities, is primarily responsible both for the "urban" character of the Western Region and for the failure of life in this region's urban milieu to affect conduct and aspirations any more than it has. The presence of 536,000 Yoruba in the Northern Region has also affected the character of urbanization in Llorin and Kabba provinces but not that of the largest Northern city, Kano, which is almost entirely non-Yoruba and Moslem. In the semi-Christian East, the urban population, while much smaller than among the Yoruba, has reflected a greater amount of European influence than have the Yoruba communities, somewhat more of whose inhabitants are Moslem than are Christian.[57] Of the Yoruba in Nigeria 53.5 per cent live in towns of 5,000 and over, 36.6 per cent in towns of 25,000 and over, and 22.1 per cent in towns of more than 100,000. The inhabitants of the Yoruba towns (of which many, unlike most African towns, are some centuries old, and of which all except Lagos are non-industrial, traditional, tribal, and non-cosmopolitan) remain engaged predominantly in farming and secondarily in crafts and trade. In consequence, while the values and attitudes of urban Yoruba of today differ somewhat from those of both their urban ancestors and their rural contemporaries, Yoruba urbanization has not disrupted "traditional tribal forms of social grouping" or generated much social or geographical mobility. Most of the social and the polit-

[56] For example, see Heads, *op. cit.*, pp. 229–37.
[57] According to P. C. Lloyd 42 per cent of the Yoruba are Moslem and 41 per cent are Christian, with relatively more of Moslem than of Christian Yoruba situated in cities. See P. C. Lloyd, "The Yoruba Town Today," *Sociological Review*, VII (July, 1959), 53.

ical relationships and some of the economic relationships encountered in Yoruba urban society remain dominated by the constraints and the ascriptive impact of patrilineal lineage and by ties of kinship.[58]

The West African town, even when the product of outside forces, continues to be linked socially and culturally "with its own hinterland"; yet West African urbanism is dynamic and it is transforming non-rural society and "gradually enfolding rural society." [59] This process of transformation will probably accelerate as industrialization, specialization, and transportation improve, and as the urban elite expands. In the end, therefore, traditional, conduct-regulating principles and constraints will give way, even in Yoruba and Moslem urban centers, to principles and constraints more in keeping with the requirements of modern life and more suited to bringing about a required decline in fertility. This transformation will proceed most rapidly, however, in towns of European origin, which includes most "modern" African towns.[60]

As has been indicated or implied, population density varies considerably from province to province and within urban areas, largely because of differences in past political and historical experience, in physical and climatic conditions, in terrain and soils, in the distribution of transport facilities, and so on. It will prob-

---

[58] See *ibid.*, pp. 45–63; William Bascom, "Urbanisation as a Traditional Pattern," *ibid.*, pp. 29–43, and "Urbanisation among the Yoruba," *American Sociological Review*, LX (March, 1955), 446–54. See also Gideon Sjoberg, "The Preindustrial City," *ibid.*, pp. 438–45; P. C. Lloyd, "The Yoruba Lineage," *Africa*, XXV (July, 1955), 235–51; Daryll Forde, ed., *Western Africa*, Part IV (London, 1951). (This report on the Yoruba is part of the many-volumed *Ethnographic Survey of Africa*, edited by Daryll Forde for the International African Institute, London, 1950 ff.) Many Yoruba cities date from the early sixteenth century. *African Abstracts*, XII (1961), item 328.

[59] See Kenneth Little's introduction to "Urbanism in West Africa," *Sociological Review*, VII (July, 1959), 5–12. Migration to towns has weakened but not wholly severed tribal or extended-family ties in Ghana. See *African Abstracts*, XII (1961), items 175, 307.

[60] "There is evidence today in many African cities of the beginnings of a social structure based on economic and cultural differences rather than on racial or tribal criteria, as in the past. . . . The development of a new culture, which will be both African and modern, is without question one of the most challenging and complex problems of the contemporary world." See UNO, *Report on the World Situation*, chap. viii on Subsaharan urbanization, esp. p. 169. See also UNO, *Special Study on Social Conditions in Non-Self-Governing Territories* (New York, 1958), *passim;* Kimble, *op. cit.*, II, chap. xviii; Moore and Feldman, *op. cit.*, pp. 49–50, 203, 227–32. International African Institute, *Some Implications of Industrialization and Urbanization in Africa South of the Sahara* (Paris, 1956), Parts I, IV.

180		*The Nigerian Political Scene*

ably be dominated in the future by the distribution of the forces
making for urbanization as such.[61] In 1952–53 density was greatest in the Eastern Region, averaging 245 per square mile, and
lowest in the Northern Region, where it averaged 60; the corresponding figures for the Western Region and Nigeria as a whole
were 134 and 84.[62] Within regions density by province ranged
from 25 to 204 per square mile in the North, from 107 to 537 in
the East, and from 81 to 365 in the West; in Lagos township density averaged 10,070. Density is even higher, of course, in some
divisions within provinces. For example, in 10 of 33 divisions in
the Eastern Region it exceeded 400 per square mile and in 6 it
exceeded 600.

(d) *Racial and tribal composition.* While the population of
Nigeria consists predominantly of two identifiable racial elements,
the "true Negro" and the Eastern branch of the Hamites (probably of Southern-Arabian origin), it is Nigeria's tribal composition that is of economic concern.[63] The population of each region
is made up largely of several principal tribal groups, most of which
are somewhat heterogeneous. In 1952–53 in the Western Region
there were, besides 4.3 million Yoruba, 446,000 Edo, 342,000 Ibo,

    [61] For example, see R. J. H. Church, *West Africa* (London, 1957), chap. x. For
maps of intraurban and interurban and other distributions of population in space
see Buchanan and Pugh, *op. cit.*, chap. ii; G. B. Stapleton, *The Wealth of Nigeria*
(London, 1958), chap. iv; J. H. Jennings, "A Population Distribution Map of the
Eastern Region of Nigeria," *Geographical Journal*, CXXIII (Sept., 1957), 416–17;
W. B. Morgan, "Farming Practice, Settlement Pattern and Population Density in
Southeastern Nigeria," *ibid.*, CXXI (Sept., 1955), 320–33. For contrasts between
the distribution of population within Nigeria and that within tropical Africa, see
G. T. Trewatha and W. Zelinsky, "Population Patterns in Tropical Africa," *Annals
of the Association of American Geographers*, XLIV (June, 1954), 135–62, and
"The Population Geography of Belgian Africa," *ibid.*, pp. 163–91. In tropical Africa
in the early 1950's the estimated number of persons per square kilometer ranged
from under 1 to 88, with Nigeria (40.3 per sq. km.) and Ruanda-Urundi (73.8 per
sq. km.) the most densely populated of the countries with more than 300,000 inhabitants, and with the whole region averaging only 7.1 persons per square kilometer.
    [62] About 1950, population per square mile in eastern and southern Asia aver-
aged 420; in western and central Europe, 310; in the northeastern United States,
180. See W. S. and E. S. Woytinsky, *World Population and Production* (New York,
1953), p. 41.
    [63] See C. S. Seligman, *Races of Africa* (3rd ed.; London, 1957), *passim;* Bu-
chanan and Pugh, *op. cit.*, pp. 79–82; Murdock, *Africa, passim.* For a Communist-
oriented interpretation, see *Die Völker Afrikas* (translated from Russian into German by D. A. Olderogge and I. I. Potechin), Vol. II (Berlin, 1961); and for an
account of tribal composition in the sixteenth and seventeenth centuries, see *African Abstracts*, XII (1961), item 302.

and about a million members of other tribes. In the Eastern Region lived 4.92 million Ibo, 737,000 Ibibio, and just over 1.5 million members of other tribes. In the more heterogeneous Northern Region lived 3.02 million Fulani, 5.49 million Hausa, and 1.3 million Kanuri, together with 773,000 Tiv, 536,000 Yoruba, 349,000 Nupe, and 167,000 Ibo; members of other tribes numbered just over 5.1 million.[64] Non-Nigerians (i.e., Europeans, Middle-Easterners, Asians) numbered only about 50,000. Nigeria is thus a multi-tribal or multi-ethnic community, but not a multi-racial one, given the extent to which the original Negro and Hamitic elements have become intermixed. Nigeria, therefore, is quite free of tension of the sort that appears to be correlated with a relatively high non-African–African population ratio, even as it is free of much of the material progress that comes with the presence of a relatively large non-African population and the tension resulting.[65]

Tribal composition is of particular economic concern when it denotes linguistic difference, for this cultural distinction reinforces other intertribal cultural differences that impede communication, reduce mobility in economic and geographic space, and prevent the social and political solidarity essential to economic growth. The language groups dominant in Nigeria belong to the Sudanic language family. The numerically most important Kwa group includes the Ibo, the Edo, the Yoruba, the Nupe, and a number of smaller groups which together form about two-fifths of the population. The Semi-Bantu group includes the Ibibio, the Tiv, and a number of smaller groups; with another Negritic-language group, the Fulani, they aggregate about one-fourth of the population. The Inner-Sudanic group comprises two subgroups, the Kanuri and related small groups, and the Hausa-Kotoko, which is dominated by Hausa speakers; it embraces about one-third of the population. Each of these linguistic groups includes

[64] See Nigeria, *Population Census of Nigeria 1952–53*, summary tables, esp. Table 6. Density figures are given in Table 2. Data are given for smaller units in the census reports on regions. Also see Murdock, *supra*, chap. i.
[65] On tension see Herskovits, *Africa*, pp. 32–34. On the progress-generating effects of tension and insecurity, see F. L. K. Hsu, "Cultural Factors," in H. F. Williamson and J. A. Buttrick, eds., *Economic Development* (New York, 1954), pp. 349–51, 356–59.

many dialects, some of which are not widely understood. There is no real *lingua franca*, though Hausa and Yoruba are understood by many and have been adapted to trading, and English is used for governmental purposes. None of these indigenous languages as it now stands is sufficiently developed to meet the needs of the modern world. Accordingly, one of these languages needs to be modernized and converted into a national language, or preferably a European tongue (e.g., English) needs to be established as the common language of the country. Until this is done, economy and universality of communication cannot be achieved, economic development will be adversely affected, and a sufficiency of political consensus or unity will hardly prove achievable. Moreover, if a sufficiency of unity is not soon achieved, and Nigeria becomes minority-ridden, the panoply of parliamentary democracy (whether in a federalistic or other guise) will be declared unsuited to the accomplishment of economic development. If this should happen power may well become concentrated in the hands of a minority, which, with the assistance of the military, will then be able to disregard local and tribal interests and to impose the burdens of economic development upon the underlying population.[66]

[66] On matters treated in this paragraph, see Peter Duignan and Lewis Gann, "The Case for the White Man," *The New Leader*, Jan. 2, 1961, pp. 16–20, as well as Herskovits's slightly different analysis, referred to earlier, in *Africa*, pp. 25–27. On linguistic groups in Nigeria, see Buchanan and Pugh, *op. cit.*, pp. 79–88, and studies that have appeared so far in the series on Western Africa as a part of the *Ethnographic Survey of Africa*, particularly Parts 3–4, 7–8, 10–13, dealing with the Ibo, the Yoruba, the Tiv, the Nupe, the Edo, the Coastal Bantus, and a number of other Nigerian peoples; also see Murdock, *Africa*, chaps. ii–iii, xiii, xvii, xxix–xxxv, lv; and Murdock, *supra*, chap. i. Herskovits, *Africa*, p. 35, is optimistic regarding the solution of the language problem, noting that African leaders in Subsaharan lands, aware that some 800 languages are now in use, are "fully cognizant of the need to be able to communicate in a world language" and of the corollary need to shape educational policy to facilitate "communication both internally and internationally." Furthermore, as Stapleton suggests, *op. cit.*, p. 53, Nigerian peoples that had not developed complicated, hierarchical social systems have "rapidly accepted the new" (for example, the Ibo); and many peoples answer to this description. It is to be noted, furthermore, that when a native language has not become the repository of a written literature (as in some Indian states), it is much easier to replace it with a superior foreign tongue. See also D. E. Apter and C. C. Rosberg, "Nationalism and Models of Political Change in Africa," in D. P. Ray, ed., *The Political Economy of Contemporary Africa* (*Symposia Studies Series No. 1*, National Institute of Social and Behavioral Science, George Washington University, Washington, 1959), pp. 7–16.

(3) *Natural Resources, Migration, Population Distribution*

Other conditions given, per capita income depends upon the ratio of a nation's population to its resources and upon the manner in which its labor force is distributed among occupations and in space. In this subsection, therefore, attention will be given to Nigeria's resource endowment and to the migratory behavior of her population.

(a) *Nigeria's resource endowment.* Nigeria enjoys a double advantage over most if not all of the new African states; its area is greater than that of most and its population is over 2½ times that of the largest of these states. Nigeria, therefore, is possessed of a potentially larger free-trade area as well as of greater opportunity for economic maneuver. Moreover, it enjoys greater economy of scale in its governmental operations and hence should experience a lower per capita governmental overhead cost than the smaller African states. Nigeria resembles most African states, however, in that, in comparison with its population, it apparently does not abound in arable land and exploitable natural resources.

Nigeria possesses a considerable though undeveloped hydropower potential, but it is not rich in inorganic raw materials. Several years ago Stapleton observed that, "as far as knowledge extends today," Nigeria is not "richly endowed either with minerals or with sources of power." In the 1950's mineral production (of which nine-tenths consisted in columbite and tin) constituted only a little over 1 per cent of the gross domestic product, whereas manufactures formed about 3 per cent; as late as 1956–57 it approximated only one dollar per capita. As of 1959 mineral exports comprised only about 3.8 per cent of all Nigeria's exports, but this fraction should rise by 1962. A twenty-year search for oil (which began to pay off in 1957) may (by 1965) eventuate in a sufficient output of relatively high cost oil to supply the country's domestic needs (about 5 per cent of all imports in the past), together with a large surplus (perhaps $30 million per year) for export (at least to neighboring countries). In view of Nigeria's over-all shortage of inorganic raw materials, it cannot rest its economic development appreciably upon their exploitation or count upon their exportation to supply foreign exchange; nor can it rely upon its mineral potential to attract foreign capital (as have South Africa, Rhodesia, and the Belgian Congo), a mode of attraction less sensitive than other modes to the investment-discouraging impact of contemporary political instability.[67]

Even Nigeria's agricultural resources (which engage nearly four-fifths of her labor force and give rise to about five-eighths of her gross domestic product and about four-fifths of her exports) are not abundant in comparison with her population, which is nearly as dense as that of Southeast Asia. Her population is much denser than that of most African states, probably because the introduction centuries ago of Malaysian and later of American plants enabled parts of West Africa to support a much denser population than was sustainable elsewhere in Subsaharan Africa; yet only about one-half her land is described as usable. While acres available per capita number about seven,[68] the amount cultivated per capita in any one year falls far short of this figure since the poorest soil may require as much as ten years of rest to restore moisture and fertility. Stamp puts the amount cultivated per capita at 1.7 acres; the International Bank report implies it to be less than 1.0.[69] Furthermore, although Nigeria's agricultural

[67] See Stapleton, *op. cit.*, chap. iii and p. 33; International Bank, *op. cit.*, percentages on pp. 346, 406–7. Buchanan and Pugh, *op. cit.*, chap. iv and p. 179, conclude that "so far there is little evidence to suggest that these resources are likely to ensure the country an important place in world markets for any appreciable time." On minerals, see also Kimble, *op. cit.*, I, chap ix; UNO, *Economic Survey of Africa since 1950*, pp. 33–36, 61–68. On the restrictedness of opportunity in Nigeria, see also F. J. Pedler, "Foreign Investment in Western Africa," *International Affairs*, XXXI (Oct., 1955), 459–68.

[68] L. D. Stamp, *Our Developing World* (London, 1960), p. 114. The significance of an acre turns, of course, on the number of SNU's (standard nutrition units equal to 1,000,000 Nutrition Calories per annum, or, allowing for a loss of 10 per cent in food preparation, to 2,460 calories per day) gotten from a cultivated acre. In Uganda this yield is 1.0 SNU per cultivated acre; in the United States and the world, respectively, 0.4 and 0.75; in France, 1.6; in Egypt, 4.0; in Burma, 1.0 (*ibid.*, p. 114). It appears to be below 1.0 in Nigeria. On soil quality, difficulties of mechanization, etc., see Church, *op. cit.*, chaps. v–vi; Stamp, *Africa* (New York, 1953), chaps. v, xiii. In 1958 inhabitants per square kilometer averaged 38 in Nigeria. Comparable densities were: Central America, 23; Ireland, 41; Southeast Asia, 45; Northwest Europe, 62. On changes in African agricultural technology and population density in the past see Murdock, *Africa*, pp. 64 ff., 245 ff.

[69] Stamp, *Our Developing World*, p. 114. According to the Bank report, about 1951, 8.8 per cent of Nigeria's 372,250 square miles were in farm crops and 1.2 per cent in tree crops; 13.8 per cent in bush fallow; 7.8 and 24.1 per cent, respectively, in forest reserves and forest; and 43.4 per cent in uncultivated bush

exports are diversified, the demand for some is not very elastic; and those that supply most of her foreign exchange may encounter increasing competition in foreign markets. The system of production presently employed, therefore, will have to be markedly improved.[70] Nigeria is not well equipped with good timber reserves, and her consumption and production (of which 40–50 per cent is exported) of timber is low when put in per capita terms.[71]

Inasmuch as Nigeria's resource endowment per capita is small, it needs to make up its resource lackings by setting its underdeveloped resources to work, by forming capital (of which its current stock is low absolutely and in per capita terms) at a high rate, by encouraging instead of discouraging foreign investment, and by increasing the personal efficiency of its labor force. As yet, however, foreign investment is relatively small and Nigeria's rate of capital formation is far below that required, in part because its per capita income is so low (about $69 in 1956 and perhaps somewhat over $80 in 1959) [72] and so little increase has been

pastures and wasteland. Built-on areas constituted only 0.9 per cent (*ibid.*, p. 200). According to the village surveys undertaken in 1951, the ratio of land under crops to land under fallow ranged from 1:9 to 1:1; the per cent of all land in uncultivated bush and waste ranged from 7 to 94. See R. M. Prothero, "The Sample Census of Agriculture, Nigeria, 1950–51," *Geographical Journal*, CXXI (June, 1955), 197–206.

[70] See R. M. Prothero, "Recent Developments in Nigerian Export Crop Production," *Geography*, XL (Jan., 1955), 18–27. He refers particularly to the need to revolutionize Nigerian agriculture and cut the production costs of cocoa, groundnuts, and oil palm products (which together in the 1950's comprised in value about four-fifths of Nigeria's exports). Limitations on the improvement of land and its use under conditions of the sort found in Nigeria and tropical Africa are discussed in D. H. K. Lee, *Climate and Economic Development in the Tropics* (New York, 1957), esp. chap. vii. See also Kimble, *op. cit.*, I, chaps. iv–v and pp. 73–79. Bruce F. Johnston is fairly optimistic regarding man's ability to increase agricultural production greatly through agronomic science. See his *The Staple Economies of Western Africa* (Stanford, 1958), chap. x. See also works by Stamp and Church cited *supra*, n. 68.

[71] UNO, *Economic Survey*, pp. 32, 170. In 1950–57 timber formed less than 3 per cent of Nigeria's exports. *Ibid.*, p. 170. On the country's forest resources see Buchanan and Pugh, *op. cit.*, chap. iv.

[72] Pedler, *op. cit.*, p. 459, in 1955 put total foreign investment in West Africa at only £ 200 million. In 1956 gross domestic capital formation amounted to about 10 per cent of gross national product, whereas expedition of the country's economic development called for a rate 2–3 times the reported rate. For rates see UNO, *Economic Survey*, pp. 15, 193, 206; Federation of Nigeria, National Economic Council, *Economic Survey of Nigeria, 1959* (Lagos, 1959). On the extent and impact of poverty in Nigeria, see D. Forde's essay in Margery Perham, ed., *The Native Economies of Nigeria*, Vol. I (London, 1945), Part I, and A. J. Brown's comments in *ibid.*, II, 328–34. S. P. Schatz believes that since the productive resources

achieved in the personal productivity of the population.[73] Nigeria's task of overcoming its capital, resource, and trained-personnel shortages, as well as that of inculcating great productive drive into the population, would be difficult even if the population were stationary; but it is greatly accentuated by the high gross and net reproduction rates now prevailing. The task is accentuated also by a disposition to put barriers in the way of the immigration of individuals possessed of skills in short supply.[74] This policy disregards the great probability that the income-increasing effect of the influx of highly qualified immigrants would greatly outweigh any adverse substitution effect experienced by certain natives.[75]

of Nigeria presently are quite underutilized for a variety of modifiable reasons, it should be possible through a restrained use of deficit financing to set these resources more fully to work and thereby augment both income and capital formation considerably. See his "Underutilized Resources, 'Directed Demand,' and Deficit Financing (Illustrated by Reference to Nigeria)," *Quarterly Journal of Economics,* LXXIII (Nov., 1959), 633–44. It needs to be remembered, of course, that in most of Africa there is little scope for deficit finance; bottlenecks are numerous and output per worker is low because productivity is low rather than because there is a great deal of disguised or other unemployment in agriculture. On capital shortage and the costliness of relatively unproductive African labor, see E. Marcus, "Some Problems of African Economic Growth and Development," in Ray, ed., *op. cit.,* pp. 16–24.

[73] On the problem of increasing personal productivity, see International Labour Office, *op. cit.,* chap. v; UNO, *Special Study on Economic Conditions in Non-Self-Governing Territories* (New York, 1960), chap. v; P. de Briey, "The Productivity of African Labour," *International Labour Review,* LXXII (Aug.–Sept., 1955), 119–39; "The Development of Wage-Earning Employment in Tropical Africa," *ibid.,* LXXIV (Sept., 1956), 239–58. De Briey emphasizes the need of the African worker to feel self-confident and psychologically and economically secure (*op. cit.,* pp. 136–37). In a paper prepared for the International Economic Association's conference in Economic Development in Africa South of the Sahara (Addis Ababa, July, 1961), D. H. Houghton reports that while it is very difficult to elevate the low productivity per worker found in almost all African agriculture, it has been possible at times greatly to reduce African labor turnover outside agriculture and even to elevate the productivity of this labor nearly to European levels. Data soon to be published suggest that total and per capita gross national product increased about 4 and 2 per cent per year, respectively, in Nigeria in 1950 and 1957.

[74] See P. T. Bauer and B. S. Yamey, "Economic Aspects of Immigration Policy in Nigeria and the Gold Coast," *South African Journal of Economics,* XXII (June, 1954), 223–32; and P. T. Bauer, *West African Trade* (Cambridge, 1954), chap. xii. The barriers are placed in the way of non-Africans in particular. These barriers slow down the development of a technically skilled labor force, for a great deal of acquired skill is gotten from contact with immigrant workers and firms, and these skills make for economic growth. On their importance, see A. G. Frank, "Human Capital and Economic Growth," *Economic Development and Cultural Change,* VIII (Jan., 1960), 170–73.

[75] The issue is discussed with respect to Asia by T. H. Silcock in "Migration Problems of the Far East," in Brinley Thomas, ed., *The Economics of International Migration* (London, 1958), chap. xviii. See also J. S. Fforde, *An International Trade in Managerial Skills* (Oxford, 1957).

(b) *Population redistribution; its motivation.* The geographical distribution of potential opportunity in a country like Nigeria depends at any given time upon the past geographical distribution of man's efforts and investment and upon the current geographical distribution of land and minerals and other elements supplied by nature (i.e., with minimal human intervention), upon actual and prospective economies of scale and agglomeration, and upon conditions external to a country and hence usually beyond its control. The elements supplied by nature may be divided into ubiquities (i.e., elements present everywhere) and non-ubiquities (i.e., elements present only at some points in geographical space). Under *ceteris paribus* conditions potential economic opportunity will be concentrated largely at certain points in proportion as the ratio of the importance of non-ubiquities to that of ubiquities is high. *Ceteris paribus* conditions may rule only in part, however. On the one hand, the relative significance of non-ubiquities may be reduced through human effort, past and present, with the result that the concentration of potential economic opportunity is less than it otherwise would have been.[76] On the other hand, as an economy evolves there come into being types of economic activity which are subject to economies of scale or to the pull of advantages associated with the agglomeration of activities and population; and these types make for the concentration of potential economic opportunity. As presently advanced economies progressed in the past, the forces making for concentration outweighed those making for dispersion; and future events may be expected to describe a somewhat similar course in Nigeria and Africa generally, despite occasional misguided efforts to Balkanize parts of Africa and perpetuate outmoded tribal subsistence economies.

So long as men are free to move, they tend to move from places where they believe economic opportunity to be less to places where they believe it to be greater, given that the difference in prospective opportunity is expected to outweigh the economic

[76] Illustrative of the incidence of man's activities upon land, landscape, plant growth, etc., see W. B. Morgan, "The Influence of European Contacts on the Landscape of Southern Nigeria," *Geographical Journal*, CXXV, Part I (March, 1959), 48–64. See also Stamp, *Our Developing World*, chaps. iii–vii.

and psychic costs of movements sufficiently to override the risks and uncertainty always associated with movement. This tendency is encountered in Nigeria and Africa as well as in advanced countries, for the individual is disposed to seek his local economic optimum, as envisaged by him to exist in the world of alternatives and tribal and other constraints known to him. In other words, he behaves as an economic-maximizing agent.[77] As his knowledge of accessible alternatives is extended, or their number increases and the tribal and other restraints to which he is subject diminish, his range of choice is enlarged, and his freedom to behave economically is augmented.[78] Whether an individual will migrate temporarily or permanently will depend largely on how he believes the difference in potential opportunity, together with obstacles to its realization, to be distributed in time. As a rule, migration is predominantly seasonal or at least temporary at first, though the annual and the cumulative numbers of permanent migrants tend to increase, at least so long as the ratio of the agricultural to the non-agricultural population remains sufficiently large. Of course, if the migrant is free to bring along his family after he has become settled in a job, he will be more disposed to cut his tribal ties and become a permanent settler. For this reason one would expect the tendency of migrants to become permanent settlers to be stronger in an African- than in a European-dominated state, since the African migrant would have few hurdles to surmount in an African state; but the propensity to immigrate into an African state might be lower.

Migration may be said to take place when either push or pull

[77] On African man's economic behavior, see W. O. Jones, "Economic Man in Africa," *Food Research Institute Studies,* I (May, 1960), 107–34; P. T. Bauer, *Economic Analysis and Policy in Underdeveloped Countries* (Durham, 1957), pp. 15–27; Bruce F. Johnston, *op. cit.,* pp. 262–63; W. J. Barber, "Economic Rationality and Behavior Patterns in an Underdeveloped Area: A Case Study of African Economic Behavior in the Rhodesias," *Economic Development and Cultural Change,* VIII (April, 1960), 237–51.

[78] For example, see P. T. Bauer, *West African Trade,* Part I. Much of this study is concerned with the impact of governmental and other forms of restrictionism. The range of choice becomes greater *ceteris paribus* as a people's economic organization becomes a "money economy." See E. K. Hawkins, "The Growth of a Money Economy in Nigeria and Ghana," *Oxford Economic Papers,* X (Oct., 1958), 339–54. Part of the increase in income associated with the monetization of an economy may be due to the fact that an increasingly large fraction of the product is being assigned a commercial value even though it had escaped such valuation under subsistence conditions.

factors are intensified, that is, when either local opportunity per capita shrinks or the significance of opportunity elsewhere increases. Illustrative of opportunity-shrinkage is the diminution in the amount of cultivable land available per capita occasioned by increase in population and the man-land ratio; this outcome is especially likely when a growing population is following either a system of bush-fallow or one of smidden agriculture (i.e., shifting cultivation) [79] and the agricultural technology in use is not very adaptable to sedentary and minimal-fallow husbandry and intensified cultivation under conditions free of erosion.[80]

Of course, should a growing population prove able to reorganize its agriculture and reduce the number of years an acre need lie fallow, it might be able within limits to offset increases in the man-land ratio.[81] Illustrative of increase in the significance of opportunity elsewhere is either an increase in the rate of remuneration to be had elsewhere or an increase in an individual's requirements or wants, which, even though the rate of pay to be earned elsewhere remains unchanged, makes him more willing to move and exchange his efforts for the money required to satisfy his augmented wants.[82] In sum, if the schedule of response of out-

[79] In Nigeria the system of bush-fallow is the one usually followed. See G. B. Stapleton, *op. cit.*, pp. 9–12, 21; Sir John Russell, *World Population and World Food Supplies* (London, 1954), pp. 283–98. On the modes of agriculture pursued in the North and the South, see essay by Forde in Perham, ed., *op. cit.*, I, Part I. On smidden agriculture, see H. C. Conklin, "The Study of Shifting Cultivation," *Current Anthropology*, II (Feb., 1961), 27–61, esp. p. 61 for the bibliography relating to African cultivation.

[80] In parts of the Eastern Region, for example, population pressure has caused the number of years land is left fallow to be reduced from 5–7 to 2–3, with the result that soil depletion has set in. See International Bank, *op. cit.*, pp. 46, 198. See also Bruce F. Johnston, *op. cit.*, pp. 9–12; Perham, *op. cit.*, I, 102–6; Buchanan and Pugh, *op. cit.*, pp. 77–79, 105–11; W. B. Morgan, "The Influence of European Contracts," *op. cit.*, p. 59, and "Farming Practice, Settlement Pattern and Population Density in South-eastern Nigeria," *op. cit.*, pp. 320–33. According to L. D. Stamp, under the bush-fallowing system in effect in 1938 in southern Nigeria, an average family of 3.6 persons cultivated 2 acres per year and farmed an acre once each 8 years, thus requiring 16 acres and permitting a maximum agricultural population density of 144 persons per square mile. The corresponding figures for northern Nigeria where a family numbered 3.3 persons were 3, 24, and 100. See "Land Utilization and Soil Erosion in Nigeria," *Geographical Review*, XXVIII (Jan., 1938), 32–45. For a careful account of the system of cultivation, the incidence of population pressure, and the difficulties attendant upon modifying prevailing farm practice, see W. B. Morgan, "Farm Practice, Settlement Pattern and Population Density in South-eastern Nigeria," *loc. cit.*

[81] For example, see Buchanan and Pugh, *op. cit.*, pp. 11–115, 123–25, 166–67.

[82] It is assumed that the increment in requirements cannot satisfactorily be supplied at his point of origin. Whereas, in an advanced economy, it is the marginal

put to inputs of effort falls, or if the schedule of demand for income (or goods) in terms of effort rises, emigration will ensue, particularly if, prior to these shifts of schedule, some individuals already were on the margin of emigrating.

What has been said relates primarily to the migration of individuals and small groups in search of better economic situations, within and outside Nigeria. It does not relate to the persisting and sometimes accelerated movements or drifts of whole peoples, a phenomenon frequently characteristic of the past settlement of Nigeria, as of Africa, and of the determination of the ethnic composition of its population at given moments in time even as it was characteristic of the settlement of Europe and the formation of the ethnic composition of Europe's population several millennia ago.[83] These movements sometimes entailed the displacement of one people by another, or the establishment of control over one people by another. Presumably the original movement, which sometimes eventuated in a series of population displacements as well as in the intermixture of peoples, usually was consequent upon the worsening of the economic situation of the initially moving people, or upon the genesis of a belief that some El Dorado lay in the distance. Nilotic peoples, pygmies, Galla, Bantu-speaking peoples, Ibo, Hausa, Fulani, Yoruba, Edo, and many others

opportunity that is conduct-determining, in a subsistence economy it may be the average opportunity or product that is determining of the reward or income enjoyed. When this situation obtains, out-migration is less than it ought to be on purely economic grounds. For example, see G. O. Gutman, "A Note on Economic Development with Subsistence Agriculture," *Oxford Economic Papers,* IX (Oct., 1957), 322–34.

[83] Presumably the moving African peoples compared not unfavorably in respect of numbers (which were quite small, as a rule), if not also of culture, with the Germanic and other peoples who moved into the Roman Empire in the centuries of its decline. Some of the indigenous east coast cultures were fairly well developed by the fifteenth century (*African Abstracts,* X [1959], item 145), and some peoples living on the east coast or in the Sudan had begun to absorb Islamic culture by the late eleventh and twelfth centuries and with it such institutions as the centralized state and the commercial city. See *ibid.,* items 28, 79, 166, 256; also Murdock, *Africa, passim.* On comparable European migrations, see F. Lot, *Les invasions barbares* (Paris, 1937), and *Les invasions germaniques* (Paris, 1945). That towns existed in Subsaharan Africa was reported even in the times of Herodotus (*History,* Bk. II, chaps. xxxii–xxxiii), who refers to a town that probably was on the river Niger, perhaps to an ancestor of nodal Timbuktu. On the trans-saharan trade routes see Seligman, *op. cit.,* map on p. 12; also Ibn Battúta, *op. cit.,* chap. xiv, also Ibn Khaldun, *The Muqaddimah* (translated by F. Rosenthal), Vol. I (London, 1958), Bk. 1, chap. i, pp. 118–20. With the coming of the Europeans to West Africa the orientation of trade and the center of economic gravity shifted away from the neighborhood of the Sahara and toward the Atlantic and the Guinea coasts. See Church, *op. cit.,* p. 168.

were involved in these movements in some capacity at one time or other.[84] While these movements sometimes eventuated in the establishment of kingdoms (e.g., in the Moslem emirates or states that overlap tribes and tribal societies in Northern Nigeria and in lands to the east and west), their boundaries usually were not clearly marked and enforced; nor were the political boundaries of subsequently established European colonies transformed into effective barriers to the movement of indigenous populations, particularly so long as European settlement remained enclave-like in character.

The subjection of interstate migration to somewhat more effective governmental control than had prevailed until recently is a quite "modern" phenomenon. Even so, interstate or interterritorial migration of the sort treated in previous paragraphs apparently is not yet being greatly interfered with, though the immigration of non-Africans has been subjected to restriction; but the increasing regulation of African migration is to be anticipated. As yet, however, measures applicable to Africans have three main objectives, particularly in European-dominated states: (i) to insure a sufficient supply of labor to labor-short areas and at the same time maintain public order; (ii) to organize migrants and protect them while they are migrating; and (iii) to prevent labor recruiters for labor-short areas from unduly depleting African communities of labor supposedly essential to the economic viability of these communities. As of now none of these objectives has assumed importance in Nigeria.[85]

(c) *Migration in Nigeria.* For purposes of analysis, the migratory movements in which the population of Nigeria has partici-

[84] For example, see Seligman, *op. cit.*, pp. 56, 67–72, 86, 135–49; *African Abstracts*, X (1959), items 79, 81, 206, 207; VI (1955), item 562; and C. R. Niven, "Nigeria Past and Present," *African Affairs*, LVI (Oct., 1957), 225 ff. Detailed information and traditional beliefs relating to the origins and movements of Africa's numerous peoples are examined in *Ethnographic Survey of Africa*. For, as Herskovits and others have pointed out, change is not new to Subsaharan Africa. Illustrative of such change is the introduction of manioc from South America into Africa by the Portuguese in the sixteenth century and its subsequent spread. See W. O. Jones, "Manioc: An Example of Innovation in African Economies," *Economic Development and Cultural Change*, V (Jan., 1957), 99–117.

[85] See "Inter-Territorial Migrations of Africans South of the Sahara," *International Labour Review*, LXXVI (Sept., 1956), 296–302; ILO, *African Labour Survey*, chap. ix.

pated, along with that of other tropical African countries, may be divided into two main categories and then further subdivided. Because of the poor quality of the statistics and because requisite vital statistical and suitable pre-1952 census data are lacking, careful quantitative analyses of the sort undertaken in Europe or America or Japan are not yet possible. But a reasonably accurate picture is to be had. The two main movements are: (1) the internal, embracing the passage of individuals from one point in Nigeria to another therein; and (2) the external, embracing the passage of individuals either into Nigeria from foreign lands, or from Nigeria into foreign lands. Individuals participating in either an internal or an external movement may be moving from: (i) a rural agricultural situation to some other rural agricultural situation; (ii) from a rural agricultural situation to one in industry, commerce, mining, or service, usually found in a town or city; (iii) from a commercial, mining, industrial, or service situation to a similar one located in another community; (iv) from a commercial, mining, industrial, or service situation to a rural situation. Each of these movements may be temporary or permanent, but with (ii) and (i) likely to be temporary, given that the destination of (i) is merely a wage-job in commercial agriculture, and with (iv) and (i) likely to be permanent, given that (iv) involves only a return to the land and that (i) merely involves replacing one farm by another located in another rural community. In the future, of course, (ii) will predominate, and the movement will be permanent if urban employment can be found.

Non-permanent migration may assume two forms, seasonal and non-seasonal. The movement of migrants who return within 6–8 months is described as seasonal; it probably embraces the bulk of Nigeria's temporary internal migration. Non-seasonal migration embracing the movement of persons who return after a lapse of 6–8 months or more, though important in some parts of Africa, appears to be of less significance in Nigeria where mining employs only a relatively small number and where migrants are free to settle as they choose.

Inasmuch as a great deal of African migration remains temporary, net and gross movements may be distinguished, though the distinction is of less importance in Nigeria than in (say) South Africa. While net movement may be of concern if an area's rate of growth is under analysis, gross movement always is of interest. For movement affects the migrant's behavior while he is moving or at his destination, and it reflects the circumstances that generate movement in the first place. Illustrative of the impact of movement upon the migrant's behavior at his destination is his efficiency as a worker; this is negatively correlated with labor turnover and a low net-gross ratio.[86]

While a great deal of interterritorial migration now takes place in Subsaharan Africa, and while some of the tribes now living in Nigeria are descendants of earlier immigrants, this form of migration, though of significance in some countries, does not play an important role in Nigeria. Not many Africans are moving in from the outside and not many are moving out of Nigeria, at least permanently. A few migrants come into the country, principally from French West Africa to work in agriculture or the mines, and a few go to Ghana, French Gabon, Fernando Po, and places not too far removed. Nigeria is too far from the two chief centers of immigration for African labor, Southern Rhodesia and the Union of South Africa, to supply labor to these countries, which draw half their wage earners from outside, mostly neighboring territories. Nigeria lacks a rich mining industry, rapidly developing manufactures, and relatively high rates of pay, all of which attract immigrants. Furthermore, average income remains relatively low, and Nigeria's domestic supply of unskilled labor is sufficient for the country's current needs.[87]

[86] For example, see "The Development of Wage-Earning Employment in Tropical Africa," *op. cit.*, pp. 256–58; "Interracial Wage Structure in Certain Parts of Africa," *International Labour Review*, LXXVIII (July, 1958), 54–55; "Inter-Territorial Migrations of Africans South of the Sahara," *ibid.*, LXXVI (Sept., 1957), 307–10. In Johannesburg labor turnover approximated 60 per cent per year. The number of Africans who make part of their living by earning wages is 3–5 times the number actually employed at any given time in representative Subsaharan-African countries. *Ibid.*, p. 295 and note. On productivity see also *supra*, n. 73. In Accra the wages of unskilled workers have been kept to the 1939 level. See *African Abstracts*, XII (1961), item 203. It should be noted that because of the sexually selective and seasonal character of much of African migration, the sex ratio of the populations of affected communities is subject to considerable variation over short periods of time.

[87] For example, see *ibid.*, pp. 302–7; "Wage-Earning Employment in Tropical Africa," *op. cit.*, pp. 253–55; *Nigeria* (report issued for 1955 and other years by

Of internal migration there is a great deal in Nigeria. Some is prompted by the pressure of population on farm land (which often can support only a relatively small number under the conditions of cultivation common in Nigeria and in much of Africa) [88] and by decline in the capacity of land to support population.[89] Some is motivated by the growing need for money to pay taxes and defray the monetary costs of goods, brides, etc. Some is generated by the fancied attractions of urban life, by the higher standards to be enjoyed in cities, and by the impression of the growing number of primary school graduates that cities alone afford them adequate opportunity.[90] These various pressures and

the British Colonial Office) (London, 1958 ff.); ILO, *African Labour Survey*, pp. 67, 130–37, 306–10, 314–15, 681–85; Lorimer and Karp, *op. cit.*, pp. 60–67; Kimble, *op. cit.*, I, 582–86; Church, *op. cit.*, p. 169; UNO, *Economic Survey of Africa since 1950*, pp. 42–43; *African Abstracts*, VIII (1957), item 439; IX (1958), item 27; XI (1960), items 6, 9, 13; XII (1961), items 3, 35, 79–81, 102; R. M. Prothero, "Migratory Labour from North-Western Nigeria," *Africa*, XXVII (July, 1957), 254–57, 260.

[88] See *supra*, n. 80. In southeastern Nigeria, according to Morgan, a system of three-year fallow can support (though at a very low level of existence) about 373 persons per square mile, and this number must be reduced if, as many believe, a five-year fallow system is required. Other estimates for this region range from under 300 to over 400 per square mile. See Morgan, "Farming Practice . . . ," *op. cit.*, p. 328; also A. T. Grove, "Soil Erosion and Population Problems in South-East Nigeria," *Geographical Journal*, CXVII (Sept., 1951), 291–306. Stamp observes "that given the existing forms of cultivation there is overpopulation in parts of Nigeria, where the density exceeds 300 persons per square mile" and that "at the moment much of Africa is supporting a maximum population." See *Africa*, pp. 136, 137. W. M. MacMillan wrote that "in South Africa, for example, South Africans will starve, even on tolerably good land, where the density is no more than 100 to the square mile." See *Africa Emergent* (rev. ed., Harmondssorth, 1949), p. 41. It should be noted also that a minimum population as well as heavy expenditure is required to make habitation possible in regions where the tsetse fly is found; Church puts this minimum at about 70 per square mile. *Op. cit.*, p. 164. The number must be large enough, under existing technology, to keep the land cleared and in use.

[89] Crops differ in calorie yield per hectare. Maize (which approximates rice in calorie yield per hectare in West Africa) is popular, but it "is one of the most soil-depleting of the grain crops." If this tendency to soil depletion is not counterbalanced, perhaps because of population pressure, it may prove necessary to shift to manioc, which is better adapted to exhausted soils and short fallows. The spread of manioc culture appears to be, at least in part, a response to soil depletion caused by population pressure. For example, see Johnston, *The Staple Food Economies*, pp. 126–27, 174–81, 185–88. But even manioc culture cannot circumvent population pressure. In Sokoto Province, with some densities of nearly 400 per square mile, "even in good years the return from land . . . is insufficient for the whole population." See Prothero, "Migratory Labour," *op. cit.*, p. 253.

[90] See Ardner *et al.*, *op. cit.*, Parts II–III; "Inter-territorial Migrations of Africans South of the Sahara," *op. cit.*, pp. 293–95. In the Union of South Africa the annual wages for unskilled African workers is 2–3 times the cash value of the crops produced by a five-member family. *Ibid.*, p. 295. At present there is considerable unemployment in the cities of Ghana and Nigeria, attributable largely

pulls, especially heavy when coupled with landlessness or with too little land, induce men to migrate and even to become wage-earners; they account for much of the migration out of the densely populated parts of Eastern and Northern Nigeria.[91]

Findings respecting migration from Sokoto Province in Northern Nigeria may be generalizable to other regions. These findings are based on a survey made of 259,000 migrants during the 1952–53 dry season. Of these migrants 73 per cent originated in Sokoto Province, 10 elsewhere in Northern Nigeria, and 17 in French territory. In number they amounted to 25–33 per cent of the province's male population aged 15–49, with this fraction approaching one-half in some districts. About 38 per cent of the migrants were going to points in Northern Nigeria, to the tin mines at Jos, to Zamfara and places where export crops are produced, and to commercial Kano and other points. Some of this migration, apparently being for short distances (20–40 miles), permitted migrants to be accompanied by their families, but much was for long distances. About 43 per cent of the migrants were going to Western and Eastern Nigeria, 17 were going to Ghana, and 2 to French territory. Most of these would travel 500–700 miles, sometimes much of it on foot. About 92 per cent of the migrants were moving to supplement their incomes, about half by exporting their strength and another quarter by trading. Most of this migration must have been seasonal or otherwise temporary, given that half the migrants had been away more than four times. However, as Prothero suggests, some of these will remain, and the fraction remaining will increase as experience makes clear the practicability and the advantages of permanent settlement.[92]

Localized territorial expansion of populations tends to diminish as land is brought under settlement and there no longer exist areas

---

to the excessive movement there of young people who have completed their primary education but lack the secondary school training many urban employments require. See Callaway, *infra*, chap. ix.

[91] For example, see Prothero, "The Population Census of Northern Nigeria . . . ," *op. cit.*, pp. 169–70, and "The Population of Eastern Nigeria," *Scottish Geographical Magazine*, LXXI (1955), 166–70. See also A. H. M. Kirk-Greene, "Tax and Travel among the Hill Tribes of Northern Adamawa," *Africa*, XXVI (Oct., 1956), 369–79; *African Abstracts*, IX (1958), item 267; XI (1960), items 49, 185; XII (1961), items 3, 35.

[92] Prothero, "Migratory Labour . . . ," *op. cit.*, pp. 251–61.

into which increasing numbers can easily expand. In the past, of course, such expansion was possible, but it usually was carried out, as in the instance of the Tiv, in accordance with tribal practice and well understood rules. Centrifugal movement was under the dominance of the lineages, though it varied with the intensity of the demand for land and was directed somewhat along the lines of least resistance.[93]

It is to be expected that internal migration will continue to predominate in Nigeria, since there are no magnetic foreign centers near that country. Movement from rural to urban areas will dominate both seasonal and permanent internal migration, each of which will be governed by the forces making for urbanization rather than by the discovery of rich natural resources. It will be accompanied by an increase in the wage-earning class, which may be expected to grow more rapidly than the population at large, as more and more individuals experience employment in a wage-earning capacity.

III. Conclusion

Nigeria, now one of the most densely populated extended areas in tropical Africa, appears to be overpopulated in some of its rural areas in that under present conditions the rural population would be better off if the man-land ratio were lower. Moreover, improvements in technology may reduce the size of the optimum man-land ratio. Regulation of Nigerian numbers is indicated, therefore, for even should the current annual rate of natural increase not exceed 1.5 per cent, the potential rate is quite high, though probably not as high as in some Asian lands. Moreover, since the country is comparatively short of good land, capital, and natural resources, and since it lacks a technically competent elite to get economic development rapidly under way now, its problems will be intensified by considerable population growth. It is unlikely, however, that Nigerian fertility will fall appreciably in the near

[93] See Paul Bohannan, "The Migration and Expansion of the Tiv," *Africa*, XXIV (Jan., 1954), 2–16.

future; it is to be expected, therefore, that numbers will double or treble in the next sixty to seventy-five years.

While emigration is not likely to be important, there being no nearby externally situated centers of attraction, internal migration will long play a major role in the country's economic development. For at present the population is not optimally distributed, rural increase exceeds rural labor requirements, and it is internal migration that brings labor to urban and other centers where labor time can be more fully and effectively used. It is internal migration that in the end will enlarge the migrants' range of choice, weaken his tribal ties, and compel the development in cities of an institutional milieu favorable to the settlement there of permanent migrants. While the ratio of net to gross migration cannot be elevated to unity, some elevation is essential to the development of skill and stability in the Nigerian labor force. Inasmuch as Nigerians are used to moving freely and far, a great deal of internal migration is to be expected, particularly as transport improves, education increases, and word of new opportunities spreads.

8

Human Resources and Economic Development in Nigeria

Frederick Harbison

I. Introduction

Of all the newly emerging African nations, Nigeria's prospects for successful economic and political development are probably the best. In terms of population it is by far the largest country on the continent. It has more native civil servants and more highly trained manpower than the other new African countries. It has made the transition from colony to state with comparative ease and stability. Its regional and federal governments, at least in form, are well designed to foster democratic political institutions. Finally, Nigeria has most of the natural resources required for balanced growth and a potentially large internal market for the goods and services that it will be capable of producing. With all these assets, if Nigeria cannot achieve successful political and economic development, then the outlook for the rest of the African continent is indeed gloomy.

The tasks ahead, however, are many, and the obstacles in the path of progress are formidable. Nigeria is short of capital and must find the means of accumulating it. It is short of high-level manpower and must find a way of developing it quickly. It lacks a sense of national unity and purpose, which it must achieve if the federal system is to work effectively.

Earlier essays have discussed the political and social aspects of Nigeria's future. Here I shall concentrate on the economic aspects, particularly on the problems of human resources.

II. The Nigerian Economy

In the decade prior to independence Nigeria's national income was presumed to be increasing at a rate of about 4 per cent per annum in real terms. Allowing for increases in population, however, the probable annual rise in income per capita often was between 2 and 2½ per cent,[1] which is about average for most countries. A 2 per cent increase in real per capita income per year might be considered as the lowest acceptable minimum rate for "successful" growth for the Federation of Nigeria. Whatever the expected rate of growth may be, Nigeria's present living standards are very low, for per capita income is less than £30 per year. On this basis, among the one hundred countries and territories in the world classified as economically underdeveloped, Nigeria falls into the poorest 20 per cent.

The government of this new nation can hardly be satisfied with a future rate of economic growth below that achieved in colonial times. Indeed, all political leaders are united in the belief that Nigeria in the next ten years can and must achieve a rate of growth much greater than that of the previous decade. They, as well as political leaders in other emerging nations, are caught up in the world-wide revolution of rising expectations. Feeling that they must increase the tempo of modernization, they are prepared to undertake a forced march toward industrialism.

The record of growth in the years just before independence is impressive, as illustrated by the following figures: [2]

Chart I.

		1947	1953	1958
Revenue of governments (excluding grants from overseas) *	(£ thousand)	14,193	51,110	81,288
Currency in circulation as of the 31st of March	(£ thousand)	23,429	51,365	55,118

[1] For a detailed description of the Nigerian economy, see Federation of Nigeria, National Economic Council, *Economic Survey of Nigeria, 1959* (Lagos, 1959). Most of the economic data contained in this essay derives from this survey.
[2] These figures are drawn from *ibid*.

Chart I. (*continued*)

		1947	1953	1958
Bank deposits as of the 31st of December	(£ thousand)	13,697	31,238	58,056
Exports and re-exports †	(£ thousand)	44,314	124,232	135,690
Imports †	(£ thousand)	32,636	108,290	167,074
Cement: imported and manufactured locally †	(tons)	107,306	297,436	573,119
Railway freight traffic *	(thousand ton-miles)	571,000	827,000	1,232,000
Commercial vehicles licensed in 1st quarter	(number)	n.a.	10,700	17,900
Private vehicles in 1st quarter	(number)	n.a.	12,300	24,150
Telephone instruments in use §	(number)	6,544	13,279	31,000
Electricity generated *	(thousand units)	85,836	164,756	331,125
Gross capital formation *	(£ thousand)	n.a.	52,157	108,938

* Year ending the 31st of March.
† Year ending the 31st of December.
§ 1947 and 1958 as of the 31st of December: 1953 as of the 31st of March.

To continue, and if possible to accelerate, this growth will require efficient government, careful development planning, judicious investment in material and human resources, and united effort.

In 1958 the population of the Federation of Nigeria and the Southern Cameroons was estimated to be approximately 35 million, and it was presumed to be growing at a rate of 2 per cent per annum. The population of the Northern Region was approximately 19 million, the Western Region 7 million, the Eastern Region 8 million, Lagos Township 350,000, and the Southern Cameroons 800,000. Most of the population lives in rural areas, and over 75 per cent of the labor force is engaged in agriculture, forestry, and animal husbandry. The urban population, however, is increasing at a very rapid rate as a result of migration from the countryside to the towns and cities.

The national income of Nigeria has been estimated at 812 million pounds a year,[3] a figure roughly equivalent, for example, to Egypt's national income. (Egypt, however, has a population of only 25 million, and thus enjoys a somewhat higher income per capita.) Agriculture accounts for at least one-half the national income of Nigeria, and agricultural products constitute 85 per cent of the country's exports. Livestock, fisheries, and forestry contribute 10 per cent of the national income. Minerals include coal, petroleum, limestone, tin, and columbite, but together these are not as yet major contributors to national income. Industry's present contribution is very small, but industrialization on a factory scale is rapidly gaining momentum. In promoting industrialization Nigeria has such significant advantages as availability of raw materials, adequate supplies of labor, expanding supplies of electric power, improved communications, and a growing internal market.

Many of the requirements for future economic growth are reasonably clear. Those that seem most apparent are first, and of primary importance, a very substantial increase in the productivity of agriculture, forestry, and animal husbandry; second, development of mineral resources, particularly petroleum; third, development of water, road, and rail transport; fourth, substantial industrial growth; and finally, a continued increase in trade and commerce.

It is obvious that Nigeria's principal source of wealth at present lies in agriculture, for it is the cultivation of field and tree crops that enables Nigeria to feed herself. In addition, agricultural exports provide needed foreign exchange. The five most important of these, accounting for 80 per cent of the total exports, are palm kernels and oil, groundnuts oil and cake, cocoa, cotton lint and seed, and rubber. Nearly all of the capital for development must come directly or indirectly from the sale of these agricultural products in the world markets.

The agricultural products mentioned above, with the exception of rubber, are purchased by the Marketing Boards in each region. Charged with the regulation of purchase prices and the control

[3] *Ibid.* A new estimate of national income is being made, and this figure may be changed considerably.

of these exports, the Marketing Boards in recent years have accumulated large surplus funds, which have been the principal source of capital to finance economic development projects. In the next few years, it is anticipated that exports of agricultural products will increase substantially, but exports of the same products from other countries are likely to increase also. These prices in the world markets may therefore fall, as has been the case already with cocoa. Thus, although it is absolutely essential that Nigeria increase its production of export crops, the prospects of continued accumulation of large funds by the Marketing Boards for development purposes are uncertain.

Other exports are hides and skins from the grazing areas of the Northern Region and logs and lumber products from the two Southern Regions. Petroleum is currently exported on a small scale, and the prospects for large exports in the future are very promising. Political leaders, particularly in the Eastern Region where oil has been discovered, are counting heavily on future petroleum revenues to finance a large share of Nigeria's development projects. It is hoped that oil revenues eventually will greatly exceed those of the agricultural Marketing Boards.

Like their counterparts in other newly developing countries, Nigerian leaders are solidly committed to a program of rapid industrial development. Existing industrial enterprises include some cotton textile mills, two cement plants, three cigarette factories, two breweries, a number of food processing plants, several metal fabrication and assembly plants, a soap factory, a growing number of small plastics factories, and several other miscellaneous establishments. There are plans and hopes for many new industries, such as a steel works, a glass manufacturing plant, several more textile mills, and a fertilizer plant. Interest by outside investors in establishing plants in Nigeria has shown a remarkable upsurge since the end of 1959, and a four- to five-fold expansion in industrial output within the next decade seems to be a reasonable target. Most political leaders hope even to exceed this. The major objective of the drive for industrialization, aside from the very important factor of prestige, is to lessen the dependency upon the relation between the world prices of Nigeria's agricultural exports and her manufactured imports. This is also the goal of almost every underdeveloped country today.

Several other economic activities deserve brief mention. Nigeria exports some tin and columbite ores. Coal of rather inferior quality is exported only in small quantities but is used extensively within the country. There has been a tendency, however, for the major consumers, such as the railways and industrial plants, to change to other sources of power, and, as a consequence, unemployment among coal miners is high. Nigeria has a good railway system, and the development of road transport, largely in the hands of Nigerian entrepreneurs, has been quite extensive. There are radio stations in all three regions and television stations in both the Eastern and Western Regions. Inland waterway transport, though not of the same importance as railways or roads, is scheduled for expansion in the future. Construction is a booming industry in Nigeria, and the erection of office buildings, schools, roads, bridges, harbor installations, and private dwellings is a common sight in most of the major towns and cities. Indeed, the city of Lagos itself has been transformed from a sprawling, overgrown town into a modern-looking metropolis in the space of only a few years, and similar transformations may be seen in a number of other developing countries. Finally, Nigeria is fairly well supplied with banks, large-scale commercial establishments (owned by foreign interests), and small traders (largely Lebanese and Syrian). There are also large and growing local markets in the principal towns where indigenous products and various imported articles are bought and sold.

For future development Nigeria needs capital. The current rate of gross capital formation is probably between 11 and 13 per cent. About 15 per cent of the total is foreign investment. Although over-all targets have not been established, it is almost certain that the rate of capital formation will have to be increased by at least 50 per cent over present levels if the country is to have an annual rate of growth of over 2 per cent per capita in real income. The problem is where to find the funds, and several solutions seem apparent. The surpluses of the Marketing Boards, for reasons explained above, are not likely to increase substantially in the future, but oil revenues are expected to rise. Outside private investment, particularly for industrial development, may be encouraged. Loans from international agencies and individual countries will be sought with vigor. Finally, an attempt may be made to increase tax revenues. Technically, it is possible for Nigeria to increase capital accumulation to the desired levels by a combination of all these measures; even so, capital accumulation alone cannot assure the success of Nigeria's development plans.

Economic growth depends upon the manner in which capital is invested as well as upon the rate of its accumulation. For example, investments in the development and improvement of roads, harbors, land, irrigation facilities, and agricultural research will bring high, long-range returns in increased productivity. Conversely, television networks, international airlines, and luxuriously appointed government and university buildings are low-return investments. For prestige purposes, however, Nigeria, in common with other countries at a comparable stage of development, has recently given fairly high priority to such investments. In addition, there has been a considerable leakage of funds through graft, corruption, and various forms of "gifts." In the new states one cannot expect complete rationality and probity in investment programs, and for this reason the total capital investment necessary to achieve a given rate of economic growth is likely to be higher than economic models might suggest. As a "political economist," I assume that Nigeria will waste a good deal of money in the course of its future development, but this in itself is no reason to be pessimistic about the prospects for reasonably rapid growth.

In my view, a much more serious problem facing Nigeria will be the accumulation of human capital, which is essential if the economy is to utilize its material capital effectively. The remainder of the paper, therefore, will focus principally on the problem of high-level manpower for Nigeria.

III. High-level Manpower Requirements

Human capital and physical capital are *both* indispensable for economic growth, and in most countries both are in short supply. In some, capital shortages constitute the more critical bottlenecks; in others, lack of high-level manpower may be the restricting factor. In my judgment, Egypt, for example, falls into the former category; Nigeria, on the other hand, faces primarily a shortage of skill—i.e., human capital. In order to employ physical capital effectively, Nigeria needs entrepreneurs, managers, and technical and professional personnel of all kinds.

High-level manpower may be defined in two ways. First, it can be defined functionally by designating occupations included in the high-level category; second, it can be described by delineating the levels of education and experience normally required to prepare persons for these high-level jobs.

By the functional definition the following occupations may be considered of the high-level category:

1. Administrators, including executives and managers of sizable groups in government, commerce, industry, education, etc.;

2. Professional personnel, including engineers, qualified accountants, doctors, dentists, veterinarians, scientists, architects, lawyers, agricultural officers and research specialists, etc.;

3. Technical, subprofessional, and supervisory personnel, such as technicians, supervisors, highly skilled craftsmen, nurses, agricultural assistants, etc.;

4. Teachers, including those employed by universities and technological institutes, secondary grammar schools, trade and vocational schools, teacher training institutions, and primary schools (provided such teachers hold Grade I certificate qualification or above);

5. Military and police officers;

6. Judges, members of parliament, government ministers, local government councilors and senior staff, and other miscellaneous occupations not falling into the above groupings.

In terms of education and experience, the category of high-level manpower would be limited to persons with a minimum of two years of post-school certificate work or its equivalent. This broad category of high-level manpower may be further divided into two groups—senior and intermediate:

(*a*) In the senior group a university degree, or advanced teachers' college degree (or its equivalent) is increasingly being considered requisite. Functionally, this group is composed of senior administrators and managers (public and private), qualified professional persons, and fully qualified teachers.

(b) In the intermediate group fall those with two or three years of post-school certificate education. Such education might have been undertaken in advanced grammar schools (6th Form), in advanced vocational or trade schools, as "preliminary work" in University College, or in some specialized "junior college" or similar institution abroad. Persons in this category usually require some technical training, but not of a professional standard, and often are in executive or supervisory, but not policy-making, positions. Functionally, this group would normally include engineering assistants, laboratory technicians, agricultural assistants, assistant chief clerks, senior draftsmen, and assistant managers.

Obviously, there are many persons employed in both the senior and intermediate groups who do not have the educational background set forth above. Yet there is probably general agreement that it would be preferable to utilize persons with the proper educational background in such positions if they were available.

In connection with the work of the "Ashby Commission," I made an estimate of the existing supply of high-level manpower in Nigeria and suggested some targets for manpower development by 1970.[4] These targets represent the probable minimum "input" of high-level manpower that would permit a rate of growth in 1960–70 equivalent to that in the decade before independence. The figures are summarized in the following charts.

The present number of persons in the high-level manpower category (both senior and intermediate) is about 30,000. This is less than 0.1 per cent of the population. The manpower targets set forth above, if achieved, would raise the percentage of high-level manpower to a little less than 0.2 per cent of the population in 1970.

Nigeria's existing numbers of high-level manpower, and even the targets set forth above, are not high in comparison with other

[4] Federation of Nigeria, Federal Ministry of Education, *Investment in Education* (Report of the Commission on Post-School Certificate and Higher Education in Nigeria) (London and Lagos, 1960).

Chart II. Senior Group: Managerial, Professional, and Administrative Personnel and Qualified Teachers

Sector	1958 reported	1960 estimated	1970 target	1970/60 net increase	Replacement factor	10-year requirement
Agriculture, forestry, and fishing	302	350	1,750	1,400	700	2,100
Mining, quarrying, petroleum	656	700	1,500	800	400	1,200
Manufacturing	621	700	2,700	2,000	1,000	3,000
Construction	1,153	1,200	2,400	1,200	600	1,800
Electricity, water, and sanitary services	297	325	525	200	100	300
Commerce	1,851	2,200	5,000	2,800	1,400	4,200
Transport, storage, and communications	1,477	1,700	3,500	1,800	900	2,700
Government services	5,313	6,000	10,000	4,000	2,000	6,000
Miscellaneous and self-employed	—	500	1,500	1,000	500	1,500
Total (excluding teachers)	11,670	13,675	28,875	15,200	7,600	22,800
Post-primary teachers (graduate qualification)	1,267	1,700	7,000	5,300	3,100	8,400
Grand Total	12,937	15,375	35,875	20,500	10,700	31,200

Chart III. Intermediate Group: Technical and Supervisory Personnel and Under-Qualified Teachers

Sector	1958 reported	1960 estimated	1970 target	1970/60 net increase	Replace-ment factor	10-year requirement
Agriculture, forestry, and fishing	231	250	2,500	2,250	750	3,000
Mining, quarrying, petroleum	198	275	1,375	1,100	400	1,500
Manufacturing	490	600	3,600	3,000	1,000	4,000
Construction	577	800	2,800	2,000	600	2,600
Electricity, water, and sanitary services	218	250	1,000	750	350	1,100
Commerce	854	1,000	3,000	2,000	500	2,500
Transport, storage, and communications	2,156	2,400	6,000	3,600	1,200	4,800
Government services	4,007	5,000	15,000	10,000	3,000	13,000
Miscellaneous and self-employed	—	500	2,000	1,500	400	1,900
Total (excluding teachers)	8,731	11,075	37,275	26,200	8,200	34,400
Post-primary teachers (qualified non-graduate)	3,431	3,700	7,000	2,500	3,000	5,500
Primary school teachers (qualified non-graduate)	567	600	11,100	10,500	3,500	14,000
Grand Total	12,729	15,375	55,375	39,200	14,700	53,900

underdeveloped countries. Ghana, for example, already has over 0.3 per cent of her population in the high-level manpower category. In more advanced countries, such as Egypt and India, high-level manpower is probably a little over 0.5 per cent, or five times Nigeria's present level. In the most advanced societies, such as the United Kingdom, the United States, Western Germany, and the Soviet Union, the range may be between 2 and 5 per cent.

One more fact is very significant. It is probable that of Nigeria's 30,000 persons in the high-level manpower category, not less than 10,000, or one-third, are expatriates. The proportion of expatriates is higher in Nigeria than in Ghana. In Egypt, the number of expatriates is probably less than 2 per cent of the total number of persons in the high-level manpower category. The Nigerianization of high-level manpower, therefore, makes the task of development more difficult. If it is assumed that only two-thirds of the 30,000 persons in the high-level manpower category are presently Nigerians, then the targets set forth in this report require more than a fivefold expansion within the next ten years.

Nigeria has not now, nor will she have in the next few years, the capacity to generate the high-level manpower necessary to make rapid economic growth possible. An examination of outputs in both the senior and intermediate categories makes this quite clear.

Of the 31,200 persons needed in the senior category, one may assume that 20,000 should have a university education or equivalent. The appropriate composition of this 20,000 might be as follows: [5]

Graduate teachers	8,500
Engineers (in all fields)	5,000
Agricultural, forestry, and fishery specialists	1,200
Veterinarians	300
Doctors	2,500
Scientists (for research institutes)	500
Others	2,000
	20,000

[5] These figures are speculative and must remain so until a basic survey can provide the existing breakdown of high-level manpower by occupation.

In arriving at the figure above, it is assumed that 10,000 persons in the senior category, mostly in managerial and administrative positions, could rise to responsible positions in commercial and industrial enterprises.

A requirement of 20,000 university graduates from 1960–70 would mean an annual output of 2,000 graduates a year. At present, less than 200 per year are being turned out in universities within the Federation. Possibly four times that number, or 800 per year, may be returning from abroad with university degrees. The existing shortfall may be at least 1,000 per year.

The shortfall is even more serious for non-graduates. If it is assumed that the ten-year requirement for persons with intermediate education is nearly 55,000, the annual requirement is 5,500. It is doubtful whether the total number of new persons with two or three years' education beyond the school certificate level exceeds 1,500 per year from Nigeria and abroad, including those who go on to university level education. Moreover, the training received by this small number in most cases is not of the kind most suitable for the country's economic and political development.

The conclusions to be drawn from these very rough and necessarily imprecise figures are these: *Nigeria's most urgent need in the near future is for expansion of intermediate education.* If funds are inadequate, this should take priority over expansion in university education within the Federation. It would be more feasible and economical to send abroad a small number of students for university education than to send a large number for intermediate training. Another obvious conclusion is that technical and scientific education, both at the university and the intermediate level, needs to be given the highest priority. But technical education is more expensive on the whole than non-technical. In university education in Egypt, for example, over two-thirds of the staff members and an equal proportion of the expenditures are in the faculties of Science, Medicine, Engineering, Agriculture, and Veterinary Medicine. Yet less than 40 per cent of the total number of students are registered in these fields. At the intermediate level also the cost of technical training greatly exceeds that of academic education. Thus, Nigeria, like other newly developing nations of modern times, must be prepared to institute educational programs that are relatively more costly than those developed prior to independence.

In Nigeria there may be a tendency, as in India and to a lesser extent in Egypt, to overinvest in education in the law and arts and to underinvest in engineering, agriculture, and science. Nigeria is fast approaching a stage where it may have a surplus of university graduates seeking to enter the *administrative ranks* of the civil service. The same situation may soon be evident in commerce and private industry. This factor needs to be given serious attention in planning higher education in Nigeria and in the counseling of young people regarding future career opportunities within their country.

Even allowing for a large error in the estimates of demand and supply set forth in the previous section, it is clear that within the next few years Nigeria cannot possibly meet her high-level manpower requirements without the employment of expatriates. Indeed, the present policy of both the Regional and Federal Governments is to encourage outside interests to bring in both capital and manpower for development projects and technical assistance programs of all kinds. Such expatriates are needed in the country only temporarily, presumably until they can train and develop Nigerians as replacements. Viewed in this way, the expatriates are really "the seed corn" for the training of Nigerians for high-level positions.

Since independence, the number of expatriates in Ghana has risen sharply, despite the Africanization program of the government. The reason is simply that Ghana's ambitious development program has a voracious appetite for high-level manpower that is not yet available within the country. Nigeria's supply of high-level manpower is inferior to that of Ghana, but her ambitions for development are just as high. Thus, the need for bringing in expatriates may be even greater than in Ghana. A most conservative guess would be that Nigeria by 1965 may need to double the present number of expatriates in employment. Many of these expatriates, of course, would be technical personnel supplied by outside agencies such as the United Nations.

The employment of additional expatriates need cause no alarm, nor should it prevent in any way the Nigerianization of high-level manpower. On the contrary, if carefully planned and controlled, the temporary employment of expatriates will expedite the Nigerianization process by providing the means for effective upgrading of Nigerian personnel. In my opinion, the ten-year objective of the Federation should be to develop its system of higher education to a point where employment of expatriates on any sizable scale becomes unnecessary after 1970. Long before that time, Nigeria should be replacing expatriates on a large scale with her own citizens. Provision is made for such Nigerianization in the replacement factor in the various manpower projections made in Charts II and III.

High-level manpower targets should not be expressed merely in terms of the number of additional persons required. Managers and administrators are developed by practical experience and by in-service training as well as by preparatory formal education. The same is true of engineers, technicians, supervisors, and teachers. As a general rule, top positions are filled only by persons who have had formal education, on-the-job training, and extensive experience.

Nigeria has a particularly urgent need to evolve programs for the more effective training of employed manpower. In many government departments, and, to a lesser extent, in private industry, persons in high positions have had little experience and almost no job training. Also, as in any rapidly expanding country with a critical shortage of high-level manpower, persons lacking the necessary pre-employment education have been employed in high positions. Thus, in any program for development of high-level manpower, measures for the training and upgrading of *employed* manpower should be given high priority. Some in-service training programs might be conducted by government departments or private businesses; others, by universities, technical institutes, or even secondary schools. A good beginning has been made in

Nigeria, but more programs are urgently needed. Also needed is an inventory of the various in-service training programs already in existence throughout the Federation. Of all investments in education, those aimed at upgrading employed manpower bring the quickest returns in economic growth.

IV. Unskilled Manpower

Ironically, Nigeria has a problem of mounting labor surpluses as well as a critical shortage of skills. Unemployment of primary school leavers is mounting with alarming speed, particularly in the Eastern Region. Even with rapid industrialization and the expansion of government services, job opportunities for primary school leavers are limited, but each year droves of young people leave the rural areas for the larger towns and cities in search of government and factory jobs, or in search of almost any employment other than traditional agriculture. The result is overcrowding in the urban areas and mounting unemployment in the growing urban labor force. Moreover, this problem is spreading throughout the Federation. While the curtailment of coal mining has aggravated conditions in the Eastern Region, unemployment among school leavers is becoming critical also in the Western Region, and the early symptoms of future difficulty are already evident in the North.

The unemployment problem is in part related to education. In the Eastern and Western Regions and in Lagos, great emphasis has been placed on achieving universal primary education as soon as possible. Well over 60 per cent of the children of normal primary school age receive some education at this level, and many of these are sent to school by their parents with the hope that they can "get a job" in the towns or cities. Since the orientation of primary education tends to stress the superiority of urban employment over traditional labor, such education changes the aspirations of youth and makes it less willing to accept the status quo. At the same time, primary education prepares young people only for more schooling and for more responsible participation as citizens, not for government jobs, factory employment, and other gainful occupations. The latter is achieved only at the secondary and post-secondary levels. However, less than 2 per cent of the age groups normally eligible can attend secondary schools, and only a minute fraction of these have an opportunity for higher education.

How then may the problem of unemployed school leavers be solved? [6] The question is difficult and there are no really good answers, but several solutions may be suggested. One possible measure might be to make the industrialization process as labor-intensive as possible. Logically, this would suggest a heavy reliance on handicraft or cottage industries, together with the use of comparatively simple machinery in the industrial plants. But Nigeria, like most other countries in a comparable stage of development, is likely to reject this approach in favor of primary reliance on factories using the most modern technology. It seems doubtful that Nigerian leaders can be persuaded to invest in antiquated steel works, textile mills, and metal processing plants when, in terms of both quality of output and the long-run costs of production, modern technology is deemed to be more efficient. Equally important, brushing aside all considerations of efficiency, Nigerians are likely to favor modern factories purely for nationalistic reasons.

As an alternative possibility, managers might be forced to use more labor than necessary in these modern factories, but this in itself would be very shortsighted. Such waste would result in the less effective use of modern equipment and machinery and a higher cost of manufactured goods. There is little to be gained by having workers underemployed within the factory gates.

If modern factories provide no solution, could jobs in petty trade, local government services, and construction absorb surplus labor? The answer would of course be yes, if new jobs such as these could be created. However, opportunities for the creation of these jobs are limited unless there is very rapid expansion of income and services at the community level. Experience, par-

---

[6] On this subject, also see the analysis and recommendations of Archibald Callaway, "School Leavers and the Developing Economy of Nigeria," *infra*, chap. ix.

ticularly in the Eastern Region, has shown that the migration of persons from rural to urban areas is likely to precede rather than to follow the expansion of economic opportunities in the cities. The presence of an army of unemployed persons in the larger urban areas is hardly conducive to economic expansion, and it thus seems doubtful that enough new local jobs could be created to reduce substantially the labor surplus.

Another alternative is to hold the surplus human resources on the land. Theoretically at least, excess labor may best be stored in the agricultural areas. But, with increasing population, the rural areas in many parts of Nigeria are already overcrowded, and disguised unemployment is becoming widespread. In any case, the effect of primary education is to make young people less willing to stay on the land. A partial answer for this dilemma might be the modernization of traditional agriculture, making it more productive and at the same time more attractive as a means of livelihood. However, such modernization might progressively result in reducing the demand for labor in the rural areas.

A final measure is to utilize surplus labor in massive programs of public works. Of all the alternatives, this holds perhaps the greatest promise for the full utilization of human resources. Here community development projects, such as those in India, might be organized to utilize local labor on a limited scale in the villages for building schools, digging irrigation canals, or improving local access roads. In this way the disguised unemployed might become a source of capital formation. However, the employment of labor on public works requires in itself a considerable amount of capital and a great deal of organization. In many cases this necessitates the diversion of scarce financial resources and high-level manpower from other development projects.

Clearly, therefore, industrialization *by itself* is not likely soon to solve the problem of surplus labor in Nigeria. Industrialization must be very rapid and extensive to absorb sizable quantities of labor. But rapid and extensive industrialization can take place only if the markets are expanding. Since Nigeria is not in a good position to export manufactured products, industrial development is dependent upon expansion of domestic markets, and this will require sharply rising incomes in all segments of the economy. For example, if incomes and employment in agriculture are rising, and if at the same time large outlays are made for labor-intensive public works, the demand for industrial products and hence industrial labor may increase. But if the other sectors of the economy are not growing, building modern factories may even increase unemployment by displacing persons from handicraft and cottage industries in greater numbers than those newly employed in the plants.

V. Policy Questions in Economic Development

Nigeria is thus plagued with two basic manpower problems: it is faced with underutilization and mounting unemployment of primary school leavers; at the same time, the shortage of high-level manpower is perhaps the principal limiting factor in future economic growth. In addition to these manpower questions, there are the problems of increasing substantially the rate of material capital formation and improving the productiveness of investment of scarce funds. We may conclude this paper by posing for discussion a number of thorny issues confronting the Nigerian leaders and the Nigerian peoples as they face an uncertain future.

First, for the next twenty to thirty years at least, Nigeria's economic growth will depend primarily on improvements in agriculture and animal husbandry. Most newly developing countries, including Nigeria, tend to downgrade investment in these areas and to overemphasize the building of factories, ultra-modern government and office buildings, and international airlines (which always operate at a loss). The highest priority manpower needs in Nigeria are agricultural officers, agricultural assistants, and veterinarians. Systems of agricultural extension services are needed far more than television networks, but educated Nigerians are not interested in agriculture or animal husbandry, particularly if they must go back to live in the bush. How then can more high-level manpower be found to bring about the modernization of agriculture? Is it possible to change the orientation of the rural primary schools so as to train young people to become better farmers instead of encouraging them to become government clerks? Can traditional agriculture be transformed without sweeping changes in the system of land tenure?

Second, as Arthur Lewis has pointed out, the current fashion of African countries, including Nigeria, is to spend lavishly on university education and on the attainment of universal primary education, while neglecting secondary education, and particularly secondary technical education. Logically, Nigeria should not increase, and preferably it should decrease, expenditures on primary education until the number of students in secondary education has increased about fivefold. But is this politically feasible in a country where the popular pressure for education is so strong?

Nigeria now has two universities and is planning several more. Should these be built on the lavish scale of University College at Ibadan, where every student is a boarder and occupies a single room? Or should the new institutions be non-residential city universities? Moreover, until the secondary school bottleneck is broken, would it not be better to continue sending most students abroad for higher education rather than building new universities in Nigeria? These questions involve more than economics. If there is a university in the Western Region, there must also be universities in the Northern and Eastern Regions. And in view of the strong regionalism in Nigeria, it will be difficult to avoid unnecessary and uneconomical duplication of expensive courses. What measures, then, can be taken to develop higher education on a more economical basis?

Third, in terms of numbers, school teachers at the secondary level and above are most needed in Nigeria. At the same time, most of the more ambitious young teachers look upon teaching not as a profession but as an avenue to politics or to jobs in the higher civil service. How then will it be possible for Nigeria to find, train, and retain the fifteen thousand new post-primary teachers that will be required in the next ten years?

Fourth, for economic development Nigeria desperately needs

both public and private foreign capital. Other countries, however, need it just as desperately. What particular measures can be taken to attract private foreign capital to the country? And how can Nigeria best present her case for public grants or loans to finance river development, dams, roads, and land-use improvement schemes?

Fifth, if a rapid rate of growth is to be achieved, personal consumption must be restricted in order to provide funds for the development of essential public services and for capital formation. Under normal circumstances this requires a high rate of savings and increased taxation. How then can Nigeria best increase taxes and promote savings?

Finally, economic development in the modern era requires effective organization and detailed planning. Nigeria has separate economic development boards in all three regions, an inter-regional economic council, and a newly created federal economic development ministry. What measures can be taken to make this machinery work effectively within the context of Nigeria's federal system of government?

These and many other crucial issues are worth discussing. As yet, in Nigeria there are no clear-cut answers to any of them. Certainly, *the means* for achieving successful economic growth are at hand. The big question is whether Nigeria has *the will* to bring it about. In order to succeed, Nigerian leaders will have to give priority to economic development over other pursuits of a more political nature. There must be co-ordination of objectives in the three Regions, and there must be a sense of Federation-wide national purpose.

The economist can easily prescribe the measures that should be taken to insure growth, but the decisions are made by the politicians. In talking about the future of the new young countries, Arthur Lewis has observed:

Politics is exciting to young countries, and politicians in these countries have attracted to themselves all the glamour which was previously reserved for priests and kings, now excluding the military parades, the salutes of guns, the yachts and country houses. We must resign ourselves to the fact that most of the new countries will be too preoccupied with other matters to give to economic development the priority which it needs.[7]

In forecasting Nigeria's future, I would not share Lewis' pessimism concerning the prospects for new countries. It would appear that Nigeria has the means and can develop the will to achieve successful growth. Of this, however, I am certain: In Nigeria, economic development is primarily a political rather than an economic question.

[7] W. A. Lewis, "Problems of New States," paper delivered at the Weizman Institute, Rehoveth, Israel. Aug., 1960.

9

School Leavers and the Developing
Economy of Nigeria [1]

Archibald Callaway

I

No social and economic problem in Nigeria is so urgent as that of finding employment for the ever-increasing number of school leavers. Nor is there any major policy issue of which the meaning and implications are so little understood. Here, through the medium of education, traditional society meets the improving economy.

Given that so many school leavers have difficulty in getting jobs, should Nigeria follow Ghana, perhaps even Guinea, with compulsory service to help build the infra-structure of the economy? What lessons do Pakistan, Israel, the Soviet Union, and the United States have to offer? These are some of the questions now being asked. Experience from other countries can be useful, but in the final resort solutions must be indigenous, growing from a knowledge of Nigerian life and work.

The danger of the school leavers' employment problem is obvious enough: in endeavoring to meet the emergency, policies

[1] The original version of this essay was read at a Conference of the Nigerian Institute of Social and Economic Research, Ibadan, Nigeria, Dec. 1960, and was published in *West Africa*, March 25, April 1, 8, and 15, 1961. The Duke University Press is indebted to NISER and to the publishers of *West Africa* for permission to reprint it in somewhat revised form in this volume. Based on extensive field research in villages and cities in selected areas throughout Nigeria, the essay deals briefly with some of the problems examined in a detailed work to be published under the auspices of the Africa Project, Center for International Studies, Massachusetts Institute of Technology.

may drift towards the adoption of expedients. To rush headlong into a scheme for harnessing school leavers into groups of general labor, for example, would be foolish in the extreme. Such schemes are much more expensive than is commonly supposed, and they carry with them the seeds of their own inefficient momentum. So far as such shortsighted policies are adopted, they could pre-empt the future course of economic progress for decades. Policies must work with economic growth, not against it.

Politicians are harassed at present; they will be besieged in the future. Jobless school leavers will become ever more numerous and there will be mounting pressures to find solutions to their problem. In the remotest parts of Western and Eastern Nigeria, for example, politicans when meeting the local villagers have found it is often better to talk about "jobs for school leavers" than about access roads. This is good politics: it is also a tribute to the respect that illiterate village people have for their young men who have gained the primary school-leaving certificate or have spent some years at secondary school. Parents and other villagers generally take it for granted that school leavers will seek employment in the towns.

At the end of each year there emerges another group of hopeful school leavers. Most expect to gain secure employment and reasonable wages—outside traditional farming. Many are disappointed. Because December, 1960, marked the completed schooling of the first intake under the Region's universal primary education scheme, Western Nigeria alone had over 180,000 boys and girls coming out of primary schools. After allowing for those going to secondary schools, there were still at least two and a half times as many school leavers in the Region seeking jobs compared with the previous year. Eastern Nigeria's school leavers increased by another 10,000, while those from the Riverain Provinces of Northern Nigeria and from Lagos grow in numbers each year. All over the Federation school leavers are meeting a progressively harder employment market.

By and large the employment problem for young school leavers in Nigeria at present affects chiefly, but not entirely, those from primary and secondary modern schools. Those who have attended secondary grammar schools are finding that they must deflate their ideas about the kind of jobs they can obtain.

Since over 75 per cent of all gainfully occupied people in Nigeria are employed in farming, most school leavers (and their teachers too) have homes in villages and parents who are farmers. A school-leaving certificate seems like a passport to newer and brighter worlds, an opportunity to escape, perhaps, from the sanctions of village life. Whatever the surrounding motives, however, the economic motive would appear to be paramount—the search for higher income, and, related to this, security of employment.[2] The youth wants an outlet for his ambitions. Several years ago a good Standard VI leaving certificate could win a job as a petty clerk or a messenger or some other more or less stable employment with prospects of advancement. The swelling of the ranks of primary school leavers because of the immense broadening of the educational base (at least in Southern Nigeria) now means that a diminishing proportion can find steady jobs.

But the school leavers keep on trying to find work. They are to be found hanging around the towns supported by their geographical or family "brothers"; they obtain a roof and food. Some do well, others find jobs which provide bare subsistence, but an increasing number cannot even cover minimum living costs, and the months go by.

A school leaver frequently describes himself as an "applicant." One young Ibo writes, "I have suffered beyond measure under applicantship in Lagos." Another says, "The duty of an applicant is to walk around. Some day I might be lucky." He visits employed members of his family group at their work premises, he calls at the Labor Exchange, and he writes applications. "If I had the money to pay the big men, I might get a job," is the feeling of one young job-seeker.

A quick look at the immense number of applications tells the story of pressure for jobs and further education: as many as 10,000 applications have been received for the few places in trade

---

[2] For a further discussion of these points, see Frederick Harbison, "Human Resources and Economic Development in Nigeria," *supra*, chap. viii.

training centers; Shell in Port Harcourt receives several thousand applications every month, and so on. Somewhat over 60 per cent of unemployed school leavers in Lagos are from the East and West, although the numbers from the North (the Riverain Provinces) who move to Lagos are increasing. The principal centers in the Regions where the few new industries have brought increased economic activity constantly attract school leavers: Port Harcourt, Onitsha, and Aba in the Eastern Region; Ibadan, Ikeja, and Benin in the Western Region; Kaduna, Kano, and Jos in the Northern Region.

The social and economic problems—and the political crosscurrents—that arise from mass unemployment of undirected youths are far-reaching. They are the "strap hangers" on the developing economy. They are to be found, among other places, at the motor parks—where the mammy wagons arrive and depart crammed with human and other cargo. They move about hoping that they will be taken on as apprentice drivers (for which they must persuade their fathers or guardians to surrender a fee, and they may or may not receive shelter or food in return). Or they may be passenger collectors or porters or petty traders. But as one comes down the list of jobs there comes a point at which employment shades into unemployment.

Unemployment is simply the inability of a school leaver (after an "experimental period" of, say, nine months) to earn enough shillings to cover costs of subsistence living. Yet, on this definition, there are many thousands of unemployed school leavers in Nigeria. Roaming the streets are a few who left school three or four years ago. For some of these there never has been a substantial period when their total earnings for odd days of casual labor or petty trading have covered costs of their shelter, food, and clothing. For a village boy living with relatives in the town, life may not always be easy: he may shift from one household to another when he senses that his presence is no longer welcome. In such cases his relatives give him shelter to which he returns in the evening—but not much else. Provision of shelter is a big concession, nevertheless: rent of a small room in Ibadan, for example (with no light, water, or compound [3]), costs £1 to 30 shillings a month.

The capacity of school leavers for not returning to the farms is extraordinary, at least at first sight. Many admit that they would do anything rather than return to work on the family farm: that would mean confession of their failure to win the higher income expected of an "educated man." Above all, they want employment with a future and they do not see this amid the harshness of bush farming. They take their cue from the evolving Nigerian economy, but the economy rejects them.

Many of the school leavers of several years ago still harbor thoughts of furthering their education; some are found studying by correspondence. The enthusiasm for education in Nigeria is a vital part of the contemporary scene, and this is shown in an almost pathetic belief in the efficacy of a certificate or diploma in securing a job.

These school leavers have high expectations of their newly independent nation. Disillusionment must not be allowed to emerge. Given competitive opportunities in all aspects of Nigeria's economic life (including farming), these school leavers can be powerful instruments of economic growth.

II

The question now arises: why are there not more jobs available to young literate Nigerians? The basic cause of the scarcity of employment outside farming is to be found within the economic growth process itself. Nigeria is still in essence a "maintenance economy." The system is underfunctioning because of lack of capital, managerial experience, and industrial skill. Thus the employment problem of young school leavers is part of the wider picture of surplus labor resources.

New industries do not absorb many employees—in relation, that is, to the numbers struggling for jobs. And while young school leavers have great potentiality for improvement, few have

[3] Yard space attached to the dwelling.

ready skills for many of the tasks of modern industry. Moreover, new industries will be established only gradually. On whatever optimistic assumptions one may make, internal savings together with imported funds—loans and private investment—make a flow of savings too small to push development fast enough to provide employment of the magnitude needed to meet the problem.

The savings required to provide employment for one Nigerian in most new industries is very high. An extreme case is the recently erected cement factory in Western Nigeria, whose capital cost was £4 million, but which will provide employment when operating at full capacity for only about 300. The proposed textile factory on the Ikeja industrial estate, Western Nigeria, will cost £1.75 million and will employ some 1,000 Nigerians. Port Harcourt's proposed oil refinery with a capital cost of £12 million will employ only 350. Manufacture of cement tiles, bitumen, aluminum products, glass, confectionery, canned foods, as well as flour milling and textile weaving in factories, will require direct capital investment often of over £1,000 per employee. The same applies to the bigger rubber and oil palm plantations. Some more capital-intensive industries may require £5,000 or more per employee.

Eventually as incomes rise and markets widen, there will be signs of a self-generating industrial system. Yet, even a decade from now, those engaged in factories cannot be expected to exceed 7 per cent of the then gainfully occupied population. (Nigeria's population is presently rising at the rate of about 2,000 net increase each day.)

In the meantime, as most new industries begin to expand, they will be found to increase output with less than commensurate increases in employees. The path to lower cost of production is to use more machines, or the existing ones more effectively, rather than to use more—or at least proportionately more—employees. As business expands the same will hold true for the larger trading establishments. All public utilities have more than enough workers. And there has been a marked slackening off in the rate of recruitment to regional and local government service. Positions as teachers in the West and East are less plentiful to unqualified school leavers. Building, on the other hand, continues to provide an increasing proportion of total employment outside farming.

In financial terms there is an inner contradiction in Nigeria's development. This arises from the high and rising proportion of regional public expenditure on education, especially primary education. Recurrent spending on education is contained under other headings in the budgets, such as maintenance of school buildings, pension payments, expatriate teacher allowances, and so on. When all these costs are included, no less than 50 per cent of the total expenditures for both Western and Eastern Nigeria and close to 30 per cent for the North are now being spent on education.

Of the three million pupils in the 18,000 schools of the Federation some 95 per cent are in primary schools. Of those in primary schools 1.25 million are in Western Nigeria and the same number in Eastern Nigeria, about 250,000 in Northern Nigeria, and some 80,000 in Lagos. Both Western and Eastern Nigeria have about doubled the number of their primary school pupils during the last five years, and both now have about 80 per cent of school-age children receiving some schooling. The withdrawal rate between starting age and finishing class, however, is very high. During the next five years the numbers of school pupils will increase by about 25 per cent; but, more important, pupils will stay at school for longer periods. This will be a costly operation.

Signs are that education is becoming more socially acceptable in the far North. Katsina Province shows stirrings of interest under its enlightened Emir; and competition among Emirs (together with pressures from within the native authorities) could account for a massive demand for educational facilities. The outstanding example was the rush to get into the Kano free primary education scheme.

The imaginative Ashby Report [4] has become an indispensable document for top administrators in the Federation; governments are alert to its advice. In case it is thought, however, that the

[4] Federation of Nigeria, Federal Ministry of Education, *Investment in Education* (Report of the Commission on Post-School Certificate and Higher Education in Nigeria) (Lagos and London, 1960).

recommendations of the report will help solve the employment problems of young school leavers in the future, the answer is easily given: it is likely to do exactly the reverse. The emphasis on higher education in order to provide the high-level, skilled manpower will tend to induce greater enthusiasm throughout the educational system, including primary schools. As a result, more children will be at schools, and for longer periods.

The implications of the report are that out of every 1000 who complete primary school education (by, say, 1970 and after) in the West, East, and Lagos, no less than 930 will look for jobs. And 225 of every 250 children who complete primary school in the North will look for jobs (assuming for the North that 25 per cent of school-age children will be at school instead of the present 10 per cent).

On current trends it is likely that in five years' time the expenses of education, most of which will be for primary schooling, could take 60 per cent or even more of the regional recurrent budgets of the West and East. The proportion to be spent on education in the North will rise similarly. This then is the contradiction: the more that is spent on education from regional budgets, the less there is left to spend on recurrent costs of further capital outlay that could provide employment.

One step toward the solution of the employment problem of young school leavers, therefore, should be a reduction in the rate of increase in the costs of primary education at the regional government level. This can be accomplished by raising the school-starting age (as was recently done in the Eastern Region), or, as a last resort, by reintroducing or raising fees for later classes at primary schools and hence encouraging a higher rate of withdrawal in earlier standards (difficult politically and perhaps inadvisable on other grounds).

Of far greater importance is the need to shift more of the rising burden of recurrent costs of primary education to local effort. All maintenance costs (of school buildings, purchase of school books, etc.) could be provided locally. Another possibility is for local authorities to pay a flat rate for all teachers and for the regional government to supplement this according to teachers' qualifications and experience. Also there is a need to review (or to re-introduce) the variable system of assumed local contributions for primary education. Regional revenues tend to follow fluctuations in foreign trade. During periods of falling proceeds from exports of primary products, the assumed local contribution system pro-vides a mechanism for further shifting of primary education costs from regional budgets. This would help to maintain employment and to meet the expected rise in expenditure on secondary, tech-nical, and other higher education.

The big lesson to be learned in Nigeria is the art of "develop-ment from below." Far too little is known about taxable capacity locally, and far too few steps have been taken towards harnessing local enthusiasm to pay for development. A campaign needs to be waged to prevent tax evasion in the towns, by smaller traders, smugglers, and others. A determined effort might also be made to prevent any further disparity between the incomes of peasant families and the salaries of civil servants and other professional people in the towns. General salary increases have occurred at regular four-year intervals in the past and should be brought to a halt: they are completely indefensible in a young, developing economy.

When this has been done, not only will regional governments be in a better position financially to afford positive programs to increase employment opportunities for the ever-growing numbers of school leavers, but Nigeria's case for international aid for higher education—beginning with teacher training programs—will be all the more valid.

III

Policies towards employing school leavers should strike a bal-ance between tradition and economic progress. They should take into account the transitions in village life, the changing fabric of the towns and cities, the aspirations of young school leavers, and the variety of their innate talents. These policies should not force, but guide by creating incentives and, wherever possible, should aim at providing employment at low capital cost.

For half a century commentators on Nigeria have said that school leavers refuse to work with their hands: "They want white-collar jobs" is an expression still frequently heard. The implication is always that the school leavers are lacking in some undefined morality. The school leaver turns out, however, to be more perceptive of economic opportunity than the commentator. Naturally the school leaver will make his strongest bid for the class of jobs with the most appealing net advantages, of which money income and its regularity are the principal ingredients. If a school leaver can win a job as a junior clerk or as a messenger in a government office at £100 a year, and if he watches his living costs carefully, very likely he will be better off than his father who is farming in the home village; and he will often be found contributing to his younger brother's education.

Present-day school leavers do work with their hands and many may be classified as general laborers. They compete first to work on town building sites rather than up-country roads. Their pay is between four and five shillings a day. Some harbor thoughts of becoming labor clerks or eventually rising to positions as headmen of the gangs. But even jobs as general laborers are not plentiful and employers often prefer more mature, stronger people, who, as it happens, are illiterate. And there is an immense surplus of this kind of labor.

A second piece of folklore about school leavers produces the belief that by making massive changes in the curricula of primary schools to include "environmental" subjects, school leavers will be encouraged to remain in villages and work on home farms. A strong case can be made for incremental changes in curricula to include a farm or craft subject where this is not being done already; in fact, however, most Nigerian schools do have subjects of this kind. More important is to have well-qualified teachers to teach them.

The truth is that school leavers' attitudes towards employment are determined almost exclusively by what is happening outside the schools, in the society and economy. No amount of instruction by itself—whether in primary or post-primary schools—can make modern farmers. The work of rural science teachers, the existence of miniature farm plots, the fostering of young farmers' clubs can have real meaning only when there exist positive policies for improved farming for those school leavers best suited to receive direct help. Combined with instruction must be a purposive and supervised settlement plan that seeks to help the young farmer to overcome the many obstacles: land tenure, lack of understanding by village farmers, frustrations due to lack of savings to finance improvements, and in some cases lack of a market for hard-earned surpluses.

This is proved by the experience of the Rural Training Center at Asaba, Western Nigeria (perhaps the most distinguished institution of its kind in West Africa). Its avowed purpose was to create modern farmers: the trainees were almost all primary school leavers and came from both Eastern and Western Nigeria. Yet during ten years few modern farmers were created, despite the efforts of the Center's devoted staff. One reason was that the training fitted school leavers for jobs at higher incomes: teachers of rural science, assistants in leper settlements, laborers and overseers in plantations, and so on. Case histories of former trainees who returned to their villages show the real obstacles to have been the unreliability of sponsors (parent or guardian) in meeting their promises of land and small amounts of capital, and the inability of settlers to plan ahead effectively.

The same lesson comes from the experience of the Kafinsoli Farm School in Katsina Province in the far North. Here the attempt was to make Primary IV school leavers into modern farmers by providing a nine-months' course of instruction in "mixed farming," based on the use of dual-purpose cattle. The experiment foundered on the lack of an effective follow-through settlement plan. The Kafinsoli attempt is impressive, nevertheless, because of its simplicity and low cost and for the measure of success that was obtained. The North would be well-advised to prize this experience when establishing much-needed farm schools to provide instruction and direction to school leavers inclined to farming in the Riverain Provinces, beginning in Kabba Province.

Among school leavers there is an almost universal view that farming in the traditional way offers nothing but hardship, low money returns, and no chance of personal success. Yet hundreds of school leavers interviewed throughout Nigeria have said that they do not reject modern farming. The farm settlement scheme of Western Nigeria [5] has become widely popular in the Region; for example, last December in the final class of one secondary modern school some 40 per cent of the boys applied to join the scheme. These farm settlements are surprisingly well known in other parts of the Federation as well; to school leavers they represent the "new look" in farming. But these farm settlements—and those proposed for Eastern Nigeria, which will also emphasize cash crops—are heavily capitalized and they absorb few school leavers (under 1000 so far have been taken into the Western Nigeria settlements). Although adjustments will be needed from time to time, these farm settlements can be made to work well. Their primary function, however, is to create a new picture in the public mind of what farming can be and to establish a goal towards which the individual farmer can aim. By the year 2000 it is possible that upwards of half the total farm production in Nigeria may come from large-scale plantations and from individual holdings comparable to those allocated to settlers on the farm settlements (20 to 40 acres). But in the meantime no government in Nigeria can afford to provide credit on the same scale (£3,000 to £4,000) for each school leaver who may want to become a farmer.

Farm settlements of this kind are not enough. Follow-up schemes should be considered to assist individual farmers or small groups of farmers who wish to make a break from traditional farming. It is imperative that a further plan for school leavers be worked out and put into operation immediately.

One such plan—which grows out of inquiries from school leavers, heads of schools, and farmers in different parts of Nigeria—is as follows. Bring together in a village those school leavers who are inclined toward farming and form a young farmers' class. Seek the co-operation of village leaders to obtain land for each school leaver of sufficient size to make an economic farming unit; encourage the formation of village committees for

[5] See the author's "School Leavers for the Farms," *West Africa*, Sept. 10, 1960.

this purpose. In most cases the land will be part of, or adjoining, the family farm. If land is not available in the village, a district committee could explore ways of obtaining land in a nearby area. Station in the village an extension worker to provide instruction in a suitable new system and in farming techniques for that area, in simple economics of farm management, in co-operative marketing, and in better family nutrition. Most of the week the school leaver works on his farm. He is taught how to grow crops and how to keep animals and poultry; his farm expands each year according to his capacity—on a prearranged plan—until it reaches full development. Some balance is decided between income now (arable crops) and income later (tree crops). Small amounts of credit supervised by the extension worker are provided for specific purposes: for labor to assist with clearing, purchases of planting material, fertilizers, and insecticides.

These school leavers thus remain in their own familiar environment; costs of living are low. Interviews with fathers in villages show that they would welcome this special opportunity for their literate sons because their education is being continued and they have the prospect of a higher money income. Village farmers will be alert to the results achieved by these young men, whose efforts will in fact convey the work of government demonstration farms to village level. Villagers will see a series of complementary changes take place in these new farms—in effect a change in the system of farming. As a result, they will be more ready to meet the farm extension workers part way and try more of their suggested improvements.

The basic plan is capable of variations to meet local conditions. When the growing of traditional crops like yams and cassava will not provide the necessary cash income to help build an expanding economic farm unit, then in some areas the newer strains of maize and rice can be introduced. In other areas it may be possible to make a beginning with mixed farming, such as beef cattle and palms. As a pilot project in a specific area, a farm implement pool might hire its machine services at full economic, or subsidized cost. Villages vary considerably in the quality of local leadership and a start could be made with those where the administration of

they cram the typing schools where instruction and practice for one hour each week-day cost six shillings a month. Because their education is being continued, these typing students are not required to pay tax, and they still make their daily rounds as "applicants" in the search for jobs.

Again—and of greater significance—school leavers are becoming apprentices to Nigerian master craftsmen and artisans in the back streets of the towns. And they are finding new chances (although still small in number) as apprentices in the service trades in the villages.

Formerly the preserve of illiterate people, this indigenous apprentice system now absorbs more and more literates. Employers in small businesses such as tailoring (garment making) and printing, and also mechanics, are often found to have a full complement of apprentices with at least Standard VI pass and some with several years of secondary school training. Illiterate traders find it profitable to take on literate apprentices, as do lorry drivers. But this is not all: school leavers are apprentices to small manufacturers, such as furniture makers, shoe or sandal makers, leather workers, textile weavers, tinsmiths and so on. They compete strongly for opportunities in the trades related to building and construction (which presently accounts for over 40 per cent of total capital formation in Nigeria): they are apprentices to carpenters, masons, bricklayers, painters, welders, plumbers, and the like.

At its best this system of apprenticing provides an excellent training for young Nigerians; at its worst, it is merely a source of cheap labor. Through this experience school leavers do receive "exposure" to the pressures of competitive business and they learn by doing. Their conditions of apprenticeship, however, vary considerably and it often costs between £10 and £30 for two to three years' instruction, an amount that in many cases represents a considerable sacrifice by fathers and guardians, many of whom are farmers in villages. Sometimes, but by no means always, the master provides shelter, food, and clothing. A clear distinction should be drawn between this back-street system and the forms of apprenticeship to be found with the larger Nigerian contractors and the expatriate firms, where payments are made to the apprentices on a normal contractual basis.

One might well ask: what would happen if the apprentice laws of a more economically advanced country were to be applied in Nigeria (meaning that masters must have certain minimum qualifications, that some money payments be made to apprentices, etc.)? In the first place, it is extremely doubtful that these laws could be enforced, but assuming that they could be, then some tens of thousands of people would lose their only means of livelihood. Much of the motor transport of the country—which is maintained (however imperfectly) by back-street mechanics—would come to a standstill. And, of course, there would be less employment for school leavers. The aim of government policies, therefore, should not be to destroy this highly competitive system but to work with it and to improve its functioning.

Of several hundred small businesses analyzed in Ibadan and other parts of Nigeria, over three-quarters of the proprietors were found to be former apprentices. Again, a few of today's more prominent Nigerian entrepreneurs had their early beginnings in this indigenous apprentice system (others have had the benefit of training as employees of the expatriate firms and government); in their turn they became master craftsmen and artisans and later grew to employ others.

All large towns in Nigeria are alive with the activities of a great variety of small businesses, each struggling to expand. Here is one of the key points of growth for the Nigerian economy. The dense population of these areas provides a ready market—an advantage Nigerian entrepreneurs have over their counterparts in other less populated areas of West Africa. Yet government economic policies have almost neglected indigenous small businesses.

To encourage these small businesses, a Business Extension Service is needed (as a counterpart to the Agricultural Extension Service operating in the Regions) with a clear set of economic principles and procedures. The Business Extension Service could arrange accelerated training programs for apprentices and masters, recruited on a selective basis, to improve technical skills—on the lines well proven in French-speaking West African countries. For small manufacturers the Business Extension Service could channel technical advice on product design to appeal to more customers and on improved use of local materials; it could assess credit needs. The Nigerian scene offers many possibilities to the small-scale industrialist for substituting local products for imported consumer goods. Footwear, specialized fabrics and clothing, electrical fittings, household utensils are some of the more obvious examples. Small industries absorb much labor in relation to capital invested, and the economies of scale are by no means always on the side of the large factory. By replacing imported goods with Nigerian-made products, foreign exchange is saved.

Another step might be an attempt to interest the large expatriate trading establishments in the pattern set by their counterparts in Latin America in providing a market for dispersed cottage industries and other small manufacturers. Moreover, there is need to re-examine the role that small-scale industrial estates of the Yaba type could play, how co-operative marketing of products could foster growth of small industries, and how training of school leavers in handicraft centers could be related to market possibilities.

Strong encouragement to these small labor-intensive industries will help in providing employment for school leavers, but the effect will be limited. And, in the meantime, the number of unemployed school leavers increases as each year passes.

Some may say that the working of the employment market will itself solve the dilemma of school leavers by forcing them back to the villages when they find that jobs at a few shillings a day are no longer available in the towns. But this is a commentary, not a solution. Many villages in Southern Nigeria already have their own cadre of school leavers who are doing nothing or grudgingly following their fathers to the farms. Again, it is said, as a last resort, cannot school leavers always engage in petty trading? It is true that a few school leavers may be able to make headway as petty traders in competition with other village people, and eventually they may accumulate a small savings fund, become bigger traders and thus earn a reasonable income while fulfilling a function within a strongly competitive system. A few others may help the produce merchants in the villages, and some may become apprentices to the local tailors, or to the mechanics who have the dual function of mending the mammy wagons that break down on bush tracks and of keeping the village cycles in good repair.

Yet it still remains true that many thousands of school leavers can find no opportunity in the towns or villages—and they see no future in traditional farming. A large number of these youths, however, could find a challenge and the promise of a higher income in improved farming as outlined in the village-level farm settlement plan. And, at the same time, they will become agents of progress.

Nigeria is characterized by the co-existence of underutilized manpower and unexploited tracts of land. A fresh look should be given to the forms of enticement to foreign capital to establish large plantations in association with regional governments and private Nigerian savings. Where land has competing uses, a firmer policy is needed on the demarcation of forest reserves and land available for plantations. Not only do new plantations absorb much labor, but school leavers might be employed to improve existing palm and rubber plantations.

A national wages policy, designed to reduce the widening disparity in incomes now existing between the great mass of people and the few and to prevent competition for salary and wage increases among the Regions, is a necessity. So too is a bolder policy towards the accumulation of the nation's savings for development.

Underemployment and unemployment are features of all young developing economies. The uniqueness of Nigeria (particularly Southern Nigeria) is that the faster pace of basic education has intensified this condition. No complete solution to the employment problems of school leavers can be found; but much can be done, nevertheless, within the incentives of the present highly competitive economic system.

Part Four

The Political Future

10

The Future for Democracy in Nigeria

Pendleton Herring

I. Prospects and Problems

The future course of events in Africa is so fateful that an effort to analyze forces and tendencies in a key country of this great continent seems appropriate even though inescapably speculative in character.

From the standpoint of the West, the most acceptable forecast would be: As Nigeria goes, so goes Africa.

Here is the largest and most populous country of the continent, a member of the British Commonwealth, a working federal system, with its own constitution, with competing political parties, a free press, and a civil service. The rule of law prevails, the courts are conducted in the British tradition, and leading members of the bar have been trained in the Inns of Court in London.

English is accepted as the language for communication throughout the Federation, and there is a profound concern with education at all levels.

Even the casual visitor senses the tremendous desire on the part of Nigerians to be on the move, to catch up with the twentieth century and to improve their economic and social conditions. There is high aspiration, great vitality, and a capacity for hard work. There is much in the recent history of the country that could be brought forward as evidence to sustain the points summarily mentioned here. In terms of most of the forms conventionally associated with self-government, it can be said that democracy in Nigeria is in "good shape" and that the prospects there are better than for the rest of the continent.

There is much, however, to be said in negative terms. The standard of living is very low and the per capita income in Nigeria places this country in the lower 20 per cent of the under-industrialized countries.[1] While Nigeria is a federation, the strong regional loyalties and the hostility that those in one region often entertain for those in another mean that forces for disunity are latent.[2] Moreover, the capacity of the civil service to carry the burdens that are being taken over from the British [3] and the ability of the politicians to achieve an effective balance between the hopes of their supporters and the facts of economic life have yet to be demonstrated.

Hence in discussing the prospects of Nigeria's future, speculation can move from the picture of the Federation of Nigeria serving as a nucleus about which newly emerging African states in the future might cluster and eventuate in a United States of Africa, to the opposite extreme of fragmentation within Nigeria itself.

Yet the prospects for democracy in Nigeria are probably as favorable as in any of the developing countries and indeed more promising than in most.

One of the most perceptive and well-informed students of colonialism in Asia and African countries, hazarding a forecast of democratic trends, states:

Over the next decades both the face and the substance of political life are sure to be drastically changed, but one can have no confidence that the change will bring an effective extension of democracy, except, perhaps, in some plebiscitary sense. The role of the rising masses, still largely illiterate and politically inexperienced, may prove to embrace not much more than the right to say "yes" after having been duly indoctrinated.[4]

[1] For a more detailed treatment of the standard of living in Nigeria, see Joseph J. Spengler, "Population Movements and Economic Development in Nigeria," *supra*, chap. vii, *passim*.
[2] The centrifugal and centripetal forces of Nigerian federalism are analyzed in Taylor Cole, "Emergent Federalism in Nigeria," *supra*, chap. iii.
[3] See Taylor Cole, "Nigerian Bureaucracy in Transition," *supra*, chap. v.
[4] Rupert Emerson, *From Empire to Nation* (Cambridge, Mass., 1960), pp. 245–46.

While this may be the over-all prospect for the developing countries, several basic factors should, in my opinion, be taken into account in considering the future of Nigeria:

(1) This nation is not faced with drastic population pressures that threaten to absorb the fruits of economic gains and leave the country as poorly or worse off despite moderate economic growth. Production has a reasonable chance of keeping pace with population.[5]

(2) Nigeria has the resources for a viable economy. Agricultural exports and industrialization can be expected to increase. The country has raw materials, water resources, and sturdy manpower. There is a large potential domestic market. On the other hand, there are any number of practical problems: questions that involve credit, manpower training, the improvement of transportation and communication facilities, the organization of plantations, co-operatives, and all sorts of productive entities. The country is living off the profits of export products. Nigeria cannot safely assume a continued and steady high level of prices. The present economy depends on the export market, and the world prices for palm oil, cocoa, groundnuts, minerals, and oil have the instability implicit in such a situation.

On balance the economic and demographic problems appear manageable—not easy but not impossible. They are matters to be dealt with politically and administratively.

(3) The country faces independence with a heritage from Great Britain that points the way to parliamentary government. "Great Britain's principal legacy to the peoples of the Commonwealth and the colonies has hitherto been her social democratic system and her concept of law and justice," Kalu Ezera writes. Moreover,

Nigerian leaders and potential leaders seem to have a strong faith in this system. As a result of the experience gained from the successful management of their internal self-government, Nigerian leaders have developed a strong conviction that they too have an equal capacity, like their counterparts in other democratic countries, to profit from

[5] International Bank for Reconstruction and Development, *The Economic Development of Nigeria* (Baltimore, 1955), p. 10.

their experience and produce in turn a modern effective democratic system.[6]

To this summary statement I would add that the Army is not a political factor in Nigerian politics. Fortunate is the democracy where such a reference can be treated as an afterthought!

A comment by Chief Awolowo is pertinent:

If we choose welfare politics it will be well with us. In a developing country with slender means, such as ours, welfare politics and power politics do not mix. A choice must be made between butter and bullets: we cannot have both, as they have managed to do in the U.S.A. and Britain.[7]

Nigerian foreign policy seems consistent with this choice. As Premier Akintola said to me, "As a country we are too young to have enemies, but we are old enough to realize that responsibilities come with independence."

These attitudes on the part of thoughtful Nigerians joined with the factors—demographic, economic, and constitutional—noted above, place Nigeria in a more favorable position than many of the developing countries. A feeling of optimism concerning the future seems justified. The prospects based on these particular variables are good. But Nigeria shares problems with other new countries that are of great significance in political development.

II. Nigerian Social Structure and
Political Implications

In Nigeria the society is marked by mass poverty and by a small, relatively wealthy elite.[8] The elite constitutes less than one-

[6] Kalu Ezera, *Constitutional Developments in Nigeria* (Cambridge, 1960), p. 259.
[7] Chief Obafemi Awolowo, *Awo: The Autobiography of Chief Obafemi Awolowo* (Cambridge, 1960), pp. 306–7.
[8] A recent study at first hand of this ruling group reports that there exists an attitude on their part of contempt for their less fortunate fellow citizens. "There is a vast gulf between a member of the elite and the masses of his countrymen. He has been educated, perhaps abroad, and has probably acquired tastes and manners considerably different from those of the working class. He associates mainly with those like himself, and his daily routine and general living are very different from those of the greater part of the population. His work is of at least white-collar status; his entertainment is limited but select. More often than not,

tenth of one per cent of the population. This class is professional and administrative; it is composed of engineers, scientists, doctors, lawyers, journalists, educators, public officials, and politicians.[9]

Lacking industry, there are no industrialists of importance. The Nigerians engaged in business are the owners and operators of the lorries that provide transportation, the merchants are Lebanese, and banking and the export trades are in the hands of businessmen from the outside.[10] The Nigerian capitalist looks for a large quick profit. The need for housing is so great that Nigerians with funds to invest can build a house for £7,000 and get £3,000 for the first three years' rent. The business firm is a highly individualistic effort and the business tends to be identified with the individual who starts it; the common pattern is for the business to deteriorate as the founder grows old and dies. At present there seems to be little that is indigenous in the native culture that would sustain the development of a business middle class with all that this has meant in terms of political stability in countries such as the United States.

One of the most interesting and possibly significant efforts under way in Nigeria is carried on by Robert Fleming with the backing of the Rockefeller Brothers Fund. He is a missionary for the idea of private enterprise. For over two years he has been conducting feasibility studies of business. Thus far his efforts have been almost entirely devoted to identifying those business enterprises that would appear profitable in Nigeria and that could be set up by combining local financing with help from abroad. He stands for integrated ownership and direction, with the directing power in the hands of the Nigerians.

An important index of future development within Nigeria in

---

he lives on a government reservation, campus, or other institutional compound, physically removed from the homes of the masses. He belongs to the social club of his city, and his other leisure is spent in visiting or being visited by his associates in work or play. As a result the elite move about within a relatively narrow circle of acquaintances and rarely have extensive contact with the man in the street." Hugh H. Smythe and Mabel M. Smythe, *The New Nigerian Elite* (Stanford, 1960), pp. 99–100.
[9] Frederick H. Harbison, "More Chiefs, Fewer Indians," *University*, No. 7 (Winter, 1961), pp. 9–12.
[10] Hugh H. Smythe and Mabel M. Smythe, "Occupation and Upper-Class Formation in Nigeria," *The Southwestern Social Science Quarterly*, XLI (Dec., 1960), p. 355.

political as well as in economic terms can, I think, be found in the success of Fleming's program in moving from a negotiating phase to a stage of actual business operations. In very concrete fashion the place and function of the entrepreneur in a developing society is being tested. It is too early to predict the outcome of these experimental efforts.

The prospects for democracy in Nigeria would seem to be enhanced if, instead of state socialism, there could be some form of mixed economy.

The private individual as a risk taker and enterpriser encounters in Nigeria an indigenous institution that runs counter to private enterprise. The extended family system means that the individual who prospers is expected to share his good fortune with his brothers and cousins. The more prosperous the individual, the greater his family responsibilities and the greater the demands made upon him. This serves not only as a drain on the bank roll but more importantly perhaps as a brake on the individual's motivation.[11]

What will happen to family loyalties over the next decade as

[11] One observer states that ". . . family loyalties tend to cut across disparities of wealth, and encourage the better-off to spend their money on their relatives rather than in raising their own standard of living. The rich earn no right to be aloof. The people of Lagos admire and envy wealth: every clerk dreams of making his way abroad to a degree and affluence, and football pools flourish. But they are not snobbish about money. The manners of an egalitarian society surmount gross inequalities of income.

". . . How long will this remain so? Will family loyalties go on working against the segregation of rich and poor? As men are promoted to the senior ranks of the civil service and commercial firms, they find themselves no longer contributors towards a mutual exchange of gifts and services, but the victims of demands which may be beyond their means: to their country cousins their wealth seems almost inexhaustible. Faced with insistent, even predatory claims, they may begin to restrict the range of relatives to whom they recognize an obligation. Then, again, they are not altogether free to spend their money on others if they wish. With the senior service post comes government quarters in a secluded suburb, designed for the commuter with his own car, and servants for his house and garden. The senior executive of a commercial firm will be expected to uphold its prestige in his social manners. And through their education they often acquire, too, a more European conception of marriage—a more companionate attitude toward their wives, a greater sensitivity to the emotional needs of their children.

"But though the prosperous may choose to spend more on their homes and their wives and children, and less on their kin, it seems to me that for the poorer people of Lagos this is not possible. They will rather sacrifice marriage for the sake of their ties with the family into which they were born. There may in time grow up a profound difference between the family life of rich and poor, a class division as exclusive and provocative as any we have known in modern Europe." Peter Marris, "Social Change and Social Class," *International Journal of Comparative Sociology*, I, 1 (March, 1960), 121.

economic conditions change? Will the loosening of family obligations with greater freedom for each individual to go his own way
make for a more democratic society or promote anomalies? Will
it make for more or less equality? The answers are far from certain.

It could be argued that with the growth of a business class,
with opportunities for the self-made man, "eliteism" can be diminished. In a situation so fluid much can be affected by ideas, by
conscious decisions, by acts of will, by emotional reactions—in a
word, by policy politically formulated.

A developing society such as Nigeria today is a society of
changing institutions. It is this flux that offers an opportunity and
a challenge to American policy-makers and to private well-wishers
also. To those who would foster democratic tendencies, there is
much in the culture that is worthy of attention.

Among the elements that characterize such a political culture
is the mobility of the population in the Eastern and Western Regions and the Hausa traders of the Northern Region. Men are
not bound to place. They are willing to move about readily in
order to seek employment or to trade. The outgoing, aggressive,
and venturesome nature of such populations may not be without
significance in appraising the forces that make for a democratic
society, nor should we overlook the role of the market women.
In the riots in 1929 they demonstrated their significance as a
force to be reckoned with in politics. They are inveterate bar-
gainers and the observer is tempted to speculate concerning a
passion for trading and a capacity for compromise in politics.
Market activity is more than economic. Indeed it may very well
be uneconomic by standards of productivity. It is clearly social.

In the indigenous culture, then, we find a readiness to organize
and to bargain. This, however, has not been carried over into the
establishment of effective labor unions. At present the organizations that exist are little more than devices for politicians to get
workers' support, or for the government to seek their acquiescence.

One of the most crucial tests of democratic advance is whether
a middle class can emerge to a position of strength. Politicians
must rely on their appeals to a great mass electorate. If political

support must be plebiscitary then the "plebes" must be conditioned, or unreason may triumph. Party leaders have appealed to the electorate by offering higher wages; one party offered to do away with the income tax. There were riots when a direct tax was imposed to pay for the new system of primary schools.

As one Nigerian economist has written:

Our governments face the basic dilemma that, in a democratic society with a preponderance of illiterate citizens, elections are won more by good politics than by good policies. The cry being always for less taxes and more spending, it takes a particularly bold government to preach the virtues of thrift and prudent expenditure.[12]

Occupations provide class distinctions along traditional lines. Some follow in their fathers' footsteps and craft skills are tied in with lineage. Modernization dislodges the customary crafts and helps break down the loyalty to occupational class.[13]

In the course of political development there will be the projection of certain indigenous factors as the growing economic and social needs of the country select some and discard others. The interplay of interests, the injection of new ideas, will result in modified institutional arrangements.

Let us next review this process with respect to (1) tribalism vs. nationalism, and (2) traditional patterns of authority vs. modern controls.

(1) *Tribalism vs. Nationalism.* Nigeria is a new nation, created out of entities brought into being by Britain as a colonial power. Even the name of the country is a British invention. Over 35 million people are distributed throughout three great regions, each with strong local loyalties, the Yoruba in the West, the Ibo

---

[12] *Ibadan,* No. 10 (Oct., 1960), p. 5.
[13] "The urban worker is aware that in the modern sector he has common occupational interests with other workers not his kinsmen, and that to protect and advance these interests it is necessary to support a labor union; but he is also sensitive to both the responsibilities imposed, and the security provided, by his lineage. African farmers or traders participating in the modern economy recognize the need for the articulation of their specific agricultural or trading interests; but they are also impressed by the fact that in many instances lineage and clan loyalties and organizations are useful, if not indispensable, aids in larger-scale enterprise and in the amassment of capital." James S. Coleman, "The Politics of Sub-Saharan Africa," in Gabriel A. Almond and James S. Coleman, eds., *The Politics of the Developing Areas* (Princeton, 1960), pp. 247–368 at 325.

in the East, and the Hausa-Fulani in the North. In addition, there are many smaller tribes acutely aware of their minority status. The linguistic diversity within the country is extraordinary: there are about 250 different languages.

The very existence of so many languages has resulted in the necessity of finding a common tongue for purposes of communication. Moreover, no one of the dominant regional groups would be accepted by the others in providing a language for the whole Federation. Thus English provides the only practical alternative.

Cultural and linguistic loyalties have a long past. Their influence upon the attainment of a sense of national unity is still a topic for debate. William Bascom, for example, argues that this poses very real problems.

For many Africans tribal stereotypes and hostilities, often sharpened by four centuries of slave wars financed and munitioned by Europeans, are still strong. It would be a mistake, for example, for Nigeria's future political leaders to underestimate the strength of these cultural and linguistic loyalties.[14]

On the other hand, James Coleman points out that while national unification may be somewhat retarded by racial and by tribal and linguistic pluralism, such differences can survive within the new nation and may in fact have a place in the development of a competitive society. "The multiplicity of tribes within a state is not everywhere an obstacle to the creation of a broader political nationality," he writes. "Indeed, the larger their number and the smaller their size, the better are the chances for effective amalgamation." [15]

With respect to both linguistic and tribal diversity, Nigeria seems fortunate in that a virtue can be made of the necessity of using a common language in supporting a federal system. Dictatorship seems unlikely in Nigeria because no one leader could readily grasp control in a country of such divergencies. Huey Long could control Louisiana, an Nkrumah can dominate Ghana, Boss Hague was powerful in New Jersey, and Tubman is boss in Li-

[14] William Bascom, "Obstacles to Self-Government," *Annals of the American Academy of Political and Social Science*, CCCVI (July, 1956), 63.
[15] *Op. cit.*, p. 368.

beria. In the protection of freedom, federalism is a factor of great importance.

Indeed, the diversity found in the power structure when Nigeria is looked upon in terms of political culture warrants the thought that the character of the society provides the most telling evidence that one of the important conditions congenial to democratic institutions is present in indigenous form. We are dealing with a highly pluralistic culture.

(2) *Traditional Patterns of Authority vs. Modern Controls.* This culture has not only great regional differences—of tribes in space—but also differences in time perspectives as well. Here are loyalties to the past that have to be reconciled to requirements of the present and the future. Traditional patterns of authority must be related to the systems of control required by the new functions that government is now called upon to perform. Yet there are tribal rulers who are held in high esteem by their followers and whose influence cannot be disregarded. It is said that "local politics in every small chiefdom, as in Benin, turned on support of the Chief or opposition to him and over this basic pattern was imposed a network of jealousies between clans and chiefdoms; allegiance to national parties has followed the divisions imposed by these local politics." [16]

This quotation from the Commission that inquired into the fears of minorities in Nigeria illustrates rather vividly how intensely local and personal loyalties create resistances that make all the more difficult the task of the politicians trying to articulate interests and create support for policies on a regional or federal basis. The Action Group in the Western Region is attempting to follow a middle course between the cultivation of democratic institutions appropriate to modern needs and a regard for the role of the tribal chiefs. How to keep such leaders politically neutral is a problem not easily solved.

The emirates in the Northern Region are still personages of

[16] Commission appointed to enquire into the fears of minorities and the means of allaying them, *Nigeria* (London, 1958, Cmnd. 505), Part II, *The Western Region,* chap. iii, "The Fears and Grievances of Minorities," p. 23.

prestige and power. This is a heritage of the practice of indirect rule followed by the British for decades. The course of change must be toward substituting for the native authorities agencies of the Federal and Regional Governments. This may help to re-assure the numerous small tribes who in the past have had good reason to fear the domination of the emirates.

The Northern System of Government is in a state of transition; in the past power was entirely in the hands of the Emirs; in the last fifty years they have been guided and advised in the use of their power by British Residents. But the Residents will now change their functions, if they remain at all, and it will be for the newly elected Government of the Northern People's Congress to guide and advise the Emirs; change is bound to come and one may suppose that there will be gradually estab-lished within the Party a balance of power between the Emirs and the elected politicians, many of whom have served an apprenticeship in public affairs in administrative posts under the Native Authorities.[17]

Once Western-trained officials go home, will the ancient power of the emirates arise again?

In Northern Nigeria there are important tendencies under way. For example, the Institute of Administration at Zaria is training officials and judges of various ranks in modern methods and con-ceptions of government, a new code of law modifying the tradi-tional Islamic code is being successfully introduced, and the na-tive judges, the al-kahli, apply the new code on certain days of the week for criminal and civil cases, and on other days the tradi-tional code in probate and domestic cases.

The readiness of officials and judges to accept new training and the support on the part of the Premier and the government of the region are very encouraging symptoms. The success of this blend-ing of cultures and this effort to train officials will have fateful consequences so far as the future is concerned. Such retraining, however, must proceed apace since the expatriate Britishers still serving in the ministries in the North seem to feel that even under favorable conditions they should not expect to remain in their posts for more than three to five years longer. It would be my guess that the situation in Northern Nigeria is more favorable

[17] *Ibid.*, Part IV, *The Northern Region*, chap. ix, "The Fears and Grievances of Minorities," pp. 60, 61.

for change than in a number of other societies with a Moslem tradition.

The political implication of Mohammedanism in Northern Nigeria is a subject worthy of the attention of a specialist. An objective analysis of the role of the Christian missions would also be very enlightening. Even when the missionaries have failed in their primary proselyting efforts their presence and the ideas they introduced contributed to the nationalistic ferment.[18]

Still another topic worthy of research attention for estimating the capacity of a new nation to achieve coherent and stable statehood is the nature and influence of indigenous religious beliefs. Some may be dysfunctional for a changing society; others may serve to fortify the attitudes that make for a smoothly operating social order. In Yoruba mythology, for example, human beings are not depicted as pulled between the forces of good and evil. Indeed good and evil are not thought of as opposing forces. The same gods can harm or protect, they can bring happiness or the reverse.

Good and evil, in other words, are but two sides of one and the same thing, just as the good citizen is not the one who obeys certain abstract ideas of civic virtue, but the one who finds the proper relationship with his fellowmen. In the same way, the realistic Paganism of the Yorubas demands of the religious man that he should achieve the proper relationship with the supernatural forces, and has no place for the theory that man is a fallen creature who should be redeemed by some absolutely good being.[19]

Just as the image of the good citizen is affected by underlying religious and ethical beliefs, so too the myths of a people are relevant to the values by which their behavior is guided. I am too aware of the pitfalls to pursue further possible analogies between tribal beliefs and democratic forms, but such parallels seem worthy of the attention of competent analysts if we are to get beneath the surface of political life.

The forces we have been considering are, of course, common

[18] James S. Coleman, *Nigeria, Background to Nationalism* (Berkeley, 1958), chap. iv.

[19] H. V. Beier, "The Historical and Psychological Significance of Yoruba Myths," *Odu, Journal of Yoruba and Related Studies*, No. 1 (Jan., 1955), p. 25.

to most societies whether called localism or tribalism, ultraconservatism or traditionalism, or irrationalism in various forms.

III. The Political Process

Let us now consider some of the distinctive attributes of the political process in a developing polity.

How have the Nigerians been made politically aware and ready to take part in the process of governance? By what steps does the tribal man become the political man? As already noted, the British under their practice of "indirect rule" used the emirs and the native authorities who discharged various functions of local government. By and large, governance was approached as an administrative or an adjudicative process. Officials, as Sutton has pointed out, were "police officers, magistrates, and omnicompetent executives who might cajole and listen to complaints, but who in the end 'told people what they were to do.' " [20] Such officials took their orders from their superiors. They might have considerable discretion in the exercise of their powers but they were not accountable to the electorate nor to popular, elected politicians. Their experience, thus, was confined to the politics of a colonial bureaucracy and it is doubtful that they had much opportunity to participate in the discussions concerned with policy formulation. When Nigerians were admitted to legislative councils they served in a tutelary capacity. All these functions were limited to a small fraction of the public.

The other type of political experience was the politics of protest. In the type of political leadership that instilled nationalistic fervor and that aroused the masses to demand independence, the skills of oratory and of organizing for one simple overriding purpose were of paramount importance. As Sutton states: ". . . passionate speeches to enthusiastic crowds that take the whole existing structure of government as a target of criticism—these have been the germinating expression of African political life." [21] The

[20] Francis X. Sutton, "Authority and Authoritarianism in the New Africa," *infra*, chap. xi, p. 278.
[21] *Ibid.*, p. 277.

reality of leadership could be achieved only by awakening the masses and mobilizing the populace as conscious political supporters and as opponents to the existing governmental authorities.

There is obviously a meaningful place for both the politicians' capacity to build a mass following and the officials' competence to carry out orders. In Nigeria, as in other newly independent countries, previous political experience has been largely of these two sorts.

Here then is a newly politicized society fostered in the politics of protest now trying to meet the problems of a "welfare state." Such a polity calls for a government operating at maximal efficiency. No heavier burden can be placed upon the political process, and the most advanced societies have a great deal to learn about the capacity of the electorate for seeing the larger issues and the readiness of special interests to realize that there are limits beyond which they cannot press for advantage without endangering their own welfare and that of the general public. It is optimistic indeed to think that a mass of voters with very limited experience in self-government can exercise the restraint that is necessary if longer-range rather than immediate objectives are to be achieved. In a country of rising expectations the economic realities will impose a delay in the fulfilment of these expectations. What the political consequences will be is anybody's guess. The self-restraint and willingness to postpone satisfactions would place a burden upon even the most mature political system. The conduct of modern government involves skills for governance to which the citizens of new nations have had relatively little exposure.

To make a democracy function, there is need for skill not only in the politics of campaigning, of vote winning, or of effective debating in legislative assemblies. There is also the skill of the negotiator exercised in the caucus room and around the committee table. Within the political party, within the legislature, or within the administrative office, the process of governance continues, and there neither ringing oratory nor loyal obedience has much relevance. There is a need for critical analysis, for inventiveness, for the capacity to co-ordinate and to uncover interrelations. A readiness to challenge and to defend and a willingness to compromise and to accept are all pertinent. The art of articulating interests and building consent is the art of government, and, like all art, that which strikes the eye of the beholder does not at once reveal the discipline and the craftsmanship that make possible the evident consummation. Politics is a way of getting things done governmentally. It is the process of making power operative. It is governance in action. As ways to get men to act we find at one end of the continuum the way that functions by command, backed by the certain knowledge that a refusal to obey will bring condign punishment and even the extreme sanction of the death penalty; at the other end of the continuum we find the way that wins men to compliance by methods short of violence. This latter way gets individuals to identify themselves with a larger purpose by appeals to reason, or to emotional loyalties. It is the way of persuasion, incentives, recognitions, and rewards. The politics of democracy draws its strength more from the permissive than the repressive parts of the governmental continuum. It attempts to provide appropriate procedures for eliciting participation, the sharing of ideas and responsibilities, in committees, in councils, and in the full array of deliberative agencies. But these devices for co-operative action remain empty forms unless the individual understands his role. The ways of democratic politics must be learned and the course is difficult to codify for the neophyte in our culture. He learns by apprenticeship rather than by the book. He learns his role from others who already know their parts.[22]

Paradoxically the best hope that these more subtle forms of political behavior may be exercised rests in indigenous experience with representative institutions in the southern parts of Nigeria before the British moved in. As Ezera states:

The Ibos and the Ibibios of Eastern Nigeria were and still are great believers in a government by discussion. Similarly, the Yorubas and related peoples of the Western Region were and still are fundamentally believers in constitutional monarchy. Hence the tribal societies of these peoples are essentially inimical to tyranny.[23]

[22] C. P. Snow, *Science and Government* (Cambridge, Mass., 1961), pp. 62–66. Here the author calls attention to committee politics, hierarchical politics, and court politics as three illustrations of political behavior akin to that discussed above.
[23] Kalu Ezera, *op. cit.*, p. 259.

The activities of age-group societies among the Ibos in building roads, schools, village halls and engaging in other community undertakings seem clearly in line with democratic values.

Further relevant testimony for our problem can be found in the role of the *oba* and his relationship to the chief and the tribal councils among the Yoruba. The functions of this religious leader might be compared to those of a constitutional monarch: the basic point being a conception of the contingency of power—i.e., authority based in some measure upon consent. Furthermore, it is of interest to recall that Lord Lugard, who had no difficulty in adapting his conception of indirect rule to patterns of governance in the North, had real difficulty in the Eastern and Western Regions in finding a counterpart to the Northern emir. The locus of power in these communities could not be so clearly identified.

African culture more broadly viewed provides evidence of practices that seem akin to the politics of the committee room and council chambers—namely, the readiness to discuss and ponder and seek agreement rather than to think that counting noses necessarily disposes of political differences.

In the aboriginal system, groups were, of course, smaller than today, but when a group could not arrive at unanimity, the minority would simply walk out of the meeting, and that would mean there would be more talk informally until a unanimous decision was reached. Now this is something that is quite difficult for us to understand; yet it works, and it is democratic.[24]

In Nigeria the strong indigenous attitudes and customs conducive to democratic practices among the Ibos and Yorubas cannot be overlooked. Political change is under way in the North. The British legacy is significant: membership in the Commonwealth, and acceptance of the "rule of law" and concepts of liberty and equality. Modernization in the economic realm breaks up old forms and new social institutions can foster greater freedom.

For a democratic order to function it must proceed from diversity toward that measure of agreement adequate for working

[24] See statement by Melville J. Herskovits in U.S. Congress, Senate, Committee on Foreign Relations, *Hearings, United States Foreign Policy—Africa*, 86th Cong., 2nd Sess., 1960, p. 117.

purposes. My purpose has been to call attention to various kinds and levels of diversity that must be reckoned with. While in the United States there is a great measure of pluralism and many competing interests, a considerable degree of coherence arises from the fact that however numerous the groups, they tend to be more or less organized and to serve as vehicles for articulating the objectives of the individuals who regard themselves as members. In Nigeria the diversity that governance must attempt to bring within the bounds of public policy and administration is characterized by many deep-seated differences.

IV. Education

As already noted, the great question in Nigeria is whether the political leadership can persuade the populace of the economic realities that face the country and whether they can remain in office on a program demanding sacrifices as well as offering promises for social welfare. The responsible leaders realize that the country needs help both in terms of money and of expert assistance from abroad. For coping with the problems facing the country now and in the future great hope is placed in education. This is the magic word and lies at the heart of most economic and social planning.

A few facts from the Report of the Ashby Commission will serve to highlight the situation.[25] As of the date of the Report, there were 2.5 million children in 17,000 schools in Nigeria. Two-thirds of the educational budget went for primary education. Eighty-two thousand teachers were engaged in this work and it is said that nine-tenths of the teachers were not properly qualified. Twenty-five thousand Nigerians were in teacher training schools. In the whole country, students in the first year of primary school numbered 648,749, in the first year of secondary school, 12,-344, and in the 6th forms, 553. There were places at University College at Ibadan for only 300 freshmen. In the University Col-

[25] *Investment in Education* (Report of the Commission on Post-School Certificate and Higher Education in Nigeria) (London and Lagos, 1960), p. 3 and *passim*.

lege at Ibadan and the Nigerian College of Art, Sciences and Technology there were about 1,800 students. About a thousand Nigerians were studying in colleges overseas in 1960. Such figures dramatically raise questions about the purpose of education and of how best to relate available educational resources to the needs of the economy and the desires of the electorate.

Education for what? The Nigerian masses have a faith in the capacity of education to improve their economic lot that seems at times comparable to the belief of the primitive Tivs that the aspirin pills of the missionaries should be able to cure any ailment from headaches to leprosy. The hopes pinned upon education are many.

It is thought of in the first instance as the surest means whereby the individual may improve his own economic and social position. It is said that every mother feels her child must have an elementary education. Parents regard education not only as good for the child but also as a form of insurance for themselves. If their child succeeds, their chances for security are increased. There are many instances of a family concentrating their resources on the education of one member in the hope that all may benefit thereby from his increased financial expectations. Education is commonly viewed in terms of fulfilling formal requirements or passing examinations to get jobs.

Graduates trained in clerical or literary skills provide recruits for the bureaucracy. Admittedly there is great need for an administrative elite and for better trained clerks, but there are also the demands of emergent industrialization for technicians and engineers. Apparently this employment does not enjoy the same prestige as clerical work. The individual sees that blue-collar jobs are not as well paid as white-collar work, although the country needs proportionately more employees in these categories as industrialization develops. The country needs veterinarians and agriculturalists. In my interview with Nnamdi Azikiwe, the Governor-General emphasized the importance of training that will enable students to become productive in economic terms. Education, in his opinion, should produce "know-how."

The desire on the part of the academic student has been to relate himself as closely as possible to what he conceives of as a

British model. The goal at times seems to be a quest for status as much as for enlightenment or for vocational training. The social prestige of the educated man, particularly the graduate of a British university, is very high indeed. To acquire education is to gain prestige, and the highest deference is accorded those who hold degrees from Oxford or Cambridge, or who have been certified by the Inns of Court in London. Here indubitably are standards of excellence and as such highly admirable, but we must also ask: How relevant are such models for the long-term developmental needs of Nigeria?

The educational pattern has an important bearing on the political attitudes of students and of the elite. The country is just at the beginning of its educational development and the models selected for imitation can be enormously influential. The need for education at all levels is so great and the popular desire for schooling is so insistent that there is the danger that education may be regarded as a panacea capable of more than formal instruction as such can ever achieve.

At the present time in Nigeria the effort to validate education by copying British models means embracing standards developed for a society very different from their own. There are, to be sure, practical reasons explaining the present situation. How, for example, as a practical matter could a British faculty in a Nigerian university with standards set by the University of London be expected to have the motivation, the flair, or the imagination for adapting European culture to an African setting? The process has been rather to bring about an adaptation on the part of the Nigerian student to British standards and values.

From the standpoint of the individual, education means opportunity and economic betterment. Since the need for men and women with some training is so great, these expectations have been fulfilled in considerable measure but already certain limitations can be seen. For example, newly educated youths expecting to step into positions of influence find that the politicians who led the movement for independence, though often not so well-trained nor so able as the oncoming generation, are nevertheless firmly entrenched.

At the other extreme of the social scale is the problem of the so-called school leavers. Here youths attracted away from agricultural pursuits find that an elementary school education does not qualify them for technical employment. They feel no incentive to return to the farms from which they came and where virtually a subsistence livelihood prevailed. Plans are afoot for land resettlement projects that may eventually put their energies to productive use. It is clear, however, that educational policy has to be related to economic development if unemployment with all that this threatens in terms of frustration and political instability is to be avoided.[26]

Education, then, in a developing country such as Nigeria, cannot be viewed solely as a matter of enhancing individual opportunity. It must be thought of as "the development of the manpower resources" of the nation.[27] This is the viewpoint so ably developed by Professor Harbison in his contribution to the Ashby Commission Report. Education unrelated to social needs and public purposes can lead to unemployment, political instability, wasteful expenditure, and the encouragement of faulty values. In brief, the advancement of education must be thought of in relation to the achievement of national goals. And in a free society the identification of these purposes, their clarification through public policy, and their realization through effective administration must be fulfilled through democratic government.

The politicians are faced with a public opinion that demands education without quite appreciating that mere literary skills do not insure economic advancement for the nation. This faith is of course to be preferred to hostility or indifference, and one can visualize a gradual change in public attitudes as progress is made from fighting illiteracy to increasing the skills needed for economic and social development.

It is to be hoped that education may indeed teach the limits of education itself as a formal process. Meeting formal standards for passing examinations, if such hurdles are treated as ends rather than means, can be a stultifying experience. On the other hand,

---

[26] For a detailed treatment of the problems related to school leavers, see Archibald C. Callaway, "School Leavers and the Developing Economy of Nigeria," *supra*, chap. ix.

[27] *Investment in Education*, pp. 49–124.

it is doubtless true that even this kind of educational experience is preferable to none at all. Our concern here, however, is with the currents that direct human aspiration and energy toward a democratic society, and if this goal is to be achieved there are elements more subtle than those provided by formal education as such. Education is a vital part of that broader process of socialization for relating the individual to his society or inducting him into his culture.

I offer as a premise that in most basic terms "democracy is built on the belief that the purpose of a society is to emancipate the intelligence and protect the integrity of the individual men and women who compose it." [28] Viewed by this standard, the support of education and the freedom of the press are of prime importance in liberating intelligence and in protecting the integrity of the individual.

Two educational forces of great importance to political socialization operate outside academic confines. The first to note is the press. In Nigeria it is free, outspoken, and has been a crucially significant factor in the rise of nationalism. The numerous papers both in English and in the vernacular are much concerned with politics. At a recent conference on the West African press a good review of the cultural conditions within which the press of Nigeria operates concluded that the climate "is not a particularly stuffy or choking one." "It is not so unhealthy as to make the Press morbid and feeble," the report continues. "It may not at present be ideally conducive to the fastest growth desirable, but it possesses all the conditions that forebode vast improvements in the future." As the report further points out, "The rate of literacy is rapid enough. The means of mass communication of new and enlightened ideas are fast increasing in number, quality and effect."

Newspaper readership bids fair to double or even treble within the next few years, what with the rapid spread of education and an advanced stage of mechanization of production. Increased readership will mean increased circulation, and therefore more advertising revenue. Increased revenue will mean higher pay and more attraction for the

[28] Rockefeller Brothers Fund (Report VI), *The Power of the Democratic Idea* (Garden City, N.Y., 1960), p. 74.

better educated recruits into the profession of journalism. This will in turn mean an improvement of literary, technical and professional standards.[29]

One of the most helpful factors in the development of the press has been the part taken by the *London Daily Mirror*. This paper with its technical skills and great financial strength set the pace of a modern newspaper devoted to reporting the news, building a large circulation, reaching widely across the country and maintaining a nonpartisan viewpoint but not hesitating to admonish when criticism seemed in order.

Coleman notes that

this infusion of external capital and expertise, devoted not only to profits but to the creation of new national communities and a discerning public opinion, has both revolutionized the pattern of communications and furthered the process of political maturation. Literate Africans in the remotest areas have been linked with their new national governments and made to feel themselves an integral part of the developing national societies to which they belong.[30]

Coleman's second point is so germane and so well stated that it must be presented in full:

The second change which has affected the communications process has been the expansion in the public relations activities of governments. At the height of agitational politics, when colonial governments were subjected to unrelenting invective by the nationalist press, the British government gave high priority to the development of public relations departments specifically charged with the task of countering nationalist propaganda and explaining government policies and programs to the masses. This engendered intense competition between nationalist propagandists and colonial governments, which led to a progressive widening and deepening of the communications process. When nationalists finally approached the threshold of political power they were determined that one of their first acts would be the dissolution of all government public relations activities. Once in power, however, they saw the utility of the official apparatus of mass communication which had been developed during terminal colonialism, particularly as they became in-

[29] Increase Coker, "The Nigerian Press: 1929–1959," in *Report on the Press in West Africa* (a report prepared for the International Seminar on "Press and Progress in West Africa" at the University of Dakar, May 31–June 4, 1960, by the Committee on Inter-African Relations), (Ibadan, Nigeria: Department of Extra-Mural Studies, University College, Ibadan, distributor), pp. 73–133 at 99.
[30] James S. Coleman, in Almond and Coleman, *op. cit.*, p. 351.

creasingly impressed with the difficulties in realizing their ambitious programs and the consequent need to rationalize and explain postponements or non-fulfillment. The result is that public relations departments acquired a new lease on life, and had their activities expanded. This growth has been matched by the mass education programs carried out by departments of education, agriculture, forestry, and health, among others. Of even greater significance is the creation of national radio networks, controlled by public corporations, exempted from politics, which give continuous coverage of events and developments throughout the new national society. With the great increase in literacy, these activities have operated to create a unified communications process, transcending existing discontinuities and pluralism, at least for certain strata of the population.[31]

Here, I submit, is intelligent and constructive action for strengthening democratic government. To demonstrate the meaning of modern technically competent journalism, to turn officials into educators and expositors of public policies, and to use the mass media to build unity and understanding is to take a positive approach to the conditions basic to democratic government.

V. The Administrative Problem

Nigeria, to attain modernization, must be conducted largely as an administered society. Educational policy, industrial development, the exploitation of resources, the improvement of agriculture, the use of foreign credits, and technical assistance—all these factors interrelate, and forethought and co-ordinated effort are therefore essential.

To pursue such goals calls for highly rational behavior and carefully calculated decisions.

It is difficult for an outsider coming from the industrialized West to appreciate at first both the limited strength of the native bureaucracy and the tremendously heavy burden that it must carry. Our administered society has, in addition to the vast bureaucracies of government at all levels, the highly organized cadres of big business, of labor, and of the host of associations and organized interests with their innumerable interlacings and over-

[31] *Ibid.*

lappings that constitute the tough fabric of a mature social order. To be realistic one must reckon with the "fragility" of the present administrative situation in Nigeria. As one experienced observer pointed out to me:

There are, in all the Governments of Nigeria only six Nigerian Administrative Officers of any real competence (two in the Federal Government, one in the Eastern Region, two in the West, and one in the North). There are perhaps five more men of competence in the Foreign Service. More than half of the Permanent Secretaries in the Eastern Region, for example, have had less than five years' experience of any kind in Government. The average age of the entire Administration (including remaining expatriates) is thirty-three. The situation in the West is a little better, but not essentially different. The North and the Federal Government are still largely staffed by expatriates, but in the case of the Northern Government, 40 per cent of the Administrative establishment is now vacant and the expatriate exodus is only beginning. The situation cannot but worsen before it betters and the years between now and 1970 will be touch and go as to whether an administrative machine can be held together at all.

Beyond the formal administrative service there are no other bureaucratic structures. This means there are no other ways of getting social purposes fulfilled that necessitate extensive organized behavior. One must, of course, reckon with the political parties as organizations. The effect of partisan participation within the bureaucracy is yet to be analyzed clearly. However, the push from the politicians and their followers is for more ministerial posts with the subordinate jobs and perquisites that accompany such additions. This in turn calls for more administrative machinery and more busy work. The strain placed upon the limited number of highly competent officials is extreme, and as crises occur they find themselves dashing about to put out fires that should never have been ignited. The identification of a dominant political party with each of the three regions tends to endorse the regional governmental loyalties and inter-region rivalries. The various ministries are tempted to develop positions on current issues and to feel that stating a position is almost as good as implementing a decision. I offer the following comments by a well-informed resident:

Inter-regional boards composed of Ministers tend to be like meetings of the [U.N.] Security Council. Each Government states its position; positive action consists largely in accepting a proposal "in principle"— which is normally the end of it—and each goes merrily along negotiating for its own steel mill, even though everyone knows that not more than one mill would be economic.

On the other hand, there is a growing volume of valuable informal collaboration and cooperation at the official level. In this respect, it should be recalled that the basic unity of this country, until the political leaders managed to unite on independence, was the unity of the British Administration. This was officially shattered with Regionalisation, but the Administrative Officers still knew one another personally and belonged to a common Colonial Service, and informal cooperation continued. The first impact of Nigerianisation was to impair this informal structure. It is now gradually rebuilding in the South—tho' not yet in the North—and I personally believe we should be most sympathetic to this development. Under the British system of administration, as you know, the permanent officials in the course of time have a very significant impact on policy; and I would hazard the guess that in the near future the emergence of a bureaucratic *esprit de corps* and sense of common purpose on a nation-wide basis will prove one of the major unifying factors, while the impact of the political process is quite likely to be divisive. At the present stage, intergovernmental cooperation even at the official level tends to be impeded by formal organisation and structure because of the consequent necessary involvement of Ministers.

The analysis of my non-Nigerian commentator is corroborated by the following points made by a competent Nigerian economist:

It seems about time that we face up squarely to the fact that the financial burden of administering this country has become far greater than our poor economy can continue to bear without serious brake on future progress. If the vast army of personnel (tied up with the process of legislation and administration) cannot be reduced—which is bound to be a sore point politically—some way must be found of scaling down salaries, allowances and other facilities which are so obviously out of tune with the country's financial capacity.

The author then argues for a political truce by the agreement among the major political parties with respect to the issue of taxation and also questions relating to wages, salaries, and allowances. "By thus seeking from time to time to remove certain vital economic issues from the arena of political bickerings," he states, "our governments will be better able to provide the high quality of political leadership which we shall need so much in the future if we are to meet the challenge of economic development more successfully than in the past."

There is obviously little precedent in the democratic experience of other countries to sustain the hope that the most important political issues can be removed from politics by agreement on political truces among parties. The values cherished by the leaders, the policies supported by the public, the social institutions that evolve to meet new conditions—all these elements must be taken into account in judging the viability of parliamentary government in Nigeria. There is no dependable basis for evaluating so many variables.

VI. Conclusion

In order to analyze, it is necessary to establish categories, and having done so, it is tempting to set priorities or to argue for relationships of cause and effect. A consequence of such thinking is to assert that one type of phenomenon (be it political, for example) is determinate of what happens to other categories (be they economic, social, tribal, or whatever).

I think the course of events in Nigeria belies any such form of analysis. Rather than seeing political factors as more basic than economic, or social as more fundamental than either, it is enough to note that an interaction exists and to remember that our categories are nothing more than constructs erected for analytical convenience. This point is worth making because it guards against the tendency to treat "democracy" as a political condition that cannot be reached until a specified series of antecedent economic and social conditions have been achieved.

It seems to me that the history of representative institutions and of constitutional government clearly demonstrates that what some writers refer to as economic and social *preconditions* of democracy in fact developed along with certain political forces and democratic forms. Thus historically we find that the spread of literacy, widened access to schools, economic improvement for the general populace, urbanization, breakdown of class barriers, and many similar factors generally accompanied or indeed sometimes followed democratic advances such as the broadening of the franchise. The argument is often advanced today that democracy cannot be successfully introduced until certain preconditions have been established, to wit, a substantial measure of material well-being, education, industrialization, and urbanization.[32]

If the Western democracies had been guided by a theory of "essential preconditions for democracy," the reform acts of the nineteenth century could never have been passed.

What we have come to call democracy is the outcome of an historical process that began with the breakup of feudalism and that became articulated during the age of the "Democratic Revolution" at the end of the eighteenth century. We must reckon with the long struggle to achieve secularization and the very recent stage of equalitarianism that advanced through electoral and social reforms in the nineteenth century concomitantly with the diffusion of economic prosperity, the fruits of technology, and the mighty changes wrought by wars and depressions.

Before democratic institutions, either social or political, could flourish, strong countervailing forces—feudal, clerical, monarchical, and aristocratic—had to be broken down. Moreover, the wealth created by the industrial revolution was a long time reaching the masses. The struggles of the have-not classes in Europe and America were not encouraged by friendly foreign powers, such as we find today, eager to see democratic values prevail. That liberty and equality as ideals and as practices have prevailed to their present extent is the result of hard struggle. As Professor Palmer states:

the great generalization of Alexis de Tocqueville, that history exhibits a centuries-long movement toward a greater equality of conditions, seems true to me only if it includes the thought, as a subordinate generalization, that men have at times fought for this increase of equality against contrary tendencies and against very positive opposition.[33]

[32] See Seymour Martin Lipset, *Political Man* (Garden City, N.Y., 1960), pp. 45–76.
[33] R. R. Palmer, *The Age of the Democratic Revolution* (Princeton, 1959), p. 407.

The struggle for freedom and equality has been the most persistent and general political aspiration over the last two hundred years. Today the prevailing ethos sustains the power of the democratic idea. Today the proponents of democracy face the threat of Communism or a nationalistic dictatorship, but these dangers increase only in the event of democratic failure. This, I submit, is a far different set of circumstances than faced by the idealists and revolutionaries of the eighteenth and nineteenth centuries. In that era the arrogance and pride of wealth and station denied that there was even a problem of popular participation. The power of quite contrary ideas held sway. In Nigeria the nationalist leaders built their case for independence upon the democratic doctrines learned while in colonial status.[34]

My conclusion is simply that while Nigeria faces a very different challenge from that faced historically by the champions of democratic values, the course for democratic advance has never been easy and it cannot be won in the future any more than it was in the past by waiting upon the establishment of "preconditions." We face, rather, a constant interplay of forces, some inimical and some supportive to democratic growth. Out of the opportunities offered each day will come whatever gain there will be for the future.

The growth of democracy can be sought in changes in class and in family relationships, in the nature of tribal, regional, and national loyalties, in a readiness to modify old beliefs and accept new practices, and in the objectives and values associated with education, with the press, and with public service.

[34] Chief Obafemi Awolowo has recently presented his view of democracy in the following realistic terms: "The ideal of democracy is not liable to modification or distortion, even though mankind has invented different methods for its realisation. In a democracy, the government must rule with the consent of the governed. The governed are inalienably entitled at periodic intervals to give this consent to the same or a different set of people who form the government. The expression of such consent must be free and unfettered; and must on no account be stultified or rigged. Furthermore, the consent must never be obtained by duress, threat or intimidation; by undue influence or fraud. These are the principles which underlie the ideal of democracy. Wherever these principles (or any of them) are tampered with or abrogated the resulting situation is anything but democracy. We all know that whilst these principles are solemnly observed in India, Britain and the United States of America, for instance, the methods of their application differ as between these countries. So the methods could differ in any African nation. But it is an affront to the African race to suggest that they are incapable of applying these principles." (*Op. cit.*, pp. 303–4.)

As the power of the democratic idea penetrates and informs a wide set of human relationships, institutions can be modified to sustain political forms appropriate for self-government. The interplay of interests expressed in current formulations of public policy can be more or less democratic. The influence of individual leaders gives voice and direction to democratic purposes, or the reverse. In a word, the conditions of democracy or of tyranny are of the here and now.

Self-government has failed in many countries—indeed it has failed more often than succeeded. It cannot succeed if all essential adjustments within the society are foisted upon the political process. The legal forms of government are but one vehicle for governance, and self-government must be carried on at many levels and through many institutions. It is well for an aspiring democracy to be aware that the government as such is not a mechanical device for wish fulfilment. Indeed, in the interest of political viability the preservation of free institutions must be treated as an end in itself, rather than as a mere means for serving short-run social or economic purposes.[35]

There is a great deal that we do not know about the viable conditions for democracy. Certainly there is a limit to the degree of ignorance, of poverty, of disease, and of frustration compatible with self-government. General prosperity and enlightenment correlate well with flourishing democracies. One can imagine a scale of indices that might diagnose a normal range for democratic health. But we can conclude that such a judgment would be based on a range of factors and not on the presence or absence of any one form or practice. The ideal of health or the ideal of democracy can, fortunately, be experienced and enjoyed. To prescribe the conditions essential for such enjoyment is another matter.

[35] In concluding a recent study, John Plamenatz offers this advice to the developing countries: "Do not suppose that because liberal democracy, to be effective in the large nation state, requires general literacy, widespread technical education, and a fairly high standard of living, you should begin by trying to improve literacy, technical education, and material conditions by all means in your power in order to get freedom and democracy the more quickly. Since time is on your side, because colonialism is on the decline, do not, in your hurry to get independence and literacy and material prosperity, jeopardize your chance of getting what you still hope for after you have got them." *On Alien Rule & Self-Government* (New York, 1960), p. 207.

To discourse on the preconditions of health would be to engage in the hortatory or the banal. So too would be such an approach to democracy. The goal is clear enough, but there is no error-proof routine to insure its realization.

11

Authority and Authoritarianism in the New Africa [1]

Francis X. Sutton

The rushing surge that brought sixteen African nations to independence in 1960 has caught up the world in the excitement of witnessing a great historical change, and it has mostly been a happy excitement. By becoming politically independent nations, the African peoples have done what most of the world felt they ought to do, and 1960 could be unaffectedly a year of multiple celebrations. But there have also been reasons for anxiety about the new era that is beginning in Africa. The distressing events in the ex-Belgian Congo have been like the descent of a wicked fairy, marring the year's celebrations and threatening a troubled future. The Congo was scarcely born before it gave lurid illustration to doubts that independence meant free and secure citizenries within African countries or that the removal of foreign domination in Africa was a sure step toward a healthier international order.

The front runners in African independence had already stirred doubts and misgivings before the 1960 independence rush. Ghana had been put to close scrutiny since 1957 for its deportation of people it found politically undesirable, for its Preventive Detention Act, and for its alleged efforts to cripple or eliminate the political opposition. Guinea presented a one-party state to the world as a matter of principle, and found sympathetic echoes all across

[1] This essay, in similar form, was published originally in' Journal of International Affairs, XV (1960), 7–17. The Duke University Press is indebted to the publishers for permission to reprint this somewhat revised version.

Tropical Africa, even in the apostle of moderation and good sense, Mr. Julius Nyerere of Tanganyika.

The West has strained to comprehend these early signs and to sympathize without condescension. There has been a vague willingness to believe African conditions are somehow different and hence that a more authoritarian form of government may be called for. The possibilities of anarchy and disorder are one evident basis. The mutiny and tribal warfare in the Congo have been only the most noted examples. Scarcely any emerging African state has escaped some manifestation of potential explosiveness. There were, for examples, the disturbances in the southern provinces of the Sudan as independence approached in 1955, the Ashanti riots of 1956 in Ghana, and the persisting terrorism in the Cameroons; even Nigeria saw independence marred by the (probably unimportant) disorder among the Tiv people in the Northern Region. Scylla and Charybdis seem very close together for these new states, squeezing out any comfortable track between tyranny and anarchy for parliamentary democracy to follow.

On the international scene the new African states have declared themselves firmly for neutralism or non-alignment. They do not immediately run to the Soviet bloc in their new freedom. But neither do they cling to the Western nations which have been their masters but have ultimately sought to bring them to independence in amity and good faith. Given the past intimacy of relations with Western countries, neutralism seems a withdrawal of loyalties. And it is a withdrawal that is no calm and simple assertion of autonomy, but is full of assaults on colonialism and capitalism, warnings against continued Western domination, and expressions of sympathy for the models of development seen in Communist countries.

These are the principal sources of disquiet about the African political future that show themselves among Western observers. Even when they have not seriously quieted the celebration of African independence, they have been troublesomely in the background. To understand what substance they may have, and how seriously one must view them, it seems essential to scrutinize recent history and actual conditions in Africa. One must not rest with a vapid assumption of historical difference but try to understand how the conditions of the era of colonialism brought forth nations with these characteristics. Understanding these nations in their genesis, one may try to assess the hopes and misgivings they arouse and distinguish their deep-running tendencies from mere rhetoric and passing circumstance.

I. The Sources and Character of Authority in the New States

The recent history of Africa has a tidiness for which future generations of school children may be grateful. A neat seventy-five years measures the Era of Colonialism in Africa. The Berlin Conference of 1884–85 does very nicely to mark its beginning and 1960 does dramatically well to mark its close.

Most of the independence celebrations of 1960 were the culmination of a long course of preparation, deliberate or inadvertent. Some of this preparation can be given clear dates and descriptions as historical record. The evolution of the Nigerian constitution from the Richards constitution of 1946 through the MacPherson constitution of 1951 to the constitution of 1954 and its amendment in the succeeding constitutional conferences makes such a record. So do the long discussions in the U.N. of the Somalia Trusteeship. But there has also been another form of preparation of independence that lies deeper and has the intangibility of pervasive things. This is the process whereby the authority that was vested in European governors and administrators in Africa gradually fell into dispute between Europeans and Africans and ultimately has fallen to Africans. The ultimate shift of sovereignty from a European metropolitan power to a new African nation is the legal and political expression of a sociological shift that has gone on over many years.

The rule of the European nations in Africa was established by the assertion and exercise of superior European power. Not that the scramble for Africa was particularly harsh or bloody. In some places it was, but much was gotten by negotiation, and adroit displays of power or minatory gestures often were humanely substituted for plain force. Whatever the pattern of conquest, there was conquest nonetheless and the position of the colonial powers in Africa was that of powerful conquerors. Europeans assumed a special status as superior people with a claim to authority, and colonial governments established a firm control over African territories that will undoubtedly seem remarkable in retrospect. The pacification of Africa became so thorough that personal security for a white man in Africa was as good or better than it was in Europe or America. It was sometimes not as good for Africans but African populations grew sharply in many places through the sheer elimination of warfare and insecurity. Remarkable records of peacefulness were attained. In Southern Rhodesia, for example, a melancholy note for 1960 was the breaking of a more than sixty-year period in which there had been no killings by police action.

The coming of African independence has depended upon a change in the structure of African societies whereby Europeans ceased to be the elite to whom the power of political control exclusively belonged. The history of African reaction to European social, economic, and political superiority is a complicated history taking many forms. For a long time the reactions of Africans to the European makers of empires could not be directly challenging without severe costs. Indeed—and this is a most important fact—the African had usually to react by accepting a subordinate and dependent position. In saying this, I mean to describe a reaction involving something more than calculated accommodation to the facts of European control and superior power. I mean something of the sort that psychologists have variously labeled "identification with the aggressor," "introjection of an authority figure," or "acceptance of a role model." That some psychological process of this sort should have happened seems clear, and it was an essential and inevitable step toward the ultimate emergence of African nations as we see them today. For it was through this process that Africans learned the values and practices and ideals of Europeans and shaped their own aspirations toward competing with Europeans in these terms. Sociological studies like those of Professor Clyde Mitchell and his associates at the Rhodes-Livingstone Institute for the Copper Belt of Northern Rhodesia,[2] or the now faintly tragic studies sponsored by UNESCO in the former Belgian Congo,[3] have made clear the depth of African involvement in the influences brought by Europeans. While not ceasing to be African, increasingly large sections of African populations have imitated Europeans and learned in various ways to aspire to the same things.

Hostile and challenging reactions to European dominance at first took covert and oblique forms. Some of the best known were religious in character and avoided a direct assault on the political kingdom. Later, Africans have come forward claiming that they should run the affairs of their country alongside or in place of the Europeans. These newer political movements did not seek to abandon or reject the institutions through which Europeans had controlled Africa. There has been little demand for a return to the pre-colonial Africa or any radical abandonment of the form of colonial territories. Rather the claim was that Africans were now prepared to behave like the Europeans who had been taking responsibility for political and administrative control of African territories.

The basis of colonial government by Europeans had legally lain with the mother countries and been clothed in various constitutional and statutory instruments like the Foreign Jurisdiction Act for the British territories. But the essentials lay in the sociological status of Europeans as a dominant elite. The legitimacy of such a government in an aggressively political setting could not be secure. It was always vulnerable to claimants of the right to represent the popular masses being governed. White men could hardly make such a claim without the embarrassments of paternalism.[4] Effective African nationalism came with the emergence of Africans who could present themselves as equipped to do what

---

[2] J. Clyde Mitchell, "Africans in Industrial Towns in Northern Rhodesia," in *H. R. H. The Duke of Edinburgh's Study Conference 1956*, Vol. II.
[3] Cf. V. G. Pons, Nelly Xydias, and Pierre Clement, "Social Effects of Urbanization in Stanleyville, Belgian Congo," in International African Institute, *Social Implications of Industrialization and Urbanization in Africa South of the Sahara* (Paris, 1956), pp. 229–492.
[4] It may be one indicator of their political uncertainty of touch that the Belgians alone tried to elevate paternalism into an explicit doctrine of colonial government. Cf. G. E. Brausch, "Le Paternalisme: une doctrine belge de politique indigène," *Revue de l'Institut de Sociologie*, 1957, pp. 191–217.

European governors and administrators had been doing and also to represent "the people." Once they did so, a new and ultimately irresistible competitor for legitimate authority was on the scene. The new authority might for a time be badly served by unsure or incompetent African leaders, but it could not long be constrained.

For there to be effective African leaders, there had to be a mobilization of their popular support. The masses of the African population had to be in some way "politicized," and this process has normally taken forms not comfortably within the institutionalized range of political expression. By this I mean to say the masses were not at first and typically drawn into political action as voters in campaigns or as engaged observers of established governments. Particularly in the British territories, there was an attempt gradually to introduce the principles of representation and elections into the government of these territories. There were African members of the Legislative Council of the Gold Coast as early as 1886. Initially appointed, these African representatives have been ultimately elected in varying ways, with gradually widening franchises. This policy may be seen as a controlled and deliberate set of moves toward "politicizing" Africans. But the nationalistic movements have outrun any such controlled tutelage. Julius Lewin is undoubtedly too harsh when he writes that the legislative councils of the British territories were "façades, rather than forums," and decries executive councils as "embryonic cabinets where the inner secrets of policy-making are still carefully guarded from African scrutiny." [5] For many new African leaders, these institutions have been schools of responsibility, but they have not had pride of place in the political education of the masses. African political awareness has come more characteristically in the movements of protest, with meetings and demonstrations on the margin of legitimate political activity as the classic settings. Listening to long-winded orators in the beer halls of Northern Rhodesia, and waiting all day Sunday in an outdoor gathering of the unfranchised for a late afternoon speech from Tom Mboya or some other leading Kenya politician have been characteristic experi-

[5] *Central African Examiner* (Salisbury), Dec. 6, 1958, pp. 15–16.

ences. Passionate speeches to enthusiastic crowds that take the whole existing structure of government as a target of criticism—these have been the germinating expression of African political life.

Cause and effect become badly jumbled in the complex movement of African nationalism. The rapidity of the African conquest of self-rule and independence is at once a cause and a consequence of the process I have depicted. Had Africans come to political consciousness more gradually through becoming aware of political institutions and their internal processes, learning of "the issues" (like the ideal voters of American liberals) in the contexts of these institutions, the forces created by enthusiastic responses to African leaders in public meetings might not have had such a free sweep. But conversely, rapid change meant little chance for the slow maturing of a response to institutions that needed much adapting if they were to be at all suited to African control.

Authoritarianism in the new African states is a particular cause and consequence of the rapid changes. It is—perhaps paradoxically—a feature of government in which there is basic continuity across the great shift from colonial to African control. For the colonial governments in Africa, however benevolent, responsible, and well-meaning they may have been, were not democratic governments in the sense that we know them in the Western world. As I have stressed, colonial administrations did not have their mandate from the governed. They might, and typically did, work through indigenous African authorities at local levels and consultation went on at all levels, including the general territorial administration. But in the end they responded not to the dictates of the electorate but to the judgments of a governor and his advisers. There was little experience of direct and legitimate challenge to the authority of the administration. The District Officers or *commandants de cercle* who ruled the territories were, as Delavignette put it, "chiefs" rather than simple administrators.[6] They

---

[6] According to Robert Delavignette, *Service Africain* (Paris, 1946), p. 31, "L'administration coloniale territoriale a un caractère d'humanité positive que prend une allure d'autorité révolutionnaire. Chargée d'introduire un régime nouveau dans la politique et l'économie du pays, concentrée dans quelques Européens, qui ne peuvent communiquer que par intermédiaires avec la masse de leurs administrés . . . et qui sont séparés d'eux par le genre de vie, la forme de pensée, le

were police officers, magistrates, and omnicompetent executives who might cajole and listen to complaints, but who in the end "told people what they were to do." A considerable measure of discretion was inseparable from diffuse and multiple powers so that one finds African nationalists today arguing that the arbitrariness of power they are accused of had ample precedents in colonial rule.

The Africans who have emerged as leaders of their people have an authority differently based but similarly diffuse. Winning leadership in the context of enthusiastic movements, they have taken on heroic stature in the eyes of their followers. Men like Azikiwe and Awolowo in Nigeria, Nkrumah in Ghana, Nyerere in Tanganyika, or Sékou Touré in Guinea have the claim to authority of men whose qualities are thought to be beyond those of ordinary men. In the term Max Weber taught us and that is now being widely applied by Africanists, they are "charismatic" leaders. It was a part of Weber's analysis to stress that charismatic authority lacks the clear definition and bounds of legal, constitutional authority, and the application to Africa seems to be supported by the facts. Thus the "authoritarianism" we now see in Africa derives in part at least from the very nature of the authority through which it has been possible for Africans to grasp control of their own affairs.

Lest all of this discussion rest doubtfully in generality, or appear more personal and original than it in fact is, I venture to illustrate with a case from recent African history that has benefited from a lucid analysis.

II. An Illustration: Nyasaland

The disturbances in Nyasaland that attracted the world's attention in 1958 and 1959 arose from a confrontation of established colonial authority with the pervasive new authority of a national-

mode de travail, comment ne serait-elle pas révolutionnaire et autoritaire? . . . Il y a dans l'administration coloniale térritoriale un principe interne qui lui est propre: l'autorité personnelle de l'administrateur et, en dernière analyse, la personnalité dan l'art de commander."

ist leader. It will be recalled that Dr. Hastings Banda, "the most distinguished of Nyasas," returned to Nyasaland in July, 1958, after an absence of many years in South Africa, the United States, Great Britain, and Ghana, during which he acquired a medical education, practiced his profession, and became known and respected among Africans from his own and other territories. He returned at the request of members of the African National Congress in Nyasaland and was immediately accepted as their leader. Subsequent to his arrival, there was a series of public disturbances; force was used to disperse African crowds, and on March 3, 1959, a state of emergency was declared and numerous leaders of the African National Congress were arrested. There was an immediate and vigorous reaction to this governmental move. A series of disturbances broke out all over the country in which forty-one lives were lost and sixty-eight persons were wounded by gunfire. In subsequent actions, aiming at restoration of law and order in the country, additional lives were lost. The Nyasaland Government issued a White Paper in which it alleged, among other things, that a plot to murder members of the Government had existed.

These events brought strong reactions in the United Kingdom and a commission was appointed by the Secretary of State for the Colonies, Mr. Alan Lennox-Boyd, to investigate the disturbances and the events leading up to them. The commission had four members, all British, under the chairmanship of Sir Patrick Devlin, and in the usual fashion, has come to be known as the Devlin Commission. In its report, this Commission remarks that the Government of Nyasaland "was a benevolent despotism." [7] It stresses the benevolence but points up the conflict between the despotism and the attitudes of a small minority of politically active Nyasalanders who had challenged the Government. The Commission notes that provision for the election of a few Africans to the Legislative Council had not altered the character of the Government. They describe the probable disappointment of the devisers of this constitutional arrangement:

[7] *Report of the Nyasaland Commission of Inquiry* (London, 1959, Cmnd. 814), p. 16.

No doubt it was hoped that the five Africans in the Legislative Council would treat the four years of the Legislature's life as a sort of probationary period during which they would put the African viewpoint with moderation and make a thoughtful contribution to a formulation of policy which remained the exclusive responsibility of the Government; this was their chance to learn how to run the estate which would someday be theirs. Instead of that, they have behaved as if they were the opposition in a full-fledged democracy whose duty it was to harass and criticize the Government. Their speeches are largely designed as propaganda to be printed in Hansard at Government expense; Hansard has become a best seller among educated Africans. But the forms of government and the attitude of the Government toward its subjects are still essentially paternal. The leaders of Congress have been pouring new wine into old skins.[8]

When Dr. Banda arrived on the scene, he intensified the issue by establishing contact with the people in enormous crowds amidst immense enthusiasm. His speeches were made in English and their content was moderate but their delivery was highly emotional and arousing. The Commissioners remarked: "We have listened to the recordings of some of them and they are the speeches of a demagogue." [9] The Devlin Commission absolves Dr. Banda of many of the charges against him. They nevertheless argue that the effect of his appearance and his oratory was to present a sort of radical challenge to the Nyasaland Government such as would not be the case in the appearance of an ordinary political leader in a democracy. The Commission illustrates and then proceeds to analyze the challenge both to Europeans and to the traditional African authorities through whom they worked:

In a democracy politicians are frequently scoffed at. If one were referred to as "a little boy of twenty-five years direct from Oxford" no one would worry. But when Dr. Banda referred to District Commissioners in these terms (not an individual but the genus) it was thought by the Administration to be dangerous. A District Commissioner cannot afford to be jeered at or insulted in public; if that is tolerated, it would lead to a loss of authority which would be fatal. Many unofficial Europeans consider that the same thing applies to them. . . . Government in Nyasaland is based on respect for authority and this applies to the

[8] *Ibid.*, p. 16.
[9] *Ibid.*, p. 27.

Chiefs as much as to the Europeans. "Contempt" of a chief is an offense that he can punish. Party demonstrations against a chief hostile to Congress might well amount to contempt. . . . The respect which by native tradition and custom is paid the chiefs is something which the Government is most anxious to preserve; one of the things about Congress which most disturbed the Government was the practice of stirring up disrespectful demonstrations against loyal chiefs. The Government's attitude is that the chiefs should be above politics. . . .[10]

In these contexts, criticism of established authority was regarded, rightly or wrongly, as a radical rejection of authority. The Commission goes on:

If, for example, Dr. Banda attacked the enforcement of the Agricultural Rules, then must it not be that he did not want them observed? If so, then was not the African confronted with a choice between obedience to Dr. Banda and obedience to the Government? The African did not think of Dr. Banda as a party leader whose policies happen to be opposed to those of the Government; they thought of him as a national leader setting up his authority against that of the Boma (the seat of government).[11]

Tragic conflict was latent and scarcely avoidable:

The real case against Dr. Banda is not that he ever advocated disobedience . . . we do not think that he ever did—but that he refused to realize that disobedience was the inevitable consequence of what he was saying and doing. . . . Congress behaved as if Nyasaland was capable of functioning as a democracy in the fullest sense and that the Government was holding things back. The Government, on the other hand, became increasingly intolerant of any opposition on Western and democratic lines because it considered it tantamount to the setting up of a rival authority. . . . This conflict of thought and feeling between a government that is still paternal in outlook and an opposition that is not yet as mature as it believes itself to be is no doubt a common feature in the emergence of democracy all over the world.[12]

The recent history of other African territories has not, I think, differed in essentials from the case of Nyasaland. Governments whose powers were not seen as explicitly and carefully defined, or subject to open critical opposition, have been challenged and then inherited by Africans. Diffuse respect for an alien elite has

[10] *Ibid.*, pp. 16–17.
[11] *Ibid.*, p. 17.
[12] *Ibid.*, p. 21.

been replaced by enthusiastic devotion to charismatic African leaders, through a period of struggle and crisis that is dangerously brief in many cases. Charges of colonial blindness and selfishness on the one hand or of African impetuosity and heedlessness on the other hand are too common nowadays. Seen against an appreciation of human frailties and an analysis of the forces with which leaders have had to deal, the wonder may be that the great change has been as well-paved as it has in cases like Ghana, Nigeria, and some of the French-speaking territories.

There are obviously other roots of the authoritarianism and the distaste for open opposition we now see in African governments. It is not to be taken for granted that a single African leader will readily establish control over a whole territory. There are notoriously great differences among the African peoples who were swept into one political entity by the colonial partition of Africa. Once political expression is possible for Africans there is a good chance that it will give voice to these differences. Well-tried machinery for accommodating opposition among African leaders is no more present than it is for the transition from European to African control. There are now abundant examples in Africa of the flaring of tribal and other hostilities once European control is lifted. Adding to the examples already given, one notes the tribal form of most parties in the ex-Belgian Congo and the resulting tragic violence in Kasai, Katanga, and elsewhere; the uncomfortable to unsafe position of migrants like the Dahomians over much of French Africa and the sharpening of measures against Southerners in Northern Nigeria. New possibilities of expression of internal differences make new demands for effective control by a government. Countries like Ghana that have taken strong measures have pointed to the ruthlessness of their opponents as justification— and with much plausibility. There seems little doubt that African governments have graver problems of security than the colonial governments had—they are more intimately involved in potentially explosive African differences. These, one ventures to think, are some of the realities behind the ideology of national unity and one-party systems which Western observers often find so disquieting. What role contemplation of models East and West may play invites further attention, and doing so brings us to the international relations of the new African states.

III. Neutralism, Independence, and Maturity

The analysis of the transition to African independence that I have given makes it sudden and reactive. The old structure of colonial societies is not abruptly destroyed; rather, places are exchanged in its fabric. Africans previously in a dependent and subordinate status throughout these societies have claimed the control of them for themselves. Lord Mountbatten recently said that he thought the Tanganyika army could not be fully Africanized for twenty years, this being the time he estimated it would take to make battalion commanders. Such a vision of Africans growing through slow and natural stages into calm and unaffected exercise of high stations and authority as Europeans did before them has not and cannot be realized. Long before, a critical mass of psychological reactions is exceeded and Africans bounce to the top.

To assume that the Africans now controlling African states are calmly confident of their capacity to run African societies unaided seems very doubtful. There are too many controverting facts—the lack of trained African professionals and technicians, and the continuing control of Europeans over most business organizations are among the potent ones. When Nkrumah and other African leaders have warned about the dangers of colonialism in covert forms, Western powers have often felt offended at the impugning of their good faith in granting independence. But anxieties of the sort must be seen as normal and real. It must be remembered that Africans and their new states remain weak and have only recently been the passive subjects of guidance by white men in most spheres. We should expect a need for emotionally tinged acts and assertions that plainly affirm independence. In the international political sphere, neutralism or open sympathy with the Communist world are natural expressions of this need. If there are dangers in it, there are also grave dangers of another sort in steadily proclaimed loyalty to the West. For this sort of loyalty threatens to undermine the bases of confidence in setting forth as an independent state.

Sympathy for the Communist world is thus in part reactive. But that there is also an intrinsic appeal of Communist models in ideology and in development policy cannot be doubted. Outside the Western world, Communism, after all, is an ideology that permits the pursuit of goals learned from an envied and respected West while being in apparent opposition to it. And it is some ideology of this sort that the African states need.

It will, therefore, be astonishing if the African states are comfortable partners of the Western world in the great game of international politics. There is more than discouragement in this prospect. For if the general analysis here is sound, a stage of fractiousness in the leadership of African states may be essential to their progress towards maturity as independent and responsible nations. By adopting an independent course Africans may have costly experiences. But they will at least be gaining experience in the exercise of independent responsibility. And through the exercise of responsibility lies the best course towards attaining a true maturity. In nations as in individuals, true independence can only be an attribute of maturity. Like anxious parents, the Western nations are now seeing the African nations go off rather headstrongly by themselves. They expect and will need further help about which they will often have to be gracelessly demanding. Guiding hands will have to be light, deft, and inconspicuous to be acceptable. But their absence will be resented and their ultimate effects not trivial.

Appendix

A Survey of Selected Social Science
Research on Nigeria Since the End of 1957

James O'Connell

Since James Coleman, *Nigeria: Background to Nationalism* (Berkeley, 1958), furnishes a comprehensive and well-assembled bibliography extending through 1957, this chapter can best begin where his bibliography ends.[1] It is impossible to list or comment on everything that has appeared since then. But, since independence was in sight by 1958 and was already achieved in practice internally, two basic trends in the 1958–61 period have been the consolidation of national unity and the drive toward economic betterment. These trends include efforts as diverse as a growing historical awareness in the country and the gradual adaptation of administration and law to new social conditions. Such trends can be used as a guiding principle in selecting and assembling publications.

History

One of the few weaknesses in Coleman's excellent study, as Thomas Hodgkin, *West Africa*, September 12, 1959, p. 717, pointed out in one of the best-written reviews of the work, was that its

[1] The author wishes to express his appreciation to his colleagues in the Department of Economics and Social Studies, University College, Ibadan, and to Mrs. R. Prince and Mr. V. M. Hogg of the Nigerian Institute of Social and Economic Research for their assistance in the preparation of this chapter. The author alone, of course, is responsible for the accuracy of the citations and the evaluation of the sources.

historical treatment was inadequate where it dealt with periods earlier than the immediate nationalist past. Coleman's study provided little basis for criticism of Rupert Emerson's statement that "Nigeria is notoriously a precarious lumping together of peoples whose separate identity is at least as real a matter as their acceptance of national unity" ("Nationalism and Political Development," *Journal of Politics*, XXII [1960], 3–28). Hodgkin, *Nigerian Perspectives* (Oxford, 1960), further shows that Emerson's observation is superficial by superbly sketching Nigerian history down to 1900 in this introduction to an anthology of historical documents. Hodgkin makes clear that though the scramble for Africa and the pattern of British conquest gave final shape to the Nigerian frontiers, these frontiers enclose peoples who hold a past and traditions in common. Five main groupings of people may be distinguished: (1) Kanem-Bornu and its dependencies; (2) the Hausa states and their southern neighbors, for example, the Nupe and the Jukun kingdoms, which from the beginning of the nineteenth century become in large part the history of the Fulani empire; (3) the Oyo empire, and the Yoruba successor-states that established themselves in the nineteenth century after the disintegration of the empire; (4) the kingdoms of Benin and Warri; and (5) the Delta states and the predominantly Ibo hinterland. These groups influenced one another down the centuries in religion, trade, and war. Hodgkin's introduction and anthology mark a decisive departure in the writing of Nigerian history from "within" rather than from "without." Written from "without," Nigerian history appears as the history of European contacts with the coast, an approach that disfigures the long-accepted work of Sir Alan Burns, *History of Nigeria* (London, 1929; 5th ed., London, 1955). A new general history by M. C. English, *An Outline of Nigerian History* (London, 1959), does fair justice to the periods before European penetration, but its more recent chronicling is marred by a condescending tone in describing African advance. Another general history by Michael Crowder is due to appear this year.

The history of the Northern peoples has been given considerable attention lately—for one thing, it is richer in documentation for its earlier periods than the history of the forest peoples. Michael G. Smith has followed up the intimate recording by his wife, Mary Felice Smith, of the autobiography of the old Hausa woman, *Baba of Karo* (London, 1954)—to which he contributed an introduction on Hausa social structure—with a study of the administrative structure of one distinctively Hausa people (*Government in Zazzau* [Oxford, 1960]). The earlier part of the book is historical; but its final section describes the administration as it functioned in 1950. One may quarrel with Smith's projecting back into the past the details of social structure that were available to him in some later documents, but his work is undeniably important for Hausa history and administration. Thomas Hodgkin, "Smith on Zazzau," *West Africa*, August 26 and September 2, 1961, pp. 933, 973, has reviewed rather critically Smith's approach and findings. Kurt Krieger, *Geschichte von Zamfara Sokoto Provinz, Nord Nigeria* (Berlin, 1959), deals with another part of the Muslim North. Krieger was unluckly in that he was denied direct access to one key document and had to content himself with a copy, whose departures from the original cannot always be clearly seen. J. Carnochan, *Africa*, XXX (July, 1960), 280, reviewing Krieger's work, is highly critical of some of his reconstructions. Alongside these works there is a briefer book by A. H. M. Kirk-Green, *Adamawa Past and Present* (Oxford, 1958), that combines a history of the area with a present-day description. Though the book falls a little between the poles of history and contemporary description, it is still an accurate account of peoples who have recently been engaged in two referendums before deciding to stay in Nigeria rather than join the Cameroon Republic. For an account of some sources of the history of the North there is A. D. H. Bivar, "Arabic Documents of Northern Nigeria," *Bulletin of the School of Oriental and African Studies*, XXII, 2 (1959), 324–49. One important side to these studies—and to the many more that are likely to follow them soon—is that they will enable young intellectuals from the South to get to know better the traditions of the North. Such acquaintance will help to foster a sympathy that is vital to national unity, introduce them to that part of Nigerian history where the manuscript tradition is strongest, and suggest the ties that link the Northern peoples to the great African empires of the past such as Songhay and Mali. E. W. Bovill, *The Golden Trade of the Moors* (Oxford, 1958), which is a revision of his *Caravans of the Old Sahara* (London, 1933), offers a great deal of readable historical material on many of the peoples who live on the edge of the Sahara. Oddly enough this material provides a solid historical background for pan-African aspirations from the peoples in Nigeria who up to the present have been least inclined to take part in the moves toward African Union.

In K. O. Dike, ed., *Eminent Nigerians of the Nineteenth Century* (Cambridge, 1960), there is a collection of short biographies of leaders of local communities, including Dan Fodio and Madame Tinubu. Though it is too much to call these people nationalists in the later sense, they did much to lay the foundation for the local participation in politics that made twentieth-century nationalism possible. R. L. Sklar in a penetrating article, "The Contribution of Tribalism to Nationalism in Western Nigeria," *Journal of Human Relations*, VIII (Spring and Summer, 1960), 407–18, suggests how such local sentiment did help make nationalist appeals meaningful to the masses of the people. Little by little—though too slowly and uncritically as yet—local history is being recorded. For that reason J. U. Egharevba, *A Short History of Benin* (Lagos, 1960), is important. An Eastern people have had their chronicler, U. E. Obio-Offiong, *A First Step to the Study of Ibibio History* (Aba, 1958). Though such works are uncritical, they help to preserve source material and arouse pride and interest in local history. Quite good articles on Nigerian history are constantly appearing now. The issues of the *Journal of the Historical Society of Nigeria* are particularly valuable. If we were to select one article rather than another in this *Journal*, it might be A. F. C. Ryder, "Missionary Activities in the Kingdom of Warri to the Early Nineteenth Century," III (December, 1960), 1–26, which shows that Portuguese contacts lasted much longer than is usually thought. A thorough study of the new beginnings of Christian missionary activities in the nineteenth century, and especially the work of Bishop Crowther, will have to await the publication of a thesis by

J. F. Ade Ajayi, "Christian Missions and the Making of Nigeria 1841–1891" (University of London, 1958). Simon Ottenberg, "Ibo Oracles and Intergroup Relations," *Southwestern Journal of Anthropology*, XIV, 3 (1958), 295–317, not only describes carefully a deep-rooted aspect of Ibo religious psychology but makes available much evidence on the nineteenth-century trade routes in the East. G. I. Jones, "Native and Trade Currencies in Southern Nigeria during the 18th and 19th Centuries," *Africa*, XXVIII, 1 (1958), 43–54, offers both interesting information and suggests an important aspect of methodology in research. In connection with historical research the importance of the Nigerian National Archives at Ibadan is growing. Its *Reports* can be consulted with profit.

For understanding the shaping of Nigeria's frontier and the beginnings of administration, Margery Perham, *Lugard: the Years of Authority 1898–1945* (Oxford, 1960), the second volume of her biography, is essential. The historical side is well done in the volume and its comment is not spoiled—as it might have been—by an uneasy conscience about Lugard's conviction that imperialist expansion was bringing great civilizing benefits to subjugated peoples. The extraordinary part of Lugard's conquest was how with a small number of British officers and some African auxiliaries he humbled the rulers of the old Fulani empire. The British forces—despite their Maxim guns—could not have stood up to a united and determined resistance. But there was a failure of nerve among the social groups that made them give way before the new forces that were beginning to penetrate. Another factor contributing to the collapse was the lack of loyalty shown by the commoners to their overlords; after one battle Lugard heard firing and discovered that the Fulani horsemen were dealing with their foot soldiers for failing to support them. Miss Perham's book makes available valuable information for the study of the beginnings of the British system of indirect rule in Nigeria. It is clear now that the autocratic Lugard initially had no intention of continuing indirect rule indefinitely. Some of his successors in the North converted the system into a doctrinal method of administration. Lugard himself protested against this development. P. C. Lloyd,

"Lugard and Indirect Rule," *Ibadan,* No. 10 (November, 1960), pp. 18–22, criticizes some of Miss Perham's emphases and does a good deal to get rid of the commonly held oversimplified notions regarding indirect rule.

The consolidation of the power of the ruling class has had important repercussions in recent politics. It is interesting to speculate on the reasons why the Northern Elements Progressive Union (NEPU) has failed to drive a wedge between the common people and the Northern Peoples' Congress (NPC), the party of the natural rulers. Undoubtedly a large part of the explanation is to be found in the way in which the emirs were able to exercise control through the administrative structure of authority and in the appeal they could make to Northern sentiment against an opposition that allied itself unwisely with strangers. But, formally at least, constitutional rule has been legally established now in the North, and it will be interesting to see how the traditional rulers will react when formal education and modern technology have exercised their influence on social structure.

Inevitably Miss Perham deals at length also with the European background to imperialist expansion in Africa. Two other books are concerned with men who played considerable roles in the acquisition of Nigeria. J. E. Flint, *Sir George Goldie and the Making of Nigeria* (London, 1960), deals with a man who employed Lugard at one stage and who through his part in organizing trade and wringing a charter from an unwilling British government helped to set the stage for the final British take-over. C. Gertzel has written a valuable review of Flint's book in "Sir George Goldie and the Making of Nigeria," *Ibadan,* No. 13 (November, 1961), pp. 20–23, which has the particular merit of suggesting the fields of study—such as the nature of the early treaties with emirs and chiefs—that are still awaiting research. Roland Oliver, *Sir Harry Johnston and the Scramble for Africa* (London, 1959), tells the story of one of the gifted and adventuresome—though by no means scrupulous—administrators who made the British Empire possible. J. F. Ade Ajayi, "The British Occupation of Lagos, 1851–61: A Critical Review," *Nigeria,* LXIX (August, 1961), 96–105, evaluates the complex motives that lay behind the complete annexation of Lagos. R. Robinson and J. Gallagher, *Africa and the Victorians* (London, 1961), consider the imperialist period on a wide canvas. They reject the view that British expansion in Africa come from motives of imperialist pride and commercial exploitation. The author's view is that

from start to finish the partition of tropical Africa was driven by the persistent crisis in Egypt. . . . So far from commercial expansion requiring the extension of territorial claims, it was the extension of territorial claims which in time required commercial expansion. The arguments of the so-called new imperialism were *ex post facto* justifications of advances, they were not the original reasons for making them. Ministers had publicly justified their improvisation in tropical Africa with appeals to imperial sentiment and promises of African progress. After 1900, something had to be done to fulfill these aspirations, when the spheres allotted on the map had to be made good on the ground. The same fabulous artificers who had galvanised America, Australia and Asia, had come to the last continent [p. 472].

They admit, however, that Nigeria is at least a partial exception to their general thesis and grant that there a reluctant government "acted to preserve existing fields of trading and missionary enterprise from foreign annexations."

C. Gertzel, "The Early Days of an African Trader," *Ibadan*, No. 10 (November, 1960), pp. 12–16, describes the fascinating enterprise of John Holt in his first trading period. We shall have to await the publication of her thesis on John Holt and the Nigerian trade before we have a full story of the penetration of the Eastern hinterland by the European traders after their long years of trading with middlemen on the coast itself. But, whatever the motives behind the European political and commercial penetration of this period and whatever the technical and cultural advantages it finally brought with it, Africans were placed for many years in an inferior position and the severest injury of colonization, the hurt to a people's self-respect, resulted. It is in this connection that lies the importance of a book like Basil Davidson, *Old Africa Rediscovered* (London, 1959). It enables people to reach back beyond the colonial period and recapture the thrill and achievement of Old African civilizations and empires. The sections of the book that deal with Nigeria are not the best, but it does make

available in a readable way the results of archeological research
going on all over the continent. W. Fagg and F. Willett, "Ancient
Ife," *Odù*, VIII (1960), 21–35, and Frank Willett, "Ife and its
Archeology," *Journal of African History*, I, 2 (1960), 231–48,
give excellent summaries of the work that has been done at Ife.

In brief, the trends in historical studies emphasize that African
history has begun to be written from within and that it has ceased
to be the history of contacts with Europe. At the same time scholars from the former colonial powers are writing with great ob-
jectivity on some of the leading personalities of the colonial period.

Political Development

Coleman's study of the Nigerian nationalist movement that led
to independence in 1960 is by far the best work on the subject.
As co-editor and collaborator in another work, *The Politics of the
Developing Areas* (Princeton, 1960), he adds no detail to the
Nigerian side of his study of nationalism. But together with his
co-editor he makes an interesting attempt to define concepts that
are useful for interpreting the politics of a country like Nigeria.
Kalu Ezera has published a revised version of his doctoral dissertation, entitled *Constitutional Developments in Nigeria* (Cambridge, 1960). It adds some later detail to Coleman's book and
provides more discussion of the constitutional conferences, but it
is much narrower in scope than Coleman's endeavor to examine
all the factors that contributed to the emergence of Nigerian nationalism. As source material for constitutional development one
must refer to the *Report by the* ad hoc *Meeting of the Nigerian
Constitutional Conference Held in Lagos in February 1958*
(Lagos, 1958), where provisions were worked out for electoral
regulations and the regionalization of the marketing boards; the
*Report by the resumed Nigerian Constitutional Conference Held
in London in September and October, 1958* (London, 1958),
which decided the issues held over from the 1957 Conference
and gave the Federation its present final shape; and the *Report*

of the ad hoc *Committee of the Conference on the Nigerian Constitution* (Lagos, 1959), where some important details were added. These conferences worked on the proposals of the *Raisman Fiscal Commission* (Lagos, 1958), which furnished the basis for the present awkward arrangements for dividing finance among the center and the Regions. Another important report was made by the Commission appointed to enquire into the fears of minorities and the means of allaying them (*Nigeria* [London, 1958, Cmnd. 505]). This Minorities Commission report is important not only for its recommendations opposing the creation of new regions and favoring a statement of human rights in the Constitution but also for the information it contained on political sentiment in several parts of the country. The Western Region Government has published *Proposals for the creation of a minority area for the midwest area and the establishment of a midwest minority council* (Sessional paper 14/1960), and some of these proposals have already been implemented. They may be important with time if a new Midwest Region is not created. T. O. Elias, *Government and Politics in Africa* (London, 1961), is the recently published lecture series that he delivered at the University of Delhi in 1956. Unfortunately the lectures were prepared before some of the best recent works were published; Dr. Elias has not revised them and they are badly dated already. The work does, however, have a certain documentary interest since the author seeks a cultural background to African nationalism in the African achievements of the past. This kind of effort has been all too rare in English-speaking Africa. There is an introductory survey prepared by the Royal Institute of International Affairs, *Nigeria: The Political and Economic Background* (London, 1960).

Two books have appeared from prominent participants in the struggle for freedom and the beginnings of self-government. Chief Obafemi Awolowo has written his autobiography, *Awo: The Autobiography of Chief Obafemi Awolowo* (Cambridge, 1960). With painstaking attention to detail Awolowo recounts many events of considerable political interest such as his decision to break away from Dr. Azikiwe and the means that he took to found his own party. The section in which he describes his premiership of the Western Region falls curiously flat, however, and it is odd that he should consider the founding of commercial television to be the pinnacle of his achievement. The final section, in which he discusses issues such as internal democracy and foreign policy, is a mature and cogent analysis. He rejects caustically the notion that African countries are ready only for an inferior brand of democracy. His foreign policy views are considerably more to the right and also less enthusiastic about African union than some of his more recent statements would suggest. A duplicated version of his speech in favor of Nigeria's associating herself with the Ghana-Guinea-Mali union is available (Ibadan, 1961). The book throws considerable light on the character of the man who wrote it, and Tunde Oloko in "Awo: Credit Wants and Politics," *Ibadan*, No. 11 (February, 1961), pp. 7–9, makes a shrewd analysis of Awolowo's career. Dr. Azikiwe has had his speeches gathered selectively into a volume, *Zik: A Selection of the Speeches of Nnamdi Azikiwe* (Cambridge, 1961). The main defect of the book is that the published speeches can in no way express the pulsating appeal that the orator could make to the assembled gatherings. Unfortunately, too, it does not contain his fine inaugural speech as Governor-General, in which he stated superbly an African point of view on colonization in Africa. This speech may be found, however, reprinted under the title, *Human Dignity* (Enugu, 1961). Apart from the constant demand for freedom in the speeches before independence was assured, the recurring emphasis is on education, since Zik understood quite well that educational improvements were essential to give freedom a proper content. Dr. Azikiwe's founding of the University of Nigeria at Nsukka forms a logical climax to this theme. A short but worthwhile comment on these speeches and on Zik's career has been made by Ukpabi Asika in "Nationalism in the Making," *Ibadan*, No. 12 (June, 1961), pp. 10–11. Dr. Azikiwe and Chief Awolowo have their biographies sketched briefly in Ronald Segal, *Political Africa: A Who's Who of Personalities and Parties* (London, 1961), an extremely well-presented African political encyclopedia that gives some excellent thumbnail portraits of other Nigerian political leaders and describes with reasonable accuracy the policies of the main Nigerian parties. Michael Crowder has some gossipy descriptions in his *Pagans and Politicians* (London, 1959). Fred Anyiam, who evidences a strongly biased sympathy for the National Council of Nigeria and the Cameroons (NCNC), has written *Men and Matters in Nigerian Politics 1934–58* (Yaba, 1959), which contains some useful information. Certainly the best study of Nigerian political parties is Richard L. Sklar, "Nigerian Political Parties" (Princeton, unpublished thesis, 1961), and one hopes that it will be published before too long. Thomas Hodgkin has just published *African Political Parties* (London, 1961), which contains many references to the Nigerian parties and offers a framework for interpretation.

The energies of political parties are basically geared to winning power through elections. K. W. J. Post, *The Nigerian Federal Election of 1959*, is in the press. Post did some research on expressions of political sentiments that is to appear in "Some Pre-Election Opinion Polls in Eastern Nigeria," *Nigerian Institute of Social and Economic Research: Conference Proceedings, 1960* (hereafter abbreviated *NISER Proceedings*). E. Awa, "The Federal Election in Nigeria, 1959," *Ibadan*, No. 8 (March, 1960), pp. 4–7, is a fairly detailed analysis of the policies of the parties and their impact on the public; in the same issue of *Ibadan*, pp. 7–9, K. W. J. Post has written "The Federal Election: An Outside View." Post, "Forming a Government in Nigeria," *Nigerian Economic Journal*, II (1960), 1–5, has described in a short article what is known of the party maneuvers preceding the formation of the present coalition government. The Federal Electoral Commission has published its *Report on the Nigerian Federal Elections* (Lagos, 1960), but it is disappointing in its lack of detail and of critical evaluation of the kind of ballot boxes, voting methods, and techniques that were used. There are two more lengthy studies of Nigerian regional elections in W. J. M. Mackenzie and Kenneth Robinson, eds., *Five Elections in Africa* (London, 1960): "The Western Region of Nigeria, May 1956," by Philip Whitaker, and "The Eastern Region of Nigeria, March 1957," by J. H. Price. The analysis of elections is valuable only when it is done in the context of a politico-sociological analysis that goes far beyond the elections themselves. Both Whitaker and Price are somewhat narrow in their approach. Yet their work is competent. Both bring out the ethnic nature of the voting. Whitaker's concluding remarks on the administrative conduct of the election in the West stresses issues such as the general absence of a belief in the fairness and impartiality of the administration. P. C. Lloyd and K. W. J. Post bring to light some of the technicalities and hazards of organizing the registration of voters in "Where Should One Vote?," *Journal of African Administration,* XII, 2 (1960), 95–106. There is a *Report of the Constituency Delimitation Commission* (Lagos, 1958), and there are also regional reports on constituency delimitation. Quite important sidelights on the running of elections can be found in the annual police reports of the Federal Police Department. It is quite clear now that to insure a minimum amount of fair play in electoral campaigns and voting it was vital to keep the police under federal control. Chief Awolowo and the Action Group, which had advocated the regionalization of the police, would themselves have been the group likely to suffer most if that had taken place.

For a general description of the Federal Constitution there is nothing as yet better than Taylor Cole, "The Independence Constitution of Federal Nigeria," *The South Atlantic Quarterly,* LX, 1 (1961) (*Duke University Commonwealth-Studies Reprint Series,* No. 6). The various papers contained in L. Brett, ed., *Constitutional Problems of Federalism in Nigeria: Record of Proceedings of a Seminar Held in Lagos, August, 1960* (Lagos, 1961), concentrate for the most part on the legal aspects of federalism. They mark the beginning of detailed comment on the Constitution. Taylor Cole, "Emergent Federalism in Nigeria," however, goes well beyond the legal field to discuss the factors that are contributing to a genuine political and social unity in the country. D. Rothchild's section on Nigeria in his *Toward Unity in Africa: A Study of Federalism in British Africa* (Washington, 1960), is primarily an historical evaluation, but it provides a brief survey of some of the tensions that went into making Nigeria a federal rather than a unitary state. Horst David, "Einheitsstaat-Bundestaat, Staatsrechtliche Probleme in Ghana und Nigeria," in *Afrika*

Heute: Jahrbuch der Deutschen Afrika Gesellschaft (Köln, 1960), compares federal and unitary tendencies. The Hansard Society has published a symposium, *What Are the Problems of Parliamentary Government in West Africa?* (London, 1958). Sir Frederick Metcalfe, the former speaker in the Nigerian parliament, describes the development of parliamentary techniques in "Nigeria's New Federal House," *West Africa*, July 9, 1960, p. 772. Dr. Elias, *Federation vs. Confederation and the Nigerian Federation* (Port of Spain, 1960), contrasts some of the proposals made for a West Indian federation and some parts of the Nigerian constitutional system. Particularly valuable is his commentary on the human rights provisions in the Nigerian Constitution. The future of the Constitution depends on the general shape of political activity in the country. Ayo Ogunsheye, "Nigeria's Political Prospects," *Ibadan*, No. 11 (February, 1961), pp. 4–7, makes some trenchant comments on conditions that are needed to insure political stability in the concrete political circumstances of the country. James O'Connell examines the political implications of bringing welfare notions and schemes into a developing economy in "Ein westafrikanischer Staat im Wandel," *Afrika Heute*, pp. 57–67. A longer study, *Nigeria: Prospects for Democracy* (London, 1961), has come from Chief H. O. Davies, who was once one of the prominent nationalist leaders. He places Nigerian prospects interestingly against an historical and comparative background (using the Sudan, for example, for comparison). But one would have liked more detailed internal analysis from one of Chief Davies' experience. In "Société traditionelle et démocratie," *Présence Africaine*, XXIII (December 1958—January 1959), 6–15, Ogunsheye lays stress on the socio-psychological factors in traditional society that should make for democratic functioning in modern African states. There has been disappointingly little published material on Nigerian foreign policy, but there are sensible remarks to be found in the views of the Nigeria Society, which are expressed in their journal, *The New Nigerian*, I, 1 (August 1961), 5–8. The essay by L. Gray Cowan, "Nigerian Foreign Policy," *supra*, Chapter VI, is a welcome addition to the limited material available.

Studies of local government are more scarce than the importance of the subject merits. There is a basic introductory book on the South by P. J. Harris, *Local Government in Southern Nigeria* (Cambridge, 1957). There are the recent revisions of Eastern law which provide the legal basis for a two-tier local structure, more rigidly controlled than previously by the Regional Government, Eastern Region of Nigeria, *Local Government Law No. 17, 1960*. I. D. Cameron and B. K. Cooper, *West African Councillor* (London, 1955), provides a manual for councilors that offers an insight into the issues and modes of procedure of concern to councilors. There is an excellent article by P. Dyson, "Local Government Training in the Western Region of Nigeria," *Journal of African Administration*, XI 4 (1959), 193–200, that deals with training for local government service. There is a short article on the same subject by Mallam Muhammadu Song, "Nigerian Local Government in Transition," *Journal of African Administration*, XII, 2 (1960), 74–76. L. Gray Cowan devotes part of his *Local Government in West Africa* (New York, 1958), to Nigeria. Cowan also contributes a chapter on Nigerian local government to Gwendolyn M. Carter and William O. Brown, eds., *Transition in Africa* (Boston, 1958). On Eastern local government mention may be made of an unpublished work by Kalu K. Ogba, "Development of Local Government in Eastern Nigeria" (Oxford, unpublished thesis, 1958). On the Yoruba West there is P. C. Lloyd, "Local Government in Yoruba Towns: An Analysis of the Roles of the Obas, Chiefs and Elected Councillors" (Oxford, unpublished thesis, 1958). E. Awa, "Local Government in a Developing Country (Nigeria)," *Seminar on Representative Government* (Ibadan, March, 1959, duplicated), has presented a paper that among other things shows how in parts of the Eastern Region real local power often lay with people who were not elected representatives at all. There are various official reports on local government elections, such as, for example, *Report on Local Government Elections in the Western Region* (Sessional paper 7/1958). But the history of local government still remains a sad account that is strewn with the wreckage of abolished councils. Political bitterness, lack of integrity, absence of adequate leadership, and inefficient administration (coming often from the lack of funds with which to employ trained staff in small administrative areas) have prevented real success up to the present. Ilorin was the pilot scheme in the North, but it failed for political reasons that can be read in *Statement of the Government on the Report of the Committee of Inquiry to investigate allegations about the Ilorin Native Authority* (Kaduna, 1958). N. C. Perkins, *Report on the Investigation into the Enugu Town Council* (Enugu, 1961), brought to light bribery and corruption that led to court charges and convictions. R. N. Rapson's investigation into the allocation of market stalls in Lagos, *Report on the Marketstalls* (Lagos, 1959), throws light on one of the most contentious issues in Nigerian local politics. There have been few cases of council corruption in Nigeria where the market stalls have not loomed large; indeed disgruntlement about their allocation has sparked off more than one inquiry. The special case of Lagos local government has led to Sir John Imrie, *Report on the Relationship between the Federal Government and the Lagos Town Council* (Lagos, 1959).

Public Administration

For a long time during the colonial era the administration and the executive coincided. There are politicians in charge now, but they can make their decisions operative only through the administration, and the administration plays no small part in helping to formulate the decisions that the political leaders make. In a developing country government is also by far the greatest employer of labor. The *Report on Employment and Earnings Enquiry* (Lagos, 1958), gave 302,200 in "public employment" against 176,100 in private, commercial, and other employment. For a long time to come state authority and enterprise will have to undertake activities that in a more advanced country could be left to private enterprise. This emphasizes the importance of the civil service and related groups, such as the employees of the public corporations. The Mbanefo Commission, *Review of Salaries and Wages* (Lagos, 1959), gives information on the salary and wage structure of the public service. The figures reveal the enormous gap between senior and junior service income. That gap may well be a source of serious social instability in the future.

A general study of the transition from expatriate to local personnel has been made by Kenneth Younger, *The Public Service in New States* (London, 1960). He discusses particularly the conditions for retaining the expatriate personnel that are needed during the early years of independence. He remarks on the blundering compensation systems that lured officers away rather than induced them to stay. He does not, however, get to the heart of internal problems facing the new states. A short review by Ukpabi Asika, *Ibadan*, No. 10 (November, 1960), pp. 34–35, takes issue on this point and adds a valuable foonote to a useful book. Great Britain, *Her Majesty's Overseas Civil Service: Statement of Policy Regarding Officers Serving in Nigeria* (London, 1958), provided an official statement of policy, but there is also the reaction of Nigerians and Nigerian officers to consider. Though Nigerianization as an issue is declining in importance, it still remains a bitter bone of contention in certain sectors. In this connection there appeared the *Final Report of the Parliamentary Committee on the Nigerianisation of the Federal Public Service* (Sessional paper 6/1959). That report was extremely critical of the slow rate of Nigerianization, and undoubtedly the committee that produced it did help to accelerate the pace. But the committee's report contained exaggerations and factual errors. The Federal Government, after some delay, issued its comments on the *Report* and put some matters back into perspective in *Matters Arising from the Final Report of the Parliamentary Committee on the Nigerianisation of the Public Service* (Lagos, 1960). The Head of the Western Region Civil Service, Chief S. O. Adebo, "The Civil Service in an Independent Nigeria," *The New Nigerian*, I, 1 (1960), 16–18, draws on his own experience to insist that "accelerated Nigerianisation is bound to involve a temporary lowering of efficiency. This is not a point against accelerated Nigerianisation. . . . There is [however] no reason why an accelerated pace of Nigerianisation should involve a lowering of the moral standards in the Service." A short unsigned article, "Nigerianisation in Ibadan," *West Africa*

(October 29, 1960), pp. 1220–21, notes that those officers just promoted in the Western Region had not been promoted out of place; they were as experienced as the expatriate officers who were working alongside them. One of the undiscussed issues of the moment, at least in publications, is the policy of Northernization in the North. Northern Region of Nigeria, *Report on the Public Service Commission* (Kaduna, 1958), declares that "it is the policy of the Regional Government to Northernise the Public Service; if a qualified Northerner is available, he is given priority in recruitment; if no Northerner is available an Expatriate may be recruited or a non-Northerner on contract terms." Such policy may be understandable from the viewpoint of the educational backwardness of the North, but it weakens the unity of the Federation. Another allied issue—the introduction of Northerners at an accelerated pace into the federal service—has also been little discussed but it is one that is causing intense dissatisfaction in Southern circles. A. H. M. Kirk-Greene, "A Training Course for Northern Nigerian Administrative Officers," *Journal of African Administration*, XI, 2 (1959), 63–71, describes one of the courses being run by the Northern Government to bring their officers up to a certain level of efficiency in a faster than normal time.

One can consider at this stage that preoccupations with Nigerianization and Northernization will be temporary and marginal. The important objective is to develop services in which recruitment and promotion are open and fair and for which talent is available. In the attainment of this objective the public service commissions play a vital role. The various reports published on work of the commissions offer source material to scholars. L. G. Coke Wallis has prepared a pamphlet, *The Public Service Commission: Its Role and Development in Western Nigeria* (Ibadan, 1960). Satisfactory studies of the actual working of the civil services have not yet been published. Taylor Cole has written a general review, "Bureaucracy in Transition: Independent Nigeria," *Public Administration*, XXXVIII (Winter, 1960), 321–37, and a revised version of this appears *supra*, Chapter V. Donald Kingsley, *Staffing, Organizational and Training Problems in the Public Service of the Western Region* (Ibadan, 1961), is an excellent study that has recently been published. There is information to be gleaned from the statement on *The Integration of Departments with Ministries* (Lagos, 1959), and from the *Administrative Organisation of the Eastern Region* (Enugu, 1958). In *NISER Proceedings, 1960,* James O'Connell has a paper, "Administrative Science and Nigeria," which discusses administration against the general political and social background, the need to combine bureaucratic and technical expertise, and the role of the university in the formation of administrators.

Sociology

It is impossible to list all the anthropological articles on Nigerian peoples that are appearing at the moment. It is consequently necessary to be even more selective than in other sections of this essay. These studies are taking on an increasingly practical importance in a rapidly changing social order. Two good family analyses are by Yoruba writers: Chief I. O. Delano, "The Yoruba Family as the Basis of Yoruba Culture," *Odù,* V (1958), 21–28, and A. Mobogunje, "The Yoruba Home," *ibid.,* pp. 28–36. One might add A. Mobogunje, "The Market Woman," *Ibadan,* No. 11 (February, 1961), pp. 14–17, which explains how the market woman combines her trading with her family responsibilities. D. C. Simmons describes aspects of the life of a people of Eastern Nigeria in "Sexual Life, Marriage and Childhood among the Efik," *Africa,* XXX (April, 1960), 153–65. A rare enough person, an African woman writer, Adetowun Ogunsheye, writes on her fellow countrywomen in "Les femmes du Nigeria," *Présence Africaine,* XXXII (1960), 121–38. A Izzett, "Family Life Among the Yoruba in Lagos, Nigeria," in A. Southall, ed., *Social Change in Modern Africa* (London, 1961), describes family life in a large cosmopolitan town. Marguerite Dupire contributes an excellent chapter, "Situation de la Femme dans une Société Pastorale" to Denise Paulme, ed., *Femmes d'Afrique Noire* (Paris, 1960), which deals with the Fulani nomads of Northern Nigeria and Niger. She describes their mental attitudes, their work, and their ambiguous religious situation in a society that is slowly being permeated by Islamic influences. Her description brings out the sharp contrast between these women and the settled Hausa women like Baba of Karo. Peter Marris, "Slum Clearance and Family Life in Lagos," *Human Organization*, XIX (1960), 123–28, deals with the adaptation forced on people in the new housing schemes. Marris has now published a longer study, *Family and Social Change in an African City* (London, 1961), that analyzes at some length how the Lagos rehousing venture provided better material living conditions but failed to cope adequately with social structure. There is still much room for schemes and building designs that more realistically suit extended family obligations and the tropical weather conditions. In an issue of the *Sociological Review*, VII, 1 (1959), that is devoted to the theme of "Urbanism in West Africa," P. C. Lloyd has a description, "The Yoruba Town Today" (pp. 45–63). He deals with the same theme in "Yoruba Towns," *Ibadan*, No. 9 (June, 1960), pp. 26–29. One might compare the knowledge of social links that W. B. Schwab distils from his description of terminology in "The Terminology of Kinship and Marriage among the Yoruba," *Africa*, XXVIII (October, 1958), 301–13, with the more phenomenological approach of Edwin Ardener to a section of the Ibos in "Lineage and Locality among the Mba-Ise Ibo," *Africa*, XXIX (April, 1959), 113–33. The study of individuals against their social background is approached somewhat unusually in Paul Bohannan, ed., *African Homicide and Suicide* (Princeton, 1960). One might refer also to P. Morton-Williams, "Yoruba Responses to the Fear of Death," *Africa*, XXX (January, 1960), 34–40, and R. Prince, "Cultural Mechanisms for the Mastering of Grief among the Yoruba" (Summary), in *NISER Proceedings*, 1958, pp. 232–33. A somber facet of life that cannot be ignored is described by Daryll Forde, "Spirits, Witches and Sorcerers in the Supernatural Economy of the Yako," *Journal of the Royal Anthropological Institute*, LXXXVIII (1958), 165–77.

Harold D. Gunn and F. P. Conant have added another volume to the *Ethnographic Survey*, a description of *Peoples of the Middle Niger Region, Northern Nigeria* (London, 1960). Worth a mention is an interesting local study by Mallam Shuaibu Na'Ibi and Alhaji Hassan, *The Gwari Tribe in Abuja Emirate* (Lagos, 1961), which is a simple but informative account of a Northern pagan people. There is another study of Northern people by E. Hopen, *The Pastoral Fulbe Family in Gwandu* (Oxford, 1958). Paul Bohannan, "The Impact of Money on an African Subsistence Economy," *Journal of Economic History*, XIX, 4 (1959), 491–503, analyzes evolving conceptions of money among the Tiv and their impact on notions of marriage and status. Two other articles on the Tiv might be read together: Paul Bohannan, "Extra-Processual Events in Tiv Political Institutions," *American Anthropologist*, LX, 1 (1958), 1–12, and J. G. Wallace, "The Tiv System of Election," *Journal of African Administration*, X (1958), 63–70. These articles help to explain the strong Tiv resistance to the Northern administration. Laura Bohannan's chapter on the Tiv in John Middleton and David Tait, eds., *Tribes without Rulers* (London, 1958), sheds more light on the egalitarian outlook of this people. Paul and Laura Bohannan have made available *Three Source Notebooks in Tiv Ethnography* (New Haven, 1958). The strong constitutionalism of Yoruba political structure is well brought out in P. C. Lloyd, "Sacred Kingship and Government among the Yoruba," *Africa*, XXX (July, 1960), 221–37. Two contributions on social status in the Muslim North are worth mentioning: M. G. Smith, "The Hausa System of Social Status," *NISER Proceedings, 1958*, pp. 180–94, and E. R. Yeld, "Islam and Social Stratification in Northern Nigeria," *British Journal of Sociology*, XI (June, 1960), 112–28. G. I. Jones discusses changing relationships among different groups in "Ecology and Social Structure among the North Eastern Ibo," *Africa*, XXXI (April, 1961), 117–34. S. O. Ottenberg, "Ibo Receptivity to Change" in William R. Bascom and Melville J. Herskovits, eds., *Continuity and Change in African Cultures* (Chicago, 1958), pp. 130–43, examines the psycho-sociological factors that have made the Ibos the most dynamic people in the country in recent years. Phoebe V. Ottenberg has contributed a chapter to the same book on "The Changing Economic Position of Women among the Afrikpo Ibo."

African society has far from ceased to be religious. Ulli Beier has followed up his *Sacred Carvings from One Small Yoruba Town*

(Lagos, 1957), with *Sacred Festivals in One Yoruba Town* (Lagos, 1959). These two books offer excellent summaries of Yoruba belief and ritual. R. E. Bradbury has a well-written article, "Divine Kingship in Benin," *Nigeria,* LXII (1959), 186–207. Robin Horton, *The Gods as Guests* (Lagos, 1960), is a delightful volume on the festivals of the Kalabari people of the Delta. The mutations that Christianity can undergo in an African religious context are described by J. C. Messenger, Jr., "Reinterpretations of Christian and Indigenous Belief in a Nigerian Nativist Church," *American Anthropologist,* LXII, 2 (1960), 268–78. The same writer has a chapter, "Religious Acculturation among the Anang Ibibio," in Bascom and Herskovits, *Continuity and Change in African Cultures,* pp. 279–99, which analyzes psychological and moral reactions to Catholic and Protestant teachings on salvation, but much of the interpretation is naïve and tends to rely on doctrinaire schematization rather than on empirical facts. From an Anglican viewpoint, Edmund Ilogu, "The Problem of Indigenization in Nigeria," *International Review of Missions,* XLIX (1960), 167–82, attempts to show how African customs can be integrated into Christian worship. The Catholic Bishops put out a pamphlet for independence, *The Catholic Church in an Independent Nigeria* (Ibadan, 1960), that deals with both religious and social questions; one of its chapters contends that the main West African pagan beliefs and practices are perfected rather than destroyed in the Christian system. A work dealing with Africa south of the Sahara and containing many references to Nigeria is B. Sundkler, *The Christian Ministry in Africa* (London, 1960). Sundkler combines a fine understanding of present-day political and social development in Africa with a sure sense of religious sociology and a sympathetic insight into the problems of the non-secular elite. J. Spencer Trimingham, *Islam in West Africa* (Oxford, 1959), is not accurate on all points of detail, but he succeeds generally in his aim "to try to assess what has been the result of the impact of Islam, the way it influences African society, and conversely, the way the African community moulds the Islam it has received." Humphrey Fisher, "The Ahmadiyya Movement in Nigeria," in *African Affairs* (*St. Antony's Papers Number Ten*) (London,

1961), pp. 60–88, is a chapter on a somewhat rationalistic and quasi-heretical Muslim sect that is making a determined effort to make up for the Muslim backwardness in schools in Southern Nigeria but one that is disliked intensely by orthodox Muslims.

The educated elite of Nigerian society have received less attention than they deserve. There are glimpses of them in a recent novel by Cyprian Ekwensi, *Jagua Nana* (London, 1961). Chinue Achebe's second novel, *No Longer at Ease* (London, 1960), is practically a documentary written around the career and temptations of a young graduate in Lagos. Even more explicitly a documentary work is Onuora Nzekwu, *A Wand of Noble Wood* (London, 1961), whose plot is built around the tensions that the traditional Onitsha marriage system creates for a young journalist. The first formal study of the Nigerian elite is disappointing. H. H. Smythe and M. M. Smythe, *The New Nigerian Elite* (Stanford, 1960), fails sadly to present a clear concept of "elite." The study does not deal properly with important issues such as the extended family ramifications of well-salaried Nigerians and the love-hatred complex of many intellectuals in the face of Western cultural influences. A rather acid and slightly unbalanced article by Colin MacInnes, "Welcome, Beauty Walk," *Encounter*, XV (October, 1960), 38–52, gives a better account of aspects of Western-educated Nigerians than does the Smythes' book. Melvin J. Lasky, "Africa for Beginners," *Encounter*, XVII (July, 1961), 32–48, has some quite good descriptions of the preoccupations of Nigerian intellectuals. He records rather well, for example, the reasons that many of them have not warmed to the cult of "Négritude" sponsored by men like Senghor. C. A. Rodgers, "A Study of Race Attitudes in Nigeria," *Rhodes-Livingstone Journal*, XXVI (December, 1959), 51–64, examines the reaction of Nigerian students to other races at the University College, Ibadan. Rodgers' penetration is not very deep but his work is at least a first statistical analysis. J. Jahn (English translation by Marjorie Greene), *Muntu: An Outline of Neo-African Culture* (London, 1961), is a poor interpretation of changing African culture, but it has some good comments on recent African creative writing. It is hardly out of place to mention here the excellent study by Increase Coker, "The

Nigerian Press," in *The Press in West Africa; Report Prepared for the Dakar Conference on the Press, 1960* (Ibadan, 1960). Coker manages to make very clear how much more developed the press is in Nigeria than anywhere else in West Africa.

Law

The study of customary law is still extremely important. In most parts of Nigeria it still governs large parts of the life of peoples, though it is doubtful if there is any area where the years of colonial administration have not in greater or lesser degree modified such law. A classic study by Paul Bohannan, *Justice and Judgment among the Tiv* (Oxford, 1957), deals with the Tiv system of courts and brings out their ideas of justice and the means they take to enforce it. Antony Allott, *Essays in African Law* (London, 1960), offers a useful general background. In the essay entitled "The Unity of African Law" he insists that "there is no universal, general African Law; there are rather a limited number of *types* of legal features, attitudes and procedures." The same kind of remark might be made concerning "Nigerian" law. P. C. Lloyd, *Yoruba Land Law*, is in the press. This study is more anthropological than legal, but it indicates the kind of work that has to be done before any worthwhile revision of land law can take place. Lloyd has also published "Some Notes on the Yoruba Rules of Succession and on 'Family Property,' " *Journal of African Law*, III (1959), 7–32. Land tenure is one of the key issues in modern development. But in many parts of the country uncertainty concerning ownership and constant bitter disputes between families or communities impede building and agricultural development. Intelligent land reform is needed to end excessive uncertainty and, at the same time, to safeguard the social values inherent in community ownership and to protect people against unscrupulous forms of exploitation. G. B. A. Coker, *Family Property among the Yorubas* (London, 1958), deals with the legal position of Lagos lands; this work, which outlines customary law on the basis of cases that have been decided in the superior

courts of Nigeria, is meant primarily for members of the legal profession. Federation of Nigeria, *The Report of the Federal Land
Department, 1956–57* (Lagos, 1959), makes available information
on legal land issues.

Some studies are available on the changing law situation. Dr.
Elias' Lugard Lectures for 1956 have been published as *The
Impact of English Law on Nigerian Customary Law* (Lagos,
1960). A series of two important articles has been written by an
administrator, F. A. Ajayi, "The Interaction of English Law with
Customary Law in Western Nigeria," *Journal of African Law,* IV,
1 (1960), 40–50, and *ibid.,* IV, 2 (1960), 98–114. P. C. Lloyd
deals with changes in land law in "Some Modern Developments
in Yoruba Customary Land Law," *Journal of African Administration,* XII, 1 (1960), 11–20. In a different area is the *Report of the
Committee on the Future of the Nigerian Legal Profession* (Lagos, 1959). There are references to Nigeria and general background material in the published report of a conference under the
title of *The Future of Law in Africa* (London, 1960), which was
edited by A. N. Allott. The Federal Government and the Regions
now publish annual *Law Reports.* These *Reports* make it possible
to follow much of the development of law in the country.

The North, with its special problems deriving not only from
changing social and political circumstances but also from the
contrasting and opposing systems of Muslim and non-Muslim law,
has had to make special efforts. It is to the credit of the Regional
Government that, in spite of fears and conservative reluctance, a
substantial amount of reform, inspired by the precedents in the
Sudan and Pakistan, has been introduced. *Statement by the Government of the Northern Region on the Reorganisation of the
Legal and Judicial Systems of the Northern Region* (Kaduna,
1958) is a white paper issued on the proposed changes. J. N. D.
Anderson, who was a member of the commission that drew up
the reforms, has written a remarkably clear and readable account
of the effort in "Conflict of Law in Northern Nigeria: A New
Start," *International and Comparative Law Quarterly,* VIII, 3
(1959), 442–56. Different points of view on legal reform in the
North are expressed in J. Price, O. Odumosu, and J. N. D. Ander-

son, "Criminal Law Reform in Northern Nigeria," *Modern Law Review*, XXIV (September, 1961), 604–25. S. S. Richardson, "Training for Penal Reform in Northern Nigeria," *Journal of African Administration*, XIII, 1 (1961), 38–45, describes the attempts being made to train personnel to apply the new laws. A good article by J. N. D. Anderson, "Relationship between Islamic and Customary Law in Africa," *Journal of African Administration*, XII, 4 (1960), 228–34, depicts the background against which the Northern reforms are being carried out. He points out that in Northern Nigeria it is often impossible in practice to say which cases should come under Muslim law and which under customary law. Unfortunately, however, an important part of the new legislation has recently been nullified. The Native Courts (Amendment) Law passed by the Northern House in October, 1961, no longer permits non-Muslims to opt out of the Alkali courts. Political pressures are evidently responsible for this backward step.

Education

A glance at two official publications, *Triennial Survey of the Work of the Federal Department of Education for the Years 1955 to 1957* (Lagos, 1959), and *Department of Education Statistics, 1960* (Lagos, 1960), suggests the tremendous advances that have taken place during the years immediately past. They also show that the Western Region is slightly ahead of the Eastern and that the Northern Region is considerably behind both. But the most important document that has appeared on Nigerian education for some time is Federation of Nigeria, Federal Ministry of Education, *Investment in Education* (Report of the Commission on Post-School Certificate and Higher Education in Nigeria, Sir Eric Ashby, Chairman) (London and Lagos, 1960). The team led by Ashby surveyed most aspects of the structure of education in the country; they rightly traced weaknesses in candidates for university education to their earlier school training, and they believed that they should make recommendations accordingly. Frederick Harbison's manpower survey provided a preface for the Report. The recommendations of the Report may face impossible financial barriers, but they are geared to needs in the country. Moreover, it is quite true, as the Report implies, that determined planning can stimulate internal effort and attract outside help. Unfortunately, the findings have been far too little discussed in public in Nigeria. A symposium held at University College, Ibadan, was not published. Ian Espie, "Decade of Decision," *Ibadan*, No. 11 (February, 1961), pp. 9–13, is a general survey of Nigerian education. J. C. Edozien, "Comments on the Recommendations on Medical Education in the Ashby Commission Report," *ibid.*, pp. 13–14, criticizes the Report's suggestions on medical training and suggests state-controlled, short, practical courses to deal with the present "under-doctored" situation. An important criticism of the Report is that its recommendations are based on an inadequate analysis of social and educational conditions in the country. It also underestimates the cost of implementing its proposals. But, in general, the major value of the Report may be that it represents a symbol of Nigerian determination to move ahead rapidly both in the cultural and technological sectors. The Banjo Commission, *Report on Education in the Western Region* (Ibadan, 1961), was meant to complete the work of the Ashby Commission in the West and to advise the regional government on immediate practical steps to improve their system. The document bears signs of haste and clearly its writers have not thought out thoroughly certain of their recommendations (such as those regarding the feeder system for secondary schools). But there is considerable information in it, and it describes several of the main problems in education that the Region faces—such as, for example, 26,000 of the 40,000 teachers are untrained and many elementary school leavers have an inadequate command of English. *Educational Development 1961–70* (Lagos, 1961) is a white paper issued by the Federal Government on the Ashby Report in which the major recommendations of the Report are accepted. Although this white paper shows the government to be sympathetic, it is less concrete in its proposals than it might have been and contains some impractical suggestions. J. N. Archer was seconded from the Commonwealth Relations Office to the Federal

Government to advise on the costing and phasing of the recommendations contained in the Ashby Report. The results of his work were made available for a restricted circle in J. N. Archer, *Educational Development in Nigeria: 1961–70* (Lagos, 1961). Another document that may be mentioned is the *Report of the Federal Advisory Committee on Technical Education and Industrial Training* (Lagos, 1959). There is still no word when the report of the Dike Commission on education in the Eastern Region is likely to be released. A brief study by D. H. Williams, *A Short Survey of Education in the Northern Region* (Kaduna, 1960), gives some information about education in the North. W. F. Jeffries, "The Literacy Campaign in Northern Nigeria," *Fundamental and Adult Education*, X (1958), 2–6, describes efforts on another level. The Ashby Commission had recommended 25 per cent primary school scholarization in the North as a target for 1970. To observers this figure looked reasonable for most parts of the Region since the educational pace would be economically feasible and not socially disruptive. But the Federal Government's white paper on the Ashby Report increased the target to 50 per cent. The Northern government has now issued its own white paper, *Educational Development* (Kaduna, 1961), in which it sets out its plans for the various stages of development.

Part of the problem of raising standards lies in the way the more able teachers have deserted, and are still deserting, the profession. This drift has not been pure loss. A great number of the political leaders were once teachers. Some of the best graduates studied for university entrance requirements while they were teaching in primary schools. But the drift must be slowed down considerably if the primary schools, in particular, are to insure quality and continuity of teaching. The answer lies largely in raising the status of the profession, and this means that teachers will, among other things, need to be better paid. Yet the Western and Eastern Regions already spend more than 40 per cent of their budgets on education. Apart from the government reports there is presently a scarcity of literature dealing with these problems. Two available studies that might be mentioned are D. R. Howell, "The Status of Teachers in Nigeria," *Overseas Education*, XXX,

3 (1958), 102–9, and Joan Foster, "Women's Teacher Training in Northern Nigeria," *ibid.*, XXXI, 4 (1960), 147–55, which describes a Northern effort to further teacher training. An allied theme is dealt with in J. O. A. Herrington, "Problem of the Inspectorate in Western Nigeria," *ibid.*, XXX, 4 (1959), 176–80.

Though the Ashby Commission recommended new university institutions to be added to those already existing, it did little to break down the proportions of graduates that might take degrees in different specialties. In most of the proposed institutions graduates in the arts and graduates trained in an academic form of science will predominate disproportionately. Though the Commission did not neglect to make recommendations about technological training, it seems that technology will continue to be relegated to secondary importance. A good service would be done if research were to continue the work that Harbison has begun, both in the Ashby Commission Report and *supra*, Chapter VIII, and were to evaluate in detail the kinds of graduates that Nigeria needs in relation to the capacities and demands of the economy.

Kenneth Mellanby, *The Birth of Nigeria's First University* (London, 1958), gives a vivid account of the problems that had to be solved in getting the University College, Ibadan, under way. Mellanby, who was the first Principal of the College, had to overcome a colonial government's reluctance to spend money, convince British academics that they were not going to ruin their careers by coming to the tropics, and combat Nigerian suspicions that the College was founded simply to reduce the number of Nigerian students who were acquiring radical ideas abroad. If Ibadan now has fine buildings, a growing international reputation, and the confidence of the country, it is in no small part owed to Mellanby. A book by the second Principal, J. T. Saunders, *University College, Ibadan* (Cambridge, 1960), compares badly with Mellanby's book. It reads like a college calendar with its lists of subjects and students and shows little insight into the educational situation of the country. Two teachers at Ibadan, John Ferguson and Adegoke Olubummo, have written *Emergent University* (London, 1960), which draws on the Ibadan experience to offer opinions on universities in developing countries. They have few novel views to present and give the impression of aligning themselves with the conservative rather than with the progressive tendencies at Ibadan. One of their colleagues, Lalage Brown, in a stimulating and forceful review, "Emergent University?," *Ibadan*, No. 11 (February, 1961), pp. 17–19, rejects convincingly several of their central contentions. An informative progress report on the university can be found in the first *Foundation Day Address* (Ibadan, 1960) of the present Principal, K. O. Dike. He stresses the difficulties that students at the College are meeting in the attempt to get scholarships and points out the anomalous nature of this problem in a country that is committed to founding several other universities. Kenneth Mellanby, *op. cit.*, was both critical and complimentary of the British university authorities with whom he dealt from Ibadan. One of the most helpful and able of them, Sir Alexander Carr-Saunders, has now presented the British version of the founding of these university institutions in *New Universities Overseas* (London, 1961).

Economic Development

Political stability and social progress are going to depend very much on economic development. At the moment we are awaiting the publication of the second survey of the national income (the report has already been submitted to the Federal Government). The previous survey made in 1950–51 gave an annual income of only £20 per person. This is much less than the income per person in Ghana, which is a poor country by Western standards. The second survey should help considerably in mapping the economy, such mapping being a prerequisite for any economic take-off. The National Economic Council has published *Economic Survey of Nigeria, 1959* (Lagos, 1959), which contains a review of the economy and a forecast of probable developments during the next few years. To understand the economic plans that are being implemented at present in the country it is important to keep in mind that the survey, IBRD, *The Economic Development of Nigeria, a Report* (Baltimore, 1955), served as a basis for present development schemes. Reports on the federal economic plan that are published as sessional papers by the Federal Government (for example, see 1/1958 and 1/1959) offer information on the progress that is being made. At present a team sponsored by the Ford Foundation and under the direction of W. Stolper of the University of Michigan is working on a new federal development plan for the period 1962–67. The statements of the economic policies of the Regions are also important: *Progress Report on the Development Finance Programme* (Kaduna, 1959); *Development Programme, 1958–62* (Enugu, 1959) and *Revised Development Programme* (Enugu, 1960); and *Western Region Development Plan, 1960–65* (Ibadan, 1959). The Western Region, which is the richest of the three Regions, plans not to increase the amount of money being spent on services during the present period of planning and to put its increased income into industrial and agricultural expansion. Ian Stewart of Edinburgh University, who worked on the first national income survey, has published a general article, "Nigeria's Economic Prospects," *The Three Banks Review*, No. 49 (March, 1961), pp. 16–28, in which he concludes that "the evidence . . . will bear two different interpretations. One is that incomes have been rising since 1950/51 at a modest rate; the other, politically much less palatable, interpretation is that so far applications of capital and technically skilled labour have not had sufficient impact on the mainspring of agricultural productivity to guarantee an improving standard of nutrition for Africa's largest single population." It is worthwhile to place the Nigerian economic situation against a general African background, such as that provided by W. A. Hance, *African Economic Development* (London, 1958), and UNO, *Economic Survey of Africa since 1950* (New York, 1959).

Basic information about the Nigerian economy is more abundant than it might appear, but it is often hard to come by. The Federal Government's quarterly *Digest of Statistics* is extremely important, and so also is the quarterly *Western Region Statistical Bulletin. The Monthly Trade Returns* and the *Annual Trade Reports* are indispensable. The various public corporations and institutions publish annual reports—the reports of the railway and electricity corporations, for example, offer particularly valuable information about many sectors of the economy. These various bodies also from time to time commission studies—for example, the Economic Intelligence Unit lately did a study of economic problems relating to the activities of the Western Region Marketing Board, which has not yet been released. In the economic sphere more than in any other, a number of valuable reports and studies have been released, usually for limited circulation. Often the only way of obtaining these documents is through personal contacts with the ministries. The quarterly *Nigeria Trade Journal* provides current information and articles on the economy. *The Handbook of Commerce and Industry* (Lagos, 1961) contains a good deal of not easily available information. *The Statistical and Economic Review*, published by the United Africa Company, reports on trade and price indices in Nigeria as well as other African countries. The *Overseas Review*, published by Barclay's Bank, gives information on current economic trends in areas where the Bank does business.

There are many references to Nigeria in J. R. Hicks, ed., *Federalism and Economic Growth* (London, 1961). Hicks, *Essays in World Economics* (Oxford, 1959), has a chapter in which he sets out principles of revenue allocation in a federation. S. P. Schatz, "The Influence of Planning on Development: the Nigerian Experience," *Social Research*, XXVII (Winter, 1960), 451–68, discusses the relation between the published development plans of Nigerian governments and the implementation of these plans. The discrepancy between planning goals and achievements draws attention to the large part that guesswork played in the preparation of the plans. Two other articles by Schatz are of interest for the study of Nigerian planning: "Underutilized Resources, 'Directed Demand' and Deficit Financing," *Quarterly Journal of Economics*, LXIII (November, 1959), 633–44, and "The American Approach to Foreign Aid and the Thesis of Low Absorptive Capacity," *Quarterly Review of Economics and Business*, I (November, 1961), 55–62. Banking and monetary policy are essential tools of planning and fortunately these aspects of the economy have begun to be increasingly studied—indeed, to such an extent that here one can do little more than list the titles of the studies. C. V. Brown, "The Supply of Bank Money in Nigeria," *Bankers' Magazine*, CXC (November and December, 1960), 301–10, and 397–402, examines the lending policies of the commercial banks; he also examines the Central Bank's monetary policy and indicates that its effectiveness is limited partly by the rudimentary character of the monetary institutions and partly by legislation. Brown develops the same theme in "The Effectiveness of Monetary Policy in Nigeria," in *NISER Proceedings, 1960.* In the same volume mention should be made of A. Ayida, "A Critical Analysis of Banking Trends in Nigeria." To the previous NISER volume, pp. 80–90, H. M. A. Onitiri had contributed "The Central Bank of Nigeria and the Problem of Domestic Monetary Stability." A. Hazlewood, "Central Banking in Nigeria," *Bankers' Magazine*, CLXXXVI (August, 1958), 115–20, and Hazlewood, "New Deal for Nigerian Federal Finance," *ibid.* (September, 1958), p. 369, also merits study. There is considerable mention of Nigeria in a recently completed thesis by J. O. W. Olakanpo, "Central Banking in Commonwealth Countries" (London, 1961). Also see Olakanpo, "Monetary Management in Dependent Economies," *Economica*, XXVIII (November, 1961), 395–408. The annual reports of the Central Bank are also relevant to the study of banking in Nigeria. In a related sphere a committee reported on *Fostering a Share Market in Nigeria* (Lagos, 1959). Already a stock exchange has been established in Lagos and dealings are taking place in a limited number of British and Nigerian shares.

A certain amount of work has been done on consumer demand. Also, research is being done currently on long-term development of supply and demand for agricultural products by a team working under Ian Stewart. Two members of this team have published preliminary studies: W. D. C. Wright has a paper that appeared in the *NISER Proceedings, 1960,* and R. C. Ogley, "Nigeria's Future Demand for Food," *Ibadan*, No. 11 (February, 1961), pp. 33–35, suggests various possible patterns of future consumption. Urban consumer reports have already appeared on Enugu (1954–55), Kaduna and Zaria (1955–56), Kano (1958–59), Lagos (1953–54), and Ibadan (1955). The agricultural situation will profoundly influence both the food situation and the internal and external trade of the country. Apart from the efforts of the marketing boards, agricultural economics remains comparatively undeveloped. H. A. Oluwasanmi, "The Agrarian Situation in Nigeria," *Journal of Human Relations,* VIII (Spring and Summer, 1960), 657–67, may serve as a useful introduction. Agricultural extension work needs to be developed, and a fair share of research might usefully be directed toward seeing how it could be expanded to the best advantage. T. Oloko, H. L. Dusenberry, and D. W. Pett have recently produced *A Handbook for Extension Workers* (Ibadan, 1961). The marketing boards have occasioned a fair amount of literature in the past. More recently there is a contribution by F. Kuiper, "Some Aspects of the Operations of Marketing Boards," *NISER Proceedings, 1958,* pp. 43–49. P. T. Bauer and B. S. Yamey, "A Case Study of Response to Price in an Under-developed Economy," *Economic Journal,* LXIX (1959), 800–805, study the improvement in the quality of cocoa in the light of price incentives, but they clearly overstated the importance of price incentives and minimized that of extension work and services provided by the boards. V. W. Hogg, "Response to Price in an Underdeveloped Economy," *Economic Journal,* LXX (December, 1960), 852–55, brought the issue back into focus in a short note.

Though Nigeria can expect a certain amount of foreign aid to help the economic take-off, the basic investment effort has to come from internal savings. An important thesis has been written on this subject by O. Aboyade, "Capital Formation in Nigeria" (Cambridge, 1960), which is due for publication in 1962. But there are many problems—the lack of experience and technical knowledge and difficulties in getting credit—that beset the Nigerian entrepreneur. S. I. Edokpayi points out some of them in "Some Problems in the Development of Indigenous Private Business Enterprise in Nigeria," *NISER Proceedings, 1960.* O. Aboyade, "Some Factors of the Building and Construction Activities in Nigeria," *ibid.,* is a specific examination of a field in which Nigerians have succeeded better than in most others. In *NISER Proceedings, 1958,* pp. 111–20, C. N. Isong, "Modernisation of the Esusu Credit Society," discusses how a traditional form of savings society might be used to stimulate savings that could be profitably invested. There is also a report by an advisory committee, of which Chief H. O. Davies was chairman, entitled *Aids to African Businessmen* (Lagos, 1959). Two surveys have been done for foreign investors. The U. S. Department of Commerce has published *Investment in Nigeria: Basic Information for United States Businessmen* (Washington, 1957), and the Federation of British Industries has offered suggestions to British businessmen in *Nigeria: An Industrial Reconnaissance* (London, 1961). An immediate problem that the country must face is the growing deficit in the balance of payments, and, unless industrialization and agricultural improvements are given substantial aid from abroad, the deficit will grow. In "Import Duties and the Nigerian Balance of External Payments," *Nigerian Journal of Economic and Social Studies*, II, 1 (1960), 26–37, H. M. A. Onitiri discusses the effects of the increased import taxes of January, 1959, on the economy generally and on the balance of payments. The entire structure of imports should be properly examined. Onitiri suggests an outline of a constructive foreign trade policy in "Nigeria's International Economic Relations: A Survey," *Nigerian Journal of Economic and Social Studies*, III, 1 (1961), 13–38.

The Federal Government has published a first comprehensive report on the employment market situation, which is based on manpower information already available and on the results of a sample survey of employing establishments at the end of March, 1961. This *Report on Employment Market Situation* (Lagos, 1961) brings out only too clearly the acute shortage of high-level Nigerian manpower. The unemployment situation appears to be deteriorating without any improvement coming about in the availability of *skilled* manpower. Each year from now on more than a quarter of a million primary school leavers are due to come on the market in the Eastern and Western Regions. Given the present slow rate of industrial growth, these young people cannot be absorbed into the towns. If, as has happened up to the present, almost all school leavers make their way to the towns, there is grave danger of an unemployment situation that may threaten social and political stability. Archibald Callaway,

"School Leavers and the Developing Economy of Nigeria," *supra,* Chapter IX, analyzes the situation of these youngsters, their aspirations, and their prospects.

There are studies available on Nigerian labor. J. I. Roper, *Labour Problems in West Africa* (London, 1958), is somewhat vaguely written, but it may serve as an introduction. A much better study that is also directly concerned with Nigeria is due to appear soon—T. M. Yesufu, *Problems of Industrial Relations in Nigeria.* W. A. Warmington, *A West African Trade Union* (London, 1960), though it deals with the workers' union in the Cameroons Development Corporation, is pertinent enough to be of use to those studying the Nigerian scene. *The African Labour Survey* (Geneva, 1958), contains information on industrial relations, technical and vocational training, labor protection, and workers' housing. Unfortunately this I. L. O. survey repeats mistaken notions about the quality of African labor. Only one scientific study of West African labor productivity has been undertaken. Peter Kilby has published the findings of his study in "African Labour Productivity Reconsidered," *Economic Journal,* LXXI (June, 1961), 273–91. It is worthwhile to quote Kilby's conclusions drawn from his detailed statistical analysis:

First, the African (Nigerian) does not possess any inherent incapacities or attitudes that are detrimental to efficient production. In fact, it can be argued that regarding continuous labour and repetitive operations he is peculiarly well-suited to modern production. Secondly, the African's willingness to work considerably exceeds that of labourers in developed economies. Thirdly, with regard to machine technology, there are certain facets of machine operation and maintenance which the African, because of his environmental background, does not naturally adapt to. Training, however, will rectify these shortcomings. . . . In the final reckoning, it is not the African labourer but his employer who must bear the stigma of imperfect performance [p. 91].

These findings reverse traditional views held in many business circles in West Africa. Kilby approaches the same question in "Some Determinants of Industrial Productivity in Nigeria," *NISER Proceedings, 1960.* The Mbanefo arbitration award, *Review of Salaries and Wages* (Lagos, 1959), which determined the salary scales of government employees, thereby also affected salaries in non-governmental sectors. This is inevitable in a country where some two-thirds of the salaried employees work in the public sector. But there has been a certain arbitrariness about the timing of government awards that has made economists and businessmen uneasy and anxious for better co-ordination between the public and private sectors of employment. Both industrial and agricultural development, especially the latter, may soon require that labor should migrate from one part of the country to another part. Some recent work has been done on migrant labor. R. M. Prothero has continued his previous work with *Migrant Labour from Sokoto Province, Northern Nigeria* (Kaduna, 1958); S. Tidjani has published "Note sur la migration humaine à la Côte du Benin," *Bulletin de l'Institut français de l'Afrique noire*, XXII, 3–4 (1960), 509–13, which studies the Zabermas who migrate from North Dahomey toward Nigeria and suggests ways in which they can be helped. In the same issue of the *Bulletin* there are studies of migratory labor in various parts of West Africa. On this subject, also see Joseph J. Spengler, "Population Movements and Economic Development in Nigeria," *supra*, Chapter VII.

One defect in the surveys of the Nigerian economy that have been made from time to time is that they have too often considered the economy exclusively from a capitalistic viewpoint. Too little inquiry has been made into the more enterprising forms of public development or into the possibilities in mixed private-public undertakings. But it is true that much public enterprise in Nigeria has not had a very happy history. The only general published work on the subject is A. H. Hanson, "Public Enterprise in Nigeria: I, Federal Public Utilities," *Public Administration*, XXXVI (1958), 366–84, and "II, Development Corporations," *ibid.*, XXXVII (1959), 21–40. In 1961 W. A. Robson submitted to the Federal Government a report on the federal public corporations, but there seems little likelihood that it will be released. The harsh lessons to be drawn from the failure of the Mokwa scheme can be read in K. D. S. Baldwin, *The Niger Agricultural Project* (Oxford, 1957). In another sphere of public finance, U. K. Hicks, *Development from Below* (Oxford, 1961), discusses the financing of local government in Nigeria.

Transport forms the arteries of the country. Gilbert Walker, *Traffic and Transport in Nigeria* (London, 1961), is still a serious contribution despite the fact that the survey on which it is based was carried out several years ago. E. K. Hawkins, *Road Transport in Nigeria* (London, 1958), is a briefer work than Walker's but it is nonetheless important as a study of the manner by which Africans came to dominate some parts of road transport. The study also offers acute comment on both the economics of road transport and on the social apparatus that has grown up around it. V. W. Hogg, "Transport Planning Problems in Nigeria," *Ibadan*, No. 9 (June, 1960), pp. 11–12, serves as an introduction to the topic of its title. Hogg, in collaboration with C. M. Roelandts, has another study that is due to appear soon, "Nigerian Motor Vehicle Traffic: An Economic Forecast." In collaboration with H. P. White, Hogg is understood to be preparing an additional study, "Transport Movements of Nigerian Export Crops." This last mentioned work is the first scientific analysis to be made of the routes used in transporting the Marketing Boards' export crops and should be useful in suggesting certain reroutings that might make possible a reduction of transportation costs. The *Report of the Commission of Inquiry into the Administration, Economics and Industrial Relations of the Nigerian Railway Corporation* (Lagos, 1961) might have provided useful analysis and made an important impact, but the work of the Commission was hastily done and much of it is inferior. V. W. Hogg criticizes its economic basis strongly in "N.R.C. and L.S.D.," *Ibadan*, No. 11 (February, 1961), pp. 24–27, and also points out that the Commission made no attempt to reconcile the economic and social welfare aspects of the railway. The Stanford Research Institute carried out an inquiry for the federal Joint Planning Committee on the "Economic Coordination of Transport in Nigeria." The report has not yet been released by the government, but it is understood that it supports strongly the development of railways. A Dutch firm, Nedeco, has prepared a report on the utilization of rivers, which is published in *River Studies and Recommendations on Improvement of Niger and Benue* (Amsterdam, 1959). The various Nigerian transport problems may gain from being examined against the general background analyzed in UNO, *Transport Problems in Relation to Economic Development in West Africa* ([New York], 1960).

A Bibliographical Note

Those who wish to keep up with current social science research in Nigeria should consult the reviews that have been frequently cited in this survey. The most useful source to consult about books and documentary material published in Nigeria is *Nigerian Publications* (Ibadan University Press). Published annually by the staff of the University College library, this volume lists all the books and pamphlets that the University College has received in the previous year under the publications ordinance. It also notes serial publications that have ceased to appear and lists recent library acquisitions dealing with Nigeria or those written by Nigerians but published abroad. An excellent source for articles is the bibliography in each issue of *Africa* (International African Institute, London). The Institute of Commonwealth Studies (Oxford) sends out duplicated lists of books and articles dealing with all the Commonwealth countries, and the section on Nigeria is always excellent. *Africa Report* (African-American Institute— monthly) usually contains some bibliographical information, including a listing of articles in the later issues. Helen F. Conover, *Nigerian Official Publications, 1869–1959* (Washington, 1959), provides a list of official documents and publications. Mary Holdsworth has been doing good work for several years in making available to the non-Russian speaking public information about Russian writings on Africa. She has gathered her work together in *Soviet African Studies 1918–59: An Annotated Bibliography* (London, 1961). However, the few publications on Nigeria by Russian writers are generally poor. Indeed it is correct to add that little work of value has been done on Nigeria in languages other than English, for most of these non-English writings have apparently borrowed heavily from English language sources. Nigeria might benefit, however, from more research by scholars trained outside British and American institutions, and it would be especially valuable if students from other parts of Africa undertook serious research on Nigeria.

Current Research

James Coleman, "Research on Africa in European Centres," *African Studies Bulletin*, II, 3 (1959), 1–33, has well presented the recent work done on Africa in Europe. United States, Department of State, Bureau of Intelligence and Research, *External Research: Africa*, ER No. 7. 16 (April, 1961), which contains a section on Nigeria (pp. 22–24), lists current studies on Africa being carried out by Americans both in the field and in the United States. The Nigerian Institute of Social and Economic Research has begun to keep a register of social studies being prepared in Nigeria, but it has as yet issued no publications on this topic.

We can list briefly some of the topics with which current research is concerned. In history, the Fulani *jihad,* the formation of Nigeria's frontiers, the expansion of the Christian Churches (including the independent Nigerian bodies), the trade on the Niger, the life of Herbert Macaulay, and the rise of Ibadan to power in Yorubaland are being studied. In politics, inquiries into voting behavior in several towns are being carried on, several studies of political parties are in progress, Ibo political institutions are being surveyed from several different viewpoints, political and legal examinations of the federal Constitution are under way, and foreign policy is being considered. Sociology and anthropology still attract most research workers. The projects are numerous: Yoruba market women, the Onitsha market, educational patterns among the Ijaw and the status of women among the Ijaw, the social structure of the Igala and of several peoples on the Jos Plateau, family and kinship among the Ibo, urbanization in Southeast Nigeria, Afikpo political and social structure, family structure and social change in Onitsha, mental disease among the Yoruba, and foreign-educated Nigerians and their status. Economic studies are increasing rapidly in number: factors affecting industrial productivity (in several industries, including the coal mining industry at Enugu), agricultural productivity, capital formation, government measures to stimulate indigenous private enterprise, various aspects of transport problems, land tenure and use, employment of school leavers, apprenticeship systems, banking, and foreign trade. Educational research is being undertaken on intelligence tests for Nigerian children and on their learning problems.

It is obvious that research should be encouraged in many spheres of Nigerian social studies. The rapidly increasing number of historical studies could well make use of oral testimony and traditions before these are lost. A great gap in political studies is the absence of careful research on the working of local councils. There is room especially for careful case histories that could provide a basis for generalizations about conditions surrounding local government in Nigeria. In the economic sector there is need for more studies that deal with the development of enterpreneurial and technical skills and with capital formation in the country. Agriculture awaits much more extensive experimental and survey work. But, in the meantime, more thought needs to be given to communicating the knowledge and skills already available and to studying how land tenure can be adjusted to foster modernization. Thorough reconsideration of the syllabi of Nigerian primary and secondary education is seriously needed. The primary school program is little geared to keeping young people on the land, and the programs could be more relevant to the African background of the pupils. It is imperative to plan technical education in relation to the phases of the economy's development. The traditional kind of descriptive anthropology has undoubtedly a certain value in Nigeria, but priorities in sociological research must increasingly be given to studies of social change that are relevant, but not subordinate, to demography, town planning, and preventive and social medicine.

Those who wish to consult schematically prepared lists of research projects in politics and administration, economics, and sociology might examine the papers issued by the working groups of the Conference on Research for Development in West Africa, which was held at the University College, Ibadan, in March, 1961. The suggestions for further research made in the present essay are meant to do little more than to supplement the bibliographical survey, but they may serve to suggest subjects that scholars new to the field of Nigerian social studies can consider in formulating their own research problems and projects.

Index